A GUIDE TO
THE HISTORY OF
MASSACHUSETTS

Recent Titles in
Reference Guides to State History and Research

A Guide to the History of Louisiana
Light Townsend Cummins and Glen Jeansonne, editors

A Guide to the History of Texas
Light Townsend Cummins and Alvin R. Bailey, Jr., editors

A GUIDE TO
THE HISTORY OF
MASSACHUSETTS

Edited by
Martin Kaufman,
John W. Ifkovic,
and Joseph Carvalho III

REFERENCE GUIDES TO STATE HISTORY AND RESEARCH

GREENWOOD PRESS
New York • Westport, Connecticut • London

Library of Congress Cataloging-in-Publication Data

A Guide to the history of Massachusetts.

(Reference guides to state history and research)
Includes index.
1. Massachusetts—History—Sources—Bibliography.
2. Massachusetts—Historiography.   3. Archives—
Massachusetts—Directories.   4. Historical libraries—
Massachusetts—Directories.   I. Kaufman, Martin,
1940-   . II. Ifkovic, John W.   III. Carvalho,
Joseph, 1953-   .   IV. Series.
Z1295.G84   1988   [F64]   016.9744   87-12026
ISBN 0-313-24564-9 (lib. bdg. : alk. paper)

British Library Cataloguing in Publication Data is available.

Library of Congress Catalog Card Number: 87-12026
ISBN: 0-313-24564-9

First published in 1988

Greenwood Press, Inc.
88 Post Road West, Westport, Connecticut   06881

Printed in the United States of America

The paper used in this book complies with the
Permanent Paper Standard issued by the National
Information Standards Organization (Z39.48-1984).

10 9 8 7 6 5 4 3 2 1

CONTENTS

INTRODUCTION

THIS VOLUME IS part of a series coordinated by Light Townsend Cummins and Glen Jeansonne, who in 1982 published *A Guide to the History of Louisiana*. The basic intention of Professors Cummins and Jeansonne was to produce a convenient one-volume guide to sources in state and local history. The Louisiana prototype consisted of an historiographical section followed by one describing the major archival repositories in the state. When the editorial staff of the Greenwood Press accepted the Louisiana guide for publication, it was decided that similar volumes for other states would be useful sources for persons who are interested in understanding the history of their state and region, and especially for those who are researching and writing state and local history.

Since Westfield State College's Institute for Massachusetts Studies publishes the *Historical Journal of Massachusetts* and coordinates annual programs on Massachusetts history, it was natural for Professors Cummins and Jeansonne to invite the staff of the institute to edit a similar volume for Massachusetts. With more than a decade of work in Massachusetts history, the staff of the institute was not only familiar with the work of the leading historians, but had also worked closely with a number of them on various projects. In addition, through editing the *Historical Journal* and through the *Journal*'s book review section, the staff of the institute was familiar with a large number of persons who have done extensive research and writing on aspects of the state's history.

After some time had been devoted to discussing possible ways to divide the chronological timeframe as well as possible major topics in Massachusetts history, it was decided to commission six chapters covering the entire period from 1600 to the present. The specific chapters focus upon the early colonial period (to 1689), the royalist period (1689 to 1763), the Revolutionary period (1763 to

1789), the early national period (1789 to 1860), the Gilded Age (1865 to 1900), and the twentieth century. In addition, it was decided to commission more extensive chapters on two major topics: urban Massachusetts, and women in Massachusetts, because those topics would cut broadly across the various time periods covered in the chronological chapters. Finally, since oral history is an important tool for the historian, and since it has been practiced in Massachusetts for some time, it was decided to include a chapter on the use of oral history in the state.

The editors were pleased to have been able to recruit contributors who were especially knowledgeable in their fields, and who were known to be dependable. Each contributor agreed to prepare an historiographical essay covering major sources and interpretations for either a chronological period or for the three topics, urban, women's, and oral history. The contributors were asked to define issues, problems, and opportunities while surveying the major historical literature, including books, articles, and dissertations.

In order to provide the contributors with an opportunity for critical analysis by other outstanding authorities, the staff of the Institute for Massachusetts Studies planned a series of three public sessions at the John Fitzgerald Kennedy Library in Boston, with funding from the Lowell Institute. At those sessions, held in the spring of 1985, the contributors' presentations were discussed by Nancy Cott of Yale University, Robert Hollister of Tufts University, Pauline Maier of the Massachusetts Institute of Technology, and Stephan Thernstrom of Harvard University, as well as by the staff of the Institute for Massachusetts Studies and members of the audience. Following the public series, the contributors were given an opportunity to revise their chapters in line with suggestions by the commentators, and to produce longer and more extensive chapters than could possibly be presented in lecture form.

As editors, we have followed certain general guidelines similar to the ones used in the Louisiana volume. Each essay was written exclusively for this volume, and each author was given great freedom to survey his or her topic. Uniformity seemed less important than providing each contributor with the opportunity to be creative. The authors were asked to describe the most important books, articles, and dissertations, as well as to analyze the changing approaches to the topic and to suggest fruitful areas for research. It was suggested to the authors that they integrate their citations into the text as much as possible to avoid having numerous footnotes that would interrupt the natural flow of ideas and information.

The second section, edited by Joseph Carvalho III, consists of descriptions of major archival repositories of the state's history, and it can provide the user with guidelines for finding topics and planning research in the state. Some of the leading repositories have published guides to their collections, while others have remained largely invisible except to specialists. We have sought to provide information on the specific holdings of archives and other repositories, and to emphasize the ones that do not have published collection guides. A complete description of the holdings of the American Antiquarian Society, the Massachusetts Historical Society, or Harvard University, for instance, would take a large number of volumes, and since there already are published guides to their holdings, extensive coverage in this book would only duplicate what is available in published form. Therefore, although some readers may be taken aback by the fact that smaller repositories have received more space than the largest and most significant collections in the state, this book is made more valuable by its coverage of the lesser-known repositories. Most of the descriptions of various collections have been prepared by professionals who presently manage those repositories and who were asked to provide the reader with an accurate overview of the strengths of their collections.

Beyond the resources listed in this volume and in the various separate archival guides published by the largest institutions, researchers should be aware of the availability of sources in other repositories. For instance, there is a wide range of resources available outside of the Commonwealth of Massachusetts. Depending upon the specific topic being researched, the Library of Congress and the National Archives in Washington, D.C., can be of immense value. Foreign repositories, especially those in the United Kingdom, should not be overlooked, especially for the colonial and Revolutionary periods. In addition, through patient and diligent detective work by the researcher, it is possible to locate and make use of a wide variety of records that have not yet been transferred to an archival or special collections repository. These would include records generated and maintained by town, city, and county governmental agencies, religious institutions, clubs and organizations, businesses, and newspapers. Finally, many public and private colleges and universities maintain archives for their institutional records; almost every local historical society maintains some local records; and museums may also possess original records relating to their collections, with the more professionally managed also maintaining useful curatorial records concerning artifacts in their possession.

This volume is designed as a general reference tool for persons interested in the history of Massachusetts and especially for those contemplating new projects. Space limitations have made it impossible for the book to be comprehensive, and as a result this guide is not intended for the use of historians seeking a complete bibliographical survey of a specialized research topic. It might prove useful to them in areas outside their expertise, however, and in helping to provide the proper historical perspective into which they may place their research. Instead of being a comprehensive bibliographical survey of the historical literature, the guide represents an attempt to provide an overview of bibliographical and archival sources. The guide, then, will furnish a starting point for the researcher, and its value should be that it collects in one volume a survey of the status of historical studies in Massachusetts. As editors, we assume complete responsibility for the guide, although the opinions and comments expressed in each of the chapters remain those of its author. We hope that readers will bring errors and omissions to our attention so that they may be corrected in subsequent editions.

The editors would like to express their thanks to John Stewart and Dan Fenn of the John Fitzgerald Kennedy Library for allowing us the use of their facility for the series entitled "Understanding Massachusetts History" and for adding the series to their annual calendar of events. In addition, we must express our gratitude to the trustees of the Lowell Institute for their financial support for that series. The editors would also like to express thanks and appreciation to Nancy Cott, Robert Hollister, Pauline Maier, and Stephan Thernstrom for their willingness to serve as commentators at the public sessions and for their critical analyses, which in many ways served to strengthen the chapters published in this volume. We also would like to express our appreciation to the contributors to this volume, who are to be congratulated for their excellent essays and for their willingness to follow the editorial guidelines, as well as for their ability to do so within the editors' timetable for completion of their work.

Finally, the editors would like to express appreciation to their families, who contributed to the success of the project by their continued support, although we may have neglected their needs in order to devote time and energy to this book. We must thank Gayle, Alyssa, and Michael Carvalho, Dorothy Ifkovic, and Henrietta, Edward, and Linda Kaufman.

PART ONE

THE HISTORICAL LITERATURE

1

FROM THE OLD WORLD TO THE NEW, 1620–1689

FRANCIS J. BREMER

"YOU ARE TO be set as lights upon a Hill more obvious than the highest Mountaine in the World; keepe close to Christ that you may shine full of his glory, who imployes you, and grub not continually in the Earth, like blind Moles, but by your amiable Conversation seek the winning of many to your Masters service." So Edward Johnson of Woburn defined the purpose behind the settlement of Massachusetts and set himself the task of enlightening his native land by writing the first published history of the colony. Johnson's *Wonder-Working Providence of Sion's Savior in New England* (London, 1654) was but one of many attempts by seventeenth-century New Englanders to explore in writing their place in God's providential scheme. Far more than their contemporaries elsewhere in British America, the colonial leaders in Massachusetts believed in the uniqueness of their undertaking. They have been repaid if in no other coin by the assiduous labor of two centuries of historians who have made the evolution of seventeenth-century Massachusetts the most thoroughly examined of all the episodes in our early history.

The colonial chroniclers and their works remain the starting place for those who would understand the Massachusetts heritage, not only because of how they interpreted the past but for their care in recording it. John Winthrop's *Journal, The History of New England*, ed. James Savage (Boston, 1825–1826), was not published for more than a century after his death, but was used extensively in manuscript and later in print by all who have written about the formative decades of the Bay Colony. In Winthrop's history the most important of the colony's early political leaders recorded major events such as the controversies that swirled around Roger Williams and Anne Hutchinson and the evolution of the colony's structure of government. But he also recorded incidents from everyday life. Winthrop's contemporary, Plymouth Colony's Governor William Bradford, composed a graceful and thorough history *Of Plymouth Plantation* (Boston, 1856). Johnson, Winthrop, and Bradford wrote in full confidence that New England was in the vanguard of God's army. The post-Restoration colonial historians, however, were confronted with a society not quite as certain of its purpose. William Hubbard, Increase Mather, and Cotton Mather turned to the past to rekindle in their own generation the sense of mission that had motivated their forebears. If Johnson's *Wonder-Working Providence* was designed to use New England's story to save England, Cotton Mather's *Magnalia Christi Americana* (London, 1702) was an effort to redeem New England and put it back on the path of righteousness.

In addition to composing works of formal history, the seventeenth-century colonists left an imposing record of their ideas and activities in the form of published works, government documents, and private papers such as diaries and correspondence. The preservation of these materials has provided later generations of historians with the bricks from which to build new interpretive structures.

The two major eighteenth-century historians of early Massachusetts had no emphatic interpretations to characterize their works. But both Rev. Thomas Prince's *Chronological History of New England in the Form of Annals* (Boston, 1736) and Governor Thomas Hutchinson's *History of the Colony and Province of Massachusetts Bay* (Boston, 1767) mined the available sources to provide detailed narratives.

Historians of the Revolutionary and early national generations continued in the filiopietistic mold of Mather, though they valued the early settlers more for their independent spirit and resistance to English oppression than for their Puritan theology. Indeed, in the popular writings of the pre–Civil War era the process was well underway of transforming the Bay Colony from the New Jerusalem to the seedbed of democracy. John Gorham Palfrey's primary interest was in "the strenuous action of intelligent and honest men in building up a free, strong, enlightened, and happy State." While racial bias and a panegyric attitude flaws the work, Palfrey's three-volume *History of New England during the Stuart Dynasty* (Boston, 1858–1864) is filled with exhaustive details on the social, political, and religious life of the colonies that makes it worthwhile reading. Animated by much the same biases as Palfrey, George Bancroft gave New England an important role in the creation of American democracy when writing his ten-volume *History of the United States* (Boston, 1834–1875). But while Palfrey and Bancroft gained recognition only slightly less than Francis Parkman and William Prescott in an age when the best of historical writing was also popular literature, equally important services were being performed in the quiet confines of numerous state historical societies.

The Massachusetts Historical Society had been founded in 1791, the first such organization in the nation, to be followed by such institutions as the American Antiquarian Society, the Essex Institute, the New England Historical and Genealogical Society, and the Colonial Society of Massachusetts. The founders of these societies were dedicated to the preservation of their heritage. They labored to acquire the manuscript records of the seventeenth century, inaugurated publication projects to make them more accessible, and encouraged research into New England's past. One of the foremost figures of the Massachusetts Historical Society, James Savage, edited and published what was long the definitive edition of Winthrop's journal and compiled a four-volume *Genealogical Dictionary of the First Settlers of New England* (Boston, 1860-1862), which remains a valuable research tool.[1]

If the celebratory tone of historians such as Bancroft was reflective of their generation's unbridled confidence in America's destiny, it was perhaps natural that the disillusionment that many intellectuals came to feel with the state of the nation in the Gilded Age should have produced critical assessments of America's roots. Additional impetus for a new interpretive framework probably came from an overreaction against the filial pride that exuded from the earlier works and that seemed the very antithesis of the scientific objectivity of the new academic history of the late nineteenth and early twentieth centuries. The turning point toward a more critical assessment of the founders of Massachusetts came with the publication within a decade of Brooks Adams' *The Emancipation of Massachusetts* (Boston, 1887) and Charles Francis Adams, Jr.'s *Three Episodes of Massachusetts History* (Boston, 1892). Both these descendants of one of the early settlers castigated their seventeenth century forebears for hypocrisy, intolerance, and cruelty, and Charles Francis stigmatized the late seventeenth century as a period when creativity was stifled by a "theological glacier." As in the case of his predecessors with whose views he disagreed, Charles Francis Adams, Jr., was a painstaking scholar whose insights are still instructive when not distorted by his lack of sympathy for his ancestors' beliefs.

Patriot groups ignored the lead of the Adams brothers and continued to celebrate the contributions of Plymouth Rock and the village green, but scholarly history—with a few exceptions such as Barrett Wendell—remained critical of the Puritans for some time. James Truslow Adams (no relation to Brooks and Charles Francis) won the Pulitzer Prize for his well-written *The Founding of New England* (Boston, 1921). If Charles Francis Adams, Jr., had no sympathy for the faith of the Puritans, James Truslow Adams had no understanding of it. A Beardian, J. T. Adams portrayed a colony where 80 percent of the population had come for material gain and were shackled by a small minority who forced on everyone a system of religious intolerance. A similar theme pervades the depiction of the Bay Colony leaders as theocratic, reactionary oligarchs in Vernon L. Parrington's *Main Currents in American Thought, vol. 1, The Colonial Mind* (New York, 1927). While J. T. Adams and Parrington castigated the Puritans for their dark ideas, a contemporary group of historians, including Herbert Osgood and Charles M. Andrews, found that the very independent spirit that Palfrey and Bancroft had celebrated was, when seen from an imperial perspective, selfish and obstructionist.

This muckraking, warts-are-all view of seventeenth-century Massachusetts had its critics in the wings who bemoaned its excesses. But not until the decade ushered in by the tercentenary celebration of the founding of Massachusetts did the tide dramatically turn in favor of what we today judge to be a more realistic approach that seeks to come to terms with the colonists as they were rather than as the historian might wish them to have been. Specialists in New England history can pinpoint the change with the appearance of Kenneth Murdock's *Increase Mather: The Foremost American Puritan* (Cambridge, 1925), a carefully crafted appreciation of Increase Mather as theologian, imperial politician, college president, and pastor that remains the best biography. But for the scholarly community in general, the decisive blow to the J. T. Adams–Parrington paradigm was dealt by Samuel Eliot Morison with the publication of *Builders of the Bay Colony* (Boston, 1930). Combining scholarship with a crisp, forceful style, Morison made the variety of Puritans he chose for his sketches not only intelligible but interesting people worth learning more about. Morison continued to feed that taste with his *The Founding of Harvard College* (Cambridge, 1935), *Harvard College in the Seventeenth Century*, 2 vols. (Boston, 1936), and *The Puritan Pronaos* (New York, 1936). Morison treated Puritan ideas seriously and sought to relate them to the broader world of the seventeenth century. So did Morison's Harvard colleague Perry Miller. With Miller the modern age of New England studies flowered.

Perry Miller developed the paradigm for colonial New England and Puritan studies by which we measure all subsequent work. Though now somewhat worn, with some wings torn down and others renovated, the structure he built still dominates the neighborhood. But too many scholars make the mistake of ignoring all that came between Cotton Mather and Miller. Hutchinson and Prince, Palfrey and Savage, and all the lesser-known scholars and amateurs who worked in their shadows produced much from which we can still learn. Knowledge of their work is not simply an exercise in historiography. In devoting most of our attention to what is new we should guard against discarding what remains valuable in the old.

The essence of Perry Miller's work on seventeenth-century Massachusetts can be found in *The New England Mind: The Seventeenth Century* (New York, 1939); *The New England Mind: From Colony to Province* (Cambridge, 1953); *Orthodoxy in Massachusetts* (Cambridge, 1933); *Roger Williams: His Contribution to the American Tradition* (Indianapolis, 1953); in the introduction to an anthology he compiled with Thomas Johnson, *The Puritans*, 2 vols. (New York, 1963); and in two collections of essays, *Errand into the Wilderness* (Cambridge, 1956) and *Nature's Nation* (Cambridge, 1967). Miller acknowledged the importance of that aspect of Puritan character that he designated "Augustinian Piety," but he chose to focus his investigations on the mind rather than the spirit of New Englanders. He believed that there emerged in early New England not a universal agreement to a code but a broad consensus on a range of religious, social, and political beliefs. This orthodoxy made extensive use of the idea of the covenant, a contractual image originally referring to the relationship between God and men but expanded by the Puritans to explain also a variety of relationships among men. In Miller's view the theological development of covenant ideas—he referred to a "Federal Theology"—signified a Puritan advance into a post-Calvinist world, the first step in a gradual accommodation to a New World and new circumstances that Miller labored to trace in his later works.

In the 1960s and 1970s it became fashionable to attack Miller's paradigm. Perhaps some scholars felt oppressed by the sense that if Miller was right, then nothing remained to students of Puritanism but filling in details. Whatever their motivation, some critics launched their assaults against what were exaggerations or misstatements of Miller's position. We have been deluged with monographs demonstrating the religious, social, and political pluralism of New England. But Miller never claimed that the region was monolithic. His focus on the dominant concepts of the society did not entail a denial of dissonance—indeed, *The New England Mind: From Colony to Province* is largely a study of the tensions that underlay and threatened orthodox consensus. To criticize Miller for postulating the late seventeenth-century declension of the Puritan society is to misread his his account of colonial perceptions as a judgment that he shared. Those who have found fault with his understanding of continental Calvinism and his subsequent claims for American innovation are on better grounds. Indeed, until recently it has been a hallmark of even the most subtle analysts of American colonial affairs that they show inadequate concern for the nuances of relevant European traditions. Such American myopia is being remedied by a new generation of scholars, and our understanding of the New England mind and its relationship to the broader Protestant tradition is clearer now than ever before. In the process, Miller's paradigm is being modified, but no new interpretive synthesis has yet emerged to replace it; at this time it seems that a new paradigm is not necessary as a tool for further understanding.

Whenever it seems as if nothing more can be learned about seventeenth-century Massachusetts, new studies appear that illuminate hitherto neglected aspects of colonial life. A complete review of the society and the literature that analyzes it is impossible in a limited space, but a survey of the highlights is still impressive.

Anthropologists and geographers have made us increasingly aware of the role that the environment plays in determining the options available for a people's social, economic, and even cultural development. The reciprocal impact that the natural environment of New England and its inhabitants exerted on each other is explored with great insight by William Cronon in *Changes in the Land: Indians, Colonists, and the Ecology of New England* (New York, 1983). Cronon's work contains a fine bibliographic essay that reviews the work of ecologists, anthropologists, geographers, and archaeologists in the field as well as studies by historians and ethnographers.

The lives of the native inhabitants of the region have been a subject of interest since the colonists themselves published observations on the local tribes. The best starting point for understanding the Indians of New England is the *Handbook of North America Indians*, vol. 15, *Northeast* (Washington, D.C., 1978), which was edited by Bruce Trigger. Neal Salisbury's *Manitou and Providence* (New York, 1982) focuses on the first four decades of the century and uses archaeological as well as historical sources in describing the character of Indian life before the coming of the *Mayflower*. Archaeological evidence on precontact Indian life is well synthesized in Dean R. Snow's *The Archaeology of New England* (New York, 1980). The picture that emerges of southern New England Indian life before the Puritan settlements is that of a society in transition, of a people who had moved into an agricultural way of life with consequences for their perceptions of space and time, yet who were still rooted through their religious beliefs in a preagricultural past.

Although the character and timing of the English migration to this New World were critical factors in the transformation of the region, our understanding of who the immigrants were and why they came is still incomplete. John Camden Hotten (*The Original Lists of Persons of Quality . . . and Others Who Went from Great Britain to the American Plantations, 1600-1700* [London, 1874]) and Charles Edward Banks (*The Planters of the Commonwealth: A Study of the Emigrants and Emigration in Colonial Times . . . 1620-1640* [Boston, 1930]) presented most of the surviving registers of ships' passengers, but those registers are not a true sample, and to generalize from them can be misleading.

The reasons that prompted the great migration from England (not all of which was directed toward New England) are studied in Wallace Notestein's *The English People on the Eve of Colonization* (New York, 1954), Carl Bridenbaugh's *Vexed and Troubled Englishmen* (New York, 1968), and Allan French's *Charles I and the Puritan Upheaval: A Study of the Causes of the Great Migration* (London, 1955). These macrostudies of the subject should be supplemented with detailed studies of English society by Alan Everitt, Alan Macfarlane, Joan Thirsk, and others and by microstudies of specific groups involved in the migration. Douglas Horton's "Two Bishops and the Holy Brood" (*New England Quarterly*, 40 [1967]) demonstrates variations in religious pressures on dissenters from diocese to diocese. T. H. Breen and Stephen Foster investigate in detail the background and experience of 273 migrants who came to Massachusetts in the year 1637 in "Moving to the New World: The Character of Early Massachusetts Immigration" (*William and Mary Quarterly*, 30 [1973]: 189-222). A thorough study of social and economic discontent in East Anglia is included in Norman Tyack's unpublished dissertation, "Migration from East Anglia to New England before 1660" (Ph.D. diss., University of London, 1951). Biographies of the first settlers and community studies also have light to shed on this subject.

One of the most fascinating developments in the study of early Massachusetts in recent years has been the rapid expansion of our knowledge of the everyday lives of the colonists. Borrowing from the works and methods of archaeologists, anthropologists, and other students of material culture, scholars are working to complement our understanding of Massachusetts' intellectual, institutional, political, and demographic reality with an appreciation of what it was like to live in the colony. While foretastes of the possibilities inherent in such interdisciplinary cooperation were available earlier (the Institute of Early American History and Culture conference on "The Lives of Early Americans" at Millersville University of Pennsylvania in 1981), the symbolic event that brought this development into focus was the 1982 exhibition "New England Begins" presented by the Boston Museum of Fine Arts (see John Demos, "Words and Things: A Review and Discussion of 'New England Begins,'" *William and Mary Quarterly*, 40 [1983]: 584-17). Much of the richness of the exhibit is preserved and even enhanced in the three-volume catalog, *New England Begins: The Seventeenth Century* (Boston, 1982). Robert Blair St. George's lengthy essay "'Set Thine House in Order': The Domestication of the Yeomanry in Seventeenth-Century New England" in volume two is a brilliantly original mining of the material culture of the region that comes to grips with the *mentalité* of the rural colonist. In fact, all the essays deserve a wider circulation. Using traditional literary sources, David Hall has achieved a tour de force in his reconstruction of "The Mental World of Samuel Sewall" (originally published in the *Proceedings of the Massachusetts Historical Society*, 92 [1981]: 21-44 and reprinted in *Saints and Revolutionaries*, ed. David Hall, John M. Murrin, and Thad W. Tate [New York, 1984]). Hall gives us a chance to understand how Sewall perceived and reacted to a wide variety of ordinary occurrences from street sounds at night, darkness, the passage of time, and the weather, to social relationships and religious devotions.

Such studies give us an opportunity not only to comprehend the character of everyday life but suggest ways in which patterns of behavior can be used as evidence of beliefs. In doing this they provide hope that we will in the future be able to achieve a greater appreciation of the relationship between the theological constructs of the colony's clergymen and the religious beliefs of the lay settlers. Darrett Rutman in *American Puritanism: Faith and Practice* (Philadelphia, 1970) and in other works questioned the assumption of a congruence between the beliefs of the elite and those of the men and women in village lanes. Inspired by studies of European popular culture, some historians are now trying to understand Puritanism as a form of evangelical Calvinist culture that was shaped by ministers and lay believers alike. David Hall has suggested such an approach in "The World of Print and Collective Mentality in Seventeenth Century New England," *New Directions in American Intellectual History*, ed. John Higham and Paul Conkin (Baltimore, 1979); in "Religion and Society: Problems and Reconsiderations," *Colonial British America: Essays in the History of the Early Modern Era*, ed. Jack P. Greene and J. R. Pole (Baltimore, 1984); and in "Towards a History of Popular Religion in Early New England," *William and Mary Quarterly*, 41 (1984): 49-55. His "Mental World of Samuel Sewall" is perhaps the best example so far of the promise of this approach.

George Selement and Bruce C. Woolley have provided a source of value for understanding popular formulations of theological concepts in their edition of *Thomas Shepard's "Confessions"* (*Publications of the Colonial Society of Massachusetts*, vol. 58 [Boston, 1981]), which is the transcribed conversion narratives of members of Shepard's congregation. Selement himself has used these narratives in "The Meeting of Elite and Popular Minds at Cambridge, New England, 1638-1645" (*William and Mary Quarterly*, 41 [1984]: 32-48) to argue that there was a close correspondence between the beliefs of those in the pew and in the pulpit. Another useful analysis of personal religious experience is Patricia Caldwell's *The Puritan Conversion Narrative* (New York, 1983). Darrett Rutman has expressed some reservations and demanded some refinements in the way these scholars investigate popular culture in "New England as Idea and Society Revisited" (*William and Mary Quarterly*, 41 [1984]: 56-61). While caution is necessary, the ongoing investigations of popular culture and the rituals and symbols that united colonists of all ranks represent one of the most promising paths of study now being pursued.

Considerable attention is still paid by historians to the formal thought of the region and especially to its theology. While Miller's work on *The New England Mind* remains the starting point for an understanding of Puritan theology, those working in the field since Miller are more concerned than he was in demonstrating the nuances and varied emphases within the tradition. They have also shown a greater continuity with continental Calvinism than Miller believed to exist. Leonard Trinterud was among the first to challenge the idea that covenant theology was unique to the Puritans ("The Origins of Puritanism," *Church History*, 20 [1951]), a point also made by Jens Møller ("The Beginnings of Puritan Covenant Theology," *Journal of Ecclesiastical History*, 14 [1963]). Recently Michael McGiffert has published a series of articles that provide the most complete and detailed treatment of the development and use of covenant concepts by English Protestants ("The Problem of Covenant in Puritan Thought: Peter Bulkeley's Gospel-Covenant," *New England Historical and Genealogical Register*, 130 [1976]; "William Tyndale's Conception of Covenant," *Journal of Ecclesiastical History*, 32 [1981]; "Covenant, Crown, and Commons in Elizabethan Puritanism," *Journal of British Studies*, 20 [1981]; "Grace and Works: The Rise and Division of Covenant Divinity in Elizabethan Puritanism," *Harvard Theological Review*, 75 [1982]; and "God's Controversy with Jacobean England," *American Historical Review*, 88 [1983]).

Norman Pettit's *The Heart Prepared: Grace and Conversion in Puritan Spiritual Life* (New Haven, 1966) examines the evolution of the doctrine of preparation from continental reformers and English Puritans to the clergy of seventeenth-century Massachusetts. Charles L. Cohen's *God's Caress* (New York, 1986) investigates the psychology of the conversion experience. William Stoever's *"A Faire and Easie Way to Heaven"* (Middletown, Conn., 1978) stresses the co-existence in Reformed thought on salvation of a language of conditionality and one of absolute grace and traces the consequences of this ambivalence for New England doctrinal disputes, particularly the Antinomian controversy. E. Brooks Holifield has written a fine study of Puritan sacramental theology in which doctrinal issues are related to the practical patterns of sacramental worship (*The Covenant Sealed* [New Haven, 1974]). Edmund Morgan similarly links theology and polity—in this case church admission standards—in his classic study, *Visible Saints: The History of a Puritan Idea* (New York, 1963). Important suggestions on the role of formal thought in Puritan religion can be found in Norman Fiering's "Will and Intellect in the New England Mind" (*William and Mary Quarterly*, 29 [1972]: 515-58), in Fiering's *Moral Philosophy at Seventeenth Century Harvard* (Chapel Hill, 1981), and Robert Middlekauff's "Piety and Intellect in Puritanism" (*William and Mary Quarterly*, 22 [1965]: 457-70). Charles E. Hambrick-Stowe has examined Puritan devotional exercises in *The Practice of Piety* (Chapel Hill, 1982).

James Fulton Maclear's "'The Heart of New England Rent': The Mystical Element in Early Puritan History" (*Mississippi Valley Historical Review*, 42 [1956]: 621-52) was one of the first studies to focus on the pietistic strain in American Puritanism and its potential for spawning what many saw as radical religious ideas. Other scholars eventually followed up on these suggestions and on the example set by students of English radical religion. Stephen Foster has advanced our understanding of the context of radical Puritanism in *News from the Caroline Underground* (Hamden, Conn., 1978), in "New England and the Challenge of Heresy, 1630 to 1660: The Puritan Crisis in Trans-Atlantic Perspective" (*William and Mary Quarterly*, 38 [1981]: 224-60), and in "English Puritanism and the Progress of New England Institutions, 1630-1660" (Hall, Murrin, and Tate, *Saints and Revolutionaries*). Philip Gura's *A Glimpse of Sion's Glory: Puritan Radicalism in New England, 1620-1660* (Middletown, Conn. 1984) explores the development of separatism, radical spiritism, anabaptism, Quakerism, and millenarianism and analyzes those views in the context of transatlantic Puritan thought. James F. Maclear has also discussed the role of millenarian views in "New England and the Fifth Monarchy: The Quest for the Millennium in Early American Puritanism" (*William and Mary Quarterly*, 32 [1975]: 223-60), as did Joy Gilsdorf in "The Puritan Apocalypse: New England Eschatology in the Seventeenth Century" (Ph.D. diss., Yale University, 1965). Also of value is James P. Walsh's "Holy Time and Sacred Place in Puritan New England" (*American Quarterly*, 32 [1980]). Clark Gilpin focuses on *The Millenarian Piety of Roger Williams* (Chicago, 1979).

Sacvan Bercovitch has written a number of studies that imaginatively examine the Puritan's sense of divine mission ("The Historiography of Johnson's Wonder-Working Providence," *Essex Institute Historical Collections*, 104 [1968]; "Typology in Puritan New England," *American Quarterly*, 19 [1967]; *The Puritan Origins of the American Self* [New Haven, 1975]; and *The American Jeremiad* [Madison, Wisc., 1978]). The role of typological analysis of Scripture receives considerable attention in Bercovitch's works, as it does in Jesper Rosenmeier's "The Teacher and the Witness: John Cotton and Roger Williams" (*William and Mary Quarterly*, 25 [1968]: 408-31). Some of Bercovitch's findings, and those of Perry Miller as well, will be challenged in a forthcoming book by Theodore B. Bozeman.

The institutional aspects of Massachusetts religion have also been the subject of scholarly investigation. Williston Walker's *Creeds and Platforms of Congrega-tionalism* (Boston, 1960) contains the major statements of New England ecclesi-astical polity with valuable introductory comments. Ola Winslow's *Meetinghouse Hill* (New York, 1952) is an old-fashioned social history with much information on the organization, financing, and practical affairs of the churches. Alice Earle's *The Sabbath in Puritan New England* (New York, 1900) is still useful but should be supplemented by the relevant portions of Winton Solberg's *Redeem the Time: The Puritan Sabbath in Early America* (Cambridge, 1977). Richard Gildrie's "The Ceremonial Puritan: Days of Humiliation and Thanksgiving" (*New England Historical and Genealogical Register*, 118 [1982]) is a valuable analysis of an important ritual. Emil Oberholzer has written on *Delinquent Saints: Disciplinary Action in the Early Congregational Churches in New England* (New York, 1956). An excellent case study is Kenneth Lockridge's "The History of a Puritan Church, 1637-1736" (*New England Quarterly*, 40 [1967]).

The best study of the colony's clergy is David Hall's *The Faithful Shepherd: A History of the New England Ministry in the Seventeenth Century* (Chapel Hill, 1972). Aspects of clerical life are treated in Robert Scholz' "Clerical Consocia-tion in Massachusetts Bay: Reassessing the New England Way and its Origins" (*William and Mary Quarterly*, 29 [1972]: 391-414) and George Selement's *Keepers of the Vineyard: The Puritan Ministry and Collective Culture in Colonial New England* (Lanham, Md., 1984) and "Publication and the Puritan Minister" (*William and Mary Quarterly*, 37 [1980]: 219-41). Stephen Foster demonstrates how the clergy was forced to adapt in order to maintain its influence in the New World. His essay, "The Godly in Transit: English Popular Protestantism and the Creation of a Puritan Establishment in America" is in *Seventeenth-Century New England*, ed. David D. Hall and David G. Allen (Boston, 1984), vol. 63 in the *Publications of the Colonial Society of Massachusetts*. Emory Elliott's *Power and Pulpit in Colonial New England* (Princeton, 1975) presents some controver-sial insights not only on the clergy but also on the general subject of New Eng-land Puritanism. Harry S. Stout's *The New England Soul: Preaching and Religious Culture in Colonial New England* (New York, 1986) is a history of the sermon.

Additional insight on the theology and church life of seventeenth-century Massachusetts can be found in the many available biographies of noted clergy-men. Among the more valuable are Larzer Ziff, *The Career of John Cotton* (Princeton, 1962); B. Richard Burg, *Richard Mather of Dorchester* (Lexington, Ky., 1976); Robert Middlekauff, *The Mathers: Three Generations of Puritan Intellectuals* (New York, 1971); Raymond P. Stearns, *Hugh Peter: The Strenuous Puritan* (Urbana, Ill., 1954); Kenneth Murdock's *Increase Mather*; George A. Cook, *John Wise* (New York, 1952); Richard F. Lovelace, *The American Pietism of Cotton Mather* (Grand Rapids, 1979); Ernest Lowrie, *The Shape of the Puritan Mind: The Thought of Samuel Willard* (New Haven, 1974); and two excellent new studies of Cotton Mather—David Levin's *Cotton Mather: The Young Life of the Lord's Remembrancer, 1663-1703* (Cambridge, 1978), and Kenneth Silver-man's *The Life and Times of Cotton Mather* (New York, 1984). John L. Sibley and Clifford K. Shipton, *Biographical Sketches of Those Who Attended Harvard College* (Boston, 1873-   ), provide excellent short studies of clergymen and lay leaders.

The first major religious dispute to divide Massachusetts centered around the teachings of Roger Williams. The issues at stake are best appreciated by turning to Edmund S. Morgan's *Roger Williams: The Church and the State* (New York, 1967). The Antinomian controversy that swirled around Anne Hutchinson has been extensively examined. Most of the key articles are collected in Francis J. Bremer, ed., *Anne Hutchinson: Troubler of the Puritan Zion* (Huntington, N.Y., 1980). The best full-length study is Emery Battis' *Saints and Sectaries: Anne Hutchinson and the Antinomian Controversy in the Massachusetts Bay Colony* (Chapel Hill, 1962). James Fulton Maclear's "Anne Hutchinson and the Mortalist Heresy" (*New England Quarterly*, 54 [1981]) provides an additional perspective. Robert Pope has thoroughly analyzed another controversial issue in *The Half-Way Covenant* (Princeton, 1969), while the resultant split in Boston's First Church is discussed by Richard Simmons in "The Founding of the Third Church in Boston" (*William and Mary Quarterly*, 26 [1969]: 241-52). The best work on the treatment of sects outside the orthodox consensus is William McLoughlin's *New England Dissent, 1630-1833*, two vols. (Cambridge, 1971). The Quaker challenge to the Bay is dealt with in Arthur Worrall, *Quakers in the Colonial Northeast* (Hanover, N.H., 1980); Carla G. Pestana's "The City upon a Hill under Siege: The Puritan Perception of the Quaker Threat to Massachusetts Bay, 1656-1661" (*New England Quarterly*, 56 [1983]); and Jonathan M. Chu's *Neighbors, Friends, or Madmen* (Westport, Conn., 1985).

While religious thought and practice in Massachusetts has been treated exhaustively, many aspects of the political life of the Bay Colony have been relatively neglected. Edmund S. Morgan's *Puritan Political Ideas, 1558-1794* (Indianapolis, 1965) is an anthology of key documents with introductory comments. Timothy H. Breen's *The Character of the Good Ruler* (New Haven, 1970) is the only full-length study of New England political thought in the seventeenth century. Despite the excellence of Breen's study, it is surprising that the subject has not attracted more attention.

The institutional development of Massachusetts government has suffered from a similar neglect. The narrative histories of the nineteenth and early twentieth centuries remain the most detailed accounts, although Edmund S. Morgan's interpretation of those developments in his biography of John Winthrop, *The Puritan Dilemma* (Boston, 1958), is superior. Robert Wall's *Massachusetts Bay: The Crucial Decade, 1640-1650* (New Haven, 1972) emphasizes and perhaps exaggerates the importance of the political disputes of that decade. Paul Lucas discusses political differences over how the colony should respond to the Restoration in "Colony or Commonwealth: Massachusetts Bay, 1661-1666" (*William and Mary Quarterly*, 24 [1967]: 88-107). The mounting challenge to the Massachusetts charter, culminating in its revocation, is dealt with in Michael Hall's *Edward Randolph and the American Colonies* (Chapel Hill, 1970). The Stuart monarchy's experiment in colonial absolutism is discussed in Viola F. Barnes, *The Dominion of New England* (New Haven, 1923).

The colony's relationship with England throughout the seventeenth century has attracted the attention of a growing number of historians. There was a steady flow of people, ideas, aid, and influence across the Atlantic in both directions. A number of dissertations deal with these types of exchange as well as with more formal relationships during the decades of England's civil wars and interregnum. Ralph Young's "Good News from New England: The Influence of the New England Way of Church Polity on Old England, 1635-1660" (Ph.D. diss., Michigan State University, 1971) demonstrates the active influence of American Congregationalists on English church organization. Francis J. Bremer, "Puritan Crisis: New England and the English Civil Wars, 1630-1670" (Ph.D. diss., Columbia University, 1972), traces and explains colonial political and religious support of the Puritan revolt and Cromwell's Protectorate. Timothy Sehr's "Colony and Commonwealth: Massachusetts Bay, 1649-1600" (Ph.D. diss., Indiana University, 1977) is especially strong on economic and political relations. Steven Crow's "'Left at Libertie': The Effects of the English Civil Wars and Interregnum on the American Colonies, 1640-1660" (Ph.D., diss., University of Wisconsin, 1974) offers a comparison between Massachusetts, Virginia, and Maryland. Bartholomew Schiavo takes a broader chronological perspective in "The Dissenter Connection: English Dissenters and Massachusetts Political Culture, 1630-1774" (Ph.D. diss., Brandeis University, 1976). Avihu Zakai focuses on the effect of English events on the colonists' sense of millennial purpose ("Exile and Kingdom: Reformation, Separation, and the Millennial Quest in the Formation of Massachusetts and its Relationship with England" [Ph.D. diss., Johns Hopkins University, 1983]). The colonists' reaction to the execution of Charles I is dealt with in Francis J. Bremer's "In Defense of Regicide: John Cotton on the Execution of Charles I" (*William and Mary Quarterly*, 37 [1980]: 103-24). The return of New Englanders to join in the struggle at home is the subject of William L. Sachs's "The Migration of New Englanders to England, 1640-1660" (*American Historical Review*, 53 [1948]: 251-78) and is also dealt with in Harry Stout's "University Men in New England, 1620-1660: A Demographic Analysis" (*Journal of Interdisciplinary History*, [1974]).

Relations between the colonists and the mother country in the decades between the Restoration and the Glorious Revolution are dealt with in Alison G. Olson's *Anglo-American Politics, 1660-1775* (New York, 1973). Theodore Lewis' "Massachusetts and the Glorious Revolution, 1660-1692" (Ph.D. diss., University of Wisconsin, 1967) is a detailed narrative. David Lovejoy's *The Glorious Revolution in America* (New York, 1972) remains the best published account of the events on this side of the Atlantic. J. M. Sosin's *English America and the Restoration Monarchy of Charles II* (Lincoln, Nebr., 1980) and *English America and the Revolution of 1688* (Lincoln, Nebr., 1982) take the royalist viewpoint with a vengeance and dismiss the colonial leaders of Massachusetts as hypocrites and bigots. A far more balanced and sensitive study is Richard R.

Johnson's *Adjustment to Empire: The New England Colonies, 1675-1715* (New Brunswick, N.J., 1981). Contacts between Puritan clergymen in Old and New England are discussed in Francis J. Bremer's "Increase Mather's Friends: The Trans-Atlantic Congregational Network of the Seventeenth Century" (*Proceedings of the American Antiquarian Society*, 94 [1984]). Stephen Webb's *1676: The End of American Independence* (New York, 1984) offers a provocative perspective on imperial relations in keeping with the interpretation of those ties that he advanced in *The Governors-General: The English Army and the Definition of Empire, 1569-1681* (Chapel Hill, 1979).

The role of law in the Bay has produced some fine studies in George Haskins, *Law and Authority in Early Massachusetts* (New York, 1960); David T. Konig, *Law and Society in Puritan Massachusetts: Essex County, 1629-1692* (Chapel Hill, 1979); Joseph Smith, ed., *Colonial Justice in Western Massachusetts* (Cambridge, 1961); Barbara A. Black, "The Judicial Power and the General Court in Early Massachusetts" (Ph.D. diss., Yale University, 1975); and John M. Murrin, "Magistrates, Sinners, and a Precarious Liberty: Trial by Jury in Seventeenth-Century New England" (Hall, Murrin, and Tate, *Saints and Revolutionaries*). An excellent collection is *Law in Colonial Massachusetts* (Boston, 1984), which is volume 62 in the *Publications of the Colonial Society of Massachusetts*. Edwin Powers' *Crime and Punishment in Early Massachusetts* (Boston, 1966) is a documentary collection focusing on punishment. Two studies that relate criminal behavior to the general society are Ronald A. Bosco, "Lectures at the Pillory: The Early American Execution Sermon" (*American Quarterly*, 30 [1978]), and Lawrence Towner, "True Confessions and Dying Warnings in Colonial New England" (*Publications of the Colonial Society of Massachusetts*, 59 [1982]).

In addition to Morgan's study of Winthrop, biographical studies of civil leaders include Lawrence S. Mayo's *John Endicott* (Cambridge, 1936); Richard Dunn's *Puritans and Yankees: The Winthrop Dynasty of New England* (Princeton, 1962); and Ola Winslow's *Samuel Sewall of Boston* (New York, 1964). Shorter sketches of other individuals are to be found in Sibley's and Shipton's Harvard volumes.

One area of political life that has attracted extensive scholarly attention is that of the franchise. Beginning in 1954, debate raged over such issues as the significance of religious qualifications for the franchise, the size of the potential and actual electorates, the differences between local and colony enfranchisement, the enforcement of voting laws, and patterns of officeholding. Questions concerning all of these were asked to determine whether Massachusetts was "democratic," a term now recognized as hindering rather than clarifying our understanding of the seventeenth century. Allowing for the fact that she has herself been a key figure in the controversy, these issues are well reviewed by B. Katherine Brown in "The Controversy over the Franchise in Puritan Massachusetts, 1954-1974" (*William and Mary Quarterly*, 33 [1976]: 212-41).

Social relationships in New England have been intelligently studied on both the theoretical and practical levels. Stephen Foster's *Their Solitary Way: The Puritan Social Ethic in the First Century of Settlement in New England* (New

Haven, 1971) provides an excellent introduction to the foundations of Puritan social thought. Timothy H. Breen and Stephen Foster's "The Puritans' Greatest Achievement: A Study of Social Cohesion in Seventeenth-Century Massachusetts" (*Journal of American History*, 60 [1973]: 5-22) both defines and seeks to explain the stability enjoyed by the colony. Breen pursues this subject further in his collection of essays *Puritans and Adventurers: Change and Persistence in Early America* (New York, 1980). Using fresh methods and an awareness of English society of the time, he makes the case for considerable persistence of English social practices in the colony, illustrating the point by examination of various institutions and reinforcing it by comparisons to seventeenth-century Virginia.

The persistence of English local practices in Massachusetts is also the theme of David G. Allen's *In English Ways: The Movement of Societies and Transferal of English Local Law and Custom to Massachusetts in the Seventeenth Century* (Chapel Hill, 1981). Allen's thoughtful study, which relates the differences in several colonial towns to differences in the English towns from which the settlers originated, is one of the latest and one of the best of a series of community studies that dates from Sumner C. Powell's *Puritan Village: The Formation of a New England Town* (Middletown, Conn., 1963). Historians inspired by the social-reconstruction methodologies of European social historians began to delve into local records, and a whole new direction for colonial studies was marked out with the appearance in 1970 of Kenneth Lockridge's *A New England Town: The First Hundred Years, Dedham, 1636-1736* (New York, 1970) and Philip J. Greven Jr.'s heavily demographic *Four Generations: Population, Land, and Family in Colonial Andover, Massachusetts* (Ithaca, N.Y., 1970). John Waters, himself the author of an excellent essay on "Hingham, Massachusetts, 1631-1661: An East Anglian Oligarchy in the New World" (*Journal of Social History*, 4 [1967-1968]), has summarized many of the early town studies in "From Democracy to Demography: Recent Historiography on the New England Town," *Perspectives on Early American History*, ed. Alden T. Vaughan and George A. Billias (New York, 1973). Among other valuable studies of rural communities are John J. Waters' "The Traditional World of the New England Peasants: A View of Seventeenth-Century Barnstable" (*New England Historical and Genealogical Register*, 130 [1976]) and Robert C. Goodman's "Newbury, Massachusetts, 1635-1685" (Ph.D. diss., Michigan State University, 1974).

A quite different story of social development can be found in studies of seaport cities and other commercial centers. Darrett Rutman's *Winthrop's Boston: Portrait of a Puritan Town* (Chapel Hill, 1969) and Richard Gildrie's *Salem, Massachusetts, 1626-1683* (Charlottesville, Va., 1975) examine some of the difficulties of maintaining social cohesion in larger communities with more transient populations. Stephen Innes' *Labor in a New Land: Economy and Society in Seventeenth-Century Springfield* (Princeton, 1983) describes a commercial community with economic and social relationships unlike those found in any other town that has been studied and warns us about generalizing too readily about the colonial experience.

Even more central than the town as a building block of Puritan society was the family. Edmund S. Morgan's *The Puritan Family* (New York, 1966) remains an excellent study. Puritan theories of marriage are carefully examined in James T. Johnson's *A Society Ordained by God: English Puritan Marriage Doctrine in the First Half of the Seventeenth Century* (Nashville, 1970) and in Edmund Leites' "The Duty to Desire: Love, Friendship, and Sexuality in Some Puritan Theories of Marriage" (*Journal of Social History*, 15 [Spring 1982]). Edmund S. Morgan's "The Puritans and Sex" (*New England Quarterly*, 15 [1942]) sought to dispel some of the myths still prevalent regarding the colonists' sexual ethic, and most students of the subject have followed his lead. Kathleen Verduin has challenged the accuracy of this view in "'Our Cursed Natures': Sexuality and the Puritan Conscience" (*New England Quarterly*, 56 [1983]), but she concentrates on showing that Puritans abhorred sexual deviancy, which none of those she criticizes would deny.

John Demos' *A Little Commonwealth: Family Life in Plymouth Colony* (New York, 1970) offers valuable insights into the dynamics of family life, as do some of the town studies mentioned earlier. The demographic literature is reviewed in Daniel Blake Smith's "The Study of the Family in Early America: Trends, Problems, and Prospects" (*William and Mary Quarterly*, 39 [1982]: 3-28). Philip Greven's *The Protestant Temperament* (New York, 1977) relates religious temperament to child-rearing practices in the home and to personality development. Gerald F. Moran and Maris A. Vinovskis offer observations on "The Puritan Family and Religion: A Critical Reappraisal" (*William and Mary Quarterly*, 39 [1982]: 29-63).

Despite the burgeoning interest in women's studies there is a paucity of material dealing with women in the seventeenth century. The best starting place is Mary Beth Norton's "The Evolution of White Women's Experience in Early America" (*American Historical Review*, 89 [1984]). Roger Thompson's *Women in Stuart England and America* (London, 1974) suggests that the sex ratio had much to do with how women were treated in different societies of the period. Lyle Koehler's *A Search for Power: The "Weaker Sex" in Seventeenth-Century New England* (Urbana, Ill., 1980) is not without value but is marred by the author's determination to read seventeenth-century events by the light of today's feminism. Though based on the northern New England colonies, the description of women's roles in Laurel Thatcher Ulrich's *Good Wives: Image and Reality in the Lives of Women in Northern New England, 1650-1750* (New York, 1982) would for the most part apply to Massachusetts as well. Specialized studies include Peter Hoffer and N. E. H. Hull, *Murdering Mothers: Infanticide in England and New England* (New York, 1981); C. Dallett Hemphill, "Women in Court: Sex-Role Differentiation in Salem, Massachusetts, 1636 to 1683" (*William and Mary Quarterly*, 39 [1982]: 164-75); Kim Lacy Rogers, "Relicts of the New

World: Conditions of Widowhood in Seventeenth Century New England," *Women's Being, Women's Place: Female Identity and Vocation in American History*, ed. Mary Kelley (Boston, 1979); James K. Somerville, "The Salem (Mass.) Woman in the Home, 1660-1770" (*Eighteenth-Century Life*, 1 [1974]);D. Kelly Weisberg, "'Under Great Temptations Heer': Women and Divorce in Puritan Massachusetts" (*Feminist Studies*, 2 [1975]); and Gerald Moran, "Sisters in Christ: Women and the Church in Seventeenth Century New England," *Women in American Religion*, ed. Janet Wilson James (Philadelphia, 1980). Children and child rearing are central subjects in many of the above family studies. Various other aspects of children's lives are dealt with in Peter Gregg Slater, *Children in the New England Mind* (Hamden, Conn., 1977), and Ross W. Beales, Jr., "In Search of the Historical Child: Miniature Adulthood and Youth in Colonial New England" (*American Quarterly*, 27 [1975]).

Education as examined by scholars in recent years includes not just formal schooling but the broader process of socialization, in which the family has a key role. This is especially evident in Lawrence Cremin's *American Education: The Colonial Experience* (New York, 1970) and James Axtell's *A School upon a Hill: Education and Society in Colonial New England* (New Haven, 1974). Still of value are Morison's *Puritan Pronaos* and his studies of Harvard. Kenneth Lockridge's *Literacy in Colonial New England* (New York, 1974) examines one measure of the system's success, but should be supplemented by David Hall's "The Uses of Literacy in New England, 1600-1850," *Printing and Society in Early America*, ed. William L. Joyce et al. (Worcester, 1983).

A subject that many scholars believe provides considerable insight into Massachusetts society is the way in which the colonists came to terms with death. The best-known work on this subject is David Stannard's *The Puritan Way of Death* (New York, 1977), but a more extensive study is Gordon E. Geddes' *Welcome Joy: Death in Puritan New England, 1630-1670* (Ann Arbor, 1981). Analyses of gravestone art are used to examine attitudes toward death as well as artistic themes. Among these are Alan Ludwig's *Graven Images* (Middletown, Conn., 1966); Dickran and Ann Tashjian's *Memorials for Children of Change* (Middletown, Conn., 1974); Edwin Dethlefsen and James Deetz' "Death Heads, Cherubs, and Willow Trees" (*American Antiquity*, 31 [1966]; and Peter Benes' *The Masks of Orthodoxy* (Amherst, 1977).

Witchcraft is another subject that, important in itself, assumes a greater significance by opening a window that enables us to see seventeenth-century colonists functioning in a condition of acute societal tension. The episode that has attracted the greatest attention is the 1692 outbreak in Salem. While Marion Starkey's *The Devil in Massachusetts* (New York, 1949) remains a powerful narrative, its interpretation has been superseded. Chadwick Hansen offers a medical explanation for the torments of the afflicted girls and suggests the force that the hysteria must have had for contemporaries in *Witchcraft at Salem* (New York, 1969). Paul Boyer and Stephen Nissenbaum, in *Salem Possessed: The Social Origins of Witchcraft* (Cambridge, 1974), investigate the sociopolitical divisions in Salem (town and village) and draw persuasive conclusions regarding why the accusations flew in the directions they did. Kai Erikson's *Wayward Puritans* (New York, 1966) places the episode in the context of cultural disorientation and the need to establish social boundaries. Sanford J. Fox examines the trials from a scientific perspective in *Science and Justice* (Baltimore, 1968). Richard Weisman's *Witchcraft, Magic, and Religion in Seventeenth-Century Massachusetts* (Amherst, 1984) contends that the Salem episode differed from previous incidents. This is also the conclusion of John Demos, who does not deal with Salem in his *Entertaining Satan* (New York, 1982), the most satisfying and stimulating book yet written on the general subject of witchcraft in seventeenth-century New England. By drawing on the insights of anthropology and psychology as well as the more traditional tools of the historian, Demos opens exciting new perspectives on various aspects of Puritan personality and social relations. The sexual tensions implicit in many witchcraft episodes are analyzed by Carol Karlsen in "The Devil in the Shape of a Woman" (Ph.D. diss., Yale University, 1980).

Much of the typical colonist's time was preoccupied with work, whether in the countinghouse, in the fields, or on the sea. The work ethic of the Bay colonists, however, has been generally neglected by historians. The dust has settled over the old debates regarding Puritanism and the spirit of capitalism between Max Weber and R. H. Tawney and their respective critics without proving very helpful to American colonialists. Many scholars assume some form of movement from a Puritan to a Yankee character and from traditionalism to capitalism, but the points of reference are not very clearly defined. Two good essays dealing with the Puritan work ethic but based on English sources are T. H. Breen's "The Non-Existent Controversy: Puritan and Anglican Attitudes on Work and Wealth, 1600-1640" (*Church History*, 35 [1966]) and Paul Seaver's "The Puritan Work Ethic Revisited" (*Journal of British Studies*, 19-20 [1978-1981]). The few studies that try to discover an economic *mentalité* make no reference to the religious ethic of the region. A study of Massachusetts religious culture that seeks to explain the economic choices made by the colonists would be of great value.

The standard study of the region's economy remains William B. Weeden's *Economic and Social History of New England, 1620-1789* (Boston, 1891), which, however, must be supplemented with the relevant portions of John J. McCusker and Russell R. Menard, *The Economy of British America, 1607-1789* (Chapel Hill, 1985). There are also studies of particular occupations pursued by the settlers, some of which touch on questions of motivation and values. Bernard Bailyn's *The New England Merchants in the Seventeenth Century* (Cambridge, 1955) remains a model study and can be complemented by William Davisson and Dennis J. Dugan, "Commerce in Seventeenth-Century Essex County, Massachusetts" (*Essex Institute Historical Collections*, 107 [1971]). Studies of maritime industries include R. G. Albion et al., *New England and the Sea* (Mystic, Conn., 1972); Raymond McPartland, *A History of the New England*

Fisheries (New York, 1911); John J. McElroy, "Seafaring in Seventeenth-Century New England" (*New England Quarterly*, 8 [1935]); and Daniel Vickers, "The First Whalemen of Nantucket" (*William and Mary Quarterly*, 40 [1983]: 560-83). Charles F. Carroll has studied *The Timber Economy of Puritan New England* (Providence, 1973), as has Carl Bridenbaugh in "Yankee Use and Abuse of the Forest in the Building of New England, 1620-1660" (*Proceedings of the Massachusetts Historical Society*, 89 [1977]). E. N. Hartley investigated the *Ironworks on the Saugus* (Norman, Okla., 1957). The three-volume catalog for the exhibit *New England Begins* contains essays and illustrations dealing with Massachusetts technology and crafts.

Richard B. Morris' *Government and Labor in Early America* (New York, 1946) is a good starting point for a study of workingmen, and Stephen Innes' *Labor in a New Land* contains valuable information on occasional work performed by farmers. Other studies include Terry Anderson and Robert Thomas, "White Population, Labor Force, and Extensive Growth of the New England Economy in the Seventeenth Century" (*Journal of Economic History*, 33 [1973]), and Eric Nellis, "Labor and Community in Massachusetts Bay, 1630-1660" (*Labor History*, 18 [1977]). Servitude is the subject of Lawrence Towner's "A Fondness for Freedom: Servant Protest in Puritan Society" (*William and Mary Quarterly*, 19 [1962]: 201-19). Slaves and free blacks are investigated by Lorenzo J. Greene, *The Negro in Colonial New England, 1620-1776* (New York, 1942), and Richard Twombley and Robert Moore, "Black Puritans: The Negro in Seventeenth-Century Massachusetts (*William and Mary Quarterly*, 24 [1967]: 224-42.

The vast majority of Massachusetts settlers labored on the colony's farms. The importance of agriculture in the colony's development is discussed by Darrett Rutman in "Governor Winthrop's Garden Crop: The Significance of Agriculture in the Early Commerce of Massachusetts Bay" (*William and Mary Quarterly*, 20 [1963]: 396-415) and Karen Friedman in "Victualling Colonial Boston" (*Agricultural History*, 47 [1973]). William Cronon's *Changes in the Land* deals with the agricultural transformation of the landscape. Darrett B. Rutman's *Husbandmen of Plymouth: Farms and Villages in the Old Colony, 1620-1692* (Boston, 1967) provides an excellent discussion of the farming technology that wrought those changes. The goals of the colonial farmer are the subject of a spirited debate between James Henretta and James Lemon. Henretta, in "Families and Farms: Mentalité in Pre-Industrial America" (*William and Mary Quarterly*, 35 [1978]: 3-32), argues that seventeenth-century farmers were premodern, rooted in a traditional subsistence agriculture centered around family concerns. Lemon's "Comment on James A. Henretta's 'Families and Farms'" (*William and Mary Quarterly*, 37 [1980]: 688-96) contends that farmers were motivated by entrepreneurial values. Those interested in these questions should read Timothy H. Breen's "Back to Sweat and Toil: Suggestions for the Study of Agricultural Work in Early America" (*Pennsylvania History*, 49 [1982]). Breen questions the categories employed by Henretta and Lemon, but also calls for an understanding of farm work in a broader cultural context.

The farms of New England did transform the landscape, and that transformation dictated the demise of Indian culture as it existed before the period of contact. Two general interpretations of the relationship between the colonists and the Indians have emerged in the past quarter century. One, best represented by Francis Jennings' *The Invasion of America: Indians, Colonialism, and the Cant of Conquest* (Chapel Hill, 1975), contends that the English were fundamentally hostile to Indian survival and dedicated themselves to crush the tribes and seize their land. The other view, while not denying the negative consequences of English colonization for Indian culture, rejects the notion that these consequences were the result of deliberate English strategy. The most persuasive representative of this point of view is Alden T. Vaughan. In *New England Frontier: Puritans and Indians, 1620–1675*, rev. ed. (New York, 1979) Vaughan examines the colonists' efforts to bring the Indians what they perceived as the transforming benefits of English Puritan civilization. He deals with the major areas of interaction between the races, including missionary efforts, extension of English law to the Indians, and warfare. More specialized studies of missionary activities include Ola Winslow's *John Eliot: Apostle to the Indians* (Boston, 1968); William Kellaway's *The New England Company* (London, 1961); Francis Jennings' "Goals and Functions of Puritan Missions to the Indians" (*Ethnohistory*, 18 [1971]); Neal Salisbury's "Red Puritans: The 'Praying Indians' of Massachusetts Bay and John Eliot" (*William and Mary Quarterly*, 31 [1974]: 27-54); and two articles by James Ronda: "'We Are Well As We Are': An Indian Critique of Seventeenth Century Christian Missions" (*William and Mary Quarterly*, 34 [1977]: 66-82) and "Generations of Faith: The Christian Indians of Martha's Vineyard" (*William and Mary Quarterly*, 38 [1981]: 369-394). Aspects of the application of English legal concepts to the Indians are dealt with in James Ronda's "Red and White at the Bench: Indians and the Law in Plymouth Colony, 1620-1691" (*Essex Institute Historical Collections*, 110 [1974]) and Chester E. Eisinger's "The Puritans' Justification for Taking the Land" (*Essex Institute Historical Collections*, 84 [1948]). Alden T. Vaughan deals with the Pequot War in "Pequots and Puritans: The Causes of the War of 1637" (*William and Mary Quarterly*, 21 [1964]: 256-69), and Douglas Leach examines King Philip's War in *Flintlock and Tomahawk* (New York, 1966). Vaughan and Daniel K. Richter reach some valuable conclusions regarding cultural interaction by studying captives and their fates in "Crossing the Cultural Divide: Indians and New Englanders, 1605-1763" (*Proceedings of the American Antiquarian Society*, 90 [1980]). Students of Indian relations in this period will also wish to read James Axtell's collection of essays, *The European and the Indian* (New York, 1981), and Axtell's *The Invasion Within* (New York, 1985).

The changes in the land wrought by the arrival of the Europeans were well developed when the charter of 1692 brought an era in the Bay's history to an end. But the landscape was not all that had changed. The dream of a "City on a Hill" had been transformed into the reality of being an imperial province. New Englanders were seeking a new identity. Yet if the light Edward Johnson held up to the world failed to effect the changes he espoused, it has served nonetheless as a beacon to generations of historians who have made the study of early Massachusetts one of the most fascinating and productive fields in all of American history.[2]

NOTES

1. A new edition of Winthrop's *Journal* has been prepared by Richard S. Dunn and Letitia Yendle. Upon its publication it should become the standard version.

2. Surveys that deal extensively with seventeenth-century Massachusetts are Francis J. Bremer, *The Puritan Experiment: New England Society from Bradford to Edwards* (New York, 1976) and Benjamin W. Labaree, *Colonial Massachusetts* (Millwood, N.Y., 1979). *Puritan New England: Essays on Religion, Society, and Culture* (New York, 1977) is a collection of articles edited by Alden T. Vaughan and Francis J. Bremer. Two excellent collections of primary sources are Alden T. Vaughan's *The Puritan Tradition in America, 1620-1730* (New York, 1972) and Alan Heimert and Andrew Delbanco's *The Puritans in America: A Narrative Anthology* (Cambridge, 1985). Two review essays of value are Michael McGiffert, "American Puritan Studies in the 1960s," *William and Mary Quarterly*, 27 (1970: 36-67) and the less comprehensive but still useful "New England Puritan Studies in the 1970s" by Laura Ricard in *Fides et Historia* (1983). A thorough bibliography, currently in the process of being revised, is Alden T. Vaughan's *The American Colonies in the Seventeenth Century* (New York, 1971).

2

BETWEEN PURITANISM AND REVOLUTION: THE HISTORIOGRAPHY OF ROYAL MASSACHUSETTS, 1689–1765

WILLIAM PENCAK

SEVENTEENTH-CENTURY MASSACHUSETTS' days, as a self-governing holy experiment can plausibly be described by the term "Puritanism." Social, economic, and political trends from 1629 to 1689 may be interpreted through the framework of the visible saints' efforts to preserve their "city upon a hill" from internal and external challenges as diverse as Quakers, Indians, "declension," English imperial regulations, and ecclesiastical infighting. Similarly, social and economic trends from the Stamp Act to the ratification of the U.S. Constitution can clearly be related to "Revolution": to Massachusetts' leading role in protesting British legislation and in framing new republican governments.

But what of the intervening three-quarters of a century, 1689 to 1765? Massachusetts as a royal province cannot be so neatly organized around a single historiographical theme with such obvious importance for all of American history. Unlike the Puritan experience, so crucial for the development of American ideas of self and mission, and Massachusetts' vital part in bringing on the Revolution, the early eighteenth century does not stand out immediately as one of the pivotal eras in our national past. It certainly has not attracted the same quantity of attention and controversy as those immediately before and after.

Nevertheless, understood as a transitional era between Puritanism and Revolution, Massachusetts' years as a royal province pose a series of questions—and provide a variety of answers—without which neither what followed nor preceded can be completely understood. How did religious commitment change? Was the early eighteenth century an abyss of worldliness separating the fervent heights of

The author thanks Pauline Maier and John M. Murrin for their careful reading of a first draft of this chapter.

the Puritan fathers from the Great Awakening? How was the Puritan dream of a "New Israel" handed down from father to son to emerge as the American dream of a promised land? To what extent did the eighteenth-century province maintain the remarkable growth that had convinced many in the seventeenth century that the Bay Colony was truly favored of God? And how did political and economic trends of the provincial period contribute to Massachusetts' unique Revolutionary significance?

If these questions are not as simple and overwhelming as "What was Puritanism?" or "Who made the Revolution and why?" provincial Massachusetts has engendered some of the most important work in the field of early American history. To cite just a few obvious examples: John M. Murrin's work on the Anglicization of provincial society; Zuckerman, Greven, Lockridge, Cook, and others on the development of New England towns; John A. Schutz on the possibility of colonial political stability through "deference" to an elite; Robert E. Brown's pathbreaking study of the colony as a homogeneous, middle-class society; and G. B. Warden's and Gary B. Nash's accounts of colonial urban life and social structure.

Studying eighteenth-century Massachusetts, then, is not only valuable as postscript to Puritanism or prelude to Revolution. The years from 1689 to 1765 witnessed repeated, severe crisis: four great wars lasted for thirty-seven of seventy-five years; currency problems caused the debates over Land Banks in 1714 and 1741 and specie redemption in 1748; religious acrimony characterized the Mathers' numerous disputes, the Great Awakening, and the "Anglican bishop" controversy of the early 1760s; the governor, the Council, and the House of Representatives quarrelled over the executive's salary, the assembly's choice of a speaker, and the right to supervise accounts with such vehemence that they jeopardized the province's charter; Boston's stagnation and declining economic opportunity in overcrowded rural towns produced effects in the political and social realms. And yet Massachusetts weathered all of these storms without serious internal violence or challenges to its fundamental institutions—the Congregational church and local and provincial government. A basically united province opposed Sir Edmund Andros' Dominion of New England in 1689, the French and Indians for seventy-five years, and royal authority in 1765. For all that Massachusetts' provincial history reads like one near catastrophe after another, any adequate historiographical account must deal with both conflict and consensus, with the unity and energy that made war and revolution on a grand scale possible despite social tensions and political factionalism. The three lines of inquiry set forth here—How was the eighteenth century significant for Puritanism and Revolution? How has writing on Massachusetts shaped colonial historiography in general? and How did the province successfully overcome or defuse its problems?—merge if the key question of this essay becomes How did institutions and individuals resist change or transform themselves under the pressures of these eighteenth-century crises? Looking at political, socioeconomic, and religious developments in turn, the historiography of royal Massachusetts takes on an added interest as we examine where different scholars place their emphases: What changed and what did not from Puritanism to Revolution? What sort of conflict prevailed? What sort of consensus? and Which was most important?

POLITICS AND IMPERIAL RELATIONS

Much of the subsequent debate over Massachusetts provincial politics, not to mention the information used by the various contenders, is contained in the first and in many ways still the greatest work on the subject: volume two and the first part of volume three of Thomas Hutchinson's *History of the Colony and Province of Massachusetts Bay*, ed. Lawrence S. Mayo (Cambridge, 1936).[1] In a work whose fair-minded willingness to examine controversies from different points of view has been praised by many of his professional successors, Hutchinson sketched a complex interpretation that manages to incorporate elements that future scholars have elevated into competing theories. Hutchinson believed that while town government was populist and democratic (Brown, Zuckerman), the lower class, inspired by popular leaders such as Elisha Cooke and the Land Bankers (Adams, Hoerder), occasionally threatened a stable provincial government headed by the prosperous and well-born (Schutz, Zemsky), who retained control until the Revolutionary crisis through respect for their competent administration of public affairs and willing acquiescence by the rank and file of the assembly. Hutchinson thus depicted a basically deferential society but one resting on a popular base, where mutual good will and the need to overcome protracted crisis restrained potentially explosive elements of class conflict and serious elite divisiveness. Similarly, Hutchinson regarded conflicts between the province and British government and governors as limited in scope and animosity rather than as forerunners of the Revolution. He did so in part because most of his history was finished before the Revolution began, but also because he realized—as John Adams did not when he announced his theory of "perpetual discordance" between Massachusetts and Britain—that stability before the Revolution needed explanation.

Compared with Hutchinson, other contemporaneous works on Massachusetts are superficial and polemical. Dr. William Douglass' *A Summary Historical and Political . . . of North America*, 2 vols. (London, 1755), devotes much of its considerable space on Massachusetts to denouncing the evils of paper money, Boston demagogues, and Governor William Shirley's war policies in the late 1740s. Most postrevolutionary eighteenth-century scholars were not seriously interested in the provincial period anyway. Like Adams, they uncritically sought to trace the revolutionary conflict back in time. Peter Oliver (*Origin and Progress of the American Rebellion*, ed. Douglas Adair and John A. Schutz [Stanford, 1963]) and Mercy Otis Warren (*History of the Rise, Progress, and Termination of the American Revolution*, 3 vols. [Boston, 1805]) for example, respectively found conspiracies against a benign imperial control and American liberty running from the *Mayflower* to the "shot heard round the world."

The most distinguished nineteenth-century scholars of New England, John Gorham Palfrey (*A Compendious History of New England* . . . , 5 vols. [Boston, 1873]) and (in their general histories) George Bancroft (*History of the United States from the Discovery of the Continent*, 6 vols. [Boston, 1876]) and Richard Hildreth (*History of the United States of America*, 5 vols. [New York, 1849-1852]), went far beyond Warren and Oliver in depth of research, balanced tone, and length, but little further in theory. As though they themselves stood at Concord Bridge, they traced a series of British encroachments on colonial rights with little sense of discontinuity within the colonial era or between the colonial and Revolutionary periods. Francis Parkman (*A Half Century of Conflict* and *Montcalm and Wolfe* [Boston, 1885]), who deals splendidly and vividly with military and strategic developments, similarly found as little sympathy for the French and Indians as his colleagues did for the English.

The imperial historians, who reacted against the strident nationalism of Whig history in the late nineteenth and early twentieth centuries, did not write much about provincial Massachusetts. Charles M. Andrews did not get beyond the seventeenth century, and Herbert L. Osgood's work (*The American Colonies in the Eighteenth Century*, 4 vols. [New York, 1924-1925]) contains little on Massachusetts not found in his Whig predecessors. Although he is sympathetic to the requirements of imperial defense and the predicament of British administrators, he basically casts the provincial period in the same mold of constitutional conflict between two competing, consistent visions of colonial behavior. The real gems of the "imperial" school are two excellent, informative biographies of Governors Joseph Dudley (*The Public Life of Joseph Dudley* [New York, 1911], by Everett Kimball) and William Shirley (*William Shirley, Governor of Massachusetts, 1741-1756* [New York, 1920], by George A. Wood). They show that Dudley and Shirley were neither heroes nor tyrants (although they appear much closer to the former), but sensitive statesmen trying to balance colonial and imperial interests, all the while hoping to acquire fortune and prestige for themselves. Although written much later, the Massachusetts chapters in Lawrence Henry Gipson's *The British Empire before the American Revolution*, 15 vols. (New York, 1936-1972), also present a version of Massachusetts' history from 1750 to 1776 that is sympathetic to Britain and valuable for its information if not theoretically remarkable.

The reverse may be said of James Truslow Adams' *Revolutionary New England, 1691-1776* (Boston, 1923), which applied to New England the "Progressive" interpretation that Carl Becker (*The History of Political Parties in the Province of New York, 1760-1776* [Madison, Wis., 1909]) and C. H. Lincoln (*The Revolutionary Movement in Pennsylvania* [Philadelphia, 1901]) had advanced for New York and Pennsylvania. Adams sought to discover a conflict between the seaboard and the frontier, the former dominated by an aristocracy that suppressed democratic discontent in the metropolis as well as in newly settled regions. Class conflict became intertwined with imperial politics as upper-class leaders in opposition to the governor courted popular support without intending to relinquish control. But Adams gave little evidence that conflicts of the sort he described actually existed; he usually assumed uncritically that disputes in Boston or on the frontier were in fact class-based. (Joseph J. Malone's *Pine Trees and Politics* [Seattle, 1964] does a more explicit job of showing how popular annoyance with enforcement of the White Pine Laws fueled the ambitions of Elisha Cooke and his wealthy supporters.)

Most recent research into the Land Bank controversy and the Boston "mob" (as it called itself) or "crowd" (as historians prefer to dignify it) has shown that however useful class analysis is for describing political conflict in New York, North Carolina, and elsewhere, it has limited applicability to Massachusetts. John C. Miller attempted to link lower-class resentment at the suppression of the 1741 Land Bank by British authorities at the behest of the "aristocratic" Silver Bankers with the more populist, less deferential religion adopted during the Great Awakening ("Religion, Finance, and Democracy in Massachusetts," *New England Quarterly*, 6 [1933]: 29-54). Analytically, if not in his conclusions, Miller's argument resembled that of Andrew M. Davis' monumental *Currency and Banking in the Province of Massachusetts Bay*, 2 vols. (New York, 1901). In keeping with respectable financial opinions around 1900, Davis regarded the Land Bankers and paper-money advocates as uninformed, lower-class supporters of this unsound practice. But George A. Billias, tracing individual supporters of the bank throughout the province, has shown that they were respectable farmers and merchants—people frequently of considerable means (*Massachusetts Land Bankers of 1740* [Orono, Me., 1954]). The most recent work on the bank, Cathy Mitten's, strikes a middle ground by showing that many Land Bankers were less wealthy and prestigious than the usual participants in provincial politics, if not representative of the lower class. She also demonstrates ("The New England Paper Money Tradition and the Massachusetts Land Bank of 1740" [M.A. thesis, Columbia University, 1979]) that while conventional wisdom is correct that Governor Shirley's wise liquidation of the bank (limiting each banker's liability to the amount of his investment) split the bankers and eliminated factionalism based on the bank itself, nevertheless lawsuits dragged on for over a quarter of a century. Thus Shirley by no means healed all the bank's wounds.

Similarly, Dirk Hoerder's efforts to prove autonomous lower-class crowd action in prerevolutionary Boston have proven less than successful ("Mobs and People: Crowd Action in Massachusetts during the Revolution, 1765-1780" [Ph.D. diss., Free University of Berlin, 1971]). Gary B. Nash, who finds such mobs in Philadelphia and New York, argues that in Boston, even if members of different classes rioted for different reasons, issues such as naval impressment and town markets cut across class lines (*The Urban Crucible: Social Change, Political Consciousness, and the Origins of the American Revolution* [Cambridge, 1979] and "The Transformation of Urban Politics, 1700-1766," *Journal of American History*, 60 [1974]: 605-32). G. B. Warden's "The Caucus and Democracy in Colonial Boston" (*New England Quarterly*, 43 [1970]: 19-45) and Alan and Katherine Day's "Another Look at the Boston Caucus" (*Journal of American Studies*, 5 [1971]: 19-42) reveal an urban "machine" that cut across class lines and ensured cooperation. On the other side of the coin, as William Pencak and Ralph Crandall show, the Caucus' nemeses, Thomas Hutchinson and the court party, also played a prominent role even in Boston town politics between the mid-1730s and early 1760s—probably due to the Caucus' inept leadership following Cooke's death and the court's administrative competence—despite their avowedly elitist ideology and propensity to relocate to country seats in towns surrounding Boston ("Metropolitan Boston before the American Revolution," *Bostonian Society Proceedings* [1985]: 55-79). The bulk of the evidence supports the contention of Pauline Maier (*From Resistance to Revolution: Colonial Radicals and the Development of an Opposition to Britain, 1765-1776* [New York, 1972], chap. 1) and John Lax and William Pencak ("The Knowles Riot and the Crisis of the 1740s in Massachusetts," *Perspectives in American History*, 10 [1976]: 163-214) that the mob acted on the part of the whole community to expel or counter actions widely perceived as opposed to the common good.

Nevertheless, perhaps they have gone too far. The Bostonian "aristocracy," such as it was—the Hutchinsons and Olivers—certainly had class consciousness, feared democracy, and on occasion (even before 1765) suffered mobbings. It might be best to argue that while class tension was present in Boston, it rarely took the form of overt class conflict because Bostonians shared most of the grievances mobs opposed. (Even Hutchinson detested and vigorously fought impressment.)[2] Peter Shaw has a good account of how colonial and Revolutionary crowds followed the forms of European lower-class charivari and the "lord of misrule" (*American Patriots and the Rituals of Revolution* [Cambridge, 1981]). Surely Alfred Young's long-awaited (and highly praised) unpublished manuscript on the Pope's Day rioters will add to the debate.

Still, all in all, it is difficult to see how the sort of conflict present in the more heterogeneous colonies could have appeared in a Massachusetts whose inhabitants were almost overwhelmingly English, Congregationalist, and descended from the first generation "Great Migration." As L. Kinvin Wroth, Lawrence Towner, Richard B. Morris, and William E. Nelson have demonstrated for sailors, blacks, servants, and the poor, New England towns, while warning out "the outsiders" who existed at the periphery of society, took care of their own. Lower-class lawsuits against upper-class abuse had as good a chance at success as not, and class apparently did not prove a barrier to New Englanders' propensity to take their adversaries to court.[3]

Modern historiographical writing about Massachusetts politics may conveniently begin with a book that took Massachusetts' basic homogeneity as its starting point: Robert E. Brown's *Middle-Class Democracy and the Revolution in Massachusetts, 1691-1780* (Ithaca, N.Y., 1955). Brown not only stimulated serious inquiry into the relationship of Massachusetts politics and society, but he questioned fundamentally the entire Progressive "class conflict" model for understanding early American history. Brown's thesis operated on two levels: socially, Massachusetts was about as democratic a society as history could reasonably produce. Education, material subsistence, and opportunity were widespread; almost all adult males could vote. (The Progressives argued for a very restricted franchise based on the percent of total population who did vote, not the percent of adult white males eligible.) Given a society uncomplicated by class tensions, then, what sort of political issues could develop? Brown had only one answer: John Adams' "perpetual discordance" between a worthy people wishing to enjoy their traditional liberties in peace and an insensitive mother country (backed by a handful of careerist politicians) angling for greater control and income.

Brown's dual thesis soon came under attack. Clifford K. Shipton, whose biographies of eighteenth-century Harvard graduates remain an indispensable source for political and social history, argued that Brown vastly oversimplified a complex situation. Leading politicians switched from the governor's (court) "faction" to the popular (country) side as their personal interest and family "connexions" dictated. The steadfast devotion to freedom Brown finds is replaced by Shipton with a Namierite struggle among the elite. If anything, Shipton's witty, amazingly well-researched portraits are partial to the more regular members of the court party. They defended colonial rights within the limits they considered compatible with good relations with Britain and escaped the infamy of raising mobs and instigating character assassinations against opponents.[4]

John A. Schutz (*William Shirley: King's Governor of Massachusetts* [Chapel Hill, 1961]) goes one step beyond Shipton in the Massachusettsization of Namier. Schutz argues that provincial politics during William Shirley's long governorship (1741-1756) were primarily shaped by the quarrels of a few leading men and families competing for such plums as military contracts and commissions during King George's War and the French and Indian War. Also, Shirley's astute handling of patronage, the Land Bank, the resumption of specie currency, and his military leadership in fact brought about a "political stability" quite at odds with the factional turmoil that had preceded. (Schutz described this era in "Succession Politics in Massachusetts, 1730-1741," *William and Mary Quarterly*, 3rd ser., 15 [1958]: 508-20, which details the machinations of Shirley and others to oust Governor Jonathan Belcher.) Schutz' biography of Thomas Pownall shows how Shirley's opponents persuaded his successor to stand up for the colony against exorbitant British demands during the French and Indian War (*Thomas Pownall: British Defender of American Liberty* [Glendale, Calif., 1951]).

The significance of Schutz' studies appears in their incorporation into the theories of colonial politics advanced by Bernard Bailyn and Jack P. Greene in the mid-1960s. In *The Origins of American Politics* (New York, 1969), Bailyn argued that Shirley's unusual opportunity as head of the colonial effort in two wars provided him with the patronage base needed to cajole recalcitrant legislators suspicious of executive power into regular cooperation with the government. And Greene's "Changing Interpretations of Early American Politics," *The*

Reinterpretation of Early American History, ed. Ray A. Billington (San Marino, Calif., 1966), pp. 151-84, ranked Shirley's Massachusetts with John Wentworth's New Hampshire as one of two provinces to achieve stable factionalism dominated by one faction.

If Greene and Bailyn borrowed from Massachusetts scholarship in their general theories of politics, Richard Bushman's article "Corruption and Power in Provincial America," (*The Development of a Revolutionary Mentality: Papers Presented at the First Library of Congress Symposium on the American Revolution* (Washington, D.C., 1972), pp. 63-91, clarified the Bailyn/Greene debate over whether colonials imitated English eighteenth-century "New Whig" ideology that feared "corruption" of a society by the "court" (Bailyn) or seventeenth-century "Commonwealth" or Revolution principles where Englishmen opposed more blatant exercises of unconstitutional power in the interest of "liberty" (Greene). Bushman shows that there was little in Massachusetts to render complaints of corruption convincing: government service jobs were time-consuming and in general paid less than the individuals who held them could earn in private business. As John Lax and William Pencak show for the 1740s, charges of corruption did become plausible in wartime, when the province budget expanded enormously. War contracts and military positions did offer more opportunity for private aggrandizement on a large scale (Lax and Pencak, "Knowles Riot"). Also in the 1740s, *The Independent Advertiser* used natural rights and Lockean theory for the first time to justify popular resistance to a costly war and arbitrary authority in the form of impressment even though the legislature acquiesced in the government's course. Paul Boyer has similarly described the pamphlet war of 1754, which arose in response to a provincial excise tax levied by the legislature, as based on the anti-corruption, anti-Walpole rhetoric that greeted the British Excise in 1733 ("Borrowed Rhetoric: The Massachusetts Excise Controversy of 1754," *William and Mary Quarterly*, 3rd ser., 21 [1964]: 328-51).

Other excellent work describes elite interaction in provincial Massachusetts: Malcolm Freiberg's sympathetic but not uncritical dissertation and article on Thomas Hutchinson ("Prelude to Purgatory: Thomas Hutchinson in Massachusetts Politics" [Ph.D. diss., Brown University, 1950] and "How to Become a Royal Governor: Thomas Hutchinson of Massachusetts," *Review of Politics*, 21 [1959]: 646-56); John J. Waters, Jr., on the Otis family (*The Otis Family in Provincial and Revolutionary Massachusetts* [Chapel Hill, 1968]); and Schutz and Waters' joint effort on the rivalry between the Otises and the Hutchinsons ("Patterns of Massachusetts Colonial Politics: The Writs of Assistance and the Rivalry between the Otis and Hutchinson Families," *William and Mary Quarterly*, 3rd ser., 24 [1967]: 543-67). These studies all do a fine job of emphasizing the interests, passions, and positions of a handful of Massachusetts' leading politicians. But Namierist studies fail to account for the great issues of war and peace and currency with which Massachusetts struggled, and why the populace and legislature followed one side or the other. Both Brown and Robert Zemsky (*Merchants,*

Farmers, and River Gods [Boston, 1971]) show that Shirley faced considerable and persistent opposition on both financial and military policy.

A second critique of the Brown thesis was that the franchise was widespread, but not really democratic. Brown seriously overestimated the number of eligible voters: Chilton Williamson (*American Suffrage from Property to Democracy* [Princeton, 1960]), J. R. Pole (*Political Representation in England and the Origins of the American Republic* [New York, 1966]), and William Pencak ("The Social Structure of Revolutionary Boston: Evidence from the Great Fire of 1760," *Journal of Interdisciplinary History*, 10 [1979]: 267-78) suggest that between 60 and 75 percent of the adult males, rather than the nearly unanimous levels argued by Brown, could meet the forty-shilling freehold or forty-pound property requirement. Shipton (in his review of Brown's book) and G. B. Warden (*Boston, 1689-1776* [Boston, 1971]) have added, to be sure, that towns did not enforce this provision to the letter, especially with respect to well-known law-abiding inhabitants and sons who had not yet inherited property. Brown did establish that far more people could vote than had previously been thought, but is that democracy? And if a sizeable fraction of the population could not meet what Brown considered a modest standard, what then becomes of his "classless" vision of a middle-class democracy?

The Brown thesis was further weakened by arguments that Massachusetts was a "deferential" rather than a democratic society. Following a point advanced by J. R. Pole in his influential article "Historians and the Problem of Early American Democracy" (*American Historical Review*, 67 [1962]: 626-46), Robert Dinkin and Robert Zemsky demonstrate that even if people could vote, they did not usually vote for issues or factions, but for respected "first characters" who held considerably more wealth than average (Dinkin, "Massachusetts: A Deferential or a Democratic Society?" [Ph.D. diss., Columbia University, 1968], and Zemsky, *Merchants, Farmers, and River Gods*). Some towns saved expenses by not sending deputies to the General Court, others pooled them; many deputies took little part in the affairs and debates of the house and contented themselves with passing on the merits of positions put forth by the "court" and "country" factions. Dinkin further shows that towns rarely instructed deputies on matters of other than local interest before the Stamp Act crisis—when they come to life en masse—and continued to seat their meeting houses according to prestige, age, and wealth throughout the colonial period.

Michael Zuckerman's *Peaceable Kingdoms: New England Towns in the Eighteenth Century* (New York, 1970) carried the notion of localism and disinterest to the furthest possible extent. Towns, he argued, were internally democratic, but generally uninterested in the wranglings of governors and assemblies; only the Coercive Acts of 1774 brought them to the provincial stage. Further, town-meeting democracy was not modern democracy, as Brown argued, but a matter of consensual communalism. Towns sought to keep internal peace at all cost and remained insular "peaceable kingdoms" that had withdrawn from the larger world once royal government had supplanted their Puritan experiment.

As with Brown's book, Zuckerman's has been subjected to severe criticism. David Grayson Allen questioned the typicality of Zuckerman's towns, claiming that they were mostly unrepresentative backwaters untouched by the currents of commercialism that gave rise to conflict elsewhere ("The Zuckerman Thesis and the Process of Legal Rationalization in Massachusetts" [with rebuttal by Zuckerman], *William and Mary Quarterly*, 3rd ser., 29 [1972]: 443-68). John M. Murrin made even more telling points in an amazing fifty-page review (*History and Theory*, 11 [1972]: 226-74) of several town studies that summarized some of the points in his still unpublished dissertation "Anglicizing an American Colony: The Transformation of Provincial Massachusetts" (Ph.D. diss., Yale University, 1966). Zuckerman failed to look at court records that detail graphically the traditional litigiousness of New Englanders, as well as interaction between towns. Murrin stresses the importance of the growth of county government and the increasing number of the non-elective justices of the peace in the mid-eighteenth century. According to Murrin, Zuckerman both overestimated the insularity of towns and underestimated the impact of provincial government on localities, especially through taxation, militia service, and the rise of a legal profession connected with the active county courts. When added to the growth in the stability of royal government, evidenced by legislative cooperation with the governor after 1735, Murrin postulated Anglicization as an alternative model for eighteenth-century Massachusetts. The Revolution marked a reaction against some forms of Anglicization while using others—Whig ideology, the "common law," and insistence on the "rights of Englishmen."[5]

If Murrin showed increasing stability after 1735, Philip Haffenden (*New England in the English Nation* [Oxford, 1974]) and (in a much better researched and more imaginative book) Richard R. Johnson (*Adjustment to Empire: The New England Colonies, 1675-1715* [New Brunswick, N.J., 1981]) have found the same development for 1689 to 1713. The loss of Massachusetts' charter in 1684, the Andros years, instability, and warfare all unsettled a social order based on "Puritanism." To survive, Massachusetts had to accommodate religious and political dissidents, such as Anglicans, and cooperate with imperial defense policy. If Murrin and Johnson are both correct, then, the "popular" party only dominated a factionally turbulent legislature for twenty or so years (1715-1735), when financial and constitutional issues monopolized attention.

Where then do we stand? Democracy or deference? Anglicization, lack of interest, or perpetual discordance? Of important recent work not yet discussed, T. H. Breen, *The Character of the Good Ruler: A History of Puritan Political Ideals, 1630-1730* (New Haven, 1970), and, to a lesser extent, G. B. Warden, in his uneven work on *Boston, 1689-1776*, both see a fairly continuous defense of American liberty on the ideological and practical levels, respectively, which connects Puritanism and Revolution. Edward M. Cook, Jr., in *The Fathers of the Towns: Leadership and Community Structure in Eighteenth-Century New England* (Baltimore, 1976) offers a sensible compromise: New England contained several types of towns. Cities such as Boston had high levels of political interest, social stratification, and a predominance of wealthy officeholders. County seats, suburban, self-contained, and frontier towns had progressively decreasing levels of stratification and roles in provincial affairs. Paul Lucas (*Valley of Discord: Church and Society along the Connecticut River* (Hanover, N.H., 1976]), Stephen Innes (*Labor in a New Land: Economy and Society in Seventeenth Century Springfield* [Princeton, 1983]), and Gregory Nobles (*Divisions throughout the Whole: Politics and Society in Hampshire County, Massachusetts, 1740-1775* [Cambridge, 1983]) reveal both a high degree of elite control and a strong undercurrent of popular unrest that climaxed during the Revolution.[6]

Is a synthesis possible without doing violence to the reality of Massachusetts provincial politics? I believe so. If Massachusetts towns were not "peaceable kingdoms," conflict did not approach the levels of the middle or southern colonies and did not challenge the legitimacy of established institutions. Most settlers were descended from the "Great Migration" of 1630-1640 and developed a sense of tradition and history missing elsewhere. Class tensions did not lead to class conflict. If there was more internal legislative factionalism in peacetime, this was counterbalanced by issues that did not challenge the well-being of most of the population. Similarly, discontent with taxation and military policy was compensated for by the need to unite in the common defense, expectation of British financial reimbursement, and prosperity at the conclusion of peace, as Jack P. Greene has shown.[7] During King George's and the French and Indian wars, for example, despite political stability in the legislature, Douglas Leach ("Brothers in Arms?—Anglo-American Friction at Louisbourg, 1745-1746," *Massachusetts Historical Society Proceedings*, 89 [1977]: 36-54) and Fred Anderson (*A People's Army: Massachusetts Soldiers and Society in the Seven Years' War* [Chapel Hill, 1984] and "Why did Colonial New Englanders Make Bad Soldiers? Contractual Principles and Military Conduct during the Seven Years' War," *William and Mary Quarterly*, 3rd ser., 38 [1981]: 395-417) have demonstrated general dissatisfaction and outright mutinies among rank-and-file soldiers upset at subjection to British officers or failure to be assigned or discharged as they had originally agreed. In sum, Massachusetts society possessed enough homogeneity and legitimacy that the social stability T. H. Breen and Stephen Foster have described as "the Puritans' greatest achievement" successfully weathered the crises of the eighteenth century as it had those of the seventeenth ("The Puritans' Greatest Achievement: A Study of Social Cohesion in Seventeenth-Century Massachusetts," *Journal of American History*, 60 [1973]: 5-22).

SOCIAL AND ECONOMIC HISTORY

Despite good descriptive work by William B. Weeden, W. T. Baxter, Roy H. Akagi, and others on Massachusetts social and economic history, modern study of this subject again begins with Robert E. Brown.[8] By endeavoring to demonstrate a "middle-class" society distinguished by widespread subsistence and an absence of class divisions, Brown provided a theory that scholars in the 1960s began to test.

Most of the work on eighteenth-century New England in fact refutes Brown's vision of society. Kenneth Lockridge (*A New England Town: The First Hundred Years, Dedham, 1636-1736* [New York, 1970] and "Land, Population, and the Evolution of New England Society, 1630-1790, and an Afterthought," *Colonial America: Essays in Political and Social Development*, ed. Stanley N. Katz, 2nd ed. [Boston, 1971]) contrasted a seventeenth-century Dedham of peace and plenty, a "closed Christian corporate community," with an early eighteenth-century town characterized by decreasing cohesion and increasing poverty and geographical mobility (both to outlying regions of the town and elsewhere). Philip J. Greven Jr.'s *Four Generations: Population, Land, and Family in Colonial Andover, Massachusetts* (Ithaca, N.Y., 1970) similarly showed how Andover's healthiness and abundance of land led to a population explosion, which in the long run reduced the size of farms and economic opportunity by the fourth generation (around 1740) of settlement. Andover sons, like those elsewhere, had to turn either to the frontier or face declining inheritance prospects in their hometowns. The decreasing size of farms and the inability of farmers to be self-sufficient is amply documented, too, in Robert Gross' work on Concord (*The Minutemen and Their World* [New York, 1976]) and Bettye H. Pruitt's on the 1771 tax assessments ("Agriculture and Society in the Towns of Massachusetts, 1771: A Statistical Analysis" [Ph.D. diss., Boston University, 1981] and "Self-Sufficiency and the Agricultural Economy of Eighteenth-Century Massachusetts," *William and Mary Quarterly*, 3rd ser., 41 [1984]: 333-62). Sarah F. McMahon, however, has shown that even pronounced inequality did not interfere with most people's "comfortable subsistence" ("A Comfortable Subsistence: The Changing Composition of Diet in Rural New England, 1620-1840," *William and Mary Quarterly*, 3rd ser., 42 [1985]: 26-65).[9]

That opportunity declined within older, settled towns as the eighteenth century progressed appears indisputable. What is debatable, however, is whether a permanent, "proletarianized" class of rural poor was being created. Douglas Lamar Jones takes issue with this hypothesis that American society was being "Europeanized." His article "The Strolling Poor: Transiency in Eighteenth-Century Massachusetts" (*Journal of Social History*, 8 [Spring 1975]: 28-54) demonstrates that the number of migrants not settled in a community who roamed eastern Massachusetts looking for temporary work or opportunity increased greatly in the mid-eighteenth century. But his book *Village and Seaport: Migration and Society in Eighteenth Century Massachusetts* (Hanover, N.H., 1981) and work by Christine Heyrman (*Commerce and Culture: The Maritime Communities of Colonial Massachusetts, 1690-1750* [New York, 1984]) and Fred Anderson ("A People's Army: Provincial Military Service in Massachusetts during the Seven Years' War," *William and Mary Quarterly*, 3rd ser., 40 [1983]: 499-527) argue that far from representing permanent impoverishment, migration functioned to move workers from declining areas to those where more opportunities existed—such as the frontier and seaports. Similarly, Anderson shows that military service in the French and Indian War did not attract predominantly the "dregs of society" as John Shy has argued ("A New Look at the Colonial Militia," *William and Mary Quarterly*, 3rd ser., 20 [1963]: 175-85). Rather, New England's massive military efforts, in which over one-third of the adult male population may have served, included the sons of well-to-do freeholders from throughout the province, not just "overcrowded" areas. Military pay and the opportunity to move to the frontier that followed 1763 thus alleviated what might have—but did not—become a serious economic problem. Still, it is difficult to refute the small acreages and high maldistribution of wealth found in many towns studied by Pruitt.

Studies of Massachusetts family life confirm that family ties were growing weaker as the eighteenth century progressed, another indication that fathers were having increasing difficulty controlling their sons by holding out the prospects of sizeable inheritances. Daniel Scott Smith has shown for Hingham what Greven has for Andover—young men married earlier and left the community ("Parental Power and Marriage Patterns: An Analysis of Historical Trends in Hingham, Massachusetts," *Journal of Marriage and the Family*, 35 [1973]: 406-18). They either took their chances elsewhere or (as Charles Grant has described for the Connecticut town of Kent) moved to other communities where their fathers had provided land through speculation.[10] Nancy Cott's work on divorce ("Divorce and the Changing Status of Women in Eighteenth-Century Massachusetts," *William and Mary Quarterly*, 3rd ser. [1976]: 586-614) and Alexander Keyssar's on widowhood ("Widowhood in Eighteenth-Century Massachusetts: A Problem in the History of the Family," *Perspectives in American History*, 8 [1974]: 83-119) respectively show that more New England couples were divorcing after the mid-eighteenth century and that more "unattached" widows—many of them impoverished—lived as single householders. Gary Nash has described efforts to employ them in Boston's spinning manufactory ("The Failure of Female Factory Labor in Colonial Boston," *Labor History*, 20 [1979]: 165-88).

Evidence for economic decline appears most strikingly in studies of eighteenth-century Boston. With the exception of G. B. Warden, all available statistical studies of the metropolis—Nash, Main, Henretta, Sachs, Kulikoff, and Pencak—show increasing and pronounced inequality, poverty, and general economic depression from the 1730s.[11] Nash and Warden also marshal more impressionistic but equally graphic evidence of distress in their accounts of the town: overtaxation, disease, the rise of Philadelphia and to a lesser degree New York, and the decline of trade due to protracted warfare. Boston may have been one of the few depressed or stagnant areas in eighteenth-century America, and the town's leading role in the American Revolution may be explainable simply on the grounds that townsfolk long suffering from taxes, impressment, and contact with British officials and regulars had reached their breaking point by the time of the Stamp Act. Ralph Crandall's dissertation on Charlestown ("New England's Haven Port:

Charlestown, 1630–1775" [Ph.D. diss., University of Southern California, 1975])
shows similar developments in Boston's smaller cross-bay neighbor.

If many towns in Massachusetts suffered economic difficulty of one sort or another, does this necessarily lead to a "social interpretation" of the American Revolution? In contrast to Lockridge's "Social Change and the Meaning of the American Revolution" (*Journal of Social History*, 6 [1973]: 403–39), Jack P. Greene has argued that while it is true that whatever is going on in society will affect political developments in some way, the causes of the Revolution lie in the conflict of British post-1763 policies and American political expectations ("Search for Identity: An Interpretation of Selected Patterns of Social Response in Eighteenth-Century America," *Journal of Social History*, 5 [1972]: 189–220). Of course he is right. But if instead of asking the question, "Why did the Revolution happen?" we ask "Why did it take the form it did in Massachusetts?"—especially in the crucial Boston area—then the economic and generational crises of the late colonial era suggest hypotheses at least as plausible as those based on what people said they were doing in print. Massachusetts' large number of young men who relied on either frontier expansion or war for a livelihood, and the long-term economic distress of Boston, clearly fueled the extraordinary bitterness manifested against the local loyalist elite. Whether the elite's personal wealth and successful careers irked the Revolutionaries more than the fact that their generation had apparently monopolized access to wealth and power, as argued by Jay Fliegelman (*Prodigals and Pilgrims: The American Revolt against Patriarchal Authority, 1750–1800* [Cambridge, 1982]) and William Pencak ("The Revolt against Gerontocracy: Genealogy and the Massachusetts Revolution," *National Genealogical Society Quarterly*, 66 [1978]: 291–304) seem complementary rather than contradictory propositions.

RELIGION

Scholars of seventeenth-century Puritanism define themselves in opposition to or agreement with Perry Miller's monumental volume one of *The New England Mind: The Seventeenth Century* (New York, 1939). Similarly, the starting point for studies of eighteenth-century Massachusetts religious history is volume two of his magnum opus—*The New England Mind: From Colony to Province* (Cambridge, 1953). For all Miller's fine descriptions of debates over currency, the frontier, and various religious and political matters, a fundamental historiographical, even moral point underlies his analysis. Miller wrote in juxtaposition to works such as Vernon L. Parrington's *Main Currents in American Thought*, vol. 1 (New York, 1927), which rejoiced in how eighteenth-century Enlightenment ideals cleared the air of the archaic and intolerant religiosity of such latter-day Puritans as Cotton Mather and Jonathan Edwards. (This was also the view of the nineteenth-century Adamses, Charles Francis and Brooks.)[12]

For the eighteenth century, Miller stood the Puritans' detractors on their heads. He basically rearticulated their own interpretation of the change. Puritanism's original coherent, intellectual worldview related the individual to community, state, and church in a rational yet emotionally satisfying manner. It embodied a profound and uplifting vision of human freedom and social order, but succumbed in the late seventeenth century to "declension." Massachusetts and its fellow New Englanders could not maintain their splendid synthesis in the face of the temptations afforded by the frontier and economic opportunity. In this context Miller views Cotton Mather as almost an irrelevant lunatic. His biography, *Jonathan Edwards* (New York, 1949), tragically depicts a genius trying to find a place for God in a mechanistic universe that disposed of metaphysical problems by Newton's cosmology and Locke's psychology. Edwards understood and absorbed these thinkers effectively, but realized that they only explained how things worked in scientific terms. They left out "why"— the purpose. Hence Edwards' doctrine of a universe held together by God's love.

Recent scholarly controversy has centered around two points raised by Miller: were the early years of the eighteenth century a period of religious decline or indifference, relieved by Mather's ravings and Solomon Stoddard's desperate attempts to open the churches to the unworthy? and what was the nature of the revival, the Great Awakening of the 1730s that peaked in 1740–1741, fueled by Edwards' sermons and conversions? James W. Jones (*The Shattered Synthesis: New England Puritanism before the Great Awakening* [New Haven, 1973]) and E. Brooks Holifield ("The Renaissance of Sacramental Piety in Colonial New England," *William and Mary Quarterly*, 3rd ser., 29 [1972]: 33–48) have argued persuasively that New England was not "dead" before the Awakening. The early decades of the century marked a renaissance in what Holifield has termed "sacramental piety"—a sincere effort by intelligent, well-regarded ministers to maintain something like Puritan standards of church membership while adjusting their language and arguments for a more secular world. Both Mather and Stoddard, the two giants of this period, have recently emerged as heroes, even progressives, rather than relics. Sacvan Bercovitch's literary exegesis (*The Puritan Origins of the American Self* [New Haven, 1975]), the biographies by David Levin (*Cotton Mather: The Young Life of the Lord's Remembrancer* [Cambridge, 1978]) and Kenneth Silverman (*The Life and Times of Cotton Mather* [New York, 1984]), and Robert Middlekauff's family history of *The Mathers: Three Generations of Puritan Intellectuals* (New York, 1971) show Mather as an important figure in American medicine. He risked violent opposition to bring smallpox inoculation to Boston, was a friend to blacks and other social outcasts, an important political figure, and a prolific and powerful writer who not only influenced how contemporary New Englanders viewed themselves, but whose interpretation of the Puritan mission significantly carried on their vision of a peculiarly chosen people. (As a political historian, I would still argue that Mather's involvement in provincial politics and his propensity to identify every change in the factional wind as a matter of apocalyptic importance hurt his reputation as much as his other activities may have helped it.)[13]

Similarly, the traditional image of Solomon Stoddard, "the Pope of the Connecticut Valley," who opened communion to the unregenerate, has been reinterpreted. James P. Walsh ("Solomon Stoddard's Open Communion: A Re-Examination," *New England Quarterly*, 43 [1970]: 97-114) believes, unlike Miller ("Solomon Stoddard, 1643-1729," *Harvard Theological Review*, 34 [1941]: 277-320), that his effort to admit most of his congregation to church membership was undertaken to subject them to church discipline. Thomas A. Schaefer, on the other hand, sees Stoddard as a "proto-Awakener" concerned with the harvesting of souls ("Solomon Stoddard and the Theology of Revival," *A Miscellany of American Christianity*, ed. Stuart C. Henry [Durham, 1963], pp. 328-61). Paul R. Lucas thinks Walsh and Schaefer were both right—for different points in Stoddard's life ("An Appeal to the Learned: The Mind of Solomon Stoddard," *William and Mary Quarterly*, 3rd ser., 31 [1974]: 257-92). Nor, apparently, was his sway in western Massachusetts any more absolute than Mather's in his struggle to keep Boston on the straight and narrow.

Despite the diversity of interpretation, two clear patterns emerge in the post-Miller scholarship on early eighteenth-century religion. First, the age witnessed a far more dynamic, if respectable, "establishment" religiosity than proponents of "declension" suspected. (As Christopher Jedrey shows in *The World of John Cleaveland: Family and Community in Eighteenth-Century New England* [New York, 1979], places like Ipswich, and there must have been many of them, maintained their traditional Puritanism without much controversy throughout the century.) Second, however, the politics of religious controversy centered in the Boston area and the Connecticut Valley, both long-established regions with well-developed elites and traditions of disputes that reached downward into society.

Whatever religious conflict characterized early eighteenth-century Massachusetts paled before the Great Awakening. Here the fundamental touchstone that has defined recent historiography is Alan Heimert's monumental *Religion and the American Mind from the Great Awakening to the American Revolution* (Cambridge, 1966). This conscious effort to carry on Perry Miller's work followed suggestions Miller tossed out in three articles: that the Awakening represented a popular, essentially democratic uprising against formalized, "dead" elitist religion.[14] Heimert went on to trace two cultures in New England. "Old Lights" were committed to reasonable Christiantiy, the ability of a not totally depraved man to prepare for his salvation, and deference both to a settled clergy judged by competent performance of their tasks and to society's "natural" political elite. "New Lights," on the other hand, believed in emotional conversion, the imminence of the millennium, the inability of worthless sinners to effect their deliverance, and a more democratic polity that rated both ministers and rulers in terms of their responsiveness to popular demands rather than their ability to perform traditionally defined duties. Here Heimert's theory has been generally accepted.

What provoked normally temperate reviewers such as Edmund S. Morgan to argue that Heimert's thesis partook "more of fantasy than of fact" was his argument that "New Lights" spearheaded the American Revolution, dragging the "Old Lights" along as moderate Revolutionaries or kicking them out as Tories.[15] On one level, Morgan is unquestionably right. It is hard to find any reluctance, or even much reason, in Boston's three leading Old Light prorevolutionary ministers, Charles Chauncy, Jonathan Mayhew, and Samuel Cooper, the subjects of fine biographies by Edward M. Griffith (*Old Brick: Charles Chauncy of Boston, 1705-1787* [Minneapolis, 1980]) and Charles Akers (*Called unto Liberty: A Life of Jonathan Mayhew, 1720-1766* [Cambridge, 1964], and *The Divine Politician: Samuel Cooper and the American Revolution in Boston* [Boston, 1982]). Edwin S. Gaustad (*The Great Awakening in New England* [New York, 1957]) has found that even Boston ministers overwhelmingly favored the Awakening (nine to three). John Murrin "No Awakening, No Revolution? More Counterfactual Speculations," *Reviews in American History*, 11 [1983]: 161-71) argues convincingly that given the deistical, Masonic, or "high church" propensities of many Revolutionary leaders, it is perfectly possible to conceive of the Revolution without any Awakening at all.[16]

But Harry Stout has saved a good deal of Heimert's thesis ("Religion, Communications, and the Ideological Origins of the American Revolution," *William and Mary Quarterly*, 3rd ser., 34 [1977]: 519-42). If Revolutionaries were not necessarily "New Lights," their emotional style of arguing, their non-deferential appeals to the people (they took politics outside established institutions much as the Awakeners took religion outside established churches), and their millennial hopes for an "Awakened" America to be a model for a corrupted world all borrowed heavily from the New Lights, who in effect co-opted their opponents. Nathan Hatch and Kerry Trask provide the necessary intermediate link between the Awakening of the early 1740s and the Revolutionary decade (Hatch, "The Origins of Civil Millennialism in America: New England Clergymen, War with France, and the Revolution," *William and Mary Quarterly*, 3rd ser., 31 [1974]: 407-30, and *The Sacred Cause of Liberty* [New Haven, 1977]; Trask, "In the Pursuit of Shadows: A Study of Collective Hope and Despair in Provincial Massachusetts during the Era of the Seven Years' War, 1748-1765" [Ph.D. diss., University of Minnesota, 1971]). They demonstrate that the energy and emotion of the Awakening was transmitted through the crusades of King George's and the French and Indian wars. Against the Roman Catholic French and pagan Indians, Old Lights could join in a holy war as easily as the most committed New Lights.

Furthermore, local studies of the Great Awakening in particular towns—John Bumsted for Norton; Philip Greven for Andover; Patricia Tracy for Northampton; and Gary Nash for Boston—all demonstrate that the Awakening in fact appealed most strongly to "outsiders": the young, the poor, and women.[17] Tracy's work (*Jonathan Edwards, Pastor* [New York, 1980]), in particular, is helpful for providing a third, socially rather than intellectually oriented alternative to the outstanding interpretations of Jonathan Edwards by Miller and Norman Fiering (*Jonathan Edwards' Moral Thought in Its British Context*

[Chapel Hill, 1981]). Miller sees a modern visionary, committed to saving Christianity in the mechanistic world of Locke and Newton; Fiering sees a traditional Judeo-Christian moral philosopher concerned with ethics, not just salvation, who believed man could attain a measure of earthly goodness, if not eternal salvation, through natural means. Tracy stresses instead that Edwards and his town were both dominated by the image of his predecessor and grandfather, Solomon Stoddard. Like Stoddard, Edwards cared deeply about overcoming local irreligiosity. But Northampton's younger generation, especially, misinterpreted his message in their efforts to achieve personal independence, whereas the theological and political establishment rightly regarded him as a threat. Then both factions joined to remove him when it became clear that he would not smooth out his difficult path to salvation in the service of political, economic, and generational factionalism. However much Edwards' complex writings lend themselves to multiple scholarly interpretations, in the end he stood alone among his flock as he stood intellectually above his contemporaries.

Edwards' ultimate practical failure epitomized New England's religious troubles in the years after 1750. C. C. Goen (*Revivalism and Separatism in New England, 1740-1800* [New Haven, 1962]) and William G. McLoughlin (*New England Dissent, 1630-1833* [Cambridge, 1971] and *Isaac Backus and the American Pietistic Tradition* [Boston, 1967]) have described how the Baptists, a small but vocal minority powerfully led by Isaac Backus, provoked increasing controversy through their demands for toleration. Carl Bridenbaugh's *Mitre and Sceptre: Transatlantic Faiths, Ideas, Personalities, and Politics, 1689-1775* (New York, 1962) still is the best account of how some "Old Lights," usually members of the upper crust, deserted the church of their fathers as insufficiently hierarchical and launched a renewed Anglican "missionary" effort. Others troubled with New Light excesses laid the groundwork for *The Beginnings of Unitarianism in America* described by Conrad Wright (Boston, 1955). As with the Glorious Revolution of 1689, the American Revolution in Massachusetts united religious antagonists. If Anglicans tended to be loyalists, and Baptists focused more on the province's "tyranny" against them, other religious factions closed ranks as they had in war.[18]

We must end with the paradox with which we began. For all the controversy and crises, political, economic, and religious, that characterize Massachusetts from 1689 to 1776, the center held. Especially alongside its non–New England sister colonies, Massachusetts appears as a paradigm of stability and religiosity, if not of prosperity. Why? The best answer I can offer is borrowed from Patricia Bonomi ("The Middle Colonies: Embryo of the New Political Order," *Perspectives on Early American History*, ed. Alden T. Vaughan and George A. Billias [New York, 1973], pp. 63-92). Thanks to its peculiar mode of settlement—most inhabitants were descended from the Congregational, English, middle-class Puritans who arrived between 1630 and 1640—Massachusetts lacked the social diversity that defined political strife elsewhere. Massachusetts' people quarrelled with each other, however fiercely, without violence and within institutionally accepted limits. But perhaps equally important, Massachusetts arguably suffered greater external challenges than any other British North American colony: the loss of its old charter in the 1680s, repeated imperial threats against its new charter until the mid-1730s, the heavy involvement in Anglo-French wars from 1689 to 1748, which other colonies only felt in a comparable way after 1754, and exceptional British attention in the 1760s. Massachusetts' homogeneity on so many points made it that much easier to unite in the face of external challenges, especially given the various internal crises brewing when these appeared.

To illustrate this point, let me close with one episode I have deliberately left for the end: the Salem witch trials of 1692. Historians have treated this incident with a range of theories comparable to that of Massachusetts in general. Perry Miller regarded the trials as an aberration too exceptional to merit much attention; they occurred in a moment of grave crisis, were never repeated, and were eventually repented. Nothing like the mass slaughter over centuries found in Europe occurred. Marion Starkey (*The Devil in Massachusetts: A Modern Inquiry into the Salem Witch Trials* [New York, 1949]) emphasized the "witch hunting" tactics of ministers and magistrates. Chadwick Hansen (*Witchcraft at Salem* [New York, 1969]) turned the tables. He found the clergy—especially the much-maligned Cotton Mather—among the more reasonable and moderate of the persecutors. He attributed much of the event to the actual practice of some forms of magic at Salem combined with physiological abnormalities among the "possessed" only explicable as demoniacal possession, given the state of seventeenth-century medicine. John Demos ("Underlying Themes in the Witchcraft of Seventeenth Century New England," *American Historical Review*, 75 [1970]: 1311-26) pointed to generational conflict: young girls, cooped up in households under their mothers' thumbs, retaliated against surrogate mother figures: "witches" of approximately their mothers' ages. Demos perhaps explains the girls' behavior, but why did Salem go along with them? Paul Boyer and Stephen Nissenbaum have argued in *Salem Possessed: The Social Origins of Witchcraft* (Cambridge, 1974) that Salem Village was a uniquely contentious town, split between the commercial, worldly port of nearby Salem Town and a more Puritanical, less prosperous farming interior. The accusers came from the latter, the accused from the former. (In neglected articles on Andover and Topsfield, Claude Fuess and Abbie Peterson Towne and Marietta Clark have argued this same point).[19] This explains Salem's behavior, but why then did the province go along? Nearly all historians have argued here that with the loss of the 1629 charter, the uncertainty of the political settlement following Massachusetts' Glorious Revolution, and the advent of a war that was going poorly, the Puritans believed that the Devil had truly singled them out. God was testing their religiosity by seeing whether they would adhere to their faith and suppress the Evil One.

Salem witchcraft is an event that may serve both as a symbol for the historiography of eighteenth-century Massachusetts and as a way of reconciling its diverse interpretations. As with politics, the economy, and religion, tensions operated at the family, local, and province level. But town, church, and province closed ranks, both during the persecution and (when it had become excessive) to end it. If the Devil himself could not successfully topple the factious city upon the troubled hill, what hope could Land Bankers, New Lights, Frenchmen, and Tories possibly retain?

NOTES

1. For a description of Hutchinson the historian, see William Pencak, *America's Burke: The Mind of Thomas Hutchinson* (Washington, D.C., 1982).

2. William Pencak, "Thomas Hutchinson's Fight against Naval Impressment," *New England Historical and Genealogical Register*, 132 (1978): 25-36.

3. L. Kinvin Wroth, "The Massachusetts Vice-Admiralty Courts," *Law and Authority in Colonial America*, ed. George A. Billias (Barre, Mass., 1965); Lawrence Towner, "Fondness for Freedom: Servant Protest in Puritan Society," *William and Mary Quarterly*, 3rd ser., 19 (1962): 201-20; Richard B. Morris, *Government and Labor in Early America* (New York, 1946); William E. Nelson, *The Americanization of the Common Law* (Cambridge, 1975).

4. Shipton's review appeared in the *Political Science Quarterly*, 71 (1956): 306-08. See also John Cary, "Statistical Method and the Brown Thesis on Colonial Democracy" (with a rebuttal by Brown), *William and Mary Quarterly*, 3rd ser., 20 (1963): 251-76; John L. Sibley (vols. 1-3) and Clifford K. Shipton, *Biographical Sketches of Those Who Attended Harvard College*, 17 vols. to date (Boston, 1873-   ).

5. John M. Murrin, "The Legal Transformation: Bench and Bar in Eighteenth Century Massachusetts," *Colonial America: Essays in Political and Social Development*, ed. Stanley N. Katz (Boston, 1971), pp. 417-49. See also Ronald K. Snell, "The County Magistracy in Eighteenth Century Massachusetts, 1692-1750" (Ph.D. diss., Princeton University, 1976), and Carl Bridenbaugh, "The New England Town: A Way of Life," *American Antiquarian Society Proceedings*, 56 (1946): 19-48, for a decline in localism.

6. See Also Edward M. Cook Jr.'s articles, "Social Behavior and Changing Values in Dedham, Massachusetts, 1700-1775," *William and Mary Quarterly*, 3rd ser., 27 (1970): 546-80, and "Local Leadership and the Typology of New England Towns, 1700-1785," *Political Science Quarterly*, 86 (1971): 586-608.

7. Jack P. Greene, "The Seven Years' War and the American Revolution: The Causal Relationship Considered," *The British Atlantic Empire before the American Revolution*, ed. Peter Marshall and Glyn Williams (London, 1980), pp. 85-105.

8. William B. Weeden, *Economic and Social History of New England, 1620-1789*, 2 vols. (Boston, 1890); W. T. Baxter, *The House of Hancock: Business in Boston, 1724-1775* (Cambridge, 1945); Roy H. Akagi, *The Town Proprietors of the New England Colonies: A Study of Their Development, Organization, Activities, and Controversies, 1620-1770* (Philadelphia, 1924); Percy W. Bidwell and John I. Falconer, *History of Agriculture in the Northern United States, 1620-1860* (Washington, D.C., 1925); Bernard Bailyn, *The New England Merchants in the Seventeenth Century* (Cambridge, 1955); George F. Dow, "Shipping and

Trade in Early New England," *Massachusetts Historical Society Proceedings*, 64 (1932): 185–201; and Daniel F. Vickers, "Maritime Labor in Colonial Massachusetts: A Case Study of the Essex County Cod Fishery and the Whaling Industry of Nantucket, 1630–1775" (Ph.D. diss., Princeton University, 1981). There is no general history of New England commerce in the eighteenth century, but John W. Tyler, *Smugglers and Patriots: Boston Merchants and the Advent of the American Revolution* (Boston, 1985) has good material.

9. See also James A. Henretta, "The Morphology of New England Society in the Colonial Period," *Journal of Interdisciplinary History*, 2 (1971): 379–98, and Alice Hanson Jones, *Wealth of a Nation to Be: The American Colonies on the Eve of the Revolution* (New York, 1980).

10. Charles Grant, "Land Speculation and the Settlement of Kent, 1738–1760," *New England Quarterly*, 28 (1955): 51–71.

11. G. B. Warden, "Inequality and Instability in Eighteenth Century Boston: A Reappraisal," *Journal of Interdisciplinary History*, 6 (1976): 585–620; Gary B. Nash, "Urban Wealth and Poverty in Pre-Revolutionary America," ibid., 545–84; Gloria Main, "Inequality in Early America: The Evidence from the Probate Records in Massachusetts and Maryland," ibid., 7 (1977): 559–81; James A. Henretta, "Economic Development and Social Structure in Colonial Boston," *William and Mary Quarterly*, 3rd ser., 22 (1965): 75–92; Allan Kulikoff, "The Progress of Inequality in Revolutionary Boston," ibid., 28 (1971): 375–412; William Sachs, "The Business Outlook in the Northern Colonies, 1750–1775" (Ph.D. diss., Columbia University, 1957); and William Pencak, "The Social Structure of Revolutionary Boston: Evidence from the Great Fire of 1760," *Journal of Interdisciplinary History*, 10 (1979): 267–78.

12. Brooks Adams, *The Emancipation of Massachusetts* (1887; rev. ed. Boston, 1919), and Charles Francis Adams, *Massachusetts: Its Historians and Its History: An Object Lesson* (Boston, 1893). Peter Gay, *A Loss of Mastery: Puritan Historians in Colonial America* (Berkeley, 1966), argues the same point.

13. See also Richard F. Lovelace, *The American Pietism of Cotton Mather* (Grand Rapids, 1979), and Phyllis Franklin, *Show Thyself a Man* (The Hague, 1967).

14. For Miller's ideas, see "The Great Awakening from 1740 to 1750," *Nature's Nation* (Cambridge, 1967), pp. 78–89; "Jonathan Edwards and the Great Awakening," *America in Crisis*, ed. Daniel Aaron (New York, 1952, pp. 3–19); and "Jonathan Edwards' Sociology of the Great Awakening," *New England Quarterly*, 21 (1948): 50–77.

15. Edmund S. Morgan, review of Heimert in *William and Mary Quarterly*, 3rd ser., 24 (1967): 454–59.

16. For an "Old Light" anti-Revolutionary, see Robert J. Wilson III, *The Benevolent Diety: Ebenezer Gay and the Rise of Rational Religion in New England, 1696–1787* (Philadelphia, 1984).

17. J. M. Bumsted, "Revivalism and Separatism in New England: The First Society of Norwich, Connecticut, as a Test Case," *William and Mary Quarterly*, 3rd ser., 24 (1967): 588–612, and "Religion, Finance, and Democracy in Massachusetts: The Town of Norton as a Case Study," *Journal of American History*, 57 (1971): 817–31; Philip J. Greven, Jr., "Youth, Maturity, and Religious Conversion: A Note on the Ages of Converts in Andover, 1740–1749," *Essex Insti-*

tute *Historical Collections*, 108 (1972): 119–34; Gary B. Nash, *The Urban Crucible: Social Change, Political Consciousness, and the Origins of the American Revolution* (Cambridge, 1979).

18. See also Gerald Goodwin, "The American Reaction to the Great Awakening," *Historical Magazine of the Protestant Episcopal Church*, 35 (1966): 343–71, and Joseph Haroutunian, *Piety versus Moralism: The Passing of the New England Theology* (New York, 1932).

19. Claude Fuess, "Witches at Andover," *Massachusetts Historical Society Proceedings*, 70 (1953): 8–20, and Abbie Peterson Towne and Marietta Clark, "Topsfield in the Witchcraft Delusion," *Topsfield Historical Society Collections*, 13 (1908): 23–38.

3

SAMUEL ADAMS' BUMPY RIDE: RECENT VIEWS OF THE AMERICAN REVOLUTION IN MASSACHUSETTS

BRUCE C. DANIELS

ASKING AN HISTORIAN to provide a short but comprehensive historiographical analysis of Revolutionary Massachusetts is more than a little unfair. Massachusetts' role in and importance to the Revolution were far greater than those of any other colony. Many loyalists believed that serious anti-British agitation originated with a cabal of Boston malcontents intent on destroying good government. Conspiratorial-minded patriots rooted the attack on their liberties in the murky, corrupt plots of a self-serving Boston junto currying favor with imperial authorities. British policymakers, long after civil war had exposed the strength of Revolutionary sentiments throughout the colonies, clung to their reassuring delusion that Massachusetts had artificially fomented the crisis and manipulated other colonies into rebellion. From the 1760s to the present, Massachusetts' leaders have been identified as the Revolution's leaders. Samuel and John Adams, James Otis, John Hancock, and Thomas Hutchinson loom over the events of the Revolution, and their names have become household words. Only Virginia's three great leaders, George Washington, Thomas Jefferson, and Patrick Henry, and Pennsylvania's Benjamin Franklin and Joseph Galloway rival those of Massachusetts for recognition. Neither Virginia nor Pennsylvania, however, can equal Massachusetts in supplying icons to the Revolution. The sloop *Liberty*, the Boston Massacre, the Boston Tea Party, the Massachusetts Government Act, the battles of Lexington, Concord, and Bunker Hill, and Shays' Rebellion are the signposts that mark the road to and from revolution.

Almost all professional historians, although willing to acknowledge the pre-eminence of Massachusetts in the prerevolutionary agitation, would probably agree that the primacy of the Bay Colony has been exaggerated. Nevertheless, Revolutionary Massachusetts has received scholarly attention nearly proportionate to its visibility in the popular mind. Heroes and villains require explanations for their behavior; their personalities and motives become historically newsworthy. Icons require explication and elaboration to retain their celebratory quality. The very sources used by modern historians lend themselves to scholarly overindulgence. The flamboyant actions of Massachusetts' leaders, mobs, and towns created a self-sustaining body of written records. New Englanders had the highest literacy rate in the colonies, and their town-meeting records surpass in bulk and detail the local political records of any other region. Even the presence of so many colleges and universities in Massachusetts with large faculties and libraries has enhanced its attractiveness as a subject. For at least a half century, the art of serious historical writing has been dominated by the professoriat; and there are a lot of professors in New England and wonderful research facilities to attract visiting ones.

As everyone no doubt suspects, these introductory remarks serve a purpose beyond merely describing how high the mountain is that I have been asked to climb. They attempt to get me off the hook, at least partially, for the things this chapter does not do and to justify those things it does do. I wish to concentrate my attention on the major works published primarily in the last two decades; and I do not wish to discuss in detail earlier work or the torrent of recent short articles and unpublished theses. To review all the secondary literature on Massachusetts' Revolutionary experience would reduce this chapter to a bibliographical essay and, I fear, obscure the forest in an effort to identify every tree.

Since the publication of Carl Becker's *The History of Political Parties in the Province of New York, 1760-1776* (Madison, Wis., 1909), American historians have seemed unable to escape dealing with the largest issues of the Revolution in terms prescribed by him. As iconoclastic a scholar as Becker would probably be appalled to know that for three-fourths of a century, historians have debated his proposition that the events of the 1760s, 1770s, and 1780s constituted both a war of independence and a social revolution in which differing social and economic classes vied for control of the Revolutionary resistance and settlement. To be fair to the historical profession, the questions raised by Becker are basic and profound, and the debate has been refined, taking some unusual and productive twists and turns along the way. To be fair to the spirit of honest self-examination, however, no one since 1909 has matched the conceptual audacity of Becker's eighteen-page first chapter. Professional historians use differing sets of terms to identify the opposing sides in this debate—Whig versus Progressive, Consensus versus Conflict, Neo-Whig versus New Left—but the essential historiographical outlines remain the same. One wonders how much intellectual energy and vitality has been expended defending or attacking Becker's thesis that might have been more profitably spent elsewhere. I had hoped to be able to say that I would avoid participating in the consensus/conflict dialogue in this essay; alas, I cannot. The nature of the secondary literature will not allow its omission; I promise, however, not to permit this old chestnut to dominate my discussion.[1]

Within the general framework so bemoaned above, some exciting new areas of investigation have been opened that have produced much and promise to produce more. Brilliance has not disappeared from the ranks of Revolutionary historians, it has just been confined. Often, historians have tried to break outside the consensus/conflict limits only to find reviewers and subsequent scholars searching their work for signs of whether it should be assigned to one camp or the other. Historiographers seem to resist anyone breaching the perimeter. In particular, six new types/methods/conceptual patterns are worth brief mention before we move to Massachusetts. They are not mutually exclusive, and many studies fall within two or more of these categories.

1. *Ideology.* Probably the most influential book of recent years, Bernard Bailyn's *The Ideological Origins of the American Revolution* (Cambridge, 1965), attracted everyone's attention to the notion that the Revolutionaries filtered a complex body of oppositional Whig, classical republican, and Enlightenment ideology through their own experiences as an outpost of the British Empire and focused this thought on the crises of the prerevolutionary years. Lockean ideas of the social compact and formal English constitutional theory, which previously had been regarded as the ideological wellsprings of the Revolution, became, under Bailyn's pen, just a part of a much more eclectic worldview held by colonists. Gordon Wood's *The Creation of the American Republic, 1776-1787* (Chapel Hill, 1969) similarly drew together the diverse strands of thought after the Revolution that were woven together in the writing of the state and federal constitutions.[2]

2. *Religion.* Although part of the ideological matrix described by Bailyn and others, religious thought and the colonists' religious background has received a special emphasis. Edmund S. Morgan's "The Puritan Ethic and the American Revolution" (*William and Mary Quarterly*, 24 [January 1967]: 3-43) tied the Revolutionaries to their seventeenth-century past as reformers with a mission to purify the world and suggested that the secular qualities of the Revolutionary generation had been overemphasized. Alan Heimert's *Religion and the American Mind from the Great Awakening to the Revolution* (Cambridge, 1966) shows clear connections between religious radicalism and the anti-authority impulses of the 1760s.[3]

3. *Localism.* No area of colonial and Revolutionary historical writing has increased as rapidly in size and explanatory importance as local history. Most of the first major studies stopped short of the Revolution and concentrated on the colonial period, but many of them commented implicitly on the Revolution, and increasingly, as the genre matured, its practitioners explicitly analyzed the Revolution from a local perspective.[4]

4. *Lower Classes.* Since Jesse Lemisch first turned that felicitous phrase, "The American Revolution Seen from the Bottom Up," during the turbulent 1960s, historians have been following the lead of their European predecessors in trying to capture the essence of life at or near the bottom of the social structure.[5] The roles of sailors, crowds, debtors, the unemployed, and so forth have

been integrated into a Revolutionary movement previously populated by merchants, lawyers, gentlemen, and substantial landowners. Jackson Turner Main's pioneering *The Social Structure of Revolutionary America* (Princeton, 1965) was the point of departure for much of this scholarship, although it has been largely superseded by those it helped inspire.

5. *Colonial Background.* Revolutionary historians, of course, have always emphasized the colonial period to a substantial degree: the rise of the assembly, the development of royal government, the imposition of trade regulations, and so forth of necessity have figured prominently as institutional preconditions for the imperial crisis. Recently, however, demographic, economic, and social historians have identified in the colonial past changes and trends in society that may have created some of the underlying societal preconditions for revolution. Kenneth Lockridge's essay, "Social Change and the Meaning of the American Revolution" (*Journal of Social History*, 6 [Spring 1973]: 403-39), was the first of many to argue that population growth, a dwindling supply of available land, and other economic difficulties created tensions in colonial society that made it rife with dissatisfaction and ripe for rebellion.[6]

6. *Previously Excluded Groups.* Many groups mentioned previously only in passing have begun to receive serious historical attention. In particular, loyalists and women, two large populations who had been viewed in the past primarily passively and in relationship to the patriot movement—loyalists were wrong or misguided; women sewed and suffered—are being studied on their own terms.[7]

The expansion of substance in the above six categories has been accompanied by an expansion or elaboration of historical methodologies. The greatest development has been in the increasing reliance on quantitative data and statistical analysis, but this should not obscure other alterations in approach that are nearly as significant. Virtually abandoned in the revolt against the Turner thesis, historical geography has again assumed a status of legitimacy. Town, county court, parish, probate, and land records probably now exceed colony archives in their use as sources. And social science theory, particularly from the disciplines of anthropology and psychology, is assuming a new importance.

All of the above is providing a richer picture of the American Revolution as a far more complex subject than anyone previously imagined. In Massachusetts, our perspective of the Revolution, prior to the last two decades, has been unduly limited despite the massive amount of secondary literature. Too much has focused on too little. If Massachusetts dominated the Revolutionary era, Boston dominated Massachusetts, the Caucus dominated Boston, and Samuel Adams dominated the Caucus. Thus, Cass Canfield, a journalist-historian, thought it appropriate to entitle his book *Sam Adams's Revolution.* Published by a serious press, Harper and Row, the book unabashedly asserts that the title is appropriate because "without Sam Adams there would have been no Declaration of Independence on July 4, 1776."[8] Canfield is unintentionally exaggerating a theme less boldly stated but implicit in much of the writing about prerevolutionary Massachusetts. The secondary literature of the past two decades, however, has eroded that reductionist proposition to the point where it is no longer tenable even in muted form. Samuel Adams was important; the Caucus was important; Boston was important; but other individuals, other groups and classes, and other communities were also important and are receiving the attention not only that they deserve but that we need if we are to understand what happened in Massachusetts between 1763 and 1789. I wish to discuss the Revolution in Massachusetts by looking at the work of historians who have viewed it from four perspectives: (1) from the top down—the role of leaders; (2) from the bottom up—the role of the lower classes; (3) from the center—the General Court and Boston; and (4) from the hinterland—the other towns and regions in the colony. These categories are in some ways confining; the work of most historians fits in more than one. For the sake of orderly analysis and brevity, however, I will assign (but I hope not consign) each of the works to one of them. Once the four views are developed, they can be superimposed on each other for a fuller picture.

FROM THE TOP DOWN

More than that of any other Revolutionary, Samuel Adams' reputation has undergone the most striking reinterpretation in recent years. Largely shunted to the sidelines by nineteenth-century historians, Adams moved to center stage in the first half of the twentieth century, but the role he played was hardly flattering. A wily agitator, seen to be suspecting British plots everywhere, Adams manufactured crises when there were none and orchestrated resistance when there should have been reconciliation. Unhampered by a concern for truth or ethical scruples, Adams became a "pioneer in propaganda" in the title of John C. Miller's biography. Clifford Shipton's entry on him in Sibley's *Harvard Graduates* further embellished the duplicity of a leader committed to revolution at any cost because of his own personal failures and neuroses.[9] A variety of scholars in the early 1970s, however, began to question both Adams' influence and malevolence. This new view had its best statement in an article on Adams by Pauline Maier that was subsequently expanded and appeared as a chapter in her book, *The Old Revolutionaries: Political Lives in the Age of Samuel Adams* (New York, 1980), which should have laid to rest forever the myth of "Sam Adams' Revolution" and with it the pejorative implication that the Revolution was somehow manufactured.[10] Maier shows Adams to be an austere man, deeply rooted in his Calvinist past and committed to a vision of republican virtue. Despite enhancing Adams' character, Maier's work ironically diminishes his relative importance, although in a further irony she uses his name as a label for the prerevolutionary decade. According to Maier, Adams "controlled" neither the crowds in the street nor the Boston Town Meeting, did not bully other leaders into submission, and did not advocate independence in the 1760s. Adams groped his way toward revolution reluctantly as the only alternative he could accept when imperial reform proved impossible.

The "other Adams," John, has received even more attention recently than his cousin, although our picture of him has not been altered as dramatically. Since the opening to scholars of the Adams' papers in the 1950s, several biographies or book-length studies of his thought or character have appeared. The first of these, Page Smith's two-volume study published in 1962, does not, as Smith frankly admits in the preface, "materially alter the picture" we already had.[11] Adams had been treated by scholars consistently as an ambitious but honest, dour but decent, conservative but revolutionary introspective intellectual haunted by a sense of duty. Smith's biography supports this view and is the most detailed account of Adams' life.

John Howe, Jr.'s analysis of Adams' political thought is more insightful and interpretive. Howe argues that the maintenance of order and stability obsessed Adams all his life. Anchored in this conservatism, Adams' specific thought changed, Howe believes, in response to changes in society. Although stubborn and unswerving in his commitments to deeply felt beliefs, the John Adams that emerges from Howe's pen is an adaptive man able to modify his thought as a result of his experience.[12]

The image of a brooding, duty-conscious John Adams has often been contrasted with the picture of his supposedly vocal, wily cousin Samuel. Peter Shaw's study of John's character, read in conjunction with Maier's reinterpretation of Samuel, shows the two cousins had much in common. John Adams also derived his essence from the moralistic past of his seventeenth-century ancestors, Shaw argues. Full of self-doubt, John was nearly as austere as Samuel and sought a state of grace the way the Puritans had through continual self-examination. He had, in Shaw's words, a "lonely struggle with ambition" and courted popularity as a recognition of his worth but also courted unpopularity as a sign to himself of courage and integrity.[13] Both John and Samuel Adams emerge as much as misplaced Puritans as they do as properly cast revolutionaries. Both disciplined themselves through self-denial, despised luxury and excess, feared venality and corruption, and suspected it in their opponents.

A third Adams, John's wife Abigail, has long been regarded as the most important and influential woman in Revolutionary and early national America. With the rise of women's history, Abigail has achieved a new prominence. Lynne Withey's sympathetic and charming biography of Abigail shows her life to have embodied a tension between domesticity and feminism. Essentially very conservative, convinced that a woman's place was in the home, Abigail nevertheless could not suppress her indignation at injustices accorded the poor, slaves, and women. A loyal wife and domineering mother, she prodded her husband to "remember the ladies" when reforming government and society and inculcated a spirit of inquiry in her children.[14]

All three Adamses believed that Thomas Hutchinson, the last royal governor of peacetime Massachusetts, was the most villainous actor in the Revolutionary drama. Neither Bernard Bailyn nor William Pencak, his two recent biographers, would agree.[15] One finishes reading Bailyn's sensitive, moving account of Hutchinson's life with a tremendous sense of sympathy for him and an admiration for his virtues. No other piece of historical literature can rival this biography in portraying individual tragedy in the Revolution. As unswerving as any of the Adamses, Hutchinson shared with them to a substantial degree the Whig fear of unchecked power. To Hutchinson, however, the greatest danger came not from imperial policy but from homegrown demagoguery within Massachusetts. Published in 1982, eight years after Bailyn's book, Pencak's analysis of Hutchinson's political and social thought argues that the loyalist-historian formulated a comprehensive, consistent, and personally satisfying conservative philosophy of politics and history. Calling Hutchinson an American Burke, Pencak reasserts the connection between loyalism and classical conservatism that American historians once wrote of and Canadian ones still do. If Bailyn tries to place Hutchinson on the conservative side but within the Whig spectrum, Pencak tries to place him in a separate ideological camp. Both scholars, however, rehabilitate his character and both admire his impressive intellectuality.

The other major new biography of a Massachusetts loyalist, Carol Berkin's *Jonathan Sewall* (New York, 1974) is equally sympathetic to a less well known man. Born to an impoverished branch of a prominent family, Sewall worked his way up the ladder of Massachusetts politics to be attorney general through ability, industry, and a capacity for leadership acknowledged by all. Rebellious as a student and young man, Sewall became a victim of his own success and his loyalty to friends. Developing a conservative sense of authority and at home in the factional politics of midcentury, Sewall never seemed to understand fully that great principles were at stake in the 1760s and 1770s and that the battles of those days were not just a continuation of politics as usual. Cautious and optimistic at first, Sewall was forced into exile in England and, like his friend Hutchinson, succumbed to depression. Sewall eventually migrated to Canada, an unhappy man whose life was blighted by events whose meaning he could not comprehend.[16]

James Otis and John Hancock, Boston's other two well-known patriots, still await modern biographers. The brief treatments of Hancock in recent books on other aspects of the Revolution suggest that the enduring view of him expressed in three earlier biographies as a "vacillating and chameleon" seeker of popularity may require some revision.[17] Otis' career and political thought have been reexamined in part by John J. Waters, Jr., in his *The Otis Family in Provincial and Revolutionary Massachusetts* (Chapel Hill, 1968), and in an article by James R. Ferguson, "Reason in Madness: The Political Thought of James Otis" (*William and Mary Quarterly*, 36 [April 1979]: 194-214). Waters attributes the seemingly erratic twists and turns of Otis' Revolutionary career to his mental instability, personal quarrels with Hutchinson and John and Samuel Adams, and to the constant jockeying for position that took place in the court-country politics of the colony's government. Ferguson sees amidst Otis' rambling and at times incoherent writings a consistent tension between the doctrine of natural law and the concept of sovereignty. Early in the 1760s when he emphasized natural rights, Otis supported the patriots' cause; when he later emphasized the sovereignty half of his political equation, he supported royal government.

Charles W. Akers' *The Divine Politician: Samuel Cooper and the Revolution in Boston* (Boston, 1982) attempts to bring a hitherto less publicized leader into the forefront of the Revolutionary movement. Cooper, pastor of the Brattle Street Church, the wealthiest and most influential church in Boston, was the friend and minister of John Hancock, John Adams, James Bowdoin, and several other patriot leaders. Akers' characterization of Cooper as a sensitive, pragmatic, conciliatory man who tried to heal the divisions in Massachusetts society through soothing sermons and personal charm is convincing. And Cooper undoubtedly did play more of a role in the years after independence was declared, particularly in promoting the French alliance, than posterity has credited him with. Yet the evidence available does not move Cooper into the first rank of Massachusetts' leaders.[18]

Another Revolutionary, however, Elbridge Gerry, not forgotten but certainly moved away from center stage since his death, does deserve the more prominent role his biographer George Billias assigns him.[19] The most important Massachusetts leader who did not make Boston his home during the years of prerevolutionary agitation, Gerry lived in Essex County and is remembered primarily for lending his name to devious methods of drawing election-district boundaries and for his alleged obstructionism in refusing to sign the federal constitution drafted in Philadelphia. In the most definitive of any of the biographies being discussed, Billias persuasively argues that a republican ideology suffused all of Gerry's actions and writings and that Gerry's pursuit of his vision of republican virtue required him not to sign the constitution even though he had played an influential role in drafting parts of it. Gerry emerges as an immensely likeable man in Billias' book and seems to be the happiest and most personally untroubled patriot leader. Along with John and Samuel Adams, Gerry shared the Puritan conception of public virtue and fear of luxury and excess. Unlike them, however, he managed to pursue austerity without becoming dour.

The only recent historian to compare explicitly the personalities of several of Massachusetts' leaders, Peter Shaw, did so in *American Patriots and the Rituals of Revolution* (Cambridge, 1981), published five years after his book on John Adams' character. Shaw also looks at the crowds in Boston during the Revolution and concludes that the speeches and writings of both patriot leaders and followers show them to be irrationally angry at English leaders and at loyalists such as Thomas Hutchinson, whom they regarded as father figures unfairly limiting their growth and curbing their personal independence. Like most children, of course, the patriots had been taught to revere their fathers, and they tried to resolve the tension in their anger/respect ambivalence, Shaw argues, through excessive zeal. Shaw's work is careful in many ways and provocative throughout, but the parent/child revolt theory does not tell us much about the Revolution. Revolutionaries often identify a mother country as an unfair parent; why did this anger manifest itself when it did? Why was Hutchinson the target? Why were certain issues identified and others not? As Charles Royster writes in a review of Shaw's work, "To diagnose is not necessarily to explain."[20]

FROM THE BOTTOM UP

Historians of Revolutionary Massachusetts surprisingly lagged behind those of some other colonies in direct and systematic examinations of the role of the lower classes. Many scholars allude to artisans, sailors, the poor, small farmers, and crowds, but the first major study focused on class was Allan Kulikoff's "The Progress of Inequality in Revolutionary Boston," published in 1971. Taking as his point of departure an article by James Henretta that contended that wealth distribution had become more skewed over the course of the prerevolutionary eighteenth century, Kulikoff argues that the trend toward greater inequality increased dramatically in Boston during the Revolutionary years.[21] Not only did the rich get richer, they also became more politically dominant. Poverty became a pressing issue as the Revolution progressed and economic and social divisions became more pronounced. Kulikoff, however, believed that the widening gap between classes did not necessarily lead to political divisions and that it certainly did not lead to political violence.

Since 1971 several historians have published articles along the lines established by Kulikoff, but most of them did not connect their societal analysis with the political events of the Revolution.[22] Three recent books, however, do connect class divisions to Revolutionary action: Dirk Hoerder, *Crowd Action in Revolutionary Massachusetts, 1765-1780* (New York, 1977); Gary B. Nash, *The Urban Crucible: Social Change, Political Consciousness, and the Origins of the American Revolution* (Cambridge, 1979); and David P. Szatmary, *Shay's Rebellion: The Making of an Agrarian Insurrection* (Amherst, Mass., 1980). Taken together, these three books constitute a major contribution to our understanding of the role of the people at the bottom of the social structure.

The most combative by far of the three, Hoerder's analysis of the crowd argues that political agitation in the streets reflected the basic divisions in Massachusetts society identified by social historians. Colonial crowd action was rare, according to Hoerder; when it occurred, it was used, as Pauline Maier has argued for the colonies as a whole, not as a means of challenging community norms but as a means of enforcing them. During and after the Stamp Act riots this changed, Hoerder contends; the riots of the 1760s "activated latent economic grievances," and the elite became increasingly frightened by forces in the street that defied control.[23] After troops sent to Boston dampened crowd action there, it grew in intensity in the countryside, where it proved even more difficult to control. Both inside and outside of Boston, according to Hoerder, local grievances frequently overshadowed ones against imperial policy.

Hoerder's sympathies are with the crowd, and he makes no attempt to conceal his ideological commitments; he does not use the term "mob" because it has a pejorative connotation; he seems to dislike all of the Revolutionary elite leaders; and he does not like the term "inarticulate" that historians frequently apply to the lower classes—they were articulate, but historians have not tried to hear what they said. The stridency and tone of Hoerder's work will probably diminish somewhat the thoughtful consideration that its substance deserves. L. Kinvin Wroth, for example, argues in a review that it is "ahistorical and value laden," that Hoerder's "focus is confined and pre-ordained," and "finding economic differences he [Hoerder] presumes social conflict."[24]

Nash's *The Urban Crucible* examines links between social divisions and political behavior in three colonial cities—Boston, New York, and Philadelphia. It has several chapters specifically on Boston, however, and this material by itself would be sufficient for a medium-sized monograph. Though agreeing in general with Hoerder and sharing his sympathies, Nash is much more judicious and restrained. He paints a picture of poverty and working-class anger in Boston that spread and intensified after Boston's economy languished in the years following the Seven Years' War. Added to economic class divisions, Nash argues, were religious ones. The religious revival of the mid-eighteenth century became a class-specific movement supported by the lower classes and opposed by the middle and upper ones. Revivalists preached an anti-entrepreneurial message suffused with communalism and a concern for economic and social justice. Nash believes that these divisions profoundly affected the origins of the Revolution because they provided the anger for tinder that was necessary to fuel Revolutionary fire. Nash is much more sophisticated than Hoerder in discussing the relationship between the laboring people and the leaders. Many of the leaders did not try to deceive the people, and laboring men often looked to sympathetic leaders such as Samuel Adams or James Otis to express their views. On the other hand, crowds in the street were not "frenzied with liquor and dancing like puppets" on the leading strings of men above them.[25] Nash, however, encounters the same basic problem that Hoerder could not solve: the link between class division and political action must be largely presumed. Little evidence exists to make a direct connection between poverty and politicization.

Szatmary's account of Shays' Rebellion is the only major piece of history from the bottom up that is written about events primarily outside of Boston. He assembles a mass of quantitative data on the Regulators in the Massachusetts backcountry and finds, not surprisingly, that they were small, debt-ridden farmers, Congregationalists, and frequently ex–Revolutionary war soldiers. The Shaysites did not turn lightly to "social banditry," Szatmary contends, but tried for two years to secure relief to no avail. Even after taking up arms, they did not become wild-eyed fanatics but planned their campaigns, picked specific targets, and were purposeful and restrained in using violence. Only after being ruthlessly suppressed by the eastern merchant interests did the rebellion turn radical and lash out indiscriminately at the social and economic elite.

Shays' Rebellion has previously engendered a certain amount of sympathy among historians; Szatmary's account will occasion both more sympathy and more respect for the Massachusetts Regulators. In many ways, their plight sounds similar to that of today's farmers who are squeezed by debt into radical anti-commercial activity. In Hampshire County, the Court of Common Pleas heard nearly 3,000 debt cases in the two years of 1784 and 1785. Nearly one-third of the county's male population over sixteen years of age was involved. Seizures of property enraged farmers; fear of the debtor's cell ran deep. Szatmary further argues that the rebellion was more than an economic class war: it represented two differing worldviews arrayed against each other. The farmers who rebelled saw themselves defending a rural, communal, family-based, agrarian way of life against an ever-encroaching commercial society threatening its existence. This clash of world views is plausible, even probable, but little evidence is adduced in its support.

An aesthetic problem that bedevils lower-class history in all fields is equally troublesome in the work of each of the above: Kulikoff, Hoerder, Nash, and Szatmary. In an effort to write about all of the people, individuals disappear to be replaced by tables, charts, and percentages. In most instances, this is virtually inevitable and is just one of the prices social historians have to pay. Alfred Young's charming biography of a shoemaker-turned-soldier moves away from quantitative data and probes the mind of a Revolutionary from near the bottom of the social scale.[26] Young is given the source material to do so because his subject, a man with the unlikely name of George Robert Twelves Hewes, became recognized as a hero fifty years after the Revolution and had several lengthy interviews recorded. Young's story of the radicalization of Hewes is a good companion piece to read in connection with Hoerder's account of the radicalization of the crowd. Hewes was in many of the crowds Hoerder describes.

In general, historians of the bottom part of Massachusetts society have securely established two propositions: (1) real social and economic division characterized town and countryside, and the plight of the poor was getting worse; (2) crowds, working-class people, and poor farmers played active roles in the Revolution, and these roles were not entirely directed by the elite. The nature of the connections between these two conclusions, however, has not been specified with any degree of certainty. In the case of Shays' Rebellion, a connection does seem to be more self-evident, but even there, going beyond the obvious relationships requires a leap of faith.

FROM THE CENTER

Robert E. Brown's *Middle-Class Democracy and the Revolution in Massachusetts, 1691-1780* (Ithaca, N.Y., 1955) remains the most aggressive statement ever published by a serious historian arguing that the Revolution was a war of independence and contained few or no elements of internal social conflict. Belligerent, unsystematic in research design and collection, and oblivious to contrary evidence, Brown's book is capable of being picked apart in dozens of places. It is, however, a monument on the historiographical landscape; many historians seem to feel that although outrageously overstated, Brown's overall thesis is more right than wrong. And, until recently, most scholars have felt constrained to deal with his argument that colonial Massachusetts was a functioning democracy that fought a war with England to preserve its democratic institutions and patterns of government that the English were trying to destroy with a new imperial policy.

Richard D. Brown's *Revolutionary Politics in Massachusetts: The Boston Committee of Correspondence and the Towns, 1772-1774* (Cambridge, 1970), a careful and judicious book, endorses in essence the Robert E. Brown thesis. Richard D. Brown's meticulous research into the connections between the Boston Committee of Correspondence and the committees of the towns leads him to argue that Boston did not create, dominate, or manipulate the towns' responses to imperial policies. The several hundred towns of the Massachusetts countryside were as prepared to defend their liberties as Boston was, and the varied nature of the towns' opinions indicates that no central body controlled the patriots' opinions. The Boston committee may have provided much of the original stimulus to move towns to action, but the localities played an increasingly active role in both the resistance to England and in the forming of a new state government and constitution. Once awakened, towns determined patriotic policy as much as they reacted to Boston's suggestions.

Brown feels that the countryside and Boston could unite because they shared to a remarkable degree a consensus on what Massachusetts had been and what it should be. He admits that differences, of course, had existed in late colonial Massachusetts over the Land Bank, currency issues, factional fighting in the General Court, and several other issues; differences existed after independence over the constitutions of 1778 and 1780 and over financial matters. Nevertheless, Brown argues, court and country factions united on most imperial matters, and party politics as we now define them did not exist. Neither truly democratic nor oligarchic, colonial and Revolutionary Massachusetts embodied a premodern view of politics and society that enabled it to realize a substantial degree of harmony and enabled its citizens to cooperate effectively during the Revolution. In essence, Brown diminishes Boston's role in the Revolution and diffuses the responsibility widely throughout the province.

Stephen Patterson's *Political Parties in Revolutionary Massachusetts* (Madison, Wis., 1973) provided the first major challenge to the views of the two Browns. As Patterson's choice of title suggests, he believes that political parties existed in the colony and its state legislature and were based on geographic, economic, and ideological differences. Massachusetts' citizens may have hated the idea of political parties and believed in the intrinsic good of harmony and consensus, but, according to Patterson, reality belied belief, and a generation of "antipartisan theory and partisan reality" characterized the background to the Revolution. During the Revolution, the sectional split became more pronounced. Patterson does not compile social and economic data to establish his claims of class division but relies rather on the manifestations of these divisions in voting patterns in the General Court. If Massachusetts was so united on basic issues, he asks, why did it fight so heatedly over the constitution of 1778 and ultimately reject it? Why was Massachusetts the last of the original thirteen states to adopt a constitution?[27]

Patterson wears no ideological blinders and does not crudely overstate his case or ignore contrary evidence. He admits that the country party neither advocated economic redistribution of goods nor articulated notions of class conflict. But, he argues, the representatives of the countryside did think that the rise of commerce on a grand scale was corrupting their society, and they did advocate reform through self-sacrifice, the abandonment of the pursuit of luxury, and a restoration of their sense of old-fashioned virtue. At the highest level in Boston, according to Patterson, the various splits among the leaders reflected their positions in favor of or against the reforms of the country party. The consequence of internal strife in Revolutionary Massachusetts, Patterson believes, lay in the creation of a more modern view of politics that accepted the legitimacy of conflict: partisan theory matched partisan reality.

William Pencak's *War, Politics, and Revolution in Provincial Massachusetts* (Boston, 1981) challenged Patterson's neo-Progressive view in the first modern narrative of the political history of the Revolution in Massachusetts. Mincing few words, Pencak is as combative in this remarkable tour de force as Hoerder was on the opposite side of the spectrum in his analysis of crowd action. According to Pencak, the Revolution was a "true peoples' revolt" and "the product neither of personal elite squabbling, a paranoid fear of British tyranny, nor class conflict." War, Pencak argues, was the most basic political fact in colonial Massachusetts between 1689 and the Revolution. It continually produced problems: inflation, high taxes, recession, social disorder, and other forms of suffering. England seemed unable or unwilling to comprehend or care about the devastating effects of nearly a century of military conflict and, Pencak believes, shamelessly used Massachusetts as an imperial pawn. After enduring generations of this treatment, Massachusetts, tired of being sacrificed to the interests of an ungrateful mother country, "rose almost unanimously" against royal government. The Revolution was, Pencak writes, a "reasonable response to severe, undeserved burdens."[28]

Pencak does not hide behind the walls of rhetoric but attacks head-on the work of Patterson, Hoerder, Nash, and other neo-Progressives. To Patterson's argument that political parties existed in the General Court, Pencak says that systematic roll-call analyses suggest they did not. Further, he believes that Patterson overestimated the amount of rivalry among elite factions in Boston. To Hoerder's and Nash's contention of significant class conflict exemplified by crowd action against the wealthy, Pencak replies that there was almost a complete absence of mob violence against wealthy Revolutionaries: it was exclusively directed against loyalists or suspected loyalists. Although Pencak agrees with Hoerder and Nash that crowds became increasingly active in the Revolutionary era, he believes that they continued to operate primarily as an extension of the institutional structure. By Pencak's count, ninety-four Boston merchants belonged to the Sons of Liberty, making it a community organization, not a workingman's crowd. Much of the rhetoric in Boston referring to the people in the street as hooligans, Pencak says, came from loyalists doing all they could to discredit the patriot cause and to spread fear of anarchy.[29]

Pencak's work is provocative and courageous. Compared to its closest interpretive counterpart, Robert E. Brown's book published a quarter century earlier, it is a model of careful research and honest argument. Reviews praise his accomplishment, but many believe that Pencak has not found division because he has looked in the wrong places. His focus on high provincial politics, for example, does not allow him to comment extensively on events in the countryside. His examination of manifest political events diminishes his appreciation of social, religious, and ethnic differences. And the voting rolls of the General Court still await a definitive analysis before the existence of parties can be either confirmed or denied.

Before we move from Boston to the hinterland for our views of the Revolution, six other books are worth brief mention. Two of them are narrative accounts of celebrated incidents: the Boston Tea Party and the Boston Massacre. The other four are legal/constitutional histories that provide a perspective different from more traditional history. Benjamin Woods Labaree's *The Boston Tea Party* (New York, 1964) and Hiller B. Zobel's *The Boston Massacre* (New York, 1970) both make wonderfully entertaining reading. Both authors are marvelous detectives, tracking down thousands of clues and details and weaving them together into good stories. Unfortunately, both subscribe to a view of the Revolution as a series of personal confrontations between manipulative patriot leaders and blundering royal officials. Labaree's work has a redeeming historical value in its discussion of the legal issues surrounding the tea ships as they lay in the harbor.

The most important of the legal histories, William E. Nelson's *Americanization of the Common Law: The Impact of Legal Change on Massachusetts Society, 1760-1830* (Cambridge, 1975), argues that a conception of consensus sustained prerevolutionary laws whereby juries determined almost all considerations of fact, law, and issue. During the Revolution, Nelson believes, tensions already straining this consensus became more pronounced, and the court system proved unable to function properly amidst the growing divisiveness. A new system emerged based not on consensus but on law codes imposed by judicial authority. Complementing this argument, Ronald M. Peters, Jr.'s *The Massachusetts Constitution of 1780: A Social Compact* (Amherst, 1978) argues that the opposing legal positions in the formation of a new constitution pitted those who wished to enshrine in it the conception of individual rights against those who favored popular sovereignty. Thus the heart of the debate was between those who wished to protect the individual and those who wished to protect society. From a textual examination of the constitution, Peters concludes that the latter prevailed and that the form of the new government reflects an anachronistic attempt to maintain a beleaguered colonial conception of society and law. Peters' analysis of the political theory embedded in the constitution makes an important contribution to our knowledge of it, but forcing the document into one or the other of the two categories seems ahistorical. The constitution was built on compromise, not on an either/or basis that included one principle to the near exclusion of the other.

John Phillip Reid's *In a Defiant Stance: The Conditions of Law in Massachusetts Bay, the Irish Comparison, and the Coming of the American Revolution* (University Park, Pa., 1977) is as eclectic and provocative as its title suggests. Reid makes the obvious but often unmentioned point that although the laws of Massachusetts were sufficient to maintain the royal government's prerogative, the conditions of enforcing the law were inadequate since the courts were partially under the colonists' control. Hence, no patriot was ever tried and found guilty of treason. The same basic laws were in place in Ireland but enforced by imperial authorities who used the courts to suppress Irish dissent. The Revolution, Reid argues, stemmed not from English tyranny but from permissiveness and laxity. M. H. Smith in *The Writs of Assistance Case* (Berkeley, 1978) makes much the same point in his study of the first major incident of the prerevolutionary years. He argues that judged by English precedent, the royal authorities had every right to press the case as they did and were not in the least overzealous, as the colonists claimed they were, in not making the writs specific but in using them as a general tool. No doubt both Reid and Smith are correct from a legal perspective; Massachusetts was treated more leniently than Ireland and there was English precedent for imperial actions in the Writs of Assistance case. Too much perspective, however, may be as bad as too little. Telling an unemployed Boston laborer that he was fortunate not to be starving in the Irish countryside would not have been any more effective in relieving his anger.

FROM THE HINTERLAND

Two books that do not explicitly deal with the Revolutionary movement are nonetheless important places to begin to gain an understanding of the countryside; they provide a context in which to place community studies and have been a point of departure for many historians. Michael Zuckerman's *Peaceable Kingdoms: New England Towns in the Eighteenth Century* (New York, 1970) maintains that Massachusetts townspeople predicated their social vision on a desire for concord and harmony. Although many scholars dispute Zuckerman's contention that a high degree of local consensus was achieved, almost everyone agrees that it was a deeply felt goal. Robert Zemsky's *Merchants, Farmers, and River Gods: An Essay on Eighteenth-Century American Politics* (Boston, 1971) analyzes the politics of mid-eighteenth-century Massachusetts towns. Zemsky agrees with Zuckerman that within towns divisions were few and most towns functioned in a relatively democratic manner. Between towns, however, Zemsky sees divisions reflected in their voting patterns in the General Court. Although primarily geographic, these divisions did not necessarily pit eastern Massachusetts against the west. Rather, Zemsky argues that there were five different regions in the colony, each of which had an identifiable pattern of behavior. The divisions may have been partly attributable to class, but Zemsky believes that location was more important. And the divisions revealed anger and serious tensions in Massachusetts.

Van Beck Hall's *Politics without Parties: Massachusetts, 1780-1791* (Pittsburgh, 1972) studies the voting behavior of all towns in the state in the decade following independence. As does Zemsky, Hall sees bitter intertown political divisions reflected in voting patterns in the General Court. He is more insistent than Zemsky, however, that intertown conflict tended to divide society along social and economic lines. Hall agrees that sectional divisions were important, but not as important as ones that derived from community types. The nature of a town's economic development predicted its voting behavior far more than its location, Hall argues. Ironically, divisions based on type of community may have somewhat mitigated sectional conflict because each region in the state had towns with sizeable and with negligible commercial development.

Edward M. Cook, Jr.'s *The Fathers of the Towns: Leadership and Community Structure in Eighteenth-Century New England* (Baltimore, 1976), a study of local officeholding, also argues that differing types of communities had differing patterns of leadership. Cook identifies five distinctive types of communities and local polities; in general, the larger and more complex a town was, the more elite and restrictive its politics were. Most importantly for our present purposes, however, Cook sees few changes in officeholding occasioned by the Revolution. The "fathers of the towns," as he calls the local patriarchs of the eighteenth century, by and large survived the Revolution with prestige and positions intact.

The most recent book to continue in the tradition of Zuckerman, Zemsky, Hall, and Cook and examine the behavior of many towns in order to arrive at some general conclusions is Gregory H. Nobles' *Divisions throughout the Whole: Politics and Society in Hampshire County, Massachusetts, 1740-1775* (New York, 1983). Of virtual necessity, Nobles engages in a dialogue with one of the most influential books written in an earlier era on the Revolution, Robert J. Taylor's *Western Massachusetts in the Revolution* (Providence, 1954). Taylor had argued that in the prerevolutionary years a few powerful leaders ruled without challenge over a conservative, quiescent population of western farmers. The Revolution, according to Taylor, politicized the farmers, who turned their fury on the elite and drove them from power. Taylor studied the western response primarily through an analysis of the elite. Nobles focuses instead on local politics in the two dozen or so towns in Hampshire County and arrives at somewhat different conclusions than Taylor's. Although peace and harmony may have been goals in western towns at mid-eighteenth century, Nobles maintains that it was never achieved, and, far from apathetic, small farmers, recently "awakened" in religious revivals and angry over a diminishing supply of land, challenged rule by the elite in the two decades prior to the 1760s. Nobles argues that division and tensions arising out of pre-existing local grievances fastened themselves upon the politics of the Revolutionary era. Agitation against the elite did not begin in the

1760s, it intensified. Nobles agrees with Taylor on the course of development during the Revolution itself. A dual revolution occurred in western Massachusetts towns: British rule ended and a local elite toppled.[30]

Despite the complaints of many reviewers about a glut of New England town studies, only two major single-community studies of Massachusetts towns during the Revolution period have been published. The first, Benjamin Woods Labaree's *Patriots and Partisans: The Merchants of Newburyport, 1764-1815* (Cambridge, 1962), surprisingly is seldom referred to in the literature. The second, Robert Gross' *The Minutemen and Their World* (New York, 1976), is widely acclaimed as one of the modern classics of local and Revolutionary history.

As its title indicates, Labaree's book on Newburyport focuses on the merchant community over a half century that includes the Revolution. Pathbreaking at the time of its publication, it has suffered the same relative neglect as Charles Grant's pioneering study of Kent, Connecticut, *Democracy in the Connecticut Frontier Town of Kent* [New York, 1961]), published a year earlier. Eclectic in interpretation, Labaree argues that Robert Brown's belief in the widespread nature of democracy in Massachusetts was wrong; over half of Newburyport's unskilled workers were disenfranchised on the eve of the Revolution, and a small interconnected elite dominated the town's politics. On the other hand, Labaree sees no major disputes or political divisions arising from the social and economic ones. From the beginning, most of the town, including the merchant elite, supported the patriotic movement. The Revolution, however, destroyed the merchants' hold on power not because they were politically attacked but because they lost their economic base. Newburyport's merchants suffered as much during the 1780s as western farmers did and collapsed as a collective entity to be replaced by a new group of entrepreneurs. Although lacking the sophisticated methodological tools developed by historians in the years since its publication, Labaree's work is careful, convincing, and of much value because it is the only detailed study of a seaport other than Boston.

The Minutemen and Their World, a history of Concord during the Revolution, deserves the praise it has received. The beauty of Gross' work is that it combines the best of two traditions: the charming personal view of history as narrative and the quantitative, demographic view of history as social science. As David Hackett Fischer writes on the book's back cover, "this book is a pleasure to read—so much so that one may easily miss the monumental research upon which it rests." Interpretively, Gross is not as original and for the most part joins debates already in progress. Economic malaise and sectional intratown rivalries produced bitter divisions in Concord prior to the Revolution. Little concerned with the world beyond their own boundaries, Concord's residents found themselves plunged into the imperial debates during the 1770s that at first seemed to end some of their long-standing divisions. Once the war began and new hardships emerged, some of the bitterness resurfaced. No dual revolution occurred in Concord, however, according to Gross. Most Concord residents were moderate Whigs, and the elite remained in power throughout the era, although traditional deference was weakened and average townspeople developed a penchant for holding their leaders accountable for their actions. Concord also resisted direction from Boston or other outside agencies such as the Continental Congress and jealously guarded its own local prerogatives. No strikingly new picture of the Revolution emerges from Gross' account, but no one else has created such a beautifully textured portrait of a Revolutionary community.

CONCLUSION

Inherently narcissistic, historiography at its best is but a useful service; at its worst it is tedious recitation of publishing details. From what may be regarded as the foregoing tedium, I would like to try to establish six general conclusions about the Revolution in Massachusetts.

1. Ideology played an important role in the minds of almost all participants, including those at the top and bottom of society and those inside and outside of the centers of action. Whether austere Calvinism, English constitutionalism, philosophical conservatism, eighteenth-century republicanism, New Light revivalism, anti-entrepreneurialism, or local resistance to outside authority, clusters of ideas crystallized in people's minds and helped shape their responses to events before, during, and after independence. Sometimes articulated and sometimes not, ideas moved individuals, crowds, and communities although no single pattern of thought or motivation prevailed.

2. The responsibility for the Revolution was diffused over a broad range of individuals, groups, and classes. All towns took part. The Revolution was not Sam Adams', it was Massachusetts'. The ranks of leaders were not dominated by any one or two individuals. Indeed, the rise in importance attributed to people such as Abigail Adams, Samuel Cooper, and Elbridge Gerry makes one suspect that this diffusion may spread yet more widely. The increasing importance and independence of thought and action attributed to crowds and to the various regions and towns of Massachusetts bespeaks an increasing complexity and multiplicity of motivations.

3. Religious thought and religious controversy played a far more important role in the Revolution than was once thought. Many leaders, and presumably many followers, had a Calvinist view of duty, morality, and human nature that conditioned their reaction to events. The Great Awakening and its political manifestations also conditioned the reactions of individuals and communities.

4. Prerevolutionary patterns of politics fastened themselves on the Revolutionary era. The factional battles and shifting alignments within royal government and local squabbles over town divisions, land availability, and leadership conditioned attitudes toward and stands taken on imperial policy and on resistance to that policy.

5. A substantial degree of consensus in Massachusetts existed before, during, and after the Revolution. People identified harmony as a goal; most citizens, including loyalists, thought the new imperial policy unwise; Revolutionaries who disagreed did so peacefully at the ballot box over such issues as the constitutions

of 1778 and 1780; much of the state recoiled in horror at Shays' Rebellion, and the Shaysites themselves embraced violence reluctantly only after they felt that peaceful dissent had failed.

6. Serious divisions did characterize Massachusetts society at all levels and in all regions. Widening gaps in the ownership of wealth increasingly characterized the colony prior to and during the Revolution. Sections, regions, and types of communities had differing perceptions of events. Within most towns from Hampshire County to Concord to Boston divisions were apparent. Debtors and creditors had different solutions to the problems of the new state.

I would like additionally to make the following six observations about the state of historical writing on the Revolution in Massachusetts:

1. The consensus/conflict debate is still a vital part of the historiography. It has not gone away and probably will not in the foreseeable future. Many scholars still address it explicitly and most do implicitly. Although we know that there were many shared values and many divisions in Massachusetts, we do not know the relative weighting and importance of consensus and conflict.

2. Historians are increasingly tending to place positive constructions on the motivations of participants in the Revolution regardless of their positions or roles. Villains are disappearing from the historical landscape. Revolutionaries, loyalists, merchants, crowds, and even the Shaysites are all being portrayed as individuals or groups with integrity. Samuel Adams may have declined in influence in the writings of recent historians, but he has increased in his stature as a person. One assumes that he would prefer his present position as being one of many steadfast fellows instead of being the singular master of deceit and manipulation.

3. The problem of definition remains serious and causes much unnecessary disagreement among historians, Richard D. Brown, Van Beck Hall, and Stephen Patterson, for example, agree substantially in their description of political maneuvering in the General Court but disagree in their choice of language to apply to this activity. Only to a small extent does this disagreement reflect real substantive differences.

4. Substantive disagreements do remain, however, and they will only be settled by more research. The degree of upheaval that accompanied the Revolution remains a subject of genuine debate. Which experience—that of Boston, Hampshire County, Newburyport, or Concord—should be used to assess what type and how much of an internal revolution occurred? Does an analysis of voting patterns in the General Court reveal the absence or presence of demonstrable, persistent, partisan activity?

5. We know a great deal about the Revolution in Massachusetts. A brilliant, rich, general history of Revolutionary Massachusetts could be written entirely from secondary sources.

6. There are some gaps in our knowledge that would not permit a few parts of the picture in the general history to be filled in, and there are some parts of the picture that would be fuzzy. For example, no systematic and comprehensive

accounts of loyalism and women exist. No major biographies have been written of leaders in the backcountry. Some Bostonians such as John Hancock and James Otis need a thorough re-examination. And the nature of the connections between social and economic tensions and manifest political activities must be spelled out more precisely.

With all this water over the historical dam, the various participants in the drama that unfolded in Massachusetts in the second half of the eighteenth century would probably be both amazed and flattered that so many intelligent men and women have spent so much energy and time trying to figure out what they did and why they did it. We know far more about their revolution than they did. A large number of them were just mad as hell at the English; some were mad as hell at the rabble-rousers; others were mad as hell at their neighbors; and some were not mad at all. It has become our task to tell them why they were or were not. Virginia's James Madison may have unknowingly provided the best contemporary explanation of the Revolution in Massachusetts. In *Federalist Number Ten*, Madison wrote that republicanism can best thrive in a society comprised of a vast multiplicity of self-interested individuals, groups, classes, economic interests, regions, and religions. In a society with only a few interests, Madison argued, one or two self-seeking ones can achieve a dominant position and impose a tyranny or create a conflict so deep or sharply focused that it will lead to civil war. In a society of dozens of competing interests, many of which are defined by ambiguous or overlapping lines, such a sharp cleavage will not occur. A consensus based on compromise will emerge, unplanned by anyone but resulting from these divisions scraping against each other in the day-to-day political, social, and economic marketplace. Colonial Massachusetts was a diverse society: its diversity may have given it the unity to fight a successful revolution.

NOTES

In an effort to limit the length of the notes to this essay, I do not list in them those works cited fully in the text. Neither do I cite page references for works from which I draw general conclusions.

1. See Stephen G. Kurtz and James H. Hutson, eds., *Essays on the American Revolution* (Chapel Hill, 1973), for a collection of essays that represent a variety of mature consensus views of the Revolution, and Alfred F. Young, ed., *The American Revolution: Explorations in the History of American Radicalism* (DeKalb, Ill., 1976), for a similar collection that represents the conflict view.

2. For other important statements see Pauline Maier, *From Resistance to Revolution: Colonial Radicals and the Development of American Opposition to Britain, 1765-1776* (London, 1973); Edmund S. Morgan, "The American Revolution Considered as an Intellectual Movement," *The Challenge of the American Revolution* (New York, 1976), pp. 60-87; and *The Development of a Revolutionary Mentality: Papers Presented at the First Library of Congress Symposium on the American Revolution* (Washington, D.C., 1972).

3. See also Catherine Albanese, *Sons of the Fathers: The Civil Religion of the American Revolution* (Philadelphia, 1976); Sacvan Bercovitch, *The Puritan Origins of the American Self* (New Haven, 1975); Rhys Isaac, *The Transformation of Virginia, 1740-1790* (Chapel Hill, 1982); William McLoughlin, "The Role of Religion in the Revolution: Liberty of Conscience and Cultural Cohesion in the New Nation," *The American Revolution*, ed. Kurtz and Hutson, pp. 197–255; and Harry S. Stout, "Religion, Communications, and the Ideological Origins of the American Revolution," *William and Mary Quarterly* (hereafter cited as *WMQ*), 34 (October 1977): 519–41.

4. For a representative sample of the eighteenth-century community studies outside of Massachusetts see Richard R. Beeman, *The Evolution of the Southern Backcountry: A Case Study of Lunenburg County, Virginia, 1746-1832* (Philadelphia, 1984); Bruce C. Daniels, *The Connecticut Town: Growth and Development, 1635-1790* (Middletown, Conn., 1979); Jessica Kross, *The Evolution of an American Town: Newtown, New York, 1642-1775* (Philadelphia, 1983); James Lemon, *The Best Poor Man's Country: A Geographical Study of Early Southeastern Pennsylvania* (Baltimore, 1972); and Stephanie Grauman Wolf, *Urban Village: Population, Community, and Family Structure in Germantown, Pennsylvania, 1683-1800* (Princeton, 1976).

5. Jesse Lemisch, "The American Revolution Seen from the Bottom Up," *Towards a New Past: Dissenting Essays in American History*, ed. Barton Bernstein (New York, 1968), p. 29. See especially the following essays in Young, *The American Revolution:* Edward Countryman, "Out of the Bounds of Law: Northern Land Rioters in the Eighteenth Century," pp. 37-70; Marvin L. Michael Kay, "The North Carolina Regulation, 1766-1776: A Class Conflict," pp. 71-124; and Ronald Hoffman, "The Disaffected in the Revolutionary South," pp. 273-318.

6. For examples of the process in individual colonies see Richard L. Bushman, *From Puritan to Yankee: Character and the Social Order in Connecticut, 1690-1765* (Cambridge, 1965), and A. Roger Ekirch, *"Poor Carolina": Politics and Society in Colonial North Carolina, 1729-1776* (Chapel Hill, 1981).

7. See, for example, Wallace Brown, *The King's Friends: The Composition and Motives of the American Loyalist Claimants* (Providence, 1965); Robert McCluer Calhoon, *The Loyalists in Revolutionary America, 1760-1781* (New York, 1973); Linda K. Kerber, *Women of the Republic: Intellect and Ideology in Revolutionary America* (Chapel Hill, 1980); Mary Beth Norton, *The British Americans: The Loyalist Exiles in England, 1774-1789* (Boston, 1973); and Norton, *Liberty's Daughters: The Revolutionary Experience of American Women, 1750-1800* (Boston, 1980).

8. Cass Canfield, *Sam Adams's Revolution, 1765-1776* (New York, 1976), dust jacket.

9. John C. Miller, *Samuel Adams: Pioneer in Propaganda* (Stanford, 1936); Clifford Shipton, "Samuel Adams," *Sibley's Harvard Graduates* (Boston, 1958), 420-65.

10. Pauline Maier, "Coming to Terms with Samuel Adams," *American Historical Review*, 81 (February 1976): 12-37. See Richard D. Brown, *Revolutionary Politics in Massachusetts: The Boston Committee of Correspondence and the Towns, 1772-1774* (Cambridge, 1970), and Charles Akers, "Sam Adams—and Much More," *New England Quarterly*, 47 (March 1974): 120-31.

11. Page Smith, *John Adams*, 2 vols. (New York, 1962), II, 10.

12. John R. Howe, Jr., *The Changing Political Thought of John Adams* (Princeton, 1966).

13. Peter Shaw, *The Character of John Adams* (Chapel Hill, 1976), pp. 10-12.

14. Lynne Withey, *Dearest Friend: A Life of Abigail Adams* (New York, 1981). See also Charles W. Akers, *Abigail Adams: An American Woman* (Boston, 1980), which also emphasizes the force and quality of Abigail Adams' mind.

15. Bernard Bailyn, *The Ordeal of Thomas Hutchinson* (Cambridge, 1974), and William Pencak, *America's Burke: The Mind of Thomas Hutchinson* (Washington, D.C., 1982).

16. See Janice Potter, *The Liberty We Seek: Loyalist Ideology in Colonial New York and Massachusetts* (Cambridge, 1983), whose examinations of loyalists in New York and Massachusetts include Hutchinson, Sewall, Peter Oliver, and Daniel Leonard.

17. Herbert Allan, *John Hancock: Patriot in Purple* (New York, 1953), pp. 1-3; W. T. Baxter, *The House of Hancock: Business in Boston, 1724-1775* (Cambridge, 1945), pp. 4-6; and Lorenzo Sears, *John Hancock: The Picturesque Patriot* (Boston, 1912), pp. 12-15.

18. Two other studies that show the role of important clergymen in the Revolution are Charles H. Lippy, *Seasonable Revolutionary: The Mind of Charles Chauncey* (Chicago, 1982), and Robert J. Wilson III, *The Benevolent Deity: Ebenezer Gay and the Rise of Rational Religion in New England, 1696-1787* (Philadelphia, 1984).

19. George Billias, *Elbridge Gerry: Founding Father and Republican Statesman* (New York, 1976). John Cary, *Joseph Warren: Physician, Politician, Patriot* (Urbana, Ill., 1961), tries similarly to elevate Joseph Warren to the first rank of Revolutionary patriots. Cary is unsuccessful in this, but the book is a valuable addition to Massachusetts biography.

20. Charles Royster, "Review of *American Patriots and the Rituals of Revolution*," *WMQ*, 39 (July 1982): 552.

21. Allan Kulikoff, "The Progress of Inequality in Revolutionary Boston," *WMQ*, 28 (1971): 375-412; and James Henretta, "Economic Development and Social Structure in Colonial Boston," *WMQ*, 22 (January 1965): 75-92.

22. See Bruce C. Daniels, "Long-Range Trends of Wealth Distribution in Eighteenth-Century New England," *Explorations in Economic History*, 11 (Winter 1973-1974): 123-35; Alice Hanson Jones, "Wealth Estimates for the New England Colonies about 1770," *Journal of Economic History*, 32 (March 1972): 98-127; and Douglas L. Jones, "The Strolling Poor: Transiency in Eighteenth-Century Massachusetts," *Journal of Social History*, 7 (Spring 1975): 28-54.

23. Dirk Hoerder, *Crowd Action in Revolutionary Massachusetts, 1765-1780* (New York, 1977), p. 372. See also Pauline R. Maier, "Popular Uprisings and Civil Authority in Eighteenth-Century America," *WMQ*, 27 (October 1970): 3-35.

24. L. Kinvin Wroth, "Review of *Crowd Action in Revolutionary Massachusetts, 1765-1780*," *WMQ*, 37 (April 1980): 323-24.

25. Gary B. Nash, *The Urban Crucible: Social Change, Political Consciousness, and the Origins of the American Revolution* (Cambridge, 1979), p. 296.

26. Alfred Young, "George Robert Twelves Hewes (1742–1840): A Boston Shoemaker and the Memory of the American Revolution," *WMQ*, 38 (October 1981): 561–623.

27. Stephen Patterson, *Political Parties in Revolutionary Massachusetts* (Madison, Wis., 1973), chap. 1.

28. William Pencak, *War, Politics, and Revolution in Provincial Massachusetts* (Boston, 1981), pp. xi, xiii, 228.

29. Ibid., pp. 3, 191, 197, 200.

30. Taylor's work was revisionist when it appeared. See Lee N. Newcomer's study of the west, *The Embattled Farmers: A Massachusetts Countryside in the American Revolution* (New York, 1953), published just one year earlier.

4

MASSACHUSETTS ENTERS THE MARKETPLACE, 1790–1860

JACK LARKIN

SURELY THE COMMONWEALTH of Massachusetts boasts the most impressive historical bibliography of any state—particularly given its small size, if measured in terms of the sheer density of monographs per acre. The presence of major centers of graduate study in American history and the natural tendency of scholars to look for available sources close to home has served to increase the number of historical studies of Massachusetts. As Massachusetts and New England as a whole have become in relative terms progressively smaller parts of the American mosaic—a decline noticed and variously lamented from the late eighteenth century on—historians focusing on more recent periods of the state's history have found it necessary to develop ever-sharper and clearer rationales for their choice of subject. Massachusetts was so large a chunk of Anglo-American society in the seventeenth and eighteenth centuries that studies of phenomena in Plymouth Colony, Dedham, or Boston seemingly needed little other warrant. At the time of the Revolution, Massachusetts had almost 15 percent of the American population; by 1790 that had become 10 percent, by 1810 7 percent, by 1830 only 5 percent, and by 1850, despite very substantial population growth in the previous decade, no more than 4 percent. Previously a formidable and unignorable major segment of America all by itself, during the period this chapter is discussing, Massachusetts became a part of a corner of a very large continental society, distinctive in its cultural inheritances and the shape of its economy, although in many ways influential beyond its size.

For the years between 1790 and 1860, Massachusetts has come to be a laboratory for case studies in social, economic, and political transformation. Where else, on a relatively manageable statewide scale, did urbanization, industrialization, and immigration become so pronounced by midcentury? Where else was the work of so many coming to be defined by the factory bell, the routines of shop and office, instead of by seasonal rhythms? Where else has so wide a range of people been at least modestly articulate, or the traces of their activities so richly recorded? While most Americans continued in their agrarian ways, the inhabitants of Massachusetts seem to have been rehearsing the main event of modernization, giving up their farms to become a society of clerks and merchants, factory workers and professionals, managers and laborers. A challenging exploratory essay in the application of sociological concepts of modernization to American social history, Richard D. Brown's *Modernization: The Transformation of American Life, 1600-1865* (New York, 1976) finds, I believe, its strongest evidence and argument in considering Massachusetts and Connecticut. It is hardly surprising that Brown's *Massachusetts: A Bicentennial History* (New York, 1978) is the most recent and most distinguished synthesis of the state's history.

Once the Revolution and its tumultuous aftermath of Constitution making, rural rebellion, and the creation of a national polity were over, the inhabitants of Massachusetts turned their attention to less overtly dramatic although no less ultimately important concerns—the reshaping of their landscape, society, economy, the patterns of their lives. A new landscape, the increasingly thorough penetration of the marketplace if not always the machine into production and consumption, changes in the pace of movement and the formation of families, new forms of social behavior and discipline, and a changed texture and scale of organizational life all marked the new social order that the first half of the nineteenth century brought into being.

Our consideration will begin with the landscape, adopting a perspective that has until recently been strange to historical scholarship but was self-evident at the time. The farms of Massachusetts had been gradually carved out of the forest at the cost of immense labor from 1620 on; by the time of the Revolution much of the eastern portion of the state, along with the Connecticut Valley, was cleared farmland, but wide areas in the west and center of the state, along with patches almost everywhere away from the coast, were heavily wooded. Interestingly enough, given a good bit of loose historical rhetoric about the commonwealth's agricultural decline, the years from 1790 to 1840 saw a remarkable acceleration of the clearing process, with the farmland being extended virtually to its ecological limits. Pastures and even plowfields pushed up the sides of hills; hundreds of miles of stone walls were laid up to enclose them, in many places now the sole reminder of Massachusetts' agricultural past. Large game had almost completely disappeared. The landscape of the 1830s to the 1860s was an agricultural one, tamed and ordered, open and unwooded, with clear sightlines from farm to farm and village to village in a way that is almost impossible to imagine in our present-day state whose land-use patterns vary between urban/suburban sprawl, highways, a few jewel-like villages, and second-growth forest.

Although farming was never as dominant in Massachusetts as it was elsewhere, with its long tradition, generated by both necessity and entrepreneurial drive, of fishing, seaborne commerce, and artisanal versatility, this landscape portrait allows us to remember that it was enormously important. Until after 1830 most Massachusetts households still made their living primarily from the soil; even in 1850 farmers and farm laborers were the largest single occupational group in the state. Yet the Bay State's open and well-tilled agricultural landscape was a paradox, because it was a landscape of agricultural saturation—of the already-achieved maximum number of farms—rather than of opportunity. For the increasing majority of those who stayed in the state as well as those coming into it, opportunity no longer lay on the land. Hugh Raup's "The View from John Sanderson's Farm" (*Forest History*, 10, no. 1 [April 1966] : 2-11) provides an account of the landscape-clearing process in Massachusetts. John Stilgoe's *The Common Landscape of America, 1560-1845* (New Haven, 1982) is a remarkably wide-ranging book but drawing heavily on Massachusetts sources and is really strongest on the farms, fields, shops, and villages of New England. William Cronon, *Changes in the Land: Indians, Colonists, and the Ecology of New England* (New York, 1983), begins before colonization but takes the history of the regional landscape up to 1800.

The story of the state's changes in population is in part a familiar one. Between 1790 and 1820 population grew far more slowly than natural increase; immigration remained infinitesimal, and Massachusetts exported people north to Vermont and central New Hampshire, east to the largely unsettled District of Maine, and west to New York State. For despite the landscape clearing, new farms could not be made in anything like sufficient numbers for the rising generations. From 1820 to 1840, movement northward was largely replaced by movement westward, with an increase in foreign immigration, some return migration to Massachusetts from the north, and a steady movement away from the Massachusetts countryside to villages and cities. From 1840 to 1860, or more strictly speaking from 1845, population growth accelerated enormously with Irish immigration and the rise of urban agglomerations of varying size across the landscape. The commonwealth's center of population, which had moved steadily west in the seventeenth and eighteenth centuries, began early in the nineteenth century to return eastward. The aggregate history of population in Massachusetts in the context of American society as a whole begins usefully with J. Potter's essay, "The Growth of Population in America, 1700-1860," *Population in History*, ed. D. V. Glass and D. E. C. Eversley (Chicago, 1965), pp. 631-88. Jesse Chickering's early *A Statistical View of the Population of Massachusetts from 1765 to 1840* (Boston, 1846) is still a work of considerable interest.

Massachusetts' urbanization set increasingly dense and wholly non-agrarian settlements in the midst of its cleared fields. Most overtly, by the federal census' crude characterization, the commonwealth moved from 13 percent urban in 1790 to 60 percent urban in 1860. Of course, the reality was more complicated and more interesting. Beginning in 1790 and probably somewhat earlier, everywhere in rural Massachusetts village populations were increasing much faster than the farming populations scattered in the countryside. The villagers were not farmers but artisans, merchants, and a few professional men, whose houses, shops, stores, and offices clustered around the town centers to serve their hinterlands and to become independent focuses of production and exchange. Equally striking from 1812 on was the growth of small-scale manufacturing villages for woolen and cotton manufacturing, chair making, and papermaking; they were environments of workers and mill agents, conspicuously transient. Highly rural Massachusetts towns had middle-class urban clusters in their center villages and working-class clusters in their mill villages. Larger urban agglomerations had haloes of prosperous farms and valuable agricultural land around them. Joseph Wood's "Elaboration of a Settlement System: The New England Village in the Federal Period" (*Journal of Historical Geography*, 10 [1984]: 331–56) provides the best account of the evolution of the commercial village landscape; for a comprehensive view of the development of mill villages in rural Massachusetts we can turn to the introduction, headnotes, and documents in Gary Kulik, Roger Parks, and Theodore Z. Penn, *The New England Mill Village, 1790–1860* (Cambridge, 1982).

Occurring alongside this rural urbanization was the growth of Boston and the steady increase in density of its environs, the emergence of subregional centers like Worcester, Springfield, and Taunton, the emergence of once-declining seaports like Newburyport and New Bedford as manufacturing cities, and the meteoric rise of textile cities like Lowell, Lawrence, and Chicopee. Francis X. Blouin, Jr., *The Boston Region, 1810–1850: A Study of Urbanization* (Ann Arbor, 1980), has provided a detailed statistical picture of the process in eastern Massachusetts. Robert Doherty's *Society and Power: Five New England Towns, 1800–1860* (Amherst, 1977) is a primarily quantitative comparative investigation of five Massachusetts towns—the agricultural hamlet of Pelham, the factory village of Ware, the relatively slow-growing county seat of Northampton, the dynamic emerging city of Worcester, and the highly urbanized old seaport of Salem. Doherty is primarily concerned with the relationships between the economic development of these communities and the geographic mobility, property and occupational mobility, and distribution of wealth of the population.

The material engines of transformation in Massachusetts were not mysterious. English textile technology was transplanted, adapted, and harnessed to the state's resources of abundant waterpower. Capital was applied with increasing intensiveness to create a dense network of improved roads and later a net of railroads. Artisanal shop-scale production was greatly multiplied and geared to distant markets.

Farmers indeed experienced an Indian summer in early nineteenth-century Massachusetts, gradually introducing better tools and techniques and adjusting and adapting to shifts in population density and transportation. Although it steadily lost ground relative to manufacturing and commerce, it was not until the very end of the period we are considering that the agricultural sector declined absolutely and the number of farms began to decrease. The traditional patterns of agricultural production and exchange—a household sufficiency of foodstuffs, complex networks of local exchange for goods and services, modest surpluses for wider trade—gave way to more market-oriented strategies. The first few decades saw a gradual expansion of production along familiar lines to meet the demands of city and village growth. Under the pressure of cheaper and better western grain, from 1830 on Massachusetts farmers began to abandon the pattern of mixed farming—cereal grains, hay, livestock, orchard—that had characterized their agriculture for almost two hundred years. Gradually, even farm households started making their bread with wheat flour from New York and Ohio. Depending on their location, they began to specialize in dairy or livestock production or market gardening. The farmers of Emerson's Concord, for instance, became more and more focused on supplying Boston with firewood, vegetables, butter, and milk. Agriculturalists in central Massachusetts towns with good transportation concentrated on raising livestock for the great Brighton market that supplied most of eastern Massachusetts with meat. Farmers in Berkshire County emphasized more transportable cheese. But in the 1850s it finally became clear that farming in some parts of the commonwealth was no longer viable; unproductive soil and small and hilly fields that made mechanization difficult pushed farmers in the hill towns farthest away from urban markets off the land or into partial abandonment. Just before the Civil War, the agricultural landscape began, slowly at first, to go back to the trees. An initial guide to understanding this process is Howard S. Russell's *A Long Deep Furrow: Three Centuries of Farming in New England* (Hanover, N.H., 1976), section 4 ("Another Beginning, 1800-1825") and 5 ("Good Growing Weather, 1825-1860"), which provides a recent and encyclopedic regional account that does not slight Massachusetts. Earlier but still important studies are Percy W. Bidwell's "Rural Economy of New England at the Beginning of the Nineteenth Century" (*Transactions of the Connecticut Academy of Arts and Sciences*, 20 [1916] : 241-399) and "The Agricultural Revolution in New England" (*American Historical Review*, 26 [July 1921] : 683-702).

Between 1820 and 1860 both city and countryside in Massachusetts were the scene of vigorous production for regional and far-flung markets. Textile production, in its large-city and mill-village forms, was the dominion of the machine and the large-scale organization of work. Elsewhere, except for nascent chair-making and papermaking factories, the scale of individual operation was much smaller but overall output was very large. Small farmers' sons became shoemakers and peppered country towns with ten-foot shops. Women and girls in rural households braided straw, made palm-leaf hats, and sewed shoes. In villages and rural neighborhoods and along city streets, small shops made edge tools, farm implements, shoe boxes, wagons, harnesses and trunks, pencils, brooms, stoves and tinware, and books. With the elaboration of the railroad network after the Civil War, rural Massachusetts would empty of this activity, with production increasingly concentrated in "genuinely" urban centers. Just how and why the Massachusetts countryside became commercialized is currently a subject of vigorous scholarly discussion, although it has not crystallized yet into a book. Robert A. Gross, "Agriculture and Society in Thoreau's Concord" (*Journal of American History*, 69 [June 1982] : 42-61), looks at how farmers changed both their culture of work and the scale of their investment in order to produce for the growing metropolitan market. Winifred B. Rothenberg's "The Market and Massachusetts Farmers, 1750-1855" (*Journal of Economic History*, 41 [December 1981]: 283-314) argues for widespread and early commercial orientation, while Christopher Clark ("The Household Economy, Market Exchange, and the Rise of Capitalism in the Connecticut Valley 1800-1860," *Journal of Social History*, 13 [Winter 1979]: 169-89) finds a dramatic shift from localistic, kinship-based patterns of rural exchange and production into more profit-seeking and cash-oriented ones.

In another powerful contrast with the patterns of colonial society, beginning late in the eighteenth century and accelerating into the nineteenth, Massachusetts became a landscape of men, women, and their families in rapid motion. A restless churning, with fewer than half of the inhabitants recorded in one census present ten years later, characterized communities from small and declining hill towns to the regional metropolis of Boston. A correct vision, then, of the antebellum commonwealth would be not of residential fixity but of individuals and households in motion yearly or even more often, seeking work, better opportunities, better housing, greater closeness to kin, even change for change's sake—the restless background of and response to other forms of change. The largest component of this flow was a semi-nomadic stream of unskilled and propertyless men and their dependents, since it was characteristic of the nineteenth-century social order that the poorest were the most transient. Massachusetts has seen some important work in the study of population movement. Peter Knights' *The Plain People of Boston, 1830-1860* (New York, 1971) is a massively researched quantitative study of the geographic and property mobility of the population of Boston. Doherty's *Society and Power* looks at spatial mobility, among other things, in five communities of different size and economic character. Their findings can be compared with those about eighteenth-century mobility in Douglas Lamar Jones, *Village and Seaport: Migration and Society in Eighteenth-Century Massachusetts* (Hanover, N.H., 1981).

Along with changes in population, settlement, and patterns of production came other alterations, changes in how people behaved. The people of Massachusetts, as early as and probably earlier than any other large population in America, began to break away from the demographic old regime of colonial America—the structure of high birth rates, large families, and households that defined much of the shape of earlier society. Large-scale studies of the state as a whole as well as intensive investigations of individual towns testify to a dramatic decline in the fertility of its population; decade by decade Massachusetts women had fewer children, and the average size of households grew considerably smaller. This was due only in part to a tendency to marry later; for the most part, it reflected conscious decisions within marriage to limit family size, although almost surely without mechanical contraception. Colonial notions of patriarchal lineages settled on the land and of children as farm and household labor gave way to new concerns about appropriate child rearing and the cost of launching children into a commercial and competitive society.

Mortality, the other pillar of the old regime, changed relatively little. Boston, in the colonial period a far more dangerous environment than the country towns, became a somewhat healthier place throughout the late eighteenth and early nineteenth centuries; even through the shocks of immigration, it maintained relatively lower mortality rates than other large American cities. The organization of medical care changed as male physicians grew rapidly in numbers and pushed midwives and folk healers aside in both city and countryside; yet medicine's effectiveness in curing disease did not improve until considerably later. Through most of the nineteenth century, the risks to health due to increased urban crowding were probably balanced by some modest improvements in hygiene and public sanitation. Because of the extent of its pre-1860 documentation, considerably more is known about early nineteenth-century demographic patterns in the commonwealth than anywhere else in America. Maris A. Vinovskis' *Fertility in Massachusetts from the Revolution to the Civil War* (New York, 1981) is the most intensive demographic study of any nineteenth-century American state. There are also two important Massachusetts family-reconstitution studies whose findings extend to the mid-nineteenth century: Nancy Osterud and John Fulton, "Family Limitation and Age at Marriage: Fertility Decline in Sturbridge, Massachusetts, 1730-1850" (*Population Studies*, 30 [1976]: 481-94), and Helena Temikin-Greener and Alan Swedlund, "Fertility Transition in the Connecticut Valley, 1740-1850" (*Population Studies*, 31 [1977]: 221-35).

The life of Massachusetts families, as well as their demographic dimensions, and the experience of women were being profoundly transformed during these years. New canons and standards of housekeeping, domestic comfort and child rearing, and patterns of female friendship and association were emerging for those "middle-class" rural and urban women who were broadly speaking the economic beneficiaries of commercial and industrial change. The most compelling study yet undertaken of the early nineteenth-century invention of domesticity is Nancy Cott's *The Bonds of Womanhood: Woman's Sphere in New England, 1780-1835* (New Haven, 1977).

Although not always easy to define precisely, a shift in manners—what we might call the "reformation of everyday life"—was well underway by the 1820s. Bundling—the practice of allowing courting couples to lie together in bed, more or less fully clothed—disappeared. Prenuptial pregnancy rates—the percentage of brides already pregnant at the time of marriage—began a striking decline. Dogs were no longer allowed to come to the meetinghouse with their masters. District school committees began to build separate boys' and girls' outhouses instead of one, or none at all. Standards of personal space changed as unrelated adults became less willing to sleep in the same beds. Flogging was decisively abandoned as a criminal punishment early in the century, and public executions, which had drawn enormous crowds, were eliminated in 1831. Some forms of personal hygiene such as bathing and brushing teeth seem to have risen in prevalence. A vigorous and successful temperance campaign drastically reduced alcohol consumption and effectively curtailed a wide variety of drinking rituals associated with work and socialization.

Arriving in great numbers in the 1840s, the unreformed Irish, particularly in matters of drink and public deportment, were thus even more culturally divergent than they might have been earlier in the century. Except in theology, they threatened newly won standards.

Agricultural work rituals such as huskings and barn raisings became attenuated in most places and in many disappeared altogether; similarly, traditional artisanal practices, like the shop rituals, patron saints, and episodic work rhythms of Lynn cordwainers or Boston printers declined under the pressure of more stringent work discipline.

The supernatural receded ever farther from the horizon of public consciousness. Farmers still used their almanacs and indications for guidance in planting crops, although appearing to take the subject far less seriously. The revivals of the second Great Awakening worked powerfully in Massachusetts, but had regard to moral conduct and the inner workings of the soul, not the invisible world. By the 1850s the folk beliefs of 1800 seemed wholly quaint and alien, relics of a bygone time, to reminiscing writers. A clear example of this process is provided by the law of evidence and perjury; Massachusetts juries were under colonial law charged to assume that testimony given under the powerful religious sanctions of an oath taken on Scripture was true; if sworn testimonies seemed to conflict, they were expected to do their best to reconcile them. During the first two decades of the nineteenth century the courts abandoned the notion that a statement's truth could be guaranteed by religious sanctions; jurymen were then instructed to weigh and compare testimony on the basis of internal logic and external evidence, as they are today. William E. Nelson, *The Americanization of the Common Law: The Impact of Legal Change on Massachusetts Society, 1760–1830* (Cambridge, 1975), provides an extensive and revealing account of how legal doctrine and procedure were transformed, as well as their social impact and cultural meaning. Robert L. Hampel's *Temperance and Prohibition in Massachusetts, 1813–1852* (Ann Arbor, 1982) is a recent and detailed study of the first phase of the temperance movement. Jack Larkin's "The View from New England: Notes on Everyday Life in Rural America before 1850" (*American Quarterly*, 34 [1982]: 245–61) discusses some of the changes in rural Massachusetts. Still the best study of change in everyday life patterns in the period from 1820 to 1860 is Francis W. Underwood's *Quabbin: The History of a Small Town with Outlooks on Puritan Life* (Boston, 1893) on Enfield, Massachusetts. Robert A. Gross sketches an important interpretation of Massachusetts' social transformation in "Agriculture and Society in Thoreau's Concord" and in "Lonesome in Eden: Dickinson, Thoreau, and the Problem of Community in Nineteenth-Century New England" (*Canadian Review of American Studies*, 14 [Spring 1983]: 1–17).

In 1790 the commonwealth's institutional web was tiny. The small-scale institutions of state government, the town meeting, local churches and religious societies, and a relative handful of urban voluntary associations were all that comprised the organized social fabric outside households and kinship networks. The first half of the nineteenth century saw a true organizational revolution in Massachusetts, the weaving of a remarkably diverse and complex web of associational life, very little of it expressly governmental. Voluntary associations emerged in nearly every community of the commonwealth by 1820 and continued their proliferation over the next four decades, giving Massachusetts almost certainly the highest density of such activity in the United States. Lyceums, charitable and religious societies, temperance and other reform associations, societies, Masonic lodges, professional and mechanics' groups, the complicated voluntary institutions that were political parties: by 1850 there were thousands of such organizations. They were as important for their form and style as for their diverse substantive goals. All organized on constitutional, republican principles, they segmented social experience and brought new dimensions of rational collaborative action and choice into people's lives. As modes of group life and action they were primarily the creation of the "new people" of antebellum Massachusetts—the commercial, professional, and manufacturing/entrepreneurial men and women of the center villages and cities, not farmers or laborers. Yet so pervasive a social form had they become that the Irish and other immigrant groups adopted them as vehicles while attempting to preserve very different values and traditions. Richard D. Brown has written two pioneering studies that define the course of the organizational revolution in Massachusetts: "The Emergence of Urban Society in Rural Massachusetts, 1760-1820" (*Journal of American History*, 61 [June 1974]: 29-51]) and "The Emergence of Voluntary Associations in Massachusetts, 1760-1830" (*Journal of Voluntary Action Research*, 2 [April 1973]: 64-75). Ronald P. Formisano's *The Transformation of Political Culture: Massachusetts Parties, 1790s-1840s* (New York, 1983) is a genuine social history of Massachusetts politics. Formisano displays a rich understanding of the local economies, religious alignments, and cultural patterns of the state's communities, rural and urban, and provides a particularly interesting account of the complex evolution and elaboration of the state's political organizations. Michael Frisch (*Town into City: Springfield and the Meaning of Community, 1840-1880* [Cambridge, 1972]) has written a useful study of how conceptions of community and institutional structures of governance changed with Springfield's urbanization. Gerald Gawalt's *The Promise of Power: The Emergence of the Legal Profession in Massachusetts, 1760-1830* (Westport, Conn., 1979) describes how Massachusetts' small and close-knit band of colonial lawyers became a large, specialized, and stratified group of practitioners, increasingly engaged with the problems of commerce and economic development. Another study of professional life, Donald M. Scott's *From Office to Profession: The New England Ministry, 1750-1850* (Philadelphia, 1978), looks at the simultaneous transformation of the ministry from authoritative communal leadership to specialized service.

Elementary or common schooling was another of the commonwealth's institutions to be decisively reshaped during the period, although the pattern of its transformation did not follow the simple, clear-cut pattern of primitive neglect giving way to progressive reform. Horace Mann brought the generation after 1840 to see the district schools of early nineteenth-century Massachusetts as chaotic, unstructured, prone to disruption, and instructionally inadequate. Yet from a longer historical perspective we can see that what went on in these thousands of small buildings scattered widely across the state was a considerable collective achievement, given both the educational conceptions and the economic resources available. Emerging from the single town schools of the earlier eighteenth century, by 1800 the district schools of Massachusetts had provided a broad if not quite universal rudimentary literacy for both sexes, continuing the position of the citizens of the commonwealth, along with those of Connecticut, as the best-schooled people in early America. Educational change in Massachusetts proceeded from this plateau of rudimentary but real achievement. Beginning in the 1830s, reform included the lengthening of school terms, the regularization of textbooks and curricula, the redesign of schoolhouses, the elimination of the very oldest and youngest pupils from "elementary" school populations, and the semi-professionalization and feminization of schoolteaching. The impulse behind these changes was a desire to regularize and rationalize—in the interests of order, decorum, and punctuality—a set of practices that were seen to be hopelessly unsystematic, haphazard, and often morally lax, but that were in fact simply the result of farming people's incorporation of schooling into the lives of their communities over the generations. As traditional ways were repudiated, standards of literacy were to be upgraded and those who had stayed outside the ambit of schooling were to be brought in. The emerging view of education in the Bay State, far different from the old order's concern that pupils be able to read a newspaper and a Bible and cipher out an account book, saw it as a bulwark of social order, a training ground for both skills and character, and eventually, in cultural clashes with the immigrants, as an agency of Anglo-American supremacy. Michael Katz' *The Irony of Early School Reform: Educational Innovation in Mid-Nineteenth Century Massachusetts* (Cambridge, 1968) looks at the development of educational institutions in the commonwealth in the context of changing power relationships and pervasive concern about social instability. Focusing on Boston, Stanley Schultz' *The Culture Factory: Boston Public Schools, 1789–1860* (New York, 1973) examines the development of the commonwealth's first urban school system, finding that rationalization and centralization, under the pressures of rapid growth and immigration, made for bureaucratization and sterility. Carl Kaestle and Maris Vinovskis (*Education and Social Change in Nineteenth-Century Massachusetts* [New York, 1980]) explore teachers' careers, pedagogy, curriculum, school attendance, and organizational development with sophisticated argument and quantitative techniques.

Lowell's story is a case in point illustrating the complexities of the commonwealth's progress toward "modernity." Created de novo out of the Chelmsford farm fields, an instant city rose, unique in its organizational scale on the American landscape, at first more completely planned than anything since the "holy experiments" of the seventeenth century. Young women from the marginal farms of

New Hampshire flowed into the mills, beginning the reversal of the tide of north-south migration within the region. At one level Lowell was an attempt to create an industrial order without disorder, disease, and discontent—a presumably docile female work force, an environment of order, loyalty, cordial relations, acceptable wages, and control—amounting almost to a single enormous New England household with paternal mill agents and loyal, hardworking daughters. At another level, of course, Lowell was a major effort of entrepreneurial creation, a way of putting capital to work, seeking its reward in the marketplace.

On both levels, things worked out differently than expected. Mill girls found sisterly solidarity in their work environments and in boardinghouses as they became the first Americans to adapt to the time-governed world of machine technology. The high profits of the early years began to diminish with increasing competition, and the masters of Lowell began to press their operatives harder in order to maintain their margins—the "stretch-out" (running more machines per worker), the "speed-up" of machinery, and the cutting of piece rates all were attempts to raise productivity while keeping wages the same. Turnouts and strikes resulted, as well as systematic agitation for the ten-hour day, and Lowell ceased to be an experiment in industrial order and became an industrial city. Pushed even harder by the ever-declining price of goods and overcapacity, Lowell's work force became increasingly proletarianized, piece rates declined, and skill levels were deemphasized. After 1845 Irish men who were willing to take work at almost any wage rates to support their families, along with their daughters, began to supplant the native women. Boardinghouse life dwindled. Lowell became an immigrant city of tenements and alleys with a Protestant managerial and business class. In his *Women at Work: The Transformation of Work and Community in Lowell, Massachusetts, 1826-1860* (New York, 1979), Thomas Dublin tells—extremely well—the single most dramatic story of social and economic change in pre-Civil War Massachusetts.

The most striking example we have of the transformation of artisanal culture and economy in the commonwealth is that of the shoemakers of Lynn. Early a center of the "sale" or mass-market shoe trade, Lynn was in the early nineteenth century a community uniquely dominated by the cordwainers, who had successfully struggled to retain some measure of crafts, skills, and independence with respect to their small-scale employers or "bag bosses." But from 1830 on, the shoe trade's relentless increase in scale and competitiveness and the emergence of wholly entrepreneurial capitalist shoe manufacturers in the place of master mechanics devalued their skills, pushed their incomes down and their hours upward, and left them with a bitter consciousness of loss and an intense solidarity as wage earners. A passionately argued and provocative social history of the commonwealth's closest-knit and most homogeneous artisanal community is found in Paul Faler's *Mechanics and Manufacturers in the Early Industrial Revolution: Lynn, Massachusetts, 1780-1860* (Albany, 1981).

Elsewhere, conscious and organized opposition to the forces of industrial order was not easy to find in antebellum Massachusetts. Lynn's mechanics were by Massachusetts standards rooted in place. Highly mobile or culturally divergent work forces of the factory were primarily concerned with survival; conflict was periodically visible but muted. The artisans and laborers of the villages and countryside lived and worked on a different scale. The most insightful interpretation of how the lineaments of an industrial society were imposed on the Massachusetts countryside can be found in Jonathan Prude's *The Coming of Industrial Order: Town and Factory Life in Rural Massachusetts, 1810-1860* (New York, 1983), which studies the rural mill towns of Webster and Dudley.

How did the overall welfare of the people of the commonwealth change over this long period? It is a much easier question to ask than to answer. A wide variety of consumer goods—textiles, shoes, clocks, chairs, school textbooks, and newspapers, for example—became cheaper and more abundant. Travel became far easier and faster, the flow of information enormously more abundant. Yet during these same years economic inequality grew strikingly in Massachusetts. The processes of population concentration, commercialization, and large-scale production engendered a widening gap between the relative few who owned a great proportion of the state's resources and the many who owned little or none. Inequality was greatest in the large cities; yet even in a small country town like Sturbridge it grew steadily from 1790 to 1850. The gap between the economic floor and the ceiling was expanding as the ceiling moved upward. Was the floor moving upward as well? In some ways, perhaps it was, but here is an area where historians know the least and argue the most.

Many members of the urban and village middle class of merchants, professionals, small manufacturers, clerks, proprietors, and highly skilled craftsmen, and a substantial number of farmers were able to make prosperous or modestly comfortable lives; theirs was the culture of the early Victorian parlor, the horsehair sofa, cookstoves, perhaps even railway excursions, and an academy or the emerging high school for their children. For most farmers and artisans and for all factory operatives and laborers, such things remained out of reach.

Movement upward in the social scale, as measured by the relatively modest accumulations of property, was not easy in antebellum Massachusetts for those who began with little in the way of skills and connections. What one historian calls "casualties"—men who had reached their forties without acquiring more than tiny amounts of property—were exceedingly common in the towns and cities of the commonwealth by 1850. These questions can revealingly be pondered for Massachusetts in Doherty's *Society and Power* and in Stephan Thernstrom's *Poverty and Progress: Social Mobility in a Nineteenth Century City* (Cambridge, 1964). Thernstrom primarily covers the years from 1850 to 1880, but his analysis of the changing social and economic order of Newburyport actually begins with the federal era and is equally as interesting as his pioneering exploration of social mobility. Gloria Turner Main's "Inequality in Early America: Evidence from Probate Records of Massachusetts and Maryland" (*Journal of Interdisciplinary History*, 7 [Spring 1977]: 559-81) presents striking evidence of the growth of inequality in nineteenth-century Massachusetts.

The Irish arrived poor and largely desperate. They were a marginal peasantry whose agricultural skills and attachment to farming had been eroded by ferocious overcrowding, exploitation, persecution, and recurrent crises of subsistence. Coming to Massachusetts, they occupied the lowest rungs on the occupational ladder of an expanding economy that did offer niches for them, however precarious. What had they gained, and what had they lost, in coming to Massachusetts? It is a complex and difficult question to answer about the first generation, or even the second. Oscar Handlin's *Boston Immigrants, 1790–1865: A Study in Acculturation* (Cambridge, 1941) was an astonishing piece of scholarship when written over forty years ago and remains an evocative and in many ways unsurpassed social history of Boston's Irish before the Civil War; it is particularly powerful on the material and organizational lives of the immigrants. Dennis P. Ryan's *Beyond the Ballot Box* (Rutherford, N.J., 1983) is a recent and incisive social history of the Boston Irish, importantly updating Handlin's conclusions about their lives in both the Old World and the New.

Massachusetts, more than any other state before the Civil War, was harnessed to the unpredictable fluctuations of the emerging business cycle. The industrial economy's trough periods, most markedly the panics and subsequent depressions of the late 1830s and 1850s, were devastating to increasingly large proportions of the population. The state's two leading industries, textiles and shoes, were deeply cyclical. While the shoe trade in particular was increasingly subject to ever-narrowing periods of prosperity between troughs of low demand, the textile industry was likewise faced with periodic crises of overproduction and declining profit margins. Textile and shoe workers were increasingly dependent on cash wages and less and less likely to have other resources such as family farms, garden plots, or alternative trades to fall back on. The market became for antebellum Massachusetts a secularized version of the inscrutable Calvinist God and his divine providence so central to the understanding of its Puritan founders. If it offered the possibilities of riches to some and comfort to many, it held out harsh imperatives for many more and grave anxieties for most. Carl Siracusa's *A Mechanical People: Perceptions of the Industrial Order in Massachusetts, 1815–1880* (Middletown, Conn., 1979) is a history of how the articulate and politically active in Massachusetts thought, wrote, and spoke about the social and economic consequences of the new technology and organization of work. Robert F. Dalzell, Jr. ("The Rise of the Waltham-Lowell System and Some Thoughts on the Political Economy of Modernization in Ante-Bellum Massachusetts," *Perspectives in American History*, 9 [1975]: 229-68), provides an important view of the state's overall industrial development in the course of demonstrating how unusual the Waltham-Lowell entrepreneurs actually were.

The years between the Revolution and the Civil War were the commonwealth's takeoff period, in which Massachusetts became a strikingly different society in almost every dimension of analysis. Yet how precisely to characterize that society is a problem. This historian is struck most vividly by the rapid creation of new social and economic forms, the striking transitionality of its institutional scale partway between the life of a premodern agricultural province and mature industrial society, and the profound ambiguity of its human costs and rewards. From the perspective of 1900, and certainly 1987, antebellum Massachusetts was a very embryonic version of what was to come. From the viewpoint of 1790, it would have been a remarkably vigorous and complex society. From the viewpoint of 1830 or 1850, it was a headlong rush into the unknown.

5

HISTORIANS AND LATE NINETEENTH-CENTURY MASSACHUSETTS

GERALD W. McFARLAND

SCHOLARS OF LATE nineteenth-century Massachusetts history have been more successful at describing individual aspects of their subject than they have been at tying the parts together into an integrated whole. Even their basic approach to the era has been divided into two quite distinct lines of inquiry: political histories (including biographies of political figures) and community studies that focus on a particular city's social and economic development. The period has not lent itself to being studied as a single unit by political historians, with the result that there is no book-length survey of the entire period from 1865 to 1900. An overall account of these years is obtained only by piecing together information from books and articles that deal with shorter chronological segments. The community studies approach has also produced a fragmented portrait of the era, in large part because no single study deals with more than two cities. But the problems of synthesis within these two genres pale beside the much greater problems that arise from the fact that political historians and community studies scholars have for the most part pursued their subjects along separate lines. Thus, although there are many good monographs on Bay State politics and numerous solid studies of the commonwealth's major cities, almost no work has been done to draw these two lines of inquiry together. The resultant fragmentation has led me to divide this chapter into three parts: an analysis of political histories and biographies, an evaluation of the community studies literature, and a discussion of the need for a full-scale synthesis of late nineteenth-century Massachusetts politics and society.

POLITICAL HISTORY AND BIOGRAPHY

At first glance it might appear that Massachusetts politics from 1865 to 1900 can be summed up in two words: Republican hegemony. In 1865 Massachusetts Republicans controlled the governorship, the legislature, both U.S. Senate seats, and the entire Bay State congressional delegation. Three and a half decades later Republican dominance was still nearly as complete, except that in 1900 there was one Massachusetts Democrat in Congress. The impression that Republicans were consistently in control is further reinforced by the fact that from 1865 to 1900 the GOP won all but five of the thirty-five annual gubernatorial elections. Nevertheless, the story of late nineteenth-century Massachusetts politics is much too complex to be summed up by the words "Republican hegemony." The Republicans did indeed generally maintain control, but the environment in which they did so was in constant flux, and the party had to adapt itself to two major changes: first, a shift from the politics of the early Reconstruction era to the radically changed political milieu of the years between 1873 and 1893, and then the emergence of a still-different electoral environment in the mid- and late 1890s.

Massachusetts party battles in the early Reconstruction period were extraordinary in two ways. First, Republicans achieved virtually unchallenged control of state politics, their dominance ensured by the demoralized condition in which their Democratic opponents had been left by prewar and wartime debates over sectional issues. Second, because the GOP had come to power by taking a hard line on such charged issues as slavery and emancipation, the party's leaders tended to disregard the process of pragmatic coalition building that usually prevails in American politics and instead continued to take uncompromising ideological stands during Reconstruction. But the party's postwar support for black civil rights proved much less popular than its earlier anti-slavery platform. Divisions soon arose within the party between the ideologically oriented members of its radical wing and more pragmatic organization politicians. For a time, however, this internal wrangling did not much weaken Republican supremacy in the state because the party commanded such huge electoral majorities. By the early 1870s, however, the tendency of the old radical leadership to focus almost exclusively on national issues and the radicals' relatively slow response to emerging local issues—workingmen's rights, women's suffrage, and prohibition—led to a gradual disintegration of the once-imposing Republican coalition. Thus, when Grant-era scandals and the depression that began in 1873 further undermined voter loyalty to the GOP, Democrats were in a position to make major gains. In 1874 they captured the gubernatorial election and six of the commonwealth's eleven congressional seats. The era of automatic Republican victories was over.

During the heyday of radical Republicanism, ideologically inclined GOP politicians from Massachusetts played a disproportionately large role in national party politics. For the most part biographers have provided good portraits of the first- and second-rank figures of the early Reconstruction period. *Charles Sumner and the Rights of Man* (New York, 1970), the second volume of David Donald's life of Senator Charles Sumner, one of the most important members of the GOP's radical wing, is exemplary in every respect. There are two solid studies of Henry Wilson, who left the U.S. Senate to become Grant's first vice-president. These are Ernest McKay's *Henry Wilson: Practical Radical, a Portrait of a Politician* (Port Washington, N.Y., 1971) and Richard H. Abbott's *Cobbler in Congress: The Life of Henry Wilson, 1812-1875* (Lexington, Ky., 1972). George S. Boutwell, another Republican leader with national clout (successively as congressman, secretary of the treasury, and U.S. senator) is the subject of a recent dissertation by Thomas H. Brown ("George Sewall Boutwell: Public Servant, 1818-1909" [Ph.D. diss., New York University, 1979]), a work that is unpublished and thus not readily available in most libraries. The controversial and combative Benjamin F. Butler is portrayed in a book-length biography by Hans L. Trefousse, *Ben Butler: The South Called Him Beast!* (New York, 1957), a study that unfortunately slights his importance in state politics. Although many insights on that subject can be gleaned from two dissertations and numerous journal articles that deal with Butler's career, these findings have not yet been pulled together in a single source. The dissertations are by William D. Mallam ("Benjamin Franklin Butler, Machine Politician and Congressman" [Ph.D. diss., University of Minnesota, 1941]) and William Vanderclock Crenshaw ("Benjamin F. Butler: Philosophy and Politics, 1866-1879" [Ph.D. diss., University of Georgia, 1976]). Among the journal articles are William D. Mallam's "Butlerism in Massachusetts" (*New England Quarterly*, 33 [June 1960]: 186-206); Richard Harmond's "'The Beast' in Boston: Benjamin F. Butler as Governor of Massachusetts" (*Journal of American History*, 55 [September 1968]: 266-80); Edward T. James' "Ben Butler Runs for President: Labor, Greenbackers, and Anti-Monopolists in the Election of 1884" (*Essex Institute Historical Collections*, 113 [April 1977]: 65-88); and Margaret S. Thompson's "Ben Butler versus the Brahmins: Patronage and Politics in Early Gilded Age Massachusetts" (*New England Quarterly*, 55 [June 1982]: 163-86).

Although there are many first-rate modern biographies of Bay Staters of secondary rank in post-Civil War politics, the careers of a few such men have been treated with not-so-benign neglect. In this latter category, the three studies most in need of updating are Fred Harvey Harrington's *Fighting Politician: Major General N. P. Banks* (Westport, Conn., 1948); Moorfield Storey and Edward W. Emerson's *Ebenezer Rockwood Hoar* (Boston, 1911); and George S. Merriam's *The Life and Times of Samuel Bowles*, 2 vols. (New York, 1885). Fortunately, Stephen G. Weisner's recently completed biography of Bowles (*Embattled Editor*, Lanham, Md., 1986) provides the long-awaited scholarly analysis of this important newspaper editor's career. One public figure whose life has not been overlooked by historians is Wendell Phillips, a leading abolitionist, on whom there are two modern biographies: an older study by Irving H. Bartlett, *Wendell Phillips, Brahmin Radical* (Boston, 1961), and a more recent book by James B. Stewart, *Wendell Phillips: Liberty's Hero* (Baton Rouge, 1986). There are also excellent book-length biographies on three of the older patrician liberals who were politically active in the early postwar period: Martin Duberman's *James Russell Lowell* (Boston, 1966); Duberman's *Charles Francis Adams, 1807-1886* (Stanford, 1968); and Samuel Shapiro's *Richard Henry Dana, Jr., 1815-1882* (East Lansing, 1961). Recent journal articles likewise provide useful information on the careers of John Quincy Adams, Jr., who was a Democrat (Robert Mirak, "John Quincy Adams, Jr., and the Reconstruction Crisis," *New England Quarterly*, 35 [June 1962] : 187-202), and such Republicans as Samuel Bowles (Richard Allan Gerber, "Liberal Republicanism, Reconstruction, and Social Order: Samuel Bowles as a Test Case," *New England Quarterly*, 45 [September 1972] : 393-407), Henry L. Dawes (Steven J. Arcanti, "To Secure the Party: Henry L. Dawes and the Politics of Reconstruction," *Historical Journal of Western Massachusetts*, 5 [Spring 1977] : 33-45), and Francis W. Bird (Donald B. Marti, "Francis William Bird: A Radical's Progress through the Republican Party," *Historical Journal of Massachusetts*, 11 [June 1983] : 82-93).

The best overall treatment of the early Reconstruction milieu in which these men worked is the most recent: Dale Baum's *The Civil War Party System: The Case of Massachusetts, 1848-1876* (Chapel Hill, 1984). Some of the same material was covered by Edith E. Ware in the solid chronology of events that she compiled in 1916 (*Political Opinion in Massachusetts during Civil War and Reconstruction* [New York, 1916]). Moreover, the chapters by Frederick W. Dallinger and Wellington Wells in volume 4 of Albert Bushnell Hart's *Commonwealth History of Massachusetts* (New York, 1930) also trace, albeit in much too congratulatory a fashion, the shift in emphasis from national to local issues that took place in Bay State politics between 1865 and 1875. But Baum's book gives the most detailed and authoritative description of both the early postwar impact of civil rights issues nationally and the later controversies over more local concerns, particularly temperance, women's suffrage, and labor legislation. Baum's book also deserves widespread attention as a model of what can be done through the statistical methods of election analysis that are being utilized by Baum and other practitioners of the so-called new political history. His account gains authority because he is able to describe so definitively the relative importance of such matters as religious and economic attitudes or Republican defections and new Democratic recruits in determining the shifting fortunes of the two parties during the period. To be sure, Baum has not said (nor claimed to have said) everything there is to say about the era's politics, and one can still profit from reading three briefer general assessments. The later pages of Paul Goodman's essay, "The Politics of Industrialism: Massachusetts, 1830-1870," *Uprooted Americans: Essays to Honor Oscar Handlin*, ed. Richard L. Bushman et al. (Boston, 1979), pp. 161-207, provide a deft sketch of the background and philosophy of the Bay State's Republican leaders. Several chapters in part 3 of Carl Siracusa's *A Mechanical People: Perceptions of the Industrial Order in Massachusetts, 1815-1880* (Middletown, Conn., 1979) describe how the reaction of Massachusetts politicians to postwar issues was influenced by their hopes and fears about the promises and problems of industrial society. Finally, Richard H. Abbott's excellent essay, "Massachusetts: Maintaining Hegemony," *Radical Republicans in the North: State Politics during Reconstruction*, ed. James C. Mohr (Baltimore, 1976), pp. 1–25, analyzes the Republican politicos' efforts to prevent a resurgence of Democratic strength after Appomattox.

Party battles in the Bay State were much more closely fought in the years between 1873 and 1893 than they had been in the 1860s. Even though Democratic successes came rather sporadically, they represented a serious threat to Republican hegemony. The first postwar Democratic governor was elected in 1874, but failed to win re-election in 1875. The second Democratic governor, Benjamin F. Butler, a former Republican whose victory in 1882 on a prolabor platform struck terror into the hearts of his former GOP colleagues, was also a one-termer. The most sustained challenge to Republican supremacy came in the early 1890s when a Yankee Democrat, William E. Russell, won three terms as the state's chief executive and his party for a time controlled a majority of the commonwealth's congressional seats. For an overview of the shifting electoral fortunes of the Bay State's two major party organizations in these years, the best source is Dale Baum's 1985 essay, "The Massachusetts Voter: Party Loyalty in the Gilded Age, 1872–1896," *Massachusetts in the Gilded Age: Selected Essays*, ed. Jack Tager and John W. Ifkovic (Amherst, 1985), pp. 37–66. An excellent introduction to the parties' problems of finding a winning strategy in Massachusetts is provided by the chapter titled "The First Stages of Pluralism" in Richard Brown's *Massachusetts: A Bicentennial History* (New York, 1978).

Broadly speaking, historians of Massachusetts politics in the years between 1873 and 1900 have faced a twofold task: first, to analyze how the Republicans adjusted to the challenges of closer two-party competition; and second, to describe the Democrats' efforts to break the GOP's grip on the Massachusetts electorate. On the Republican side of this story, the decline of the party's supremacy dated from the early 1870s when various ethnic, economic, and geographic interest groups either slipped away from or failed to join the Republican coalition. The most detailed description of these developments is found in the later chapters of Dale Baum's *The Civil War Party System*, which can be supplemented by Richard Abbott's 1976 essay ("Massachusetts: Maintaining Hegemony") and, perhaps, by Charles Blank's unpublished 1972 dissertation ("The Waning of Radicalism: Massachusetts Republicans and Reconstruction Issues in the Early 1870s" [Ph.D. diss., Columbia University, 1966]). Republican politicos responded to the new milieu by trying a variety of techniques: appeals to wartime loyalties, emphasis on the benefits of the party's protective tariff policy, and clumsy and often self-defeating attempts to exploit ethnocultural biases. Richard Harmond's 1974 article, "Troubles of Massachusetts Republicans during the 1880s" (*Mid-America*, 56 [April 1974]: 85–99), and his unpublished dissertation, "Tradition and Change in the Gilded Age: A Political History of Massachusetts, 1878–1893" (Ph.D. diss., Columbia University, 1966), sketch the broad outlines of these shifting GOP strategies.

One interest group's defection from the Republican ranks that has been thoroughly studied (some would say overstudied) is the Mugwump bolt of 1884. Large sections of Geoffrey Blodgett's *The Gentle Reformers: Massachusetts Democrats in the Cleveland Era* (Cambridge, 1966) and Gerald W. McFarland's *Mugwumps, Morals, and Politics, 1884-1920* (Amherst, 1975) are devoted to the topic, as is the whole of Alan W. Proctor's "Patterns of Diversity among the Massachusetts Mugwumps of 1884" (Ph.D. diss., Boston University, 1977). Other aspects of the Mugwump movement are described in the following journal articles: Philip Putnam Chase, "The Attitude of the Protestant Clergy in Massachusetts during the Election of 1884" (*Massachusetts Historical Society Proceedings*, 64 [1930-1932]: 467-98); Claude M. Fuess, "Carl Schurz and Henry Cabot Lodge in 1884" (*New England Quarterly*, 5 [July 1932]: 453-82); Gordon S. Wood, "The Massachusetts Mugwumps" (*New England Quarterly*, 33 [December 1960]: 435-51); and Dale Baum, "'Noisy But Not Numerous': The Revolt of the Massachusetts Mugwumps" (*The Historian*, 41 [February 1979]: 241-56).

Other organized political causes of the era—prohibition, nativism, women's suffrage, and workingmen's rights—have not been explored as exhaustively as the Mugwump bolt, but each has attracted at least some scholarly scrutiny. On the topic of prohibition, George F. Clark's *History of Temperance Reform in Massachusetts, 1813-1883* (Boston, 1888) must be supplemented by Baum's *The Civil War Party System* and Harmond's "Troubles of Massachusetts Republicans during the 1880s," both cited earlier, and by Peter Haebler's "Liquor and Ethnicity: French Canadians in Politics, Holyoke, 1885-1910" (in Tager and Ifkovic, eds., *Massachusetts in the Gilded Age*, pp. 67-100). Barbara M. Solomon's *Ancestors and Immigrants: A Changing New England Tradition* (Cambridge, 1956) is still a good starting point for the study of nativism. On women's issues, including suffrage, one should see Dale Baum, "Woman Suffrage and the 'Chinese Question': The Limits of Radical Republicanism in Massachusetts, 1865-1876" (*New England Quarterly*, 56 [March 1983]: 60-77); James J. Kenneally, "The Opposition to Woman Suffrage in Massachusetts, 1868-1920" (Ph.D. diss., Boston College, 1963); Kenneally, "Catholicism and Woman Suffrage in Massachusetts" (*Catholic Historical Review*, 53 [1967-1968]: 43-59); and Judith B. Ranlett, "Sorority and Community: Women's Answer to a Changing Massachusetts, 1865-1895" (Ph.D. diss., Brandeis University, 1974). Sources on labor reform and workingmen's issues are even more scattered, but the interested reader should consult Geoffrey Blodgett's *The Gentle Reformers* for the Cleveland Democrats' contribution, along with Arthur Mann's *Yankee Reformers in the Urban Age* (Cambridge, 1954), David Montgomery's *Beyond Equality: Labor and the Radical Republicans, 1862-1872* (New York, 1967), and the works on Benjamin Butler cited earlier.

Although the Republicans generally controlled statewide elections in Massachusetts between 1873 and 1893 and decisively regained statewide supremacy in the mid- and late 1890s, the story of their victories lacks some of the drama of the Democrats' efforts to oust them. Perhaps this is because the Democratic side of the story contains a fascinating subplot, the rise of the Irish in Massachusetts politics. The growth of Irish power became highly visible in the early 1880s when Irish Catholic Democrats were elected mayors of Lawrence (1881) and Boston (1884) and when Patrick A. Collins won a seat in Congress (1882). With urban workers as their power base, Irish bosses pressed their cause within the Democratic party. However, as Geoffrey Blodgett points out in *The Gentle Reformers*, the best single source on Bay State Democrats from 1884 to 1900, the Irish and Yankee Democrats still had to work together if their party was to have a realistic chance of achieving statewide victories over the GOP. In addition to Blodgett's book, his article "Yankee Leadership in a Divided City, 1860–1910" (*Journal of Urban History*, 8 [August 1982]: 371-96) is especially useful. Yankee and Irish Democrats forged what Blodgett shows to have been a sometimes uneasy alliance that had low-tariff policies, workingmen's rights, and electoral reform as its programmatic focus. It was this combination of interest groups and issues that enabled the so-called Cleveland Democrats to bring about the only period of sustained Democratic successes in the late nineteenth century: the 1890, 1891, and 1892 victories that put William E. Russell in the governor's office and kept him there for three terms.

The Cleveland Democrats' triumph was short-lived. The start of a severe depression in 1893 and the Bryan election debacle of 1896 (when few Democrats outside the party's Irish core voted for "the Commoner") returned the GOP to statewide supremacy. The only remaining bastions of Democratic power were those cities where the Irish dominated. Historians have not yet produced a fully integrated account of the 1890s, despite the existence of excellent monographs on selected topics in Massachusetts history during those years. Michael E. Hennessy's contemporary writings remain the only attempts at an overall sketch of Bay State politics and party battles during the decade. These include *Twenty-Five Years of Massachusetts Politics, 1890-1915* (Boston, 1917); *Four Decades of Massachusetts Politics, 1890-1935* (Norwood, Mass., 1935); and "Social and Political Readjustments, 1889-1929" in volume 5 of Hart's *Commonwealth History of Massachusetts* (New York, 1930). Another useful source is Solomon B. Griffin's *People and Politics Observed by a Massachusetts Editor* (Boston, 1923). Although Dale Baum has provided a convincing analysis of the voting returns from the Republicans' landslide victory in 1896 in "The Massachusetts Voter," except for his work only limited scholarly attention has been given to the GOP leadership's campaign strategies during the 1890s. More is known about the changing fortunes and shifting policies of the Democrats, mainly because those topics have been skillfully discussed by Geoffrey Blodgett. Hennessy, Blodgett, and Richard Abrams (*Conservatism in a Progressive Era: Massachusetts Politics, 1900-1912* [Cambridge, 1964]) all noted that Massachusetts was a leading industrial state whose legislature dealt in a progressive way with such modern problems as business regulation, social welfare, and factory conditions long before progressivism became commonplace on the national scene. But as these scholars were quick to observe, progressivism was a very complex phenomenon, for progress had many meanings. To the workers described in Henry F. Bedford's *Socialism and the Workers in Massachusetts, 1886-1912* (Amherst, 1966), progress meant socialism; to the Anglo-Saxon nativists portrayed in Barbara Solomon's *Ancestors and Immigrants*, progress meant applying "scientific" immigration restrictions; to the social activists sketched in Arthur Mann's *Yankee Reformers*, progress meant a wide variety of things—among them, Social Gospel Christianity, trade unionism, feminism, and Bellamy Nationalism.

There are more glaring deficiencies in the biographies of leading Bay Staters from the 1880s and 1890s than among those of public figures from the Reconstruction era. This is not to say that good biographies are lacking. Hugh Hawkins' portrait of Harvard's president, *Between Harvard and America: The Educational Leadership of Charles W. Eliot* (New York, 1972), and Edward C. Kirkland's biography of the railroad reformer and business executive, *Charles Francis Adams, Jr. 1815-1915: Patrician at Bay* (Cambridge, 1966), are both solid studies. Similarly, some of Eliot's and Adams' Mugwump allies who were more directly engaged in party politics—Thomas Wentworth Higginson and Moorfield Storey—are the subjects of quality monographs by Tilden G. Edelstein (*Strange Enthusiasm: A Life of Thomas Wentworth Higginson* [New Haven, 1968]) and William B. Hixon, Jr. (*Moorfield Storey and the Abolitionist Tradition* [New York, 1972]). There are also good modern biographies of the utopian socialist Edward Bellamy (Sylvia E. Bowman, *The Year 2000: A Critical Biography of Edward Bellamy* [New York, 1958]) and the Indian rights advocate Helen Hunt Jackson (Evelyn I. Banning, *Helen Hunt Jackson* [New York, 1973]). However, works on leading Republicans are less satisfactory. Richard E. Welch, Jr.'s volume on Senator George Frisbee Hoar's career is the best of the lot (*George F. Hoar and the Half-Breed Republicans* [Cambridge, 1971]), more informative than the available books and articles on Hoar's fellow Republicans, Henry Cabot Lodge and John D. Long (John A. Garraty, *Henry Cabot Lodge: a Biography* [New York, 1953]; Philip Putnam Chase, "A Crucial Juncture in the Political Careers of Lodge and Long," *Massachusetts Historical Society Proceedings*, 70 [1950-1953]: 102-27; and James W. Hess, "John D. Long and Reform Issues in Massachusetts Politics, 1870-1889," *New England Quarterly*, 33 [March 1960]: 57-73). The career of Senator Henry L. Dawes, another GOP leader who was at least as important as Hoar, if not more so, has not been traced.

Prominent Democrats from the era have been even more neglected, most strikingly three-term governor and presidential hopeful William E. Russell. Article-length studies of Josiah Quincy (Geoffrey Blodgett, "Josiah Quincy, Brahmin Democrat," *New England Quarterly*, 38 [December 1965]: 435-53), Nathan Matthews (Robert A. Silverman, "Nathan Matthews: Politics of Reform in Boston, 1890-1910," *New England Quarterly*, 50 [December 1977]: 626-43), and Patrick J. Maguire (John T. Galvin, "Patrick J. Maguire: Boston's Last Democratic Boss," *New England Quarterly*, 55 [September 1982]: 392-415) provide some insights into the Democratic party's workings at the local level. However, the absence of a published modern study of Patrick A. Collins or (as mentioned earlier) of a book-length biography of Benjamin Butler that includes coverage of his career in state and local affairs is a minor historiographical scandal. Michael P. Curran's *Life of Patrick A. Collins* (Norwood, Mass., 1906) is badly out of date, and Sister M. Jeanne d'Arc O'Hare's "The Public Career of Patrick Andrew Collins" (Ph.D. diss., Boston College, 1959) remains unpublished. The fact that the available books on some of the leading genteel reformers—among them Bliss Perry's *Richard Henry Dana, 1851-1931* (Boston, 1933), Perry's *Life and Letters of Henry Lee Higginson* (Boston, 1921), and Henry G. Pearson's *An American Railroad Builder, John Murray Forbes* (Boston, 1911)— are outdated is perhaps more forgivable, considering the extensive scrutiny that the Mugwumps, including these men, have received collectively.

COMMUNITY STUDIES

Late nineteenth-century Massachusetts was a leading industrial state with a highly urbanized and multiethnic population. Industrial growth was not, of course, new to the Bay State in the post–Civil War period, but from 1865 to 1900 a new era of development was marked by a decided shift away from older small-scale manufacturing methods to the factory system. The growth of factories stimulated urbanization as industrial workers were drawn to the commonwealth's cities. The 1875 state census showed that just over 50 percent of the state's population lived in cities. In 1900, only two and a half decades later, more than three-quarters of Bay Staters were urban residents. Yankees who were city-born or who had quit farming to move to urban centers were joined by successive waves of immigrants—first the Irish, then French-Canadians, and finally Eastern and Southern Europeans—crowding the commonwealth's cities. By the century's end, metropolitan Boston's population had topped one million, and the city boasted a rich mix of industrial and commercial enterprises. The state's smaller industrial cities were more often identified with a single major industry—Lowell, Fall River, and Lawrence with textiles, Lynn and Haverhill with shoes, Holyoke with paper, and Chicopee with bicycles.

Community studies, the product of research that focuses on cities and their inhabitants, has long been the most dynamic subdiscipline within the field of late nineteenth-century Massachusetts history. Virtually every major industrial community in the commonwealth—Boston, Chicopee, Fall River, Holyoke, Lawrence, Lowell, Lynn, New Bedford, Newburyport, Springfield, Waltham, and Worcester—has been the subject of one or more book-length studies. As we will see below, community studies can vary greatly in their topical focus and methodology. However, all of them have in common an underlying assumption that scholarly research into the life and institutions of a single city can yield fruitful insights about such important topics as class status, worker adjustment to factory conditions, ethnic conflict, social mobility, and family history. In other words, community studies scholars work out of a conviction that individual cities are social units small enough to be studied in great detail, but not so small that a hypothesis based on such research will be irrelevant to everything outside a given city's boundaries.

In the fifty years since the first modern monographs on Massachusetts cities began to appear in the mid-1930s, the study of the commonwealth's urban communities has gone through a gradual interpretive evolution marked by several generational shifts. Most of the pioneer studies made during the pre-World War II period focused on urban economic development. Vera Shlakman's *Economic History of a Factory Town: A Study of Chicopee, Massachusetts* (Northampton, 1935), Constance M. Green's *Holyoke, Massachusetts: A Case History of the Industrial Revolution in America* (New Haven, 1939), and Margaret T. Parker's *Lowell: A Study in Industrial Development* (New York, 1940) can serve as representative examples. These able scholars traced the emergence of urban institutions—modern transportation systems, large-scale factories, and class-segregated residential districts—and collected valuable statistical data on industrial production, corporate growth, and working conditions. A second generation of community studies scholars, profoundly influenced by Oscar Handlin's seminal work, *Boston's Immigrants, 1790-1880: A Study in Acculturation*, rev. ed. (Cambridge, 1959), gave greater attention to the ethnic experience, social mobility (or lack of same), and class attitudes of urban workers—subjects that were brought into particularly sharp focus by Stephan Thernstrom in his landmark study of Newburyport workers, *Poverty and Progress: Social Mobility in a Nineteenth Century City* (Cambridge, 1964). In the past ten years community studies scholarship, as exemplifed by Roy Rosenzweig's study of leisure-time activities of Worcester's workers (*Eight Hours for What We Will: Workers and Leisure in an Industrial City, 1870-1920* [New York, 1983]), has begun to explore more intensely laboring people's lives outside the workplace.

It is instructive to note that what Rosenzweig and most contemporary community studies scholars mean when they use the word community is something quite different from what their predecessors meant fifty years earlier. For scholars working in the 1930s, *the* community was the city, and workers were simply one subgroup among many in the city that were adjusting (albeit at some cost) to the imperatives of modern industrial life. The assumption underlying this interpretive framework was that the faster the workers adjusted to the modernization process the better it would be for all concerned. By contrast, when recent scholars use the word community, they are generally referring to working-class subcultures (including various working-class ethnic groups). In coming at their subject from, as it were, the bottom up, these younger scholars have tended to adopt a sympathetic stance toward the workers' struggle to protect their traditional communal values against the demands of society at large.

As a teacher and scholar, Oscar Handlin has had an enormous impact on the field of community studies. Although his published writings have not dealt extensively with post-Civil War Massachusetts history, his major monographs— *Boston's Immigrants: A Study in Acculturation* and (with Mary Handlin) *Commonwealth: A Study of the Role of Government in the American Economy:*

Massachusetts, 1774-1861, rev. ed. (Cambridge, 1969)—sketched out issues that his doctoral students subsequently pursued. Among the veterans of Handlin's Harvard seminars, Donald B. Cole, Alan Dawley, Arthur Mann, Barbara Solomon, Stephan Thernstrom, and Sam Bass Warner, Jr., have made particularly important contributions to the history of late nineteenth-century Massachusetts. These works include Donald B. Cole's *Immigrant City: Lawrence, Massachusetts, 1845-1921* (Chapel Hill, 1963); Alan Dawley's *Class and Community: The Industrial Revolution in Lynn* (Cambridge, 1976); Arthur Mann's *Yankee Reformers*; Barbara Solomon's *Ancestors and Immigrants*; Stephan Thernstrom's *Poverty and Progress*; and Sam Bass Warner, Jr.'s *Streetcar Suburbs: The Process of Growth in Boston, 1870-1900* (Cambridge, 1962). But the Handlin legacy does not end there. In recent years historians who are students of Handlin's students have begun to come of age in the profession. Of these, John T. Cumbler and Roy Rosenzweig have already produced significant books. In his *Working-Class Community in Industrial America: Work, Leisure, and Struggle in Two Industrial Cities, 1880-1930* (Westport, Conn., 1979), Cumbler (a Warner student) did a comparative analysis of Lynn and Fall River, with particular attention to the influence of each city's physical contours on the social and political life of its workers. In Lynn the concentration of business in a central district near working-class residential areas fostered working-class solidarity, whereas in Fall River the dispersed geographic locations of factories and working people's neighborhoods had the opposite effect, undercutting working-class political action. In his *Eight Hours for What We Will*, Rosenzweig (a Thernstrom student) showed how drinking, boisterous play, and raucous conduct at 4th of July celebrations enabled Worcester's workers to take control of their lives outside of the factories even as they were losing control within the workplace.

In addition to providing a vast amount of new data about late nineteenth-century Massachusetts, books by Handlin's students have often sparked significant interpretive debates. For example, Stephan Thernstrom's monograph on Newburyport workers explicitly challenged the work of W. Lloyd Warner and his associates, the authors of *Yankee City* (the one-volume abridged edition, New Haven, 1963), an earlier study of Newburyport's social structure. Warner's perspective had been that of a cultural anthropologist, a fact that influenced both his research methods (which relied heavily on subjective judgments drawn from interviews and surveys) and his working hypothesis that a functional equilibrium prevailed in the city's class structure. In common with many practitioners of the "new urban history," Thernstrom, whose book was excerpted in New Left anthologies, wanted to highlight social conflicts that were traceable to the American class system. He charged that Warner's approach was ahistorical in that it ignored instances of class conflict and social change that were inconsistent with the image of social equilibrium to which Warner was attached. Thernstrom substituted economic measures (occupation and income) for Warner's subjective indices of class standing and showed that although some Newburyport workers achieved a small amount of upward mobility, they rarely escaped from lower-class status. In an analysis of the distinctions between Warner and Thernstrom ("Yankee City and the New Urban History," *Journal of Urban History*, 6 [May 1980]: 321-38), Steven L. Olsen argues that Warner's and Thernstrom's findings supplement rather than totally contradict each other. For instance, Thernstrom discovered many cases in which worker behavior was determined less by economic class (i.e., by occupational status, the "objective" measure Thernstrom applied to define class standing) than by various cultural allegiances—religion, ethnicity, and even political party ties. These affiliations, Olsen suggests, not only cut across class lines but are implicitly compatible with the broad subjective criteria that Warner used in defining social status.

Alan Dawley's *Class and Community: The Industrial Revolution in Lynn* is another case in which a Handlin student challenged widely held scholarly ideas about late nineteenth-century Massachusetts. Dawley's target was the so-called Wisconsin School of labor history that had been advanced by John R. Commons and his students. Commons' perspective was that of an early twentieth-century progressive for whom industrialization was an impersonal modernizing process through which outmoded preindustrial craft production of goods had been replaced by a corporation-controlled factory system. Commons was convinced that within this particular evolutionary progression the logical thing for industrial workers to do was to avoid radical political challenges to corporate control (the growth of which he felt was inevitable), to organize themselves into trade unions to bargain with employers over bread-and-butter issues, and, where bargaining failed to achieve decent conditions, to look to progressive liberals to pass ameliorative legislation. For examples of Commons' approach, one should see John R. Commons et al., *History of Labour in the United States*, 4 vols. (New York, 1918-1935), and Commons, "American Shoemakers, 1648-1895: A Sketch of Industrial Evolution" (*Quarterly Journal of Economics*, 24 [November 1909]: 39-84).

The obvious preference of the Wisconsin School for conservative unionism and Commons' desire that workers accept rather than reject corporate capitalism were biases that, according to Dawley, led Commons to downplay or even ignore evidence that "the American economic system engendered bitter class conflicts."[1] Dawley, by contrast, argued that Lynn's workers rejected the middle-class myth of success, saw nothing inconsistent about combining union membership with radical political activity, and preferred the ideal of social equality to the goal of harmony within hierarchical corporate structures.

In a perceptive evaluation of *Class and Community*, "Artisan Origins of the American Working Class" (*International Labor and Working Class History*, 19 [Spring 1981]: 1-22), Sean Wilentz concluded that despite its many virtues, Dawley's final synthesis was "a flawed effort."[2] Wilentz credits Dawley with persuasively demonstrating that class consciousness and class conflict did accompany the industrial revolution in Lynn. He also believes that Dawley successfully rebutted Commons' description of American workers as totally pragmatic and wage-conscious in their goals. But on other points Wilentz does not find Dawley quite as convincing. He complains that Dawley's political terminology is so vague that it is unclear whether the workers' talk of equal rights owed more to working-class radicalism or to an American tradition of republican political aspirations. Dawley's case for a radical interpretation is weakened by the relative ease with which Lynn's workers were soon assimilated into the two mainstream political parties. Similarly, Dawley asserted that the Lynn workers' experience was a microcosm of industrial laborers' experiences everywhere in the United States, but the Lynn strike of 1860 and subsequent independent worker political activism in Lynn were not typical of Massachusetts labor history. Moreover, the fact that Lynn's workers, like laborers in New Bedford, Holyoke, Newburyport, and elsewhere, sought middle-class respectability through membership in churches, temperance organizations, and the two major political parties seems to conform better to Commons' paradigm of labor history than to Dawley's. Both Dawley and Commons can be read with profit.

Many topics that are covered in community studies—economic development, ethnicity, family life, occupational and geographic mobility, and working-class experiences—can be and have been separated out and exploited as themes in specialized studies. Two economic histories, Edward C. Kirkland's *Men, Cities, and Transportation: A Study of New England History, 1820-1900*, 2 vols. (Cambridge, 1948) and Robert W. Eisenmenger's *The Dynamics of Growth in New England's Economy, 1870-1964* (Middletown, Conn., 1967), stand out in that category.

There are dissertations, monographs, or journal articles on most ethnic groups, including the Irish, French-Canadians, Italians, blacks, Chinese, and Jews. On the blacks, one should consult Elizabeth H. Pleck, *Black Migration and Poverty: Boston, 1865-1900* (New York, 1979), and Joseph P. Lynch, "Blacks in Springfield, 1868-1880: A Mobility Study" (*Historical Journal of Western Massachusetts*, 7 [June 1979]: 25-34). The Chinese are described by Frederick Rudolph in "Chinamen in Yankeedom: Anti-Unionism in Massachusetts in 1870" (*American Historical Review*, 53 [October 1947]: 1-29). There are more works on French-Canadians than on any other group except the Irish. These include Ralph D. Vicero, "Immigration of French-Canadians to New England, 1840-1900: A Geographical Analysis" (Ph.D. diss., University of Wisconsin, 1968); Frances H. Early, "French-Canadian Beginnings in an American Community: Lowell, 1868-1886" (Ph.D. diss., Concordia University, 1980); and two articles by Early: "The French-Canadian Family Economy and Standard-of-Living in Lowell, 1870" (*Journal of Family History*, 7 [Summer 1982]: 180-219) and "The Rise and Fall of Felix Albert: Some Reflections on the Aspirations of Habitant Immigrants to Lowell in the Late Nineteenth Century" (*The Quebec and Acadian Diaspora in North America*, ed. Raymond Breton and Pierre Savard [Toronto, 1982], pp. 25-38). Another historian who has extensively researched the history of the French-Canadians in a Massachusetts city is Peter Haebler, in "Habitants in Holyoke: The Development of the French-Canadian Community in a Massachusetts City, 1865-1910" (Ph.D. diss., University of New Hampshire, 1976) and in three articles: "Holyoke's French-Canadian Community in Turmoil: The Role of the Church in Assimilation, 1869-1887" (*Historical Journal of Western Massachusetts*, 7 [January 1979]: 5-21); "Educational Patterns of French-Canadians in Holyoke, 1868-1910" (*Historical Journal of Massachusetts*, 10 [June 1982]: 17-29); and "Liquor and Ethnicity: French Canadians in Politics, Holyoke, 1885-1910" (in Tager and Ifkovic, eds., *Massachusetts in the Gilded Age*, pp. 67-100).

For the Irish, representative studies include Albert G. Mitchell's "Irish Family Patterns in Nineteenth-Century Ireland and Lowell, Massachusetts" (Ph.D. diss., Boston University, 1976); William W. Millett's "The Irish and Mobility Patterns in Northampton, 1846-1883" (Ph.D. diss., University of Iowa, 1980); Timothy J. Meagher's "'The Lord is Not Dead': Cultural and Social Change among the Irish in Worcester" (Ph.D. diss., Brown University, 1982); and William F. Hartford's "Paper City: Class Development in Holyoke, Massachusetts, 1850-1920" (Ph.D. diss., University of Massachusetts, 1983). On the Jews, one should consult James A. Gelin's *Starting Over: The Formation of the Jewish Community of Springfield, 1840-1905* (Lanham, Md., 1984); for the "new" immigrants of one city, see Philip T. Silvia, Jr.'s "The Position of 'New' Immigrants in the Fall River Textile Industry" (*International Migration Review*, 10 [Summer 1976]: 221-32).

The maturation of the fields of women's history and social history has led to a proliferation of published material, much of it of very high quality, on family history, fertility patterns, childbearing, and household structure in Massachusetts. A sampling of articles and other sources on these subjects should include Tamara K. Hareven and Maris A. Vinovskis, "Marital Fertility, Ethnicity, and Occupation in Urban Families: An Analysis of South Boston and the South End in 1880" (*Journal of Social History*, 8 [Spring 1975]: 69-93); Paul N. Dubovik, "Housing in Holyoke and Its Effects on Family Life, 1860-1910" (*Historical Journal of Western Massachusetts*, 4 [Spring 1975]: 40-50); Howard P. Chudacoff, "New Branches on the Tree: Household Structure in Early Stages of the Family Cycle in Worcester, 1860-1880" (*Proceedings of the American Antiquarian Society*, 86 [October 1976]: 303-20); Tamara K. Hareven and Maris A. Vinovskis, "Patterns of Childbearing in Late Nineteenth-Century America: The Determinants of Marital Fertility in Five Massachusetts Towns in 1880" (*Family and Population in Nineteenth-Century America*, ed. Tamara K. Hareven and Maris A. Vinovskis [Princeton, 1978], pp. 85-125); Myfanwy Morgan and Hilda H. Golden, "Immigrant Families in an Industrial City: A Study of Households in Holyoke, 1880" (*Journal of Family History*, 4 [Spring 1979]: 59-68); Jerome E. Wilcox III, "Tenacious Families, Mighty Forces: Household Structure in Hampshire and Hampden Counties, Massachusetts, during the Period of Industrialization" (Ph.D. diss., University of Massachusetts, 1981); and Jerry Wilcox and Hilda H. Golden, "Prolific Immigrants and Dwindling Natives? Fertility Patterns in Western Massachusetts, 1850 and 1880" (*Journal of Family History*, 7 [Fall 1982]: 265-88).

In another relatively new subfield, sport history, Stephen Hardy's *How Boston Played: Sport, Recreation, and Community, 1865-1915* (Boston, 1982) is a particularly welcome addition to the literature on late nineteenth-century Massachusetts. Other works on sport history include Hardy's "Parks for the People: Reforming the Boston Park System, 1870-1915" (*Journal of Sport History*, 7 [Winter 1980]: 5-24) and David Quentin Voigt, "The Boston Redstockings: The Birth of Major League Baseball" (*New England Quarterly*, 42 [December 1970]: 531-49).

Marvin Lazerson's *Origins of the Urban School: Public Education in Massachusetts, 1870-1915* (Cambridge, 1971) is a solid monograph in the history of education, although it and other recent publications in the field lack some of the interpretive sparkle that Michael B. Katz brought to his study of an earlier period (*The Irony of Early School Reform: Educational Innovation in Mid-Nineteenth Century Massachusetts* [Cambridge, 1968]). Two other works on education that should be consulted are Thomas W. Leavitt, "Textile Manufacturers and the Expansion of Technical Education in Massachusetts, 1869-1904" (*Essex Institute Historical Collections*, 108 [July 1972]: 244-51) and Carl F. Kaestle and Maris A. Vinovskis, *Education and Social Change in Nineteenth-Century Massachusetts* (New York, 1980).

A traditional research topic that continues to draw much scholarly attention is labor history, under which a wide array of studies on strikes, labor legislation, union organizations, and factory conditions may be grouped. On labor laws, the courts, and workplace safety, representative sources include Susan Myra Kingsbury, *Labor Laws and Their Enforcement with Special Reference to Massachusetts* (New York, 1911); Robert Asher, "Business and Workers' Welfare in the Progressive Era: Workmen's Compensation Reform in Massachusetts, 1880-1911" (*Business History Review*, 51 [Winter 1969]: 452-75); and three articles by Carl Gersuny: "Work Injuries and Adversary Processes in Two New England Textile Mills" (*Business History Review*, 51 [Autumn 1977]: 326-40); "Industrial Casualties in Lowell, 1890-1905" (*Labor History*, 20 [Summer 1979]: 435-42); and "New England Mill Casualties, 1890-1910" (*New England Quarterly*, 52 [December 1979]: 467-82). For a history of certain strikes one should consult Horace G. Wadlin, *Strikes and Lockouts, 1881-1886* (Boston, 1889), and Martin H. Dodd, "Marlboro, Massachusetts, and the Shoeworkers' Strike of 1898-1899" (*Labor History*, 20 [Summer 1979]: 376-97). The best source on unemployment is Alexander Keyssar's *Out of Work: The First Century of Unemployment in Massachusetts* (New York, 1986). Two scholarly articles that provide valuable insights about late nineteenth-century unions are John P. Hall's "Knights of St. Crispin in Massachusetts, 1869-1878" (*Journal of Economic History*, 18 [June 1958]: 161-75) and Kenneth Fones-Wolf's "Boston Eight Hour Men, New York Marxists, and the Emergence of the International Labor Union: Prelude to the AFL" (*Historical Journal of Massachusetts*, 9 [June 1981]: 47-59).

On women workers, representative sources include Carl Gersuny, "'A Devil in Petticoats' and Just Cause: Patterns of Punishment in Two New England Textile Factories" (*Business History Review*, 50 [Summer 1976]: 131-52); Judith A. McGaw, "'A Good Place to Work'. Industrial Workers and Occupational Choice:

The Case of Berkshire Women" (*Journal of Interdisciplinary History*, 10 [Autumn 1979]: 227-48); Keith Melder, "Women in the Shoe Industry: The Evidence from Lynn" (*Essex Institute Historical Collections*, 115 [October 1979]: 270-87); and Mary Blewett, "Shared But Different: The Experience of Women Workers in the Nineteenth Century Work Force of the New England Shoe Industry" (*Essays from the Lowell Conference on Industrial History, 1980 and 1981* [Lowell, 1981], pp. 77-85).

Useful sources on a variety of other topics in labor history include William J. Mulligan, Jr., "Mechanization and Work in the American Shoe Industry: Lynn, 1852-1883" (*Journal of Economic History*, 41 [March 1981]: 59-64); Mulligan's "The Family and Technological Change: The Shoemakers of Lynn during the Transition from Hand to Machine Production, 1850-1880" (Ph.D. diss., Clark University, 1982); Marianne Pedulla, "Labor in a City of Immigrants: Holyoke, 1882-1888" (*Historical Journal of Massachusetts*, 13 [June 1985]: 147-61); and Jeffrey G. Williamson, "Consumer Behavior in the Nineteenth Century: Carroll D. Wright's Massachusetts Workers in 1875" (*Explorations in Entrepreneurial History*, 2nd ser., 4 [1966-1967]: 98-135).

The state's rural population has attracted few historians, but Hal S. Barron's recently published *Those Who Stayed Behind: Rural Society in Nineteenth-Century New England* (New York, 1984) exemplifies what can be done when an able scholar focuses on the topic. On the experience of one rural family whose members became itinerant photographers, see Gerald W. McFarland, "The World of the Howes Brothers" (*New England Reflections 1882-1907*, ed. Alan B. Newman [New York, 1979], pp. xi-xx).

THE PROBLEM OF SYNTHESIS

Historians of late nineteenth-century Massachusetts have distinguished themselves by producing a significant number of first-rate monographs, the importance of which extends well beyond the state's borders. Among the political histories, Dale Baum's *The Civil War Party System* and Geoffrey Blodgett's *The Gentle Reformers* deserve to be included in any thorough list of major books on nineteenth-century American politics. Many list compilers might also mention Barbara Solomon's *Ancestors and Immigrants* and David Donald's *Charles Sumner and the Rights of Man* for their trenchant treatments of their subjects. But it is community studies scholars who have consistently made very impressive contributions to American historiography over the past five decades. A rich vein of outstanding community studies books extends back at least to Constance Green's pioneer monograph on Holyoke and includes such seminal works as Oscar Handlin's *Boston's Immigrants*, Stephan Thernstrom's *Poverty and Progress*, Sam Bass Warner, Jr.'s *Streetcar Suburbs*, and Alan Dawley's *Class and Community*. Perhaps Roy Rosenzweig's recently published *Eight Hours for What We Will* eventually will also win a place in this distinguished company. Although each of these monographs was restricted to the study of a single Massachusetts city, each of them raised interpretive points that scholars in such diverse fields as urban, labor, and immigration history found it impossible to ignore.

Despite the availability of many excellent monographs on specific aspects of late nineteenth-century Massachusetts history, scholars have not yet produced a book-length synthesis of the years from 1865 to 1900. In part, this may simply indicate that these three and a half decades, although an appropriate time span for a bibliographical essay, are not necessarily a natural timeframe for synthesis. Certainly in the area of political history one reason for the absence of an overall synthesis of the period is that it breaks down into two or three subperiods, each with its own distinctive traits. Similarly, in the field of community studies, scholars have no single, agreed-upon timeframe within which to divide the study of the type of developments they want to trace. Thernstrom, for instance, started his study of Newburyport workers by examining the pre-Civil War period and ended it in 1880 (a choice dictated in part by the availability of census records), while his student, Roy Rosenzweig, adopted the years from 1870 to 1920 as the timeframe appropriate to his book on Worcester's workers. The numerous variations—for example, 1840-1880 (Michael H. Frisch in *Town into City: Springfield and the Meaning of Community, 1840-1880* [Cambridge, 1972]), 1850-1890 (Howard M. Gitelman in *Workingmen of Waltham: Mobility in American Urban Industrial Development, 1850-1890* [Baltimore, 1974], 1845-1921 (Donald Cole on Lawrence), 1870-1900 (Warner on Boston's suburbs), and 1865-1900 (Thomas A. McMullin in "Industrialization and Social Change in a Nineteenth-Century City: New Bedford, 1865-1900" [Ph.D. diss., University of Wisconsin, 1976])—hardly inspire confidence that there will be an easy consensus on a single timeframe. Doubtless the specific theme (mobility, workers' leisure, etc.) and the specific cities under study often dictate these choices, but if, for instance, one author makes the 1890s a turning point and another does not even discuss that decade, obvious problems of comparison and synthesis arise.

Community studies scholars seem to have pursued their research on individual cities on the assumption that the parts will eventually add up to a whole, but this does not necessarily follow. Not only were the dominant industries of various cities often more notable for their differences than their similarities, but one city was frequently distinct from another in many other ways. For example, Thernstrom found that a remarkably high percentage of Newburyport's working-class residents became home owners, but he acknowledged that the same might not have been true for Boston's workers, many of whom were renters in inner-city tenement districts. Similarly, although Dawley argued that Lynn "exemplified the larger processes of American economic development," the fact that Lynn's workers were more radical and more politicized than, for instance, their fellow workers in Fall River (as described by John T. Cumbler) makes generalization difficult.[3] Moreover, as Thomas A. McMullin observes in "The Immigrant Response to Industrialism in New Bedford, 1865-1900" (in Tager and Ifkovic, eds., *Massachusetts in the Gilded Age*, pp. 101-21), the commonwealth's many ethnic groups had distinctly different responses to industrialization. McMullin illustrates the point by contrasting English and French-Canadian textile workers. Multiply this case by all the possible variations based on the Bay State's different industries, cities, and ethnic groups, and it is easy to see why, although there is a crying need for some scholar to gather these loose ends and to tie them together, the task has not been undertaken.

Even assuming, as I do, that a full-scale synthesis of the community studies data is possible, its completion would still leave us short of an overall synthesis of late nineteenth-century Massachusetts history. As mentioned earlier, political historians and community studies scholars have tended to work along separate lines, each group exploring its distinctive agenda and developing its largely unique bibliography. It is entirely possible that the two groups, like two teams of workers tunneling through a mountain from different directions, will never meet, even though the mountain under which they are working is all of a piece. But any prediction that the two will never meet may be premature, since in the years from 1976 to 1985 there have been some significant attempts to draw together data from these two lines of inquiry. For example, Alan Dawley's *Class and Community* (1976) was an especially thoughtful effort by a community studies scholar to explore the political activities of a given city's workers, while Dale Baum's *The Civil War Party System* (1984) was the most sophisticated inquiry yet by a political historian into the socioeconomic roots of the electorate's voting behavior during the era. Carl Siracusa's *A Mechanical People* (1979) tested another strategy for describing the political impact of industrialization, a method that did not, however, sufficiently utilize the data from community studies sources. Richard D. Brown's chapter "The First Stages of Pluralism" in his bicentennial history (1978) and Jack Tager's introduction (1985), "Massachusetts and the Age of Economic Revolution" (in Tager and Ifkovic, eds., *Massachusetts in the Gilded Age*, pp. 3–28), were other insightful, albeit brief, overviews of the era's social and political themes. It may be that these are harbingers of a full-scale synthesis yet to come. Even if they are not, they outline the shape that such a synthesis would have to take, and that is itself a welcome step forward in the study of late nineteenth-century Massachusetts history.

NOTES

1. Alan Dawley, *Class and Community: The Industrial Revolution in Lynn* (Cambridge, 1976), p. 194.

2. Sean Wilentz, "Artisan Origins of The American Working Class," *International Labor and Working Class History*, 19 (Spring 1981): 8.

3. Dawley, *Class and Community*, p. 8.

6

MASSACHUSETTS IN THE TWENTIETH CENTURY

ROBERT O'LEARY

IN 1980, SHORTLY after joining the Reagan White House staff, James Baker, when asked if he had ever visited a Communist country, replied, "Well, I have been to Massachusetts." Mr. Baker's remark reflects the widespread belief that Massachusetts is among the most liberal states in the country. It is a perception that has been reinforced by its twentieth-century tradition of sending relatively liberal congressmen to Washington and by its widely publicized support for George McGovern in 1972. In some respects the commonwealth's progressive reputation is well deserved, for it has frequently been at the forefront of reform both at the state and federal level. Yet a close examination of its recent history reveals a more complex political tradition, oftentimes deeply conservative, rarely concerned with ideological issues, and largely defined by ethnic and cultural divisions.

The political history of Massachusetts in the twentieth century is the story of the arrival of immigrant groups to positions of power. The revolution began in Boston in 1885 when the first Irish Catholic, Hugh O'Brien, was elected mayor. Although he was succeeded by a Yankee Protestant, the Irish again occupied the office with the election of Patrick Collins in 1902. But it was not until 1910 and the emergence of John F. Fitzgerald that the transition within Boston was complete. Fitzgerald's career has been chronicled by J. H. Cutler in *"Honey Fitz": Three Steps to the White House—The Life and Times of John F. ("Honey Fitz") Fitzgerald* (Indianapolis, 1962), a breezy and informal biography that is of limited value to the historian. It tells the familiar story of the Irish Potato Famine and the family's immigration to America. Fitzgerald began as a poor but ambitious young man who became popular in his North End neighborhood and subsequently embarked on a political career that included service as a common councilor, state senator, U.S. congressman, and mayor of Boston. His two terms as mayor were marred by controversy and an absence of any notable achievements, but his career is noteworthy because he was among the first to regularly employ the political techniques of the newly developing ethnic machines and because he was John F. Kennedy's grandfather.

Although Fitzgerald's success symbolized the changing character of local politics, his political impact was not the most enduring. That honor more properly belongs to James Michael Curley. Curley was born in Roxbury and as a young man became involved in ward politics. After two defeats he was elected a common councilor, later an alderman, then a city councilor, and eventually a U.S. congressman. But like many of his contemporaries, his greatest ambition was to be mayor, and in 1914, after a near confrontation with Fitzgerald, he achieved his goal by defeating the Yankee's "good government" candidate, James J. Storrow. Eventually he would serve three more terms as mayor, one as governor, and one more as a congressman. In between he was twice sent to prison and once appeared on the floor of the 1932 Democratic Convention as Alcalde Jaime Miguelo Curleo, chairman of the Puerto Rican delegation and supporter of FDR.

Curley brought a whole new style to Massachusetts politics, a style that enraged his numerous enemies but endeared him to many of the powerless who vicariously shared in his antics. During campaigns he eloquently vilified his opponents, regularly dismissed Yankee reformers as "Goo Goos," and characterized the phrase "Codfish Aristocracy" as "a reflection on the fish." In office he reshaped public policy into an epic struggle between good and evil and reduced the political process to an elaborate system of personal favors. At one point a political reporter estimated that 30,000 people were direct beneficiaries of the mayor's personal intervention and could be counted as hard-core supporters.

Curley has been the object of a great deal of well-deserved attention but emerges from it all as something of an historical enigma. While still active politically, he wrote his autobiography, *I'd Do It Again: A Record of All My Uproarious Years* (Englewood Cliffs, N.J., 1957), which unapologetically celebrates his accomplishments. Although it is uneven and a bit disorganized, its bombastic style and sometimes outrageous claims perfectly capture the personality of the man who, when asked by a reporter if it were true that he would "take the false teeth out of the mouth of his followers," replied, "Why not? I put them there, didn't I?" Joseph Dinneen wrote a full-length biography entitled *The Purple Shamrock: The Honorable James Michael Curley of Boston* (New York, 1949) that provides a nicely balanced but contemporary account of Curley's career. William V. Shannon also includes a chapter on Curley in his book *The American Irish* (New York, 1962), which beautifully analyzes the man's ambiguous character. He concludes by arguing that despite some notable achievements, Curley failed to transcend the boundaries of his own personal ambition and ultimately did both Massachusetts and himself a disservice by squandering his talent and debasing the moral tone of political life. The author does concede, however, that

Curley was "the victim as well as the protagonist of this tragedy . . . a prisoner of the sad history" of Irish Catholic and Yankee Protestant relations in Massachusetts.

Curley is also discussed at some length by Francis Russell in the final two chapters of *The Great Interlude: Neglected Events and Persons from the First World War to the Depression* (New York, 1964) and is the inspiration for Edwin O'Connor's novel, *The Last Hurrah* (Boston, 1956). Ralph G. Martin assigns him a chapter in his book *The Bosses* (New York, 1964) and portrays his political campaigns and accomplishments in a sympathetic manner. But Reinhard H. Luthin in *American Demagogues: Twentieth Century* (Boston, 1954) argues that the Boston politician was an unscrupulous exploiter of ethnic and religious hatreds.

Curley has also been the major or secondary focus of numerous articles and doctoral dissertations. Among the more notable articles are Francis Russell's "The Last of the Bosses" (*American Heritage*, 10 [June 1959]: 21-25) and Joseph F. Dinneen's "Boston's Incredible Curley" (*Collier's*, [August 19, 1946]). Herbert Marshall Zolot's unpublished dissertation, "The Issue of Good Government and James Michael Curley: Curley and the Boston Scene from 1897-1918" (Ph.D. diss., S.U.N.Y., Stony Brook, 1975), reviews his early relationship with other ethnic groups. And in Maurice Baskin's "Ward Politics in Boston, 1896-1921" (Ph.D. diss., Harvard University, 1975), the author points out that the political environment from which Curley emerged was different from that of many other major American cities because there were no citywide machines. Each ward boss was a feudal lord, and city politics was an unfolding drama of temporary alliances interspersed with bitter infighting. Even though Curley was a product of this tradition, he never joined the system, preferring to run as an anti-machine candidate.

Curley's political career, of course, extended beyond that of his early contemporaries and involved not only local, but also state and federal offices. Easily the best and most comprehensive analysis of him during the twenties and thirties is contained in Charles H. Trout's *Boston, The Great Depression, and the New Deal* (New York, 1977). Curley's unusually prolonged political appeal and his eventual demise is discussed by William V. Shannon in "Ex-Mayor of the Poor" (*The Reporter*, January 17, 1950) and by Vincent A. Lapomarda in "Maurice Joseph Tobin: The Decline of Bossism in Boston" (*New England Quarterly*, 43 [September 1970]: 355-81) in which he traces the relationship between Maurice Tobin and James Michael Curley. According to the author, Tobin began his political career as a protégé of Curley, but by 1936 "Curleyism" and bossism had become synonymous in many people's minds, increasingly making the aging governor a liability for a young politician building an image as a reformer. When they both chose to run for the office of mayor in 1937, the battle lines were drawn and the struggle ensued. Tobin won and again defeated Curley in 1941, subsequently moving on to the governorship and finally to a cabinet position in the Truman administration. Tobin's record of achievement was impressive, and his success as a politician was evidence, according to Lapomarda, of the waning appeal of "Curleyism," which was unable to compete with the social welfare programs associated with the New Deal.

While Curley successfully transcended ward politics, others embraced it; the most noteworthy of these was Martin Lomasney, "the Mahatma" of Boston's West End. Lomasney has attracted a substantial amount of historical attention, not only because of his importance to both city and state politics, but because much of his career challenges traditional interpretations of the period. Well-known historians such as George Mowry (*The Era of Theodore Roosevelt* [New York, 1958]) and Richard Hofstadter (*The Age of Reform* [New York, 1955]) have argued that machine politics and politicians interfered with and limited progressive reform, but local historians have concluded otherwise. Leslie G. Ainsley wrote a well-documented biography entitled *Boston Mahatma* (Boston, 1949) that has been followed by several articles, most notably A. D. Van Nostrand's "The Lomasney Legend" (*New England Quarterly*, 21 [December 1948]: 435-50) and John D. Buenker's "The Mahatma and Progressive Reform: Martin Lomasney as Lawmaker, 1911-1917" (*New England Quarterly*, 44 [September 1971]: 397-419).

All agree that the famous "Czar of Ward Eight" was either atypical of his breed or simply a good example of the extent to which some reforms were embraced by urban Democrats in Massachusetts. Ainsley labels Lomasney a "liberal . . . one who has done much for progressive ideas in lawmaking," and Buenker persuasively contends that the Mahatma's career as a local ward boss and state legislator is a powerful argument against the traditional view of big-city machine politics as the antithesis of liberal government. According to Buenker, Lomasney's record was one of constant sympathy and support for liberal reforms as long as they were consistent with the interests of his constituents. He supported such Progressive principles as the direct election of senators, women's suffrage, labor legislation, and laws promoting greater governmental responsibility for the public's welfare. At the same time, he opposed attempts to legislate cultural conformity (including a ban on Sunday baseball), Prohibition, and a state constitutional amendment prohibiting Catholic access to public funds, an amendment that he would later reshape into a more inclusive prohibition against public support for any private institution. In general, he was an advocate of cultural pluralism, a protector of the rights of minorities, and, along with other Boston representatives to the legislature, an active reformer.

If Democratic machine politicians such as Lomasney, Fitzgerald, and even Curley can be labeled Progressives, then what role did their Republican opponents play in Massachusetts politics during the Progressive Era? In a classic study, *Conservatism in a Progressive Era: Massachusetts Politics, 1900-1912* (Cambridge, 1964), Richard Abrams argues that at the outset of the twentieth century Massachusetts had already adopted many of the reforms that were later associated with the Progressive movement in other states. These early achievements were largely the work of native New Englanders, typically old-stock middle- and upper-class Protestant Republicans who were imbued with a commitment to what they considered the public good and were willing to sacrifice their own narrow commercial interests to achieve it. But at the outset of the twentieth century, while Republicans in much of the rest of the country embraced reform, their Massachusetts counterparts appeared to abandon their earlier convictions.

The developing conservative bias of Massachusetts' native middle class has been further explored by Richard B. Sherman in "Foss of Massachusetts, Demagogue v. Progressive" (*Mid America*, 43, no. 2 [April 1961] : 75-94) and "Charles Sumner Bird and the Progressive Party in Massachusetts" (*New England Quarterly* 33 [September 1960] : 325-40). In the Foss article, for example, Sherman points out that eleven key pieces of Progressive legislation submitted to the 1911 legislature were supported by 81 percent of the Democrats but by only 28 percent of the Republicans. He also found further evidence of growing Republican indifference to reform in the brief political career of Charles Sumner Bird. Bird, a well-known businessman, was the 1912 gubernatorial candidate of the newly founded Progressive Republican League, a group that in theory should have been the driving force of Progressive legislation within the state. Instead, Bird spoke out against labor unions, viewed social issues from a paternalistic perspective, and argued that political reform and middle-class values were one and the same.

While the Democrats began the twentieth century by winning political control of Boston, the Republicans maintained their dominance in the state legislature and over statewide offices. For the first two decades they controlled both U.S. Senate seats in the persons of Winthrop Murray Crane (1904-1913), John Wingate Weeks (1913-1919), and Henry Cabot Lodge (1893-1924). John A. Garraty's *Henry Cabot Lodge: A Biography* (New York, 1953) focuses largely on the senator's personality and the extent to which it influenced his positions on contemporary political issues. Much attention is given to the bitter struggle between the chairman of the Foreign Relations Committee and Woodrow Wilson over the issue of the League of Nations. The author contends that Lodge's opposition was largely motivated by partisan politics and not by any grand vision of America's role in the world. *The Lodges of Massachusetts* by Alden Hatch (New York, 1973) indulgently traces the history of the entire family from 1699 through the 1960s, pointing out its dedication to public service especially in terms of international affairs. But probably the most satisfactory account of Lodge still rests with his own *Early Memories* (New York, 1913) and to a lesser extent with Karl Schriftgiesser's *The Gentleman from Massachusetts* (New York, 1944).

Although they occurred with less regularity and with more propriety, the Republican party of Massachusetts was not without its own internal squabbles. An article by Richard E. Welch Jr., "Opponents and Colleagues: George Frisbie Hoar and Henry Cabot Lodge, 1898-1904" (*New England Quarterly* 39 [June 1966] : 182-209), and an unpublished senior honors thesis by Peter Stanley, "Hoar and Lodge on the Philippine Question" (Harvard University Archives, 1962), discuss an early struggle between the two Republican senators over the issue of acquiring the Philippines. Hoar, an anti-imperialist, argued that the acquisition would imperil the democratic principles of the U.S. Constitution, while Lodge believed that it was America's destiny to play a greater role in world affairs. For personal and political reasons they both avoided public confrontations in Massachusetts and confined their disagreements to the floor of the Senate. In the end, Hoar tended to defer to his junior colleague.

David I. Walsh, the state's first Irish Catholic governor and later senator, was also a major political figure during this period. Dorothy G. Wayman's *David I. Walsh: Citizen-Patriot* (Milwaukee, 1952) is a straightforward, non-critical, and inadequate account of his career. It is clear from her study that Walsh was originally an ally of William Jennings Bryan and later Woodrow Wilson. But Walsh's commitment to Wilson had its limits, as John H. Flannagan, Jr., has pointed out in "The Disillusionment of a Progressive: U.S. Senator David I. Walsh and the League of Nations Issue, 1918–1920" (*New England Quarterly*, 4 [December 1968] : 483–504). According to the author, Walsh began his Senate career committed to supporting Wilson's foreign policy but later became disillusioned with the president over the Treaty of Versailles, particularly with its failure to insist on Ireland's right to self-determination. The best comprehensive and balanced account of Walsh can be found in an unpublished dissertation by William J. Grattan, "David I. Walsh and His Associates: A Study in Political Theory" (Ph.D. diss., Harvard University, 1958).

Calvin Coolidge also deserves some attention and has been the object of several excellent biographies, including William Allen White's *A Puritan in Babylon: The Story of Calvin Coolidge* (New York, 1938) and Donald R. McCoy's *Calvin Coolidge: The Quiet President* (New York, 1967), both of which focus largely on his role as president. His earlier tenure as Massachusetts' governor was, however, relatively undistinguished, and had it not been for the Boston police strike of 1919 he probably would have disappeared into well-deserved historical obscurity. But the strike caused Coolidge to become the unwitting beneficiary of his own inactivity. Francis Russell, in *A City in Terror: 1919, The Boston Police Strike* (New York, 1975), recounts the governor's early efforts to ignore the crisis and his subsequent mishandling of events. Ironically, the public came away convinced that Coolidge had acted forcefully and promptly elected him to the vice-presidency.

There are several well-written comprehensive histories of Massachusetts politics in the first half of the twentieth century. Among the best is one that has already been mentioned, Richard Abrams' *Conservatism in a Progressive Era*. Abrams contends that in the latter part of the nineteenth century Massachusetts established a record of reform legislation that was among the most progressive in the entire nation. He argues that this was largely the work of middle- and upper-class native-born Republican elites, who shared a common vision and were willing to sacrifice selfish commercial interests. Among their opponents were labor unions, urban workers, and immigrant groups, all of whom either actively opposed or largely ignored the efforts of those they contemptuously labeled liberal "do-gooders."

In the twentieth century, however, the parties reversed themselves. Fearful of the newly emerging ethnic minorities and persuaded by the business community to abandon a relatively rigorous commitment to high standards of business regulation, the Massachusetts Republicans moved abruptly to the right, abandoning their earlier association with reform. Meanwhile, their Democratic counterparts traveled in the opposite direction and increasingly supported Progressive legislation because they realized it could satisfy the "bread-and-butter" needs of their constituents. Abrams concludes that the Progressive impulse that historians like George Mowry and Richard Hofstadter have ascribed to the middle and professional classes does not accurately characterize political change in Massachusetts, at least not in the early part of the twentieth century.

A different but equally valuable comprehensive study of statewide politics during the first half of the twentieth century is J. Joseph Huthmacher's *Massachusetts People and Politics, 1919-1933* (Cambridge, 1959). He analyzes not only political and economic events but also the state's growing ethnic and cultural tensions. He divides the population into three major groups: the "old stock" made of native Yankees plus easily absorbable Northern Europeans, the Irish, and "the newer races," mostly made up of Jews, Italians, and blacks. He argues that the dominant Republican party alienated both the Irish and the "newer races" over such issues as Prohibition, immigrant restriction, and one hundred percent Americanism. Eventually, the alienated joined with the largely Irish Catholic Democratic party and displaced the older Republican establishment, a transformation that was symbolically consummated when Massachusetts voted for Al Smith in 1928.

Edgar Litt's *The Political Cultures of Massachusetts* (Cambridge, 1965) deals with some of the same issues but from the perspective of a political scientist rather than that of an historian. Litt divides the state into four dominant cultures: the Patricians, whose traditions were those of the old native elite and whose interests were similar to although not identical with those of State Street; the Yeomen, who were small-town old-stock natives forming the bedrock of the state's Republican party; the Workers, who were laborers and ethnics sharing a suspicion of governmental change and a deep allegiance to family and neighborhood; and the Managers, who were an emerging group convinced of the benefits of change and free of any deep party loyalties. Litt argues that the Yeoman and the Worker were the most adversely impacted by the mid–twentieth-century growth of the federal government's economic influence and the relative decline of manufacturing in Massachusetts. Sharing a common interest in the past, they have resisted change, oftentimes by using state institutions and the political process as a buffer. But power within the commonwealth, according to Litt, has increasingly shifted to the Managers, and in time the character of state politics should reflect this development. A less valuable description of the period is chronicled in *Four Decades of Massachusetts Politics, 1890–1935* by Michael E. Hennessy (Norwood, Mass., 1935). It is a straightforward account of Massachusetts politics, short on critical analysis but long on biographies of prominent individuals. Although it does contain some valuable tidbits of information, it lacks both footnotes and a bibliography and is not particularly useful.

Charles H. Trout's *Boston, The Great Depression, and the New Deal* is a much more detailed and well-researched study. It focuses on the social, political, and economic influence of the New Deal and concludes that it did not have as profound an effect on the city as most scholars have argued. Municipal leaders who implemented the federal reforms did so in a way that preserved predepression ways of doing things. "Bostonians," he declares, "were willing to clap for new arrangements with one hand only." Why? Part of the answer goes beyond Boston, and Trout argues that the New Deal, although it appeared to be a sharp break with the past, actually lent itself to local modifications. Part of the answer also rests with the tendency of local groups to resist Roosevelt's policies. Both the Boston business community and the powerful Catholic church were "so afraid of a left wing they [wouldn't] go near one, even [if it] was on a chicken." Many of Boston's elite linked the despised Curley and the New Deal and dismissed them as equally wasteful. According to a popular contemporary rhyme:

> The King is in the White House,
> Handing out the money.
> The Queen is on the front page,
> Looking very funny.
> The Knave is up in Boston,
> Picking up the plums,
> While the country alphabetically
> Is feeding all the bums.

Even traditionally supportive groups such as social workers, labor union leaders, and hard-core Democrats were critical of the New Deal and twisted it to serve their narrow ends. Frustrated by a lack of cooperation, federal officials often denied local politicians access to federal funds, and in their place recruited Yankee Progressives as program managers.

Thus although Boston and Massachusetts were clearly affected by the New Deal, much of the community's underlying political character remained intact. Ethnic rather than ideological divisions continued to define the public debate, and politics was reduced to questions of personality and local leadership. State and city government remained relatively conservative, and there was an absence of real reform. For example, efforts to metropolitanize city services failed, the state legislature continued to dominate city government, and welfare programs continued to be administered in a parsimonious manner more characteristic of a private charity than public relief. In the end, although Massachusetts was never quite the same after the Great Depression and the New Deal, it was, nonetheless, not much different.

An article by Robert K. Massey, Jr., entitled "The Democratic Laggard: Massachusetts in 1932" (*New England Quarterly*, 44 [December 1971]: 553-74) recounts the struggle within the state's Democratic party over whom to support for president at the 1932 National Convention. Virtually everyone within the party leadership with the notable exception of James Michael Curley supported Governor Al Smith. Curley, the perennial maverick, cast his lot with FDR, not because of any deep philosophical commitment, but because he was convinced that the country would not elect a Catholic and because he believed that only Roosevelt could defeat Hoover. For Curley, that was reason enough; he warned an audience in Worcester that if "we have another era of Hoover, Ghandi would be the best-dressed man in America."

Two themes emerge from Massey's article that are consistent with Trout's book. One is the extent to which personalities and local issues dominated the political debate. The fight between Curley on one side and Walsh and Ely on the other was more a product of personal animosities than a reflection of the philosophical differences between Smith and Roosevelt. The second is the extent to which the Democratic leadership within the state supported Smith because he was an Irish Catholic and sought to promote his candidacy as a statement of religious and ethnic pride.

Post-New Deal Massachusetts politics has not yet attracted much historical attention. The Kennedys, of course, have been the object of a vast amount of literature, but their historiography is beyond the scope of this paper and is predominantly of national significance. There have been several biographies of prominent individuals such as Henry Cabot Lodge, Jr., Thomas "Tip" O'Neill, and Leverett Saltonstall, but they suffer somewhat from a contemporary perspective. There are no comprehensive political histories, and there is a surprising lack of dissertations on the period.

The historians' reluctance to write about recent political history in Massachusetts has not been shared by the political scientists. There are numerous articles and several books that focus on the emerging trends and the changing mechanics of New England politics. These include Earl Latham's *Massachusetts Politics* (New York, 1975) and Duane Lockhard's *New England State Politics* (Princeton, 1959). Lockhard traces the extent to which Massachusetts politics was a function of the struggle between "old New England stock" and the Irish-led ethnic groups. Although he suspects that ethnic and racial considerations are beginning to decline, he does allow that such loyalties in politics are an elusive matter and should not be dismissed casually.

However, Massachusetts and its politics are changing. The Republican party lost control of the House of Representatives in the 1930s and 1940s and of the Senate in 1958. According to Charles E. Coates in "The Making of a Minority: A Study of the Decline of the Republican Party in the Massachusetts State Legislature, 1946-1966" (Senior Honors thesis, Harvard University, 1970), Massachusetts has evolved into a one-party state. The shift was caused by a variety of factors, including the Democratic sweep in 1948, the subsequent power of incumbency, and the enormous appeal and political influence of the Kennedys, shown particularly by John F. Kennedy's re-election to the Senate in 1958. John Kenneth White, in *The Fractured Electorate: Political Parties and Social Change in Southern New England* (Hanover, N.H., 1983), offers a more perceptive analysis of the changes that have swept through the state in the years since World War II. According to White, the state has entered a "post-industrial" phase with an unprecedented commitment to intellectual rather than manual activities. New social classes have emerged, producing new political and class alignments. Education has replaced culture and religion as the most important factor in people's political preference. The state's Democratic party, which possesses a three-to-one advantage in registration, is divided between its "blue-collar" past and its "professional" future and is having difficulty adjusting to the changes. Meanwhile, the Republican party has "unraveled," becoming more doctrinaire and irrelevant to the issues that face the state.

As one would expect, many of the forces that shaped Massachusetts' political history in the twentieth century have also influenced its social, economic, and intellectual development. The dominant social issue of the first half of the century was the growing number and character of the newly arrived and the response of the native community. Although it deals with the nineteenth century and is both dated and judgmental, Oscar Handlin's *Boston Immigrants, 1790–1880: A Study in Acculturation* (Cambridge, rev. ed., 1959) is a good place to begin because it offers a comprehensive background for what will follow. The bulk of the social literature focuses on the Irish because they were the first, the largest, and the most influential group. William V. Shannon's *The American Irish: A Political and Social Portrait* (New York, 1966) has an unfortunately brief but well-written chapter entitled "The Boston Irish" that analyzes the difficulties faced by the newcomers. He points out that unlike other immigrants, they came to a city and to a state that had a well-entrenched and homogeneous native community that was jealously protective of its history and its institutions. For most of the nineteenth century, the Irish were the only alien group present. And despite the twentieth-century arrival of other nationalities, social relations remained essentially "two-dimensional," a division that was further burdened by a sluggish local economy. Ultimately, both sides withdrew into their respective communities, setting the stage for the emergence of what Shannon labeled the "master demagogue," James Michael Curley.

But what appeared to Shannon to be a two-dimensional confrontation was actually a more complex social experience. Dennis P. Ryan in *Beyond the Ballot Box: A Social History of the Boston Irish, 1845–1917* (Rutherford, N.J., 1983), writes that the Boston Irish were "not of one mind." Frequently quarrelling among themselves, they rejected ideological positions and coped with community problems on an individual basis. An examination of the development of Boston social agencies reveals, for example, an elaborate commitment by the Irish to help their needy counterparts. Largely under the auspices of the Catholic church, they organized a network of social institutions, including orphanages, homes for unwed mothers, temperance societies, and the like. Yet despite papal prodding they avoided the obvious, failing to build parochial schools because of their apparent satisfaction with the public system. Ryan concludes by devoting some attention to the relative inability of the Irish to advance socially and economically and argues unpersuasively that the wound was largely self-inflicted.

A much more detailed and insightful analysis of social mobility is contained in a major quantitative study by Stephan Thernstrom, *The Other Bostonians: Poverty and Progress in the American Metropolis, 1880-1970* (Cambridge, 1973). Drawing heavily on city directories, marriage listings, and tax files, the author convincingly demonstrates that because of the continual flow in and out of "human raw material," the city's lower socioeconomic community and its corresponding social structure were in a constant state of flux. The main focus of the book is, however, the relative social mobility of the city's major religious and ethnic groups: native versus immigrant, Catholic versus Jew versus Protestant, and white versus black. In the first chapter, not surprisingly, native Yankees, with advantages in culture, language, and timing, moved more rapidly than newcomers up the occupational ladder. Within ethnic groups the Irish and Italians made the slowest gains, the former in menial white-collar jobs and the latter in small businesses. Russian and British Jews did remarkably well, and French-Canadians and Swedes tended to be concentrated in the skilled trades. Among religious groups Jews achieved the most dramatic gains, followed by Protestants and finally Catholics. Of all the groups, blacks were the most socially and economically immobile and appear to have suffered from additional burdens. Why did different groups have different rates and levels of achievement? It is a difficult question with a complicated set of answers. In the case of the different religious groups, Thernstrom considers various possibilities such as discrimination, background handicaps, different fertility rates, "institutional completeness," and residential segregation and speculates that the answer may be rooted more in cultural values than anything else.

Donald B. Cole, *Immigrant City: Lawrence, Massachusetts, 1845-1921* (Chapel Hill, 1963), also seeks to illuminate the social and economic conditions of immigrants but does so by focusing on one community. Cole traces the establishment of the city of Lawrence and the successive waves of various immigrant groups, beginning with the Irish, followed by the French-Canadians, the Germans, and the Italians. Each began living and working in wretched conditions but eventually established churches, clubs, and newspapers to ameliorate its situation. Eventually, the newcomers moved on to politics, to be replaced at the bottom of the ladder by a different group, whereupon the whole process began anew. Although there is much truth to Cole's contention that Lawrence and its successive populations were part of an American success story, it is a complex tale that the author tells too simply.

Although they have not attracted as much attention as the Irish, the Jews have played a prominent role in the twentieth-century history of Massachusetts. Unfortunately, there is no well-written comprehensive history of their contribution, and one is reduced to piecing together their story from a variety of sources. Arthur Mann's *Growth and Achievement: Temple Israel, 1854-1954* (Boston, 1954) ably relates the history of Boston's oldest reform congregation. Barbara Miller Solomon's *Pioneers in Service* (Boston, 1956) provides a similar service for the Association of Jewish Philanthropies. And Francis Russell's "The Coming of the Jews" (*Antioch Review*, 50 [Spring 1955]: 19-38) is a personal but worthwhile discussion of Dorchester's reaction to the sudden influx of Jews after the Chelsea fire of 1908.

The Italian community also suffers from a lack of adequate attention. William M. DeMarco's *Ethnics and Enclaves: Boston's Italian North End* (Ann Arbor, 1981) argues that the city's major Italian community was never a unified whole but was rather a collection of Italian subcultures. The author contends that the traditions of "la famiglia" (the family) and "la via vecchia" (the village), which were growing in importance in southern Italy, were transferred substantially intact to Boston. But DeMarco's book owes many of its historical insights to an earlier work by Herbert Gans, *The Urban Villagers: Group and Class in the Life of Italian-Americans* (New York, 1962), a classic study of a largely Italian neighborhood and the extent to which its inhabitants successfully reproduced Old World values and created a viable community. It was also a belated plea to halt the destructive urban renewal programs of the 1950s, arguing that despite external appearances, working-class neighborhoods like Boston's West End were very good places to live. Marc Fried's *The World of the Urban Working Class* (Cambridge, 1973) is an elaboration of a similar theme, arguing that the West End was "both a harbor and a haven for the working class of foreign birth." Edwin Fenton's "Immigrants and Unions, A Case Study: Italians and American Labor, 1870-1920" (Ph.D. diss., Harvard University, 1957) describes the widely used padrone system and Italian workers' relationship with the state's Irish labor leaders.

Because it touched on both political and social issues, the Sacco-Vanzetti case of 1920-1927 has produced an enormous amount of worthwhile historical literature. Francis Russell's *Tragedy in Dedham: The Story of the Sacco-Vanzetti Case* (New York, 1962) is among the best, with the author apparently concluding that Sacco was guilty and Vanzetti was not. David Felix's *Protest: Sacco-Vanzetti and the Intellectuals* (Bloomington, Ind., 1965) is a failed effort to explain the intellectual community's fascination with the case, a task more successfully undertaken by the contemporary jurist Felix Frankfurter in his *The Case of Sacco-Vanzetti* (Boston, 1927).

Like other ethnic groups, Massachusetts blacks have suffered at the expense of the Irish from a lack of historical attention. What little literature there is deals almost exclusively with the nineteenth century, leaving the twentieth century to either our collective memory or to our imagination. A brief but valuable article by William B. Hixon, Jr., "Moorfield Storey and the Struggle for Equality" (*Journal of American History*, 55 [December 1968]: 533-34), discusses his leadership of the NAACP during the early part of the twentieth century. Stephen

R. Fox's *The Guardian of Boston: William Monroe Trotter* (New York, 1970) is an individual study that contains some indirect insights into the black community. Fox argues that Trotter anticipated the civil rights movement of the 1950s through his attacks on the accommodating policies of Booker T. Washington. But Fox labels Trotter a member of an "elitist militancy" who never related well to Boston's impoverished black community.

The response of the native community to the influx of immigrants in the nineteenth and early twentieth centuries is the focus of Barbara Miller Solomon's *Ancestors and Immigrants: A Changing New England Tradition* (Cambridge, 1956). In this classic study Solomon analyzes the "Old Stock's" eroding optimism and growing animosity toward the newcomers. By the turn of the century, with some notable exceptions, the native community withdrew from public involvement, indulged in racial discrimination, and eventually sought to legally restrict immigration through the establishment of the Immigration Restriction League.

Studies of the Catholic church of Massachusetts are also valuable for understanding the state's social history during the twentieth century. The third volume of the *History of the Archdiocese of Boston* (Boston, 1945) by Robert Lord et al. is the most comprehensive, but because it covers much of Cardinal O'Connell's administration, under whose auspices the history was commissioned, it is not as well done as the two earlier volumes. The best introduction to Catholic thought in the early part of the twentieth century is Donna Merwick's *Boston Priests, 1848-1910: A Study of Social and Intellectual Change* (Cambridge, 1973). Merwick argues that O'Connell's appointment as archbishop in 1906 was a troubling turning point, replacing local diversity and local autonomy with a highly centralized and Romanized administration. James Gaffney, "The Changing of the Guard" (*Catholic Historical Review*, 59 [July 1973]: 225-44) comes to a similar conclusion while detailing the local clergy's unsuccessful efforts to block O'Connell's appointment. Both are extremely well done but have a tendency to overstate the degree and misconstrue the source of diversity that preceded O'Connell's arrival. Robert O'Leary's "Cardinal William O'Connell: A Social and Intellectual Biography" (Ph.D. diss., Tufts University, 1980) argues that the profoundly conservative cardinal sought to establish an elite Catholic-Protestant alliance based on a common commitment to conservative political and social principles. John Deedy's "William Henry O'Connell: The Prince of Yesterday's Prototypes" (*The Critic*, 35 [1977]: 54-61) is also a very useful study.

There is a shelf full of books on Cardinal Richard Cushing, but all of them are contemporary accounts that tend to be excessively laudatory. Among the best are *Cardinal Cushing of Boston* (New York, 1970) by J. H. Cutler and *Cushing of Boston: A Candid Portrait* (Boston, 1965) by Joseph Dever. Donald F. Crosby's "Boston Catholics and the Spanish Civil War, 1936-1939" (*New England Quarterly*, 44 [March 1971]: 82-100) analyzes the influence of conservative Catholic values on American foreign policy.

Other Massachusetts institutions have been the subject of individual studies, but probably no group deserves more attention than the state's colleges and universities. There are scores of institutional studies that vary enormously in quality, but most, unfortunately, are eulogies that would have little interest to anyone but their faithful alumni. Samuel Eliot Morison's *Three Centuries of Harvard, 1636-1936* (Cambridge, 1936) is among the most famous, and Harold Whiting Cary's *The University of Massachusetts: A History of One Hundred Years* (Amherst, 1962) is a good history of a public institution. But individual biographies of educational leaders are oftentimes more valuable vehicles for understanding the twentieth-century history of higher education in Massachusetts. As president of Harvard University from 1869 to 1909, Charles W. Eliot was probably the most influential educator in the early twentieth century and is ably treated by Hugh Hawkins in *Between Harvard and America: The Educational Leadership of Charles W. Eliot* (New York, 1972). The book emphasizes Eliot's educational leadership, his widely imitated elective system, and his nurturing of a national university during difficult times. But none of these studies focuses on the growing social, intellectual, and economic impact of higher education on the state of Massachusetts.

There is a vast array of books, articles, and dissertations of uneven quality on both public and private secondary and elementary schools. Most are narrow in focus, but of particular note is Marvin Lazerson's *Origins of the Urban School: Public Education in Massachusetts, 1870-1915* (Cambridge, 1971), which traces the difficult transition from antebellum educational reform to the early twentieth-century progressive experience. Lazerson argues that the late nineteenth-century schools sought to promote change while their twentieth-century counterparts sought to impose middle-class values on the poor and the newly arrived, a neat dichotomy that glosses over the socialization efforts of nearly all public schools. But the state's twentieth-century educational leaders were clearly disturbed by the changes associated with industrialization, urbanization, and immigration, and hoped that an extended public school system would preserve the stability and homogeneity that they believed had prevailed in nineteenth-century Massachusetts.

There is no satisfactory economic history of twentieth-century Massachusetts, but there are two excellent, although dated, regional studies. *The Economics of New England: Case Study of an Older Area* (Cambridge, 1952), by Seymour E. Harris, traces the relative decline of manufacturing in the area during the mid-twentieth century but rejects such widely held explanations as high taxes or powerful labor unions. He does believe that the relative absence of natural resources was a major factor but also assigns blame to the federal government, arguing that throughout the 1930s and 1940s federal spending in the region never equaled federal revenues. With great foresight, he calls for better management, greater efforts to develop overseas markets, and an improved relationship with the federal government. *The Dynamics of Growth in New England's Economy, 1870-1964* (Middletown, Conn., 1967), by Robert W. Eisenmenger, explores similar issues in a somewhat more detailed fashion, enumerating the area's classic shortcomings, including raw-material costs, transportation costs, and its inadequate soil resources. According to the author, New England's development as an important commercial and manufacturing center is an historical accident, and were it not for the Puritans, Massachusetts would likely have become an economic backwater. But at the time of its publication in 1967, the author identified some positive trends, such as proximity to numerous metropolitan areas and relatively low wage rates, and concluded that New England's economic future holds promise.

Although not yet complete, the twentieth century has brought both continuity and change to Massachusetts. In 1900 local and state politics were largely non-ideological struggles between competing personalities and ethnic groups. The Republican party dominated most levels of government and increasingly resisted the political ambitions of the newly arrived. The cohesiveness of the state appeared threatened by a tidal wave of immigrants and by the added burden of what appeared to be an intractable confrontation between the Yankees and the Irish. At that time many believed that these divisions could not be overcome and were convinced that the state's historic pre-eminence was threatened. Massachusetts continued to be economically vital, but there were nagging doubts about its ability to compete and its early signs of relative economic decline.

By the 1980s some of these earlier problems had been resolved, but new concerns have quickly filled the void. For example, many of the earlier ethnic and cultural differences have faded, but there is little evidence that contemporary state politics has abandoned its earlier fascination with personalities. The Republican party's political monopoly has come to an end, but instead of a healthy two-party system, we unfortunately have substituted its Democratic equivalent. The large number of immigrants who appeared to threaten the cohesive character of the state have been successfully assimilated and ultimately have established a more pluralistic and more viable social environment. The vast social and economic gap between the Irish and the Yankees has largely disappeared and is increasingly the property of historians and folklore. But the process of social and economic assimilation is far from complete. The present plight of Massachusetts' black community, the Boston "School Bus Crisis," and the recent riots among the Puerto Ricans in Lawrence raise questions about the continuing ability of the state to successfully integrate different ethnic and racial groups. Finally, Massachusetts made a necessary but painful economic transition, abandoning a declining manufacturing base and moving toward a more promising technological and service sector. But the state's long-term prosperity is still in doubt. There are questions about its vulnerability to foreign competition, its ability to sustain viable levels of economic growth, and its willingness to preserve a healthy business environment.

The history of Massachusetts since World War II is largely unwritten. Most of the major figures associated with government, business, and various other institutions, who rose to power in the postwar period and who are now fading from the scene, have yet to attract scholarly analysis. There is cornucopia of topics that cry out for examination. For example, the state's recent economic history, involving such issues as the increasing significance of the federal government, the burgeoning electronics industry, the powerful impact of higher education, and the shift away from manufacturing to a service-based economy have yet to be placed in the proper historical perspective. The history of the state legislature, particularly its leadership and its almost feudal-like relationship with state agencies, also needs to be explored. But most of all there is a need for a comprehensive study that weaves together the massive detail of the recent past while successfully delineating its major trends. It will be a difficult but rewarding task.

7

URBAN MASSACHUSETTS

JACK TAGER

ALL TOO OFTEN reference to Massachusetts history is couched solely in terms of its justifiably rich colonial and Revolutionary past. More recently the early nineteenth century has become the object of considerable attention by a new breed of social historians whose emphasis is on the daily lives of the Bay State's ordinary citizens rather than on the movers and shakers of the political scene. But the post-Civil War period and the twentieth century have been virtually ignored by most scholars of Massachusetts history. Particularly vulnerable to this historical oversight is the commonwealth's urban revolution. What exactly is meant by the term "urban Massachusetts," and when did urbanization begin?

Did urbanization originate with the first settlement in 1630, a "city in the wilderness"? In a controversial article, "The Emergence of Urban Society in Rural Massachusetts, 1760-1820" (*Journal of American History*, 61 [June 1974]: 29-51), Richard D. Brown argued that the American Revolution unleashed forces that reduplicated Boston's urban characteristics throughout the state, making them a "generalized feature of Massachusetts society." Perhaps urban Massachusetts becomes identifiable when the commonwealth industrialized and people moved to the cities during the mid-nineteenth century. Should attention then be focused on the history of Boston from its incorporation in 1822, or instead from its development as a metropolis around the end of the century? Since the U.S. census of 1900 classified 76 percent of the state's inhabitants as urbanites, does that signify that all subsequent Massachusetts history should be regarded as urban history ipso facto?

The Massachusetts citizen not residing in Boston or its metropolitan area probably finds it even more difficult to grasp the elusive concept of urban Massachusetts. Massachusetts' westerners, those on the "wrong side" of Interstate 495, have long complained of being ignored by the political pundits in the State House who seem to limit their beneficence to the eastern portion of the state. Western "provincials" often confront sentiments such as Jane Holtz Kay's, "Boston remains the state's point of reference," she wrote in her new introduction to *The WPA Guide to Massachusetts* (New York, 1983, originally published in Boston, 1937). "The universe of Massachusetts radiates from that golden dome, sometimes to the chagrin of its westerners, who remind you that the state doesn't tilt into the sea." John Updike's cryptic but telling description of Jane, one of *The Witches of Eastwick* (New York, 1984, p. 29), accentuates the symbolic significance of the "golden dome." "She came from Boston originally and that gave her something there was no unknowing." Eventually, the western observer must agree that the eastern part of Massachusetts is the most urbanized, the most populous, with the most jobs and economic riches, and with the most serious urban problems. It is the heartland of urban Massachusetts.

If one looks at the commonwealth as a composite of metropolitan areas, a clearer picture emerges. The less densely populated west contains the northern portion of the Springfield-Hartford metropolis, an area that extends over two states, from communities as far north as Northampton and Amherst to the multitude of suburbs surrounding Hartford, all tied to the Interstate 91 pathway. In central Massachusetts, Worcester lacks both the populous suburbs and the large satellite towns or cities to rank as a true metropolis. The major urban region is to the east. It stretches over three states: ten counties in Massachusetts, all five of Rhode Island, and five counties of New Hampshire. A series of key highways radiates out of Boston, connecting cities like Nashua, New Hampshire, and Providence, Rhode Island, as well as Brockton, Fall River, Haverhill, Lawrence, Lowell, New Bedford, and Taunton, Massachusetts. Interstate 495, seeking out I-95 in the northeast and I-195 in the south, is the outer circumference enveloping the "golden ring" of the commuting region, Route 128.

This urban system, suggested Sam Bass Warner, Jr., is a "gathering of interacting people and institutions." In his splendid attempt to re-educate us, Warner's *The Way We Really Live: Social Change in Metropolitan Boston since 1920* (Boston, 1977, pp. 2 and 9), characterized this urban territory as a "human settlement." He saw it as a "place where human beings cluster together in daily activities, talking to each other, buying and selling, making things, taking care of each other, raising children, and playing." To understand how Massachusetts arrived at this particular urban condition means uncovering the origins of the urbanization process. In that vein, Boston will be considered as the colonizing agent of the present-day urban empire, similar to the crucial role played by imperial England in the eventual birth of the Republic.

The first step in unraveling the conundrum of urbanized Massachusetts is to determine when the Bay State changed from a society of small property owners, mostly self-employed farmers, to a place of people working for others, now clustered together in congested cities. For agricultural shifts, the historian must see the classic works of Percy W. Bidwell, "The Agricultural Revolution in New

England" (*American Historical Review*, 26 [1921]: 684-702) and "Population Growth in Southern New England, 1810-1860" (*Quarterly Publications of the American Statistical Association*, no. 120 [December 1917]: 817-28), and Percy W. Bidwell and John I. Falconer, *History of Agriculture in the Northern United States, 1620-1860* (Washington, D.C., 1925). In addition, one should consult Clarence H. Danhof, *Change in Agriculture: The Northern United States, 1820-1870* (Cambridge, 1969). The industrial revolution and its results, such as the mechanization of agriculture, the rise of the factory system, and the emergence of the railroad, altered life for all Americans. Henry Adams lamented in his autobiography: "The generation between 1865 and 1895 was already mortgaged to the railways, and no one knew it better than the generation itself."[1] The oft-quoted statement that "the industrial revolution of Massachusetts is the economic history of the United States in miniature" illuminates the consequential connection between industrialization and urbanization.[2] According to Carl Siracusa's trenchant analysis of industrialization, *A Mechanical People: Perceptions of the Industrial Order in Massachusetts, 1815-1880* (Middletown, Conn., 1979, p. 22), Massachusetts by 1880 "was the most thoroughly industrialized state" in the Union and the first to become urbanized.

Massachusetts was to herald the birth of the new industrial metropolis, a condition described by planner Hans Blumenfeld as "an extremely rare event in the history of mankind." A new form of human settlement came into being—the "switch," wrote demographer Kingsley Davis, "from a spread-out pattern of human settlement to one of concentration in urban centers."[3] Francis X. Blouin, Jr., in his study, *The Boston Region, 1810-1850: A Study of Urbanization* (Ann Arbor, 1980, p. 2) wrote: "When the population of a region urbanizes, one assumes that there is a greater concentration of population at specific points in the geography and that the population is increasingly engaged in non-agricultural pursuits." Of interest are two Ph.D. dissertations that cast light on economic change in the state, Christopher F. Clark's "Household Market and Capital: The Process of Economic Change in the Connecticut Valley of Massachusetts, 1800-1860" (Harvard University, 1982) and Gary J. Kornblith's "From Artisans to Businessmen: Master Mechanics in New England, 1789-1850" (Princeton University, 1983).

It was during the early decades of the nineteenth century that capitalists known as the Boston "associates" established the economic "linkages" that generated the urbanization process for the state. Blouin's *The Boston Region, 1810-1850* examined the spread of economic activity and the connecting links that involved 9 counties and 219 cities and towns. Boston acted as central bank, port, wholesale and distribution market, communications center, and subsidiary manufacturing location for an interdependent hinterland that was effectively colonized. Between 1810 and 1850 the economic base of the region shifted from commercial to industrial. Blouin argues convincingly that urbanization within the individual cities and towns was not an independent process. Rather, the pace and progress of urbanization in one area both depended on and affected the level of urbanization elsewhere in the region.[4] On the importance of an increasing capital-labor ratio in maintaining advances in productivity, one should consult Pamela J. Nickless, "A New Look at Productivity in the New England Cotton Industry, 1830-1860" (*Journal of Economic History*, 39 [December 1979]: 889-910).

There were many reasons for this symbiosis of industrialization and urbanization to begin first in Massachusetts. An already-depressed agricultural system further declined because of growing western competition. The state had in place a diversified economy in trades and crafts, one that in terms of skill and know-how was suitable for changeover to industrial production. Abundant capital available from a profitable maritime trade allowed the Boston "Brahmins" to develop manufacturing in cottons, woolens, shoes, paper, machinery, and other durables; in the course of establishing new industries they inspired the creation of colonized communities called factory towns.

In *The Coming of Industrial Order: Town and Factory Life in Rural Massachusetts, 1810-1860* (New York, 1983), Jonathan Prude provides a case study of industrialization in the rural towns of Dudley, Oxford, and Webster, focusing on the influence of Samuel Slater and the impact of the factory system upon the older farm-oriented lifestyle. Prude argues that the first factory workers were hostile to the workplace demands of the factory system, resisting innovation and imposing rural attitudes whenever possible upon reluctant managers. Another recent work on Samuel Slater is Barbara M. Tucker's *Samuel Slater and the Origins of the American Textile Industry, 1790-1860* (Ithaca, N.Y., 1985). Adding to our understanding of the transition from a rural to an urban society are a number of works, including Richard Holmes' *Communities in Transition: Bedford and Lincoln, Massachusetts, 1729-1850* (Ann Arbor, 1980); Gary J. Kornblith's "The Rise of the Mechanic Interest and the Campaign to Develop Manufacturing in Salem, 1815-1830" (*Essex Institute Historical Collections*, 121 [January 1985]: 44-65); Judith A. McGaw's "The Sources and Impact of Mechanization: The Berkshire County Paper Industry, 1801-1885" (Ph.D. diss., New York University, 1977); Mary A. Feldblum's "The Formation of the First Factory Labor Force in the New England Cotton Textile Industry, 1800-1848" (Ph.D. diss., New School for Social Research, 1977); and John W. Lozier's "Taunton and Mason: Cotton Machinery and Locomotive Manufacture in Taunton, Massachusetts, 1811-1861" (Ph.D. diss., Ohio State University, 1978).

Richard Brown's solid and lively general survey, *Massachusetts: A Bicentennial History* (New York, 1978), posited the notion that "large-scale urbanization" based on industrialization required "large-scale capital expenditures." In a splendid summary chapter titled "The Hive of Industry" (pp. 129-56) he described the pivotal role of Bostonians, such as Francis Cabot Lowell and Nathan Appleton, in organizing new technologies based upon infant automation techniques. To understand the ideas and motivations of the Boston capitalists, one should consult Oscar Handlin's "Laissez-Faire Thought in Massachusetts, 1790-1880" (*Journal of Economic History*, 3, supplement [December 1943]: 55-65) and Paul Goodman's "Ethics and Enterprise: The Values of a Boston Elite, 1800-1860" (*American Quarterly*, 18 [Fall 1966]: 437-51). Accounts of the industrialization process can be found in Paul F. McGouldrick, *New England Textiles in the Nineteenth Century: Profits and Investments* (Cambridge, 1968); Robert B. Zevin, *The Growth of Manufacturing in Early Nineteenth-Century New England* (New York, 1975); and Christopher Clark, "The Household Economy, Market Exchange, and the Rise of Capitalism in the Connecticut Valley, 1800-1860" (*Journal of Social History*, 13 [Winter 1979]: 169-89).

Several works analyze capitalist investment activities. These include three articles by Lance E. Davis: "Sources of Industrial Finance: The American Textile Industry, a Case Study" (*Explorations in Entrepreneurial History*, 9 [1957]: 189-203); "Stock Ownership in the Early New England Textile Industry" (*Business History Review*, 32 [1958]: 204-22); and "The New England Textile Mills and the Capital Market: A Study in Industrial Borrowing, 1840-1860" (*Journal of Economic History*, 20 [December 1960]: 1-30); also see Robert V. Spalding, "The Boston Mercantile Community and the Promotion of the Textile Industry in New England, 1813-1860" (Ph.D. diss., Yale University, 1963). For the role of the federal government in the process, see Carl Prince and Seth Taylor, "Daniel Webster, the Boston Associates, and the United States Government's Role in the Industrializing Process, 1815-1830" (*Journal of the Early Republic*, 2 [1982]: 283-94).

Still the best analysis of the economic, sociological, cultural, and psychological factors making up the Brahmin "caste" is that of Frederic Cople Jaher, *The Urban Establishment* (Urbana, Ill., 1982). For further insights into this group, one should consult Robert F. Dalzell, Jr., "The Rise of the Waltham-Lowell System and Some Thoughts on the Political Economy of Modernization in Ante-Bellum Massachusetts" (*Perspectives in American History*, 9 [1975]: 229-68), and E. Digby Baltzell, *Puritan Boston and Quaker Philadelphia* (New York, 1979). A truly groundbreaking investigation by Vera Shlakman, *Economic History of a Factory Town: A Study of Chicopee, Massachusetts* (Northampton, 1935), painstakingly reveals the creation of the Boston associates' complex system of interlocking directorates, enabling Boston's elites to monopolize the burgeoning textile industry. On the unique role of the family structure in these capitalist enterprises, one should see Peter Dobkin Hall, "Family Structure and Economic Organization: Massachusetts Merchants, 1700-1850" (*Family and Kin in Urban Communities, 1700-1930*, ed. Tamara K. Hareven [New York, 1977], pp. 38-61). A detailed analysis of a large investment house controlled by Brahmins is Gerald T. White, *A History of the Massachusetts Hospital Life Insurance Company* (Cambridge, 1955). For individual sketches and group portraits of the Boston associates, see Gregory Frances, *Nathan Appleton: Merchant and Entrepreneur, 1779-1861* (Charlottesville, Va., 1975); Kenneth Porter, *The Jacksons and the Lees: Two Generations of Massachusetts Merchants, 1765-1844* (Cambridge, 1937); and Carl Seaburg and Stanley Paterson, *Merchant Prince of Boston: Colonel T. H. Perkins, 1764-1854* (Cambridge, 1971). The political attitudes of these industrialists are examined in Thomas O'Connor, *Lords of the Loom: The Cotton Whigs and the Coming of the Civil War* (New York, 1968).

Searching for methods to cut labor costs and to avoid what Nathan Appleton called "the degradation" of English cotton workers, the Boston associates introduced labor-saving techniques based upon waterpower coupled with a novel labor force. Building their mills in rural areas, they brought women and children into the factory system and out of the home, itself a revolutionary social process. In her pathbreaking study of female factory operatives in the textile mills, *The Early New England Cotton Manufacture: A Study in Industrial Beginnings* (Boston, 1924, p. 59), Caroline Ware touched upon E. B. Bigelow of Boston, who in 1842 patented a series of devices "for making the carpetloom automatic, so that the costly labor of man might be dispensed with and the whole process of weaving be conducted by women and boys." As the cost of labor was the one factor that could be manipulated, the factory owners concocted a unique system of paternalism called the "Waltham system," which brought thousands of young Yankee farm girls to factory-owned boardinghouses in which behavior was rigidly controlled.

For many years a belief in the benefits of the "Waltham system" derived from that famous anthology of letters, stories, essays, and sketches written in the literary magazine of the mill women of Lowell, *The Lowell Offering*, ed. Benita Eisler (Philadelphia, 1977). A differing view by contemporary scholars stresses the onerous effects of this inflexible system of social control. The best single case study is Thomas Dublin's *Women at Work: The Transformation of Work and Community in Lowell, Massachusetts, 1826-1860* (New York, 1979). Dublin's book is a carefully researched, indispensable guide to the daily existence of factory women and the cohesive community of support that they created in order to survive the often insensitive and harsh demands of their employers. Dublin also edited a fascinating compilation of insightful letters of five factory women and their relatives, who wrote in minute detail of their daily lives (*Farm to Factory: Women's Letters, 1830-1860* [New York, 1981]). Other works that should be consulted include Mary H. Blewitt, "Work, Gender, and the Artisan Tradition in New England Shoemaking, 1780-1860" (*Journal of Social History*, 17 [Winter 1983]: 221-48); Philip S. Foner, ed., *The Factory Girls* (Urbana, Ill., 1977); Paul Faler, "Cultural Aspects of the Industrial Revolution: Lynn Shoemakers and Industrial Morality, 1826-1860" (*Labor History*, 15 [1974]: 367-94); and Carl Gersuny, "'A Devil in Petticoats' and Just Cause: Patterns of Punishment in Two New England Textile Factories" (*Business History Review*, 50 [1976]: 131-52).

With the expansion of the textile industry and increased competition, with the public sale of stock and the rise of absentee managerial control, the "excessive" cost of moral uplift spelled the doom of employer interest in the "Waltham system." Norman Ware's magnificent study, *The Industrial Worker, 1840-1860* (Boston, 1924), recorded the changeover from labor paternalism to a strict laissez-faire that left the worker to the capricious laws of supply and demand.

An excellent detailed study that contains pertinent material on conditions in Massachusetts is Edith Abbott's *Women in Industry* (New York, 1913). Two useful works are Keith Melder's "Women in the Shoe Industry: The Evidence from Lynn" (*Essex Institute Historical Collections*, 115 [October 1979]: 270-88) and Libby Zimmerman's "Women in the Economy: A Case Study of Lynn, Massachusetts, 1760-1974" (Ph.D. diss., Brandeis University, 1977). For a later look at women workers in 1884 Boston, see the rich analytic study by Carroll D. Wright, *The Working Girls of Boston* (Boston, 1889). In Lowell it did not take long befoie the female workers began to express outrage at the changing factory conditions. For more on this important development, see Thomas Dublin, "Women, Work, and Protest in Early Lowell Mills: 'The Oppressing Hand of Avarice Would Enslave Us'" (*Labor History*, 16 [1975]: 99-116), and Laurie Nisonoff, "Bread and Roses: The Proletarianization of Women Workers in New England Textile Mills, 1827-1848" (*Historical Journal of Massachusetts*, 9 [January 1981]: 3-14).

The erosion of employer paternalism after the 1840s allowed the mill owners to make use of a new and cheaper labor supply, now made available by a massive foreign migration to the United States. Initially, the first of these newcomers, the Irish, were denigrated to perform as day laborers, the men as "hewers of wood and drawers of water" and the women as "scrubbers" and "wastepickers." But the rapid expansion of markets and the steady decline of Yankee women in the labor pool opened the mills to successive generations of immigrants who were to make up the teeming populations of the mushrooming factory towns. Several of Massachusetts' nineteenth-century factory towns have had their share of able chroniclers, who described in detailed fashion the human story that unfolded there.

In a study of mobility in Waltham (*Workingmen of Waltham: Mobility in American Urban Industrial Development, 1850-1890* [Baltimore, 1974]), Howard M. Gitelman provides an impressive description of the watch and textile industries and the crucial role played by the city's Irish. In addition to his book, Gitelman has published two important articles on the impact of the Irish on the industrial city ("The Waltham System and the Coming of the Irish," *Labor History*, 8 [1967]: 227-53, and "No Irish Need Apply: Patterns of and Responses to Ethnic Discrimination in the Labor Market," *Labor History*, 14 [1973]: 56-68). Another study of Waltham is Charles W. Moore's *Timing a Century: History of the Waltham Watch Company* (Cambridge, 1945).

For Lowell, Thomas Dublin's work is crucial, but in addition there are several studies that provide information on the city's origins and evolution. These include Margaret Parker's *Lowell: A Study of Industrial Development* (New York, 1940), which is useful on the city's origins and is filled with a reservoir of plentiful factual data. *Cotton Was King: A History of Lowell, Massachusetts*, ed. Arthur L. Eno, Jr. (Somersworth, N.H., 1976), is a "group" history of the city by prominent Lowellians. While sometimes weak on analysis, this book of essays is excellent on subjects such as the establishment of Lowell, the building of the canals, and the capital investments, with a particularly good chapter on women laborers. Other works that should be consulted are John D. Coolidge's *Mill and Mansion: A Study of Architecture and Society in Lowell, 1820-1850* (New York, 1942); Frances H. Early's "Mobility Potential and the Quality of Life in Working-Class Lowell: The French Canadians ca. 1870" (*Labour/Le Travailleur*, 2 [1977] : 214-28); Steven J. Dubnoff, "The Family and Absence from Work: Irish Workers in a Lowell Cotton Mill, 1860" (Ph.D. diss., Brandeis University, 1976); Steven D. Lubar, "Corporate and Urban Contexts of Textile Technology in Nineteenth-Century Lowell: A Study of the Social Nature of Technical Knowledge" (Ph.D. diss., University of Chicago, 1983); and A. Gibbs Mitchell, Jr., "Irish Family Patterns in Nineteenth-Century Ireland and Lowell" (Ph.D. diss., Boston University, 1976).

The one and only significant work on Lawrence is Donald B. Cole's peerless *Immigrant City: Lawrence, Massachusetts, 1845-1921* (Chapel Hill, 1963). Fall River, and particularly Lynn, have been recently studied by a new generation of class-conscious social historians trained in the mold of English historian E. P. Thompson. Paul Faler's *Mechanics and Manufacturers in the Early Industrial Revolution: Lynn, 1780-1860* (Albany, 1981), with its focus on the shoe industry, is a brilliant example of the "new left" labor history. The same holds true for John Cumbler's thorough examination of working-class consciousness in Fall River and Lynn (*Working-Class Community in Industrial America: Work, Leisure, and Struggle in Two Industrial Cities, 1880-1930* [Westport, Conn., 1979]) and for Allen Dawley's *Class and Community: The Industrial Revolution in Lynn* (Cambridge, 1976). In addition to these studies, other works of interest on Lynn include Martin Blatt's "From Bench Laborer to Manufacturer: The Rise of Jewish Owners in the Declining Shoe Industry in Lynn" (*Essex Institute Historical Collections*, 115 [October 1979] : 256-70); William H. Mulligan, Jr., "Mechanization and Work in the American Shoe Industry: Lynn, 1852-1883" (*Journal of Economic History*, 41 [March 1981] : 59-63); Mulligan's "The Family and Technological Change: Shoemakers of Lynn during the Transition from Hand to Machine Production, 1850-1880" (Ph.D. diss., Clark University, 1982); and Naomi L. Rosenblum, "The Housing of Lynn's Shoe Workers in 1915" (*Essex Institute Historical Collections*, 115 [October 1979] : 221-232). In addition to Cumbler's study of Fall River, one should see Theresa A. Murphy's "Labor, Religion, and Moral Reform in Fall River, 1800-1845" (Ph.D. diss., Yale University, 1982).

Roy Rosenzweig's *Eight Hours for What We Will: Workers and Leisure in an Industrial City, 1870-1920* (Cambridge, England, 1983) imaginatively diagrammed the outpouring of intense class conflict in urbanizing Worcester. Although powerless in the factory, the workers of Worcester successfully maintained their autonomy and control over their leisure hours in the face of upper-class efforts to socially control them. Other works on Worcester include Charles C. Buell, "The Workers of Worcester: Social Mobility and Ethnicity in a New

England City, 1850-1880" (Ph.D. diss., New York University, 1974), and
Vincent E. Powers, "Invisible Immigrants: The Pre-Famine Irish Community in
Worcester, from 1826 to 1860" (Ph.D. diss., Clark University, 1976).

Michael Frisch's *Town into City: Springfield and the Meaning of Community,
1840-1880* (Cambridge, 1972), a study of Springfield's early growth as a diversified commercial, industrial, and financial center, continues to stand alone, although Richard D. Brown's *Urbanization in Springfield 1790-1830* (Springfield,
1962) should also be consulted. Constance Green's factual yet sprightly narrative,
Holyoke, Massachusetts: A Case History of the Industrial Revolution in America
(New Haven, 1939), is the best available on that city, though the competition is
beginning to flourish in many fine recently written dissertations. These include
William F. Hartford's "Paper City: Class Development in Holyoke, Massachusetts,
1850-1920" (Ph.D. diss., University of Massachusetts, 1983) and Peter Haebler's
"Habitants in Holyoke: The Development of the French-Canadian Community
in a Massachusetts City, 1865-1910" (Ph.D. diss., University of New Hampshire,
1976). Haebler's "Liquor and Ethnicity: French Canadians in Politics, Holyoke,
1885-1910" (*Massachusetts in the Gilded Age: Selected Essays*, ed. Jack Tager
and John W. Ifkovic [Amherst, 1985], pp. 67-100) casts added light on political
history in nineteenth-century Holyoke.

Gilded Age New Bedford is the subject of a good dissertation and article by
Thomas A. McMullin ("The Immigrant Response to Industrialism in New Bedford, 1865-1900" [Tager and Ifkovic, eds., *Massachusetts in the Gilded Age*, pp.
101-21] and "Industrialism and Social Change in a Nineteenth-Century Port City:
New Bedford, 1865-1900" [Ph.D. diss., University of Wisconsin, 1976]). Henry
B. Hough's *Wamsutta of New Bedford* (New Bedford, 1946) should also be
noted. As previously mentioned, the classic model for any factory-city monograph is Vera Shlakman's influential history of Chicopee. Published in 1935,
Economic History of a Factory Town is not only a brilliant example of the use
and correlation of statistical data, but it provides persuasive conceptualizations
on the relationship of class theory to capitalistic endeavors. Other useful works
on aspects of the development of the industrial city in Massachusetts include
John S. Garner, *The Model Company Town* (Amherst, 1984); Agnes Hannay, "A
Chronicle of Industry on the Mill River" (*Smith College Studies in History*, 21
[1935]: 7-142); Mark Camposeo, "The History of the Canal System between
New Haven and Northampton, 1822-1847" (*Historical Journal of Western
Massachusetts*, 6 [Fall 1977]: 37-53); Ronald Savoie, "The Silk Industry in
Northampton" (*Historical Journal of Western Massachusetts*, 5 [Spring 1977]:
21-32); Elizabeth A. Baker, "Blackinton: A Case Study of Industrialization,
1856-1876" (*Historical Journal of Massachusetts*, 9 [January 1981]: 15-26);
and Robert P. Donnell, "Locational Response to Catastrophe: The Shoe and
Leather Industry of Salem after the Conflagration of June 25, 1914" (*Essex
Institute Historical Collections*, 113 [April 1977]: 105-16). Aside from the
many works of boosterism and countless antiquarian studies, several important

Massachusetts towns and cities, such as Brockton, Haverhill, Taunton, and Pittsfield, to name only a few, are without competent historical analyses of their nineteenth-century origins.

A convenient general approach to help illustrate the growth of Massachusetts cities is to look at how people moved about, either changing domicile or commuting daily as a response to industrial forces. Robert W. Eisenmenger's informative study, *The Dynamics of Growth in New England's Economy, 1870-1964* (Middletown, Conn., 1967), associates economic growth with population movement. Even when native-born residents left nineteenth-century Massachusetts in great numbers to seek opportunities in New York, Pennsylvania, and the West, their places were taken by immigration from overseas and by a substantial intraregional migration from northern New England. Eisenmenger wrote: "Thus, the region's labor force has responded to higher income opportunities available in its better located areas."[5] For analyses of the relation between population movement and the significance of economic location, see Edgar M. Hoover, *Location Theory and the Shoe and Leather Industries* (Cambridge, 1937); Robert G. Leblanc, *Location of Manufacturing in New England in the Nineteenth Century* (Hanover, N.H., 1969); John B. Sharpless, *City Growth in the United States, England, and Wales, 1820-1861: The Effects of Location, Size, and Economic Structure on Inter-Urban Variations in Demographic Growth* (New York, 1976); John D. Black, *The Rural Economy of New England: A Regional Study* (Cambridge, 1950); and Hal S. Barron, *Those Who Stayed Behind: Rural Society in Nineteenth-Century New England* (New York, 1984).

In a world beginning to urbanize, the uprooting of static rural populations was startling. In *The Plain People of Boston, 1830-1860* (New York, 1971), Peter R. Knights postulated that beginning in the 1840s, the infusion of Irish immigrants depressed the labor market and impelled nativeborns to leave the city in large numbers. Further studies of population turnover are Peter R. Knights, "Population Turnover, Persistence, and Residential Mobility in Boston, 1830-1860" and Leo Schnore and Knights, "Residence and Social Structure: Boston in the Antebellum Period," both in *Nineteenth Century Cities*, ed. Stephan Thernstrom and Richard Sennett (New Haven, 1969, pp. 258-74 and 247-57 respectively). Stephan Thernstrom's *The Other Bostonians: Poverty and Progress in the American Metropolis, 1880-1970* (Cambridge, 1973) ascertained that by the 1880s workers held many different jobs and traveled to many places for these jobs during their lifetimes. For more on social mobility, one should see Stephan Thernstrom, *Poverty and Progress: Social Mobility in a Nineteenth Century City* (Cambridge, 1964), as well as two articles by Thernstrom: "Immigrants and WASPs: Ethnic Differences in Occupational Mobility in Boston, 1890-1940" (Thernstrom and Sennett, *Nineteenth Century Cities*) and "Urbanization, Migration, and Social Mobility in Late Nineteenth Century America" (*American Urban History*, ed. Alexander Callow, 2nd ed. [New York, 1973, pp. 125-64 and 263-73 respectively). Also helpful is Steven L. Olsen, "Yankee City and the New Urban History" (*Journal of Urban History*, 6 [May 1980]: 321-38). Old, but still valuable for raw data are the works of Massachusetts Commissioner of Labor Statistics Carroll D. Wright, *An Analysis of the Population of the City of Boston* (Boston, 1885), and South End settlement-house worker Frederick A. Bushee, "The Growth of Population in Boston" (*American Statistical Association Publications*, 6 [June 1899] : 239-74).

A factory system embedded in city life inexorably affected both the structure of society and the daily folkways of the common people. Alex Keyssar, in an essay on "Social Change in Massachusetts in the Gilded Age" (Tager and Ifkovic, eds., *Massachusetts in the Gilded Age*, pp. 132-47), noted that "at some point in the Gilded Age the typical resident of the Commonwealth became a city dweller rather than an inhabitant of a small town. . . the gulf between city and country narrowed almost to the vanishing point."[6] The abrupt reshaping of society generated complex needs, as indicated by Charles W. Cheape in *Moving the Masses: Urban Public Transit in New York, Boston, and Philadelphia, 1880-1912* (Cambridge, 1980). Crowds, congestion, increased traffic, and a growing sense of anomie were not figments of the imagination but stark realities of a new urban lifestyle. Nowhere was the experience more marked than in Boston.

Boston, our imperial centerpiece, went through a massive physical rearrangement by 1900 that culminated in its emergence as a metropolis of over one million disparate souls. That masterpiece of social history, *Boston's Immigrants: 1790-1880*, rev. and enl. ed. (New York, 1972), by Oscar Handlin, artfully recounted the preindustrial stage of Boston's urbanization. Fleeing starvation and oppression, penniless Irish peasants arrived in the 1840s to a crowded city that had both a hostile Yankee population and an uninviting economic environment. However, the Irish provided a cheap and abundant supply of labor that eventually would catapult Boston into the industrial era. Handlin wrote: "It was the vital function of the Irish to thaw out the rigidity of the system. Their labor achieved the transition from the earlier commercial to the later industrial organization of the city."[7] Boston's new and diversified industrial base attracted people like a magnet; in response the city's capitalists frantically competed for open land to expand business operations and to erect profitable residential communities.

After the Civil War the annexations of towns, the completion of the fill-ins of the South End and the Back Bay, the development of electric trolleys and rapid transit systems, and technological breakthroughs in sanitary practice all allowed for greater land use in Boston. In his genteel "random observations" on the evolution of Boston, Walter Muir Whitehill's graceful architectural history *Boston: A Topographical History* (Cambridge, 1959 and 1968, 2nd enlarged ed.) charted the continuous quest for land development. Sam Bass Warner Jr.'s brilliant monograph, *Streetcar Suburbs: The Process of Growth in Boston, 1870-1900* (Cambridge, 1962), analyzes the laissez-faire creation of a system of class-oriented neighborhoods and suburbs. "Privatistic" drives permitted developers, financial institutions, individual investors, and thousands of homeowners to build 22,500 homes for 167,000 new residents by 1900. The uncontrolled expropriation of land for residential purposes began a tide of suburbanization that was to be a mixed blessing for the future of Boston.

Warner commented on the effects of the "segregation of metropolitan life": "In the face of the continually expanding size of the metropolis, by contrast to the continual waves of poor immigrants that flooded the central city and destroyed its old residential neighborhoods, the new suburbs offered ever new areas of homogeneous middle class settlement."[8] Suburbanization revealed the "openness" of Boston society, and that social mobility was a practical reality for one-half of Boston's families. If suburban life was the reward for economic achievement, a substantial number of people whose incomes did little more than provide subsistence were left to the congestion and deterioration of inner-city neighborhoods. Other works on the evolution of Boston's neighborhoods include Henry C. Binford, *The First Suburbs: Residential Communities on the Boston Periphery, 1815-1860* (Chicago, 1985); two articles by David Ward, "Industrial Revolution and the Emergence of Boston's Central Business District" (*Economic Geography*, 42 [April 1966]: 152-71) and "The Emergence of Central Immigrant Ghettoes in American Cities, 1840-1920" (*Annals of the Association of American Geographers*, 58 [June 1968]: 343-59); and Robert A. Woods and Albert J. Kennedy, *The Zone of Emergence: Middle and Upper Working Class Communities in Boston, 1905-1914* (Cambridge, 1962).

In the same vein, Stephan Thernstrom's *The Other Bostonians: Poverty and Progress in the American Metropolis, 1880-1970* (Cambridge, 1973), a searching quantitative examination of social mobility, pointed out that while there were "significant opportunities for advancement," there were also many limitations. "Those who started at a lower level had good chances of moving upward a notch or two but not moving to the highest level."[9] That unique central city phenomenon—the immigrant ghetto—became the symbolic counterpoint to the affluent suburbs, epitomizing Boston's and the state's two societies of haves and have-nots. Ronald Dale Karr's "The Evolution of an Elite Suburb: Community Structure and Control in Brookline, 1770-1900" (Ph.D. diss., Boston University, 1981) provides information on upper-class control.

The immigrant tide inundated the cities and towns of Massachusetts, taking up the space left by the middle classes who pursued the rural myth to suburbia. Each new immigrant wave created a surging demographic flow that transformed neighborhoods overnight, essentially rearranging the nature of community life. A turn-of-the-century Boston social scientist, Frederick A. Bushee, assiduously collected data on immigrant life in *Ethnic Factors in the Population of Boston* (New York, 1903), accounting for each group's peculiar demographic meanderings. His coworkers at Boston's South End settlement, Andover House, under the direction of social reformer Robert A. Woods, meticulously studied the immigrants' every move in order to discover which methods could best be used to assimilate and Americanize them. Of special interest are three studies by Robert Woods: *Americans in Process: A Settlement Study* (Boston, 1903); *The City Wilderness: A Settlement Study, South End, Boston* (Boston, 1898); and

The Neighborhood in Nation-Building: The Running Comment of Thirty Years at the South End House (Boston, 1923).

Since the pioneering efforts by Bushee and Woods, many studies have been produced about immigrant life in Massachusetts. The state's first major ghetto was Boston's Irish North End, surveyed in a fine general work by Paula J. Todisco (*Boston's First Neighborhood: The North End* [Boston, 1976]). In *Ethnics and Enclaves: Boston's Italian North End* (Ann Arbor, 1981), William DeMarco charted the area's changeover to Italian dominance by the turn of the century. Arnold Weidner examined the first Jewish community there in *The Early Jewish Community of Boston's North End* (Waltham, 1969). For the adventures of a young Jewish settlement-house worker in the North End, see Philip Davis, *And Crown Thy Good* (New York, 1952). William F. Whyte portrayed Italian social structure and conflict in his book, *Street Corner Society: Social Structure of an Italian Slum* (Chicago, 1943), and in an article, "Race Conflicts in the North End of Boston" (*New England Quarterly*, 12 [December 1939] : 623-42). Of particular value for scholars is Nathan Kantrowitz, "Racial and Ethnic Residential Segregation in Boston, 1830-1970" (*Annals of the American Academy of Political and Social Science*, 441 [January 1979] : 41-54).

For Boston's Irish there are significant references in the well-known general works of William Shannon (*The American Irish* [New York, 1963]) and Carl Wittke (*Irish in America* [Baton Rouge, 1956]). A more recent study of unusual interest about Irish women and their migration patterns is Hasia R. Diner's *Erin's Daughters in America: Irish Immigrant Women in the Nineteenth Century* (Baltimore, 1983). In addition to Oscar Handlin's *Boston's Immigrants*, there are Dennis P. Ryan's provocative *Beyond the Ballot Box: A Social History of the Boston Irish, 1845-1917* (Rutherford, N.J., 1983) and John Stack's competent study, *International Conflict in an American City: Boston's Irish, Italians, and Jews, 1935-1944* (Westport, Conn., 1979).

Also available are a wide variety of other works that focus on Irish drinking habits, family patterns, and successful examples of assimilation. Among the best of these are Perry Duis, *The Saloon: Public Drinking in Chicago and Boston, 1880-1920* (Urbana, Ill., 1983); Richard Stivers, *A Hair of the Dog: Irish Drinking and American Stereotypes* (University Park, Pa., 1982); Maurice F. Parmelee, "Inebriety in Boston" (Ph.D. diss., Columbia University, 1909); Albert G. Mitchell, "Irish Family Patterns in Nineteenth-Century Ireland and Lowell" (Ph.D. diss., Boston University, 1976); and Timothy J. Meagher, "'The Lord is Not Dead': Cultural and Social Change among the Irish in Worcester" (Ph.D. diss., Brown University, 1982). The most heralded success story is that of John Boyle O'Reilly, a first-generation immigrant who became a successful poet and editor of the Boston *Pilot*. His story is ably portrayed by Francis R. Walsh in "The Boston *Pilot*: A Newspaper for the Irish Immigrant, 1829-1908" (Ph.D. diss., Boston University, 1968) and in several articles, including "John Boyle O'Reilly, the Boston *Pilot*, and Irish-American Assimilation, 1870-1890" (Tager and Ifkovic, eds., *Massachusetts in the Gilded Age*, pp. 148-63). Other works on

O'Reilly are Francis G. McManamin, *The American Years of John Boyle O'Reilly, 1870-1890* (New York, 1976), and James J. Roche, *Life of John Boyle O'Reilly* (Boston, 1891), written by a disciple who took over the editorship of the *Pilot.*

Aside from the Irish, other immigrant groups have received little scholarly attention. Regrettably, there is no single extant analysis of the Italian or Jewish immigrant experience in Boston or the commonwealth. Aside from Isaac Fein's laudatory and too-general narrative account of Boston's Jews from settlement to the 1970s (*Boston—Where It All Began: An Historical Perspective of the Boston Jewish Community* [Boston, 1976]) and Arthur Mann's finely etched yet narrow tale of the clash of religion and culture in one congregation, *Growth and Achievement: Temple Israel, 1854-1954* (Cambridge, 1954), there remains only a variety of reminiscences. Noteworthy is Mary Antin's autobiography of her journey from Russia as a little girl to Boston and the salutary process of Americanization, *The Promised Land* (Boston, 1912), and *From Plotzk to Boston* (New York, 1899), a series of letters to Russian relatives translated from the Yiddish, published when she was eleven. For an account of a young boy growing up in the Jewish East Side of Worcester, see Samuel N. Behrman, *The Worcester Account* (New York, 1954). Two books that stress current issues of Jews escaping from deteriorating neighborhoods are Albert Gordon's *Jews in Suburbia* (Boston, 1959) and Yona Ginsberg's *Jews in a Changing Neighborhood: The Study of Mattapan* (New York, 1975). Also useful is Morris Axelrod et al., *A Community Survey for Long Range Planning: A Study of the Jewish Population of Greater Boston* (Boston, 1967). For a fascinating account of the early years of Springfield's Jewish community, see James A. Gelin, *Starting Over: The Formation of the Jewish Community of Springfield, 1840-1905* (Lanham, Md., 1984). When one turns from the Jews to the Italians, one finds far fewer studies. One Italian immigrant who told his story of arriving as a penniless sailor in 1902 to a harsh and unwelcoming Boston was Constantine Panunzio, *The Soul of an Immigrant* (New York, 1921). Bryan Thompson's "Settlement Ties as Determinants of Immigrant Settlement in Urban Areas: A Case Study of an Italian Neighborhood in Worcester, 1875-1922" (Ph.D. diss., Clark University, 1971) is a useful study.

Except for the very able articles of Peter Haebler on Holyoke and Thomas McMullin on New Bedford, which have been mentioned earlier in this chapter, there exists no published general study of the French-Canadians in Massachusetts. (See, however, Gerard Brault, *The French-Canadian Heritage in New England* [Hanover, N.H., 1986].) For an interesting description of "The Role of the Church in Assimilation, 1869-1887," see Haebler's "Holyoke's French-Canadian Community in Turmoil" (*Historical Journal of Western Massachusetts*, 7 [January 1979]: 5-21). There is one dissertation, however, Ronald A. Petrin's "Ethnicity and Political Pragmatism: The French Canadians in Massachusetts, 1885-1915" (Ph.D. diss., Clark University, 1983). There are useful studies by Frances H. Early, "French-Canadian Beginnings in an American Community: Lowell, 1868-1886" (Ph.D. diss., Concordia University, 1980), and "The French-Canadian Family Economy and Standard-of-Living in Lowell, 1870" (*Journal of Family History*, 7 [Summer 1982]: 180-99). Also useful is Iris S. Podea, "Quebec to 'Little

Canada': The Coming of the French Canadians to New England in the Nineteenth Century" (*Uncertain Americans: Readings in Ethnic History*, ed. Leonard Dinnerstein and Frederic C. Jaher [New York, 1977], pp. 173-80). Brigitte M. Lane, "Franco-American Folk Traditions and Popular Culture in a Former Milltown: Aspects of Ethnic Urban Folklore and the Dynamics of Folklore Change in Lowell" (Ph.D. diss., Harvard University, 1983), provides an interesting perspective to the subject. See also Ralph Vicero, "Immigration of French-Canadians to New England, 1840-1900: A Geographical Analysis" (Ph.D. diss., University of Wisconsin, 1968). Finally, there is a booklet on Springfield's French and French-Canadian community, published with other similar studies during the bicentennial in 1976 (*Springfield's Ethnic Heritage: The French and French Canadian Community* [Springfield, 1976]).

Jerry Williams' *And Yet They Come: Portuguese Immigration from the Azores to the United States* (New York, 1982) on Portuguese immigration to New Bedford, Fall River, and Providence, Rhode Island, stands alone. There are scattered works on other ethnic groups, including Federal Writers Project, *The Armenians in Massachusetts* (Boston, 1937); Federal Writers Project, *The Albanian Struggle in the Old World and New* (Boston, 1939); and George T. Eliopoulos, "Greek Immigrants in Springfield, 1884-1944" (*Historical Journal of Western Massachusetts*, 5 [Spring 1977]: 46-56). For a narrative of the first Chinese in North Adams, brought in as strikebreakers in 1870, see Brent Filson, "Calvin Sampson's Chinese Experiment" (*Yankee Magazine*, 49 [February 1985]: 93-97, 133-37).

New works are just emerging on immigrant fertility patterns, family life, culture building, and residential trends. Sociologists have demonstrated that in Holyoke, for instance, "the French Canadians of 1880 and the Irish of 1850 and 1880 clearly had higher fertility than their native-born counterparts in the region." Studies that are useful in this area include Jerry Wilcox, "Tenacious Families, Mighty Forces: Household Structure in Hampshire and Hampden Counties, Massachusetts, during the Period of Industrialization" (Ph.D. diss., University of Massachusetts, 1981) and Wilcox and Hilda H. Golden, "Prolific Immigrants and Dwindling Natives? Fertility Patterns in Western Massachusetts, 1850 and 1880" (*Journal of Family History*, 7 [Fall 1982]: 265-88). Also useful are Myfanwy Morgan and Hilda H. Golden, "Immigrant Families in an Industrial City: A Study of Households in Holyoke, 1880" (*Journal of Family History*, 4 [Spring 1979]: 59-68); Maris A. Vinovskis, *Fertility in Massachusetts from the Revolution to the Civil War* (Ann Arbor, 1981); and two articles by Tamara Hareven and Maris Vinovskis: "Marital Fertility, Ethnicity, and Occupation in Urban Families: An Analysis of South Boston and the South End in 1880" (*Journal of Social History*, 8 [Spring 1975]: 69-93) and "Patterns of Childbearing in Late Nineteenth-Century America: The Determinants of Marital Fertility in Five Massachusetts Towns in 1880" (*Family and Population in Nineteenth-Century America*, ed. Tamara Hareven and Maris Vinovskis [Princeton, 1978], pp. 85-125).

In addition to these sociological and demographic studies, some beginnings are apparent in exploring the growth of Boston's Chinatown and the newly significant Hispanic communities. The useful studies in this area include Rhoads Murphey, "Boston's Chinatown" (*Economic Geography*, 28 [July 1952] : 244-55); Charles Sullivan and Kathyln Hatch, *The Chinese in Boston, 1970* (Boston, 1970); Adriana Gianturco and Norman Aronin, *Boston's Spanish Speaking Community: Findings of a Field Study* (Boston, 1970); and Massachusetts State Advisory Committee to the United States Commission on Civil Rights, *Issues of Concern to Puerto Ricans in Boston and Springfield* (Boston, 1972). Overall, however, the fields are unploughed, with the harvest yet to come.

As the cities grew, so did the necessity of improving means of transportation, providing for the public health, educating the masses, and, as a means of social control, devising leisure-time outlets suitable to the newly regimented hours demanded by factory and office. The best and most recent study of mass transit is that of Charles W. Cheape's *Moving the Masses.* Other useful works are Edward S. Mason, *The Street Railway in Massachusetts: The Rise and Decline of an Industry* (Cambridge, 1980); O. R. Cummings, *Trolleys along the Turnpike* (Cambridge, 1975); and Abraham E. Pinanski, *The Street Railway System of Metropolitan Boston* (New York, 1908).

In the history of public health, there is a larger number of works by competent historians. These include Morris J. Vogel, *The Invention of the Modern Hospital: Boston, 1870-1930* (Chicago, 1981); Virginia Drachman, *Hospital with a Heart: Women Doctors and the Paradox of Separatism at the New England Hospital, 1862-1969* (Ithaca, N.Y., 1984); Gerald W. Grob, *The State and the Mentally Ill: A History of Worcester State Hospital, 1830-1920* (Chapel Hill, 1966); Barbara G. Rosenkrantz, *Public Health and the State: Changing Views in Massachusetts, 1842-1936* (Cambridge, 1972); and Fern L. Nesson, *Great Waters: A History of Boston's Water Supply* (Hanover, N.H., 1983).

Education, like public health, has attracted a number of competent specialists. A detailed study of the Boston school system from 1789 to the Civil War that argues that the school movement was in direct response to the "urban crisis" brought on by immigration is that by Stanley K. Schultz, *The Culture Factory: Boston Public Schools, 1789-1860* (New York, 1973). A similar view is posited by Marvin Lazerson, *The Origins of the Urban School: Public Education in Massachusetts, 1870-1915* (Cambridge, 1971). An interpretation that suggests that the public school movement was originally the work of the old Yankee elite attempting to control an emerging working class is that by Michael Katz, *Irony of Early School Reform: Educational Innovation in Mid-Nineteenth Century Massachusetts* (Cambridge, 1968). In a second volume, Katz argues that efforts at social control through school reform shifted from elites to dominance by bureaucrats, who were class-oriented and racist, working with a small at-large elected school committee to dismantle popular influences and to enhance dominant social values (*Class, Bureaucracy, and Schools: The Illusion of Educational Change in America* [New York, 1971]). Another work that should be consulted is James W. Fraser, Henry Allen, and Sam Barnes, eds., *From Common School to Magnet School: Selected Essays in the History of Boston's Schools: An*

Annotated Reading List (Boston, 1977), along with George H. Martin, *The Evolution of the Massachusetts Public School System: A Historical Sketch* (New York, 1915). Among the best specialized studies are Gary L. Courchesne, "The Growth of Public Education in Holyoke, 1850-1873" (*Historical Journal of Western Massachusetts*, 7 [June 1979]: 15-24); James W. Fraser, "Mayor John F. Fitzgerald and Boston's Schools, 1905-1913" (*Historical Journal of Massachusetts*, 12 [June 1984]: 117-30); Richard W. Hale, Jr., *Tercentenary History of the Roxbury Latin School, 1645-1945* (Cambridge, 1946); Edwin D. Mead, *The Roman Catholic Church and the School Question* (Boston, 1888); Timothy Meagher, "The Delayed Development of Parochial Education among Irish Catholics in Worcester" (*Historical Journal of Massachusetts*, 12 [January 1984]: 44-59); Reed Ueda, "Suburban Social Change and Educational Reform: The Case of Somerville, 1912-24" (*Social Science History*, 3 [October 1979]: 167-203); Janet R. Wilkie, "Social Status, Acculturation, and School Attendance in 1850 Boston" (*Journal of Social History*, 2 [Winter 1977]: 179-92); David Gould, "Policy and Pedagogues: School Reform and Teacher Professionalization in Massachusetts, 1840-1920" (Ph.D. diss., Brandeis University, 1977); Annette M. Hodess, "A Study of the History of the WPA Nursery Schools of Boston," (Ed.D. diss., Boston University, 1983); and Polly Kaufman, "Boston Women and School Committee Politics: Women on the School Committee, 1872-1905" (Ed.D. diss., Boston University, 1978).

The history of recreation in Massachusetts is a growing area of scholarship. Stephen H. Hardy, *How Boston Played: Sport, Recreation, and Community, 1865-1915* (Boston, 1982), details how sporting activities were a product of "a change in community, and a search for it." There are a number of studies on parks, including Stephen Hardy's "Parks for the People: Reforming the Boston Park System, 1870-1915" (*Journal of Sport History*, 7 [Winter 1980]: 5-24); Gerald K. Marsden's "Philanthropy and the Boston Playground Movement, 1885-1915" (*Social Science Review*, 35 [1961]: 48-58); Roy Rosenzweig's "Middle-Class Parks and Working-Class Play: The Struggle over Recreational Space in Worcester, 1870-1910" (*Radical History Review*, 21 [Fall 1979]: 31-46); and Cynthia Zaitzevsky's *Frederick Law Olmsted and the Boston Park System* (Cambridge, 1982). On sports, the best works are Ronald A. Smith, "Harvard's Response to Excellence and Winning in College Athletics, 1869-1909" (Tager and Ifkovic, eds., *Massachusetts in the Gilded Age*, pp. 164-90); David Q. Voigt, "The Boston Redstockings: The Birth of Major League Baseball" (*New England Quarterly*, 42 [December 1970]: 531-49); Henry Berry, *Boston Red Sox* (New York, 1975); Joe Falls, *Boston Marathon* (New York, 1977); Allan Forbes, *Sport in Norfolk County* (Boston, 1938); Jack Mahoney, *The Golf History of New England* (Wellesley, 1973); and David Paine, "Prominent Country Clubs" (*New England Magazine*, May 1905, pp. 322-36).

Urbanized and industrialized Massachusetts was both a society seething with tension and conflict and, not surprisingly, a place of conciliation and cooperation. Doubtless, a factory system based upon a free-market economy generated labor and employer conflict, beginning with the walkouts of the "daughters of freemen" in early Lowell and continuing to the futile attempts of the Knights of Labor in the 1880s to create one great union to protect the workers. Massachusetts records indicate that at least 7,257 strikes and lockouts took place between 1887 and 1929. Noteworthy were the "general strike" at Lawrence in 1912 and the Boston police strike of 1919. Yet in the face of such worker dissatisfaction society in general seemed to be making great strides toward a more stable social order. In addition to the accounts of strikes and labor unrest found in the books and articles described in the section on the growth of the factory system, three works should be noted: George W. Coleman, "Labor and the Labor Movement, 1860-1930" (*Commonwealth History of Massachusetts*, ed. Albert Bushnell Hart, vol. 5 [New York, 1930], pp. 429-54); Carroll D. Wright, *Strikes in Massachusetts, 1830-1880: Eleventh Annual Report, Massachusetts Bureau of Statistics of Labor* (Boston, 1880); and James Leiby, *Carroll Wright and Labor Reform: The Origins of Labor Statistics* (Cambridge, 1960). A study of the Knights of Labor and New England town politics is Leon Fink's "Politics as Social History: A Case Study of Class Conflict and Political Development in Nineteenth-Century New England" (*Social History*, 7 [January 1982]: 43-58).

Other specialized studies are Henry Bedford, *Socialism and the Workers in Massachusetts, 1886-1912* (Amherst, 1966); James A. Gross, "The Making and Shaping of Unionism in the Pulp and Paper Industry" (*Labor History*, 5 [1964]: 183-208); John P. Hall, "The Knights of St. Crispin in Massachusetts, 1869-1878" (*Journal of Economic History*, 18 [June 1958]: 161-75); Jama Lazerow, "The Workingman's Hour: The 1886 Labor Uprising in Boston" (*Labor History*, 21 [1980]: 200-220); Katherine D. Lumpkin, *Shutdowns in the Connecticut Valley, Smith College Studies in History Series*, 19 [Northampton, 1934]); and Frederick Rudolph, "Chinaman in Yankeedom: Anti-Unionism in Massachusetts in 1870" (*American Historical Review*, 53 [October 1947]: 1-29). Three early sources that are useful are Horace G. Wadlin, "The Sweating System in Massachusetts" (*Journal of Social Science*, 30 [October 1892]: 86-102); Mary Trueblood, "Social Statistics of Workingwomen" (*Massachusetts Labor Bulletin*, 18 [May 1901]: 21-49); and Robert A. Woods and Albert J. Kennedy, eds., *Young Working Girls: A Summary of Evidence from Two Thousand Social Workers* (Boston, 1913).

A number of doctoral dissertations cast further light on the history of labor in Massachusetts. These include Joshua Chasan, "Civilizing Worcester: The Creation of Industrial and Cultural Order, 1848-1876" (Ph.D. diss., University of Pittsburgh, 1974); Christopher D. Dale, "From Household Laborers to Millhands: A Study of Women in the Transition to Industrial Capitalism in Antebellum New England" (Ph.D. diss., University of Kentucky, 1984); Edwin Fenton, "Immigrants and Unions, A Case Study: Italians and American Labor, 1870-1920" (Ph.D. diss., Harvard University, 1957); Alexander Keyssar, "Men out of Work: A Social History of Unemployment in Massachusetts, 1870-1916" (Ph.D. diss.,

Harvard University, 1980); and Carole Srole, "'A Position That God Has Not Particularly Assigned to Men': The Feminization of Clerical Work, Boston, 1860–1915" (Ph.D. diss., University of California, Los Angeles, 1984).

Specific studies on the Lawrence strike of 1912, in addition to material found in Cole's *Immigrant City*, include Melvin Dubofsky, *We Shall Be All: A History of the Industrial Workers of the World* (Chicago, 1969); John B. McPherson, *The Lawrence Strike of 1912* (Boston, 1912); and Henry F. Bedford, "'Not Enough Pay': Lawrence, 1912" (in Bedford, *Trouble Downtown: The Local Context of Twentieth Century America* [New York, 1978]). On the Boston police strike of 1919, specific studies include Francis Russell, *A City in Terror: 1919, The Boston Police Strike* (New York, 1975); Randolph Bartlett, "Anarchy in Boston" (*American Mercury*, 26 [December 1935]: 456-64); Richard L. Lyons, "The Boston Police Strike of 1919" (*New England Quarterly*, 20 [June 1947]: 147-68); Frederick M. Koss, "The Boston Police Strike" (Ph.D. diss., Boston University, 1960); and Jonathan R. White, "A Triumph of Bureaucracy: The Boston Police Strike and the Ideological Origins of the American Police Structure" (Ph.D. diss., Michigan State University, 1982).

In an essay on social change and the apparent fragmentation and disorder generated by urbanization, Alex Keyssar concluded that "the sources of social cohesion proved to be stronger than the sources of division, and the boundaries between classes and ethnic groups eventually softened rather than hardened."[10] Moreover, studies by Theodore Ferdinand ("The Criminal Patterns of Boston since 1849," *American Journal of Sociology*, 73 [July 1967]: 84-99) and Roger Lane ("Urbanization and Criminal Violence," *Journal of Social History* 2 [Dec. 1968]: 156-63) have demonstrated that serious crime actually declined in Boston from 1850 to 1950. The industrial revolution inspired a general rise in the standard of living of a majority of Massachusetts' urbanites, and that prosperity bears marked connection to a lessening of social violence and a promotion of orderliness. Other works of related interest include Barbara M. Brenzel, *Daughters of the State: A Social Portrait of the First Reform School for Girls in North America, 1856-1905* (Cambridge, 1983); Leonard V. Harrison, *Police Administration in Boston* (Cambridge, 1934); Robert Silverman, *Law and Urban Growth: Civil Litigation in the Boston Trial Courts, 1880-1900* (Princeton, 1981); Sam Bass Warner, Sr., *Crime and Criminal Statistics in Boston* (Cambridge, 1934); Warner and Henry B. Cabot, *Judges and Law Reform: Survey of Crime and Justice in Boston* (Cambridge, 1936); and Mary J. Bularzik, "Sex, Crime, and Justice: Women in the Criminal Justice System of Massachusetts, 1900-1950" (Ph.D. diss., Brandeis University, 1982). For an examination of preindustrial urban violence in Boston, see Theodore Hammett, "Two Mobs of Jacksonian Boston: Ideology and Interest" (*Journal of American History*, 62 [March 1976]: 845-68).

To a lesser degree, class tensions were somewhat ameliorated by the paternalistic efforts of a wide variety of upper- and middle-class social reformers. Their strenuous efforts to "uplift" and "civilize" the poor certainly raised public consciousness and resulted in the passage of a host of significant social welfare legislation by the Massachusetts General Court. Still the best work on urban reform in Boston in the late nineteenth century is Arthur Mann's *Yankee Reformers in the Urban Age: Social Reform in Boston, 1880-1900* (Cambridge, 1954). Also useful are Nathan I. Huggins' *Protestants against Poverty: Boston's Charities, 1870-1900* (Westport, Conn., 1971) and Robert Kelso's *The History of Public Poor Relief in Massachusetts, 1620-1920* (New York, 1921). Among the numerous studies of specific reform organizations are J. Leslie Dunstan, *A Light to the City: 150 Years of the City Missionary Society of Boston, 1816-1966* (Boston, 1966); Barbara M. Solomon, *Pioneers in Service: The History of the Associated Jewish Philanthropies of Boston* (Boston, 1956); and Anne M. Boylan, "Women in Groups: An Analysis of Women's Benevolent Organizations in New York and Boston, 1797-1840" (*Journal of American History*, 71 [December 1984]: 497-523).

There are numerous works by and about social reformers. A sampling includes Irving H. Bartlett, *Wendell Phillips, Brahmin Radical* (Boston, 1961) and *Wendell and Ann Phillips: The Community of Reform* (New York, 1983); Deborah P. Clifford, *Mine Eyes Have Seen the Glory: A Biography of Julia Ward Howe* (Boston, 1978); Allon Gal, *Brandeis of Boston* (Cambridge, 1980); Tilden G. Edelstein, *Strange Enthusiasm: A Life of Thomas Wentworth Higginson* (New Haven, 1968); Mercedes M. Randall, *Improper Bostonian: Emily Greene Balch* (New York, 1964); and Eleanor H. Woods, *Robert A. Woods: Champion of Democracy* (Boston, 1929). The portraits of Mary Antin and Emily Greene Balch in Sam Bass Warner, Jr., *Province of Reason: American Lives in a New Age of Science* (Cambridge, 1984), also are exceedingly useful.

A number of dissertations cast light on reform in urban Boston, including Mania K. Baghdadi, "Protestants, Poverty, and Urban Growth: A Study of the Organization of Charity in Boston and New York, 1820-1865" (Ph.D. diss., Brown University, 1975); Walter F. Carroll, "Social Change and the Family: New Bedford, 1860-1880" (Ph.D. diss., American University, 1983); Barbara M. Hobson, "Sex in the Marketplace: Prostitution in an American City, Boston, 1820-1880" (Ph.D. diss., Boston University, 1982); Peter C. Holloran, "Boston's Wayward Children: Social Services for Homeless Children, 1800-1930" (Ph.D. diss., Boston University, 1982); Paul Hughes, "Edward Everett Hale and the American City" (Ph.D. diss., New York University, 1975); Susan L. Porter, "The Benevolent Asylum—Image and Reality: The Care and Training of Female Orphans in Boston, 1800-1840" (Ph.D. diss., Boston University, 1984); and Susan S. Walton, "To Preserve the Faith: Catholic Charities in Boston, 1870-1930" (Ph.D. diss., Boston University, 1983).

For the pivotal role played by the state legislature both in realizing the social reformer's aims and in readjusting party politics to fit new constituencies, see Richard Abrams, *Conservatism in a Progressive Era: Massachusetts Politics, 1900-1912* (Cambridge, 1964); Alec Barbrook, *God Save the Commonwealth: An Electoral History of Massachusetts* (Amherst, 1973); Geoffrey Blodgett, *The*

Gentle Reformers: Massachusetts Democrats in the Cleveland Era (Cambridge, 1966); Michael Hennessy, *Four Decades of Massachusetts Politics, 1890-1935* (Norwood, Mass., 1935); J. Joseph Huthmacher, *Massachusetts People and Politics, 1919-1933* (Cambridge, 1959); Richard Harmond, "Tradition and Change in the Gilded Age: A Political History of Massachusetts, 1878-1893" (Ph.D. diss., Columbia University, 1966); and Dale Baum, *The Civil War Party System: The Case of Massachusetts, 1848-1876* (Chapel Hill, 1984).

For urban Massachusetts, the primary avenue for societal accommodation among contending groups, thus promoting a valid moral order based upon real economic progress, was the openness of the political system. A democratic system imbued with the capitalist drive for individual achievement—"equality of opportunity"—prompted a continually expanding material prosperity. For those newly arrived urban groups initially outside the corridors of Yankee power in Massachusetts, majoritarian politics provided the vehicle for both individual social mobility and for group social welfare. Martin Lomasney, the "Mahatma" of Boston's Ward Eight, conceived of politics as pure utilitarianism when he described the function of his political organization, the Hendricks Club, as "a machine for getting votes. And it gets them, by working 365 days a year, caring for people, being a big employment agency, being a generous benefactor, viewing with charitable and forgiving eyes lapses of human conduct." The colorful four-time mayor of Boston, James Michael Curley, wanted to be remembered "as the Mayor of the Poor."[11] For an account of how the party system worked "to improve order" in Boston, one should consult Ronald P. Formisano, "Boston, 1800-1840: From Deferential-Participant to Party Politics" (*Boston, 1700-1980: The Evolution of Urban Politics*, ed. Ronald P. Formisano and Constance K. Burns [Westport, Conn., 1984], pp. 29-58). The path to power for Massachusetts' ethnics was to be an arduous and complicated journey, made up first of compliant compromise and then, when power was actually within grasp, of bitter infighting and almost suicidal bickering.

Clearly, the notion of absolute Irish supremacy in Boston and elsewhere in the state is largely mythical. The Irish never made up more than one-third of the city's population. By 1920 the Irish comprised 31.9 percent, the Jews 15.7 percent (of various nationalities but with substantial Russian/Polish immigrants), the Italians 14 percent, with a variety of other groups for a total of 71.6 percent, making Boston second only to New York City in total percentage of first- and second-generation foreign stock. Between 1885 and his death in 1933, Martin Lomasney's Ward Eight in the West End dramatically changed population mix from predominately Irish to Jewish and then to Italian. All the while as "clan chief" he maintained absolute political control by bridging the polyglot ethnic gap and providing jobs and service to all. As the premier immigrant group the Irish dominated ethnic politics, but only because they were adept conciliators and compromisers.[12]

Reluctant compromise with lesser enemies was the first political lesson learned by Massachusetts' urban Irish. As Geoffrey Blodgett pointed out superbly in *The Gentle Reformers*, the initial stage in Irish inclusion in political power required humiliating subservience to Yankee Democrats. This "fragile alliance inside the Democratic party between an elite Yankee leadership and a growing Irish working-class majority" finally disintegrated after 1900 when feisty second-generation Irish leaders, such as John F. Fitzgerald and James Michael Curley, renounced subordination to reconstruct the Democratic party around working-class and ethnic lines. After ousting the Yankee elites, the ward bosses and Irish leaders, particularly Lomasney, Fitzgerald, and Curley, ferociously attacked each other, thus preventing any one group from emerging triumphant. Peter Eisinger argued that this internal squabbling in Boston allowed a small Yankee contingent of independents to work closely with a Republican-dominated state legislature to hamstring the Irish politicians through "good government" crusades and continual charter reform. Feuding Irish chieftains and seesawing alliances with Yankee reformers were to typify Boston politics until Maurice Tobin's mayoral victory in 1937 and the supposed "decline of bossism." Although Curley kept reappearing on the political scene like the proverbial bad penny, the election of Mayor John Hynes in 1949 and the growing middle-classification of the electorate heralded a new epoch for politics in Boston and the state.

Significant accounts of the political divisions in Boston are Geoffrey Blodgett's "Yankee Leadership in a Divided City: Boston, 1860-1910" (*Journal of Urban History*, 8 [August 1982]: 371-96) and "Josiah Quincy, Brahmin Democrat" (*New England Quarterly*, 38 [December 1965]: 435-53). An important article is Peter Eisinger's "Ethnic Political Transition in Boston, 1884-1933: Some Lessons for Contemporary Cities" (*Political Science Quarterly*, 93 [1978]: 217-39). Others who discuss this extraordinary alliance are Thomas O'Connor, *Bibles, Brahmins, and Bosses: A Short History of Boston* (Boston, 1976); Paul Kleppner, "From Party to Factions: The Dissolution of Boston's Majority Party, 1876-1908" (Formisano and Burns, *Boston, 1700-1980*, pp. 111-32); John T. Galvin, "The Dark Ages of Boston City Politics" (*Massachusetts Historical Society Proceedings*, 89 [1977]: 88-111); and Galvin's "Patrick J. Maguire: Boston's Last Democratic Boss" (*New England Quarterly*, 55 [September 1982]: 392-415). For a flattering biography of the "good government" Yankee who ran for mayor unsuccessfully against John Fitzgerald in 1910, see Henry G. Pearson, *Son of New England: James Jackson Storrow, 1846-1926* (Boston, 1932). Constance K. Burns examined Storrow's reform activities, suggesting that he could "transcend ethnic interests" on the school issue, but that he failed in politics when he could not reach out to the Irish, in "The Irony of Progressive Reform: Boston, 1898-1910" (Formisano and Burns, *Boston, 1700-1980*, pp. 133-63). For an uncritical look at another Republican leader, see John T. Galvin, "Henry Lee Shattuck: Ideal Politician" (*New England Quarterly*, 50 [March 1977]: 3-29). Maurice Tobin's political career has been scrutinized by Vincent Lapomarda in "Maurice Joseph Tobin: The Decline of Bossism in Boston" (*New England Quarterly*, 43 [September 1970]: 355-81), as well as in his dissertation, "Maurice

Joseph Tobin, 1901-53: A Political Profile and an Edition of Selected Public Papers" (Ph.D. diss., Boston University, 1968).

It has been some years since the classic work of Robert Merton (*Social Theory and Social Structure* [New York, 1949]) ended the simplistic myth of boss corruption and misrule. Today the consensus is that machine politics played an important social and economic function in providing order and opportunity for urban dwellers. Indeed, in his recent analysis of several nineteenth-century cities, Jon Teaford has made an excellent case for the fact that "cities like Boston successfully met the challenge of the age."[13] Yet Boston lacks a history of its municipal politics in the twentieth century. Thus it is difficult if not impossible to untangle the full truth about Boston's political life from 1900 to the present, largely because of the dearth of scholarly studies of the major figures and their contributions.

In a recent article, "Curley of Boston: The Search for Irish Legitimacy" (Formisano and Burns, *Boston, 1700-1980*, pp. 164-95), Charles Trout dared to suggest that there is convincing evidence that Curley was a liberal social reformer. Trout's book on the Curley administration in the depression, *Boston, The Great Depression, and the New Deal* (New York, 1977), mainly focuses on the impact of New Deal policies upon the city, but he promises us a full biography of Curley. William V. Shannon agreed with this positive interpretation of the Irish dominance of Boston. In "Boston's Irish Mayors: An Ethnic Perspective" (Formisano and Burns, *Boston, 1700-1980*, pp. 199-214), he wrote that the Irish established a "rudimentary welfare state" in a Boston that was sorely lacking any system of help for the poor. In "Reaction and Reform in Boston: The Gilded Age and the Progressive Era" (Tager and Ifkovic, eds., *Massachusetts in the Gilded Age*, pp. 232-46), Jack Tager has made a case for both Fitzgerald and Curley as spending more for reform measures—bathhouses, parks, recreation, business initiatives, and the like—than their progressive counterparts. John D. Buenker's analysis of "The Mahatma and Progressive Reform: Martin Lomasney as Lawmaker, 1911-1917" (*New England Quarterly*, 44 [September 1971]: 397-419) argues that the Mahatma "was in tune with the progressive currents of the day." More on Lomasney can be gleaned from Albert D. Van Nostrand, "The Lomasney Legend" (*New England Quarterly*, 21 [December 1948]: 435-50) and Henry L. Shattuck, "Martin Lomasney in the Constitutional Convention of 1917-1919" (*Proceedings of the Massachusetts Historical Society*, 71 [1953-1957]: 299-311). Incredibly, John F. Fitzgerald has been totally ignored by serious scholars. The only works on him are Francis Russell's "John the Bold: Boston's John F. 'Honeyfitz' Fitzgerald" (*The Great Interlude* [New York, 1964], pp. 162-90) and J. H. Cutler's *"Honey Fitz": Three Steps to the White House* (Indianapolis, 1962). Robert A. Woods wrote a fascinating study of the competition between Lomasney and Fitzgerald, "Traffic in Citizenship" (*Americans in Process*, pp. 147-89). Except for the welcome addition of Melvin G. Holli and Peter d'A. Jones, eds., *Biographical Dictionary of American Mayors* (Westport, Conn., 1981), which lists all of Boston's mayors, Boston politics in the age of the Irish bosses is yet to be done. Unfortunately, the best book on Curley is his unreliable but enjoyable autobiography, *I'd Do It Again* (Englewood Cliffs, N.J., 1957). Francis Russell has written a short biographical portrait, "The Last of the Bosses" (*The Great Interlude*, pp. 191-211). Joseph Dinneen's *The Purple Shamrock* (New York, 1949) suffers from the same superficiality as does his work on Lomasney, *Ward Eight* (New York, 1936). For a specific study of Irish encounters with other ethnic groups, see Herbert M. Zolot, "The Issue of Good Government and James Michael Curley: Curley and the Boston Scene from 1897-1918" (Ph.D. diss., State University of New York, Stony Brook, 1975). Robert A. Silverman has written a good article on Yankee Democrat Nathan Mathews, "Nathan Mathews: Politics of Reform in Boston, 1890-1910" (*New England Quarterly*, 50 [December 1977]: 626-43). George R. Nutter's *Nathan Mathews* (Cambridge, 1928) is one of those "memorial" biographies that eschew analysis for flattery. For a progressive's view of the troubled administration of Mayor Andrew Peters (1918-1922), see William B. Munro, "Peters of Boston: A Reform Mayor Who Did Not Fail" (*National Municipal Review*, 11 [February 1922]: 85-88).

An uncritical yet fact-filled account of Boston city government is John Koren's *Boston, 1822-1922: The Story of Its Government and Principal Activities during One Hundred Years* (Boston, 1923). For an introduction to city charter reform as a tool of Yankee opposition to bossism, see A. Chester Hanford, "The Government of the City of Boston, 1880-1930" (*Fifty Years of Boston: A Memorial Album*, ed. Elisabeth M. Herlihy [Boston, 1932], pp. 84-115), and William Marchione, "The 1949 Boston Charter Reform" (*New England Quarterly*, 49 [September 1976]: 373-98).

To achieve any understanding of the politics of post-World War II Boston and urban Massachusetts first requires an examination of the major economic changes that befell Massachusetts—particularly the decline of the textile and shoe industries, the rise of the high-technology and service industries, and the subsequent politics of urban renewal. The decline of Massachusetts' old industrial system in the twentieth century brought ruin and decay to the once-prosperous factory cities; the tensions of metropolitan life were drastically increased when economic change once again moved people around the commonwealth in search of jobs. The very industries that had converted Massachusetts into an urban society in the nineteenth century were virtually dead by 1980. The death knell for the factory towns actually began late in the nineteenth century and was halted only momentarily by the upsurge in demand brought about by two world wars. The South, with its more favorable labor conditions, close proximity to raw materials, and cheaper transportation costs, undermined the once-pre-eminent position of New England in general and Massachusetts in particular as a leader in textiles and shoes. Of 264,000 New England textile workers employed in 1930, there were only 61,000 such jobs remaining by 1970. Economists Seymour E. Harris (*The Economics of New England: Case Study of an Older Area* [Cambridge, 1952]) and R. C. Estall (*New England: A Study in Industrial Adjustment* [New York,

1966]) believed that excessive concentration on manufacturing created a critical dependence upon the response of business management and labor attitudes to market changes that turned out to be both shortsighted and deficient. Estall wrote: "More than any other region the prosperity of manufacturing underpins the rest of the economy."[14] Loss of jobs in highly specialized industrial communities forced people to move to other regions in hope of finding employment.

Massive desertions by the labor force had already occurred during the bleak depression years and were to continue after World War II. Thomas Russell Smith's *Cotton Textile Industry of Fall River: A Study of Industrial Localization* (New York, 1944) and Seymour L. Wolfbein's *The Decline of a Cotton Textile City: A Study of New Bedford* (New York, 1944) told the woeful tale of plant closings and removals and of staggeringly high rates of unemployment and large-scale migration to Boston and elsewhere. Horace B. Davis, in *Shoes: The Workers and the Industry* (New York, 1940), painted the same gloomy picture for the shoe industry in Brockton, Haverhill, and Lynn. A 1954 report of the New England Committee of the National Planning Association (A. A. Bright, ed., *The Economic State of New England*, 2 vols. [New Haven, 1954]) showed that the labor force in Massachusetts was already undergoing a metamorphosis: the number of industrial workers had declined to 42.98 percent, while a new high of 54.89 percent were represented in service areas.[15]

Other works on the decline of textiles and shoes and on population movement are Thomas L. Norton, *Trade Union Policies in the Massachusetts Shoe Industry, 1919-1929* (New York, 1932); William Cole, Jr., "Brockton: A History of the Decline of a Shoe Manufacturing City, 1900-1933" (Ph.D. diss., Boston University, 1968); Bruce A. Hardy, "American Privatism and the Urban Fiscal Crisis of the Interwar Years: A Financial Study of the Cities of New York, Chicago, Philadelphia, Detroit, and Boston, 1915-1945" (Ph.D. diss., Wayne State University, 1977); Stewart Holbrook, *The Yankee Exodus: An Account of Migration from New England* (New York, 1950); and James Green and Hugh C. Donahue, *Boston's Workers: A Labor History* (Boston, 1944). An analysis of the limited impact of defense industries on women textile workers of Lowell is found in Marc Miller, "Working Women and World War II" (*New England Quarterly*, 53 [March 1980]: 42-61). Other works related to economic conditions are James Truslow Adams et al., *New England's Prospect: 1933* (New York, 1933); Federal Writers Project, *Boston Looks Seaward: The Story of the Port, 1630-1940* (Boston, 1941); George French, ed., *New England: What It Is and What It Is to Be* (Boston, 1911); Herman Nelson, "Some Aspects of Manufacturing in Worcester" (Ph.D. diss., Clark University, 1954); Samuel E. Hill, *Teamsters and Transportation: Employee-Employer Relationships in New England* (Washington, D.C., 1942); Thomas Beal, *The Second National Bank of Boston* (New York, 1958); Allan Forbes, *Forty Years in Boston Banking* (New York, 1948); N. S. B. Gras, *The Massachusetts First National Bank of Boston, 1784-1934* (Cambridge, 1937); and Millard C. Faught, *Falmouth: Problems of a Resort Community* (New York, 1945).

The shift from durables to services was not taking place on the older manufacturing sites. Harvey Boulay's *The Twilight Cities: Political Conflict, Development, and Decay in Five Communities* (Port Washington, N.Y., 1983) (Lynn, Lawrence, Lowell, Brockton, and New Bedford) described their mutual predicaments: declining populations, departure of industry, the flight of the middle class to the suburbs, lowering property values and rising property taxes, unemployment rates higher than average, and older ethnic groups in competition with newer arrivals. It was in the newer service areas largely based in suburbs that urban Massachusetts was to find its economic salvation. Works on the economic revival include Russell B. Adams, Jr., *The Boston Money Tree* (New York, 1977); John C. Hoy and Melvin H. Bernstein, *Business and Academia: Partners in New England's Economic Revival* (Hanover, N.H., 1981); Bennett Harrison, *The Economic Development of Massachusetts* (Boston, 1974) and *Rationalization, Restructuring, and Industrial Reorganization in Older Regions: The Economic Transformation of New England since World War II* (Cambridge, 1982); David Lowenthal, *Environmental Assessment: A Comparative Analysis of Four Cities* (New York, 1972); Craig L. Moore and Steven M. Rosenthal, *Massachusetts Reconsidered: An Economic Anatomy of the Commonwealth* (Amherst, 1978); and Carl H. Reidel, *New England Prospects: Critical Choices in a Time of Change* (Hanover, N.H., 1982).

Ironically, the tensions of the Cold War fired the furnaces of a new industry for the commonwealth, particularly for northeastern Massachusetts, downtown Boston, and many of its suburbs along Route 128. Huge federal outlays for research and development in missiles, electronics, and computer systems, coupled with the brainpower and expertise in the higher education system of Boston and Cambridge, resulted in the development of hundreds of new firms in the suburbs. The fact that an Adams, Charles Francis, was from 1948 to 1964 the head of Raytheon, producer of Sparrow and Hawk missiles, was both a sign of change and a symbol of tradition. People marched to the suburbs, deserting Boston's middle-class and working-class neighborhoods for life alongside Route 128. Dotted with high-technology companies, Route 128 enclosed greater Boston—a sixty-five–mile loop with the densest population of the Bay State. Thus between 1950 and 1980 Boston lost 30 percent of its population. For a description and analysis of these developments, one should consult Otto J. Scott, *The Creative Ordeal: The Story of Raytheon* (New York, 1974); H. Green, "Hinterland Boundaries of New York City and Boston in Southern New England" (*Readings in Urban Geography*, ed. Harold Mayer and Clyde Kohn, [Chicago, 1959], pp. 185-201); Allen Wakestein, "Boston's Search for a Metropolitan Solution" (*Journal of the American Institute of Planners*, 38 [September 1972]: 285-96); Katherine McNamara, ed., *The Boston Metropolitan District: Its Physical Growth and Governmental Development* (Cambridge, 1946); Melvin R. Levin et al., *The Boston Regional Survey, Prepared for the Massachusetts Transportation Commission* (Cambridge, 1963); Ralph Gakenheimer, *Transportation Planning as Response to Controversy: Participation and Conflict in the Boston*

Case (Cambridge, 1976); and Lawrence Susskind, ed., *The Land Use Controversy in Massachusetts: Case Studies and Policy Options* (Cambridge, 1975). In addition, there are three useful dissertations: D. E. Buerle, "Some Measures of Boston and New York City Social Influence on Their Common Hinterland" (Ph.D. diss., Clark University, 1965); George H. McCaffrey, "The Political Disintegration and Reintegration of Metropolitan Boston" (Ph.D. diss., Harvard University, 1937); and James E. Vance, Jr., "The Growth of Suburbanism West of Boston: A Geographic Study of Transportation-Settlement Relationships" (Ph.D. diss., Clark University, 1952). Finally, an analysis of the effect of these developments on politics is provided by Edgar Litt, *The Political Cultures of Massachusetts* (Cambridge, 1965).

Large-scale suburbanization took jobs and housing opportunities away from the central city. Sixty percent of all jobs in Boston today are held by people who live outside the city, with only 20 percent of the entire suburban work force employed there. Robert Ryan, former director of the Boston Redevelopment Authority, said in 1984: "The city functions as the economic engine for the entire region."[16] In 1979 the median family income in Boston was $16,253, while it was $22,813 for its suburbs; the poverty rate was 20 percent for Boston versus 9.7 percent for the suburbs. As of 1984 Bostonians paid the highest rents in the nation, and the city ranked among the ten highest in the nation for its cost of home ownership. With jobs increasing only by 2 percent between 1972 and 1979, the growth rate for the suburbs was 23 percent. We have arrived at the condition that Sam Bass Warner, Jr., labeled a "divided society"—so divided physically and politically that the "metropolis was helpless to solve its problems."[17]

Our inability to cope with the metropolis is the core argument of John H. Mollenkopf's *The Contested City* (Princeton, 1983), a provocative look at the relationship between federal policies and urban redevelopment. Mollenkopf stressed the fact that the federal government's support of Boston's sustained building boom of the 1960s benefited a suburban white-collar work force to the detriment of the various neighborhoods in the city. The coming together of "progrowth coalitions"—Boston's capitalists personified by the "Vault," the Hynes and Collins mayoralties, and Edward Logue's Boston Redevelopment Authority activities—with the traditional urban largesse of national Democrats, served to "Manhattanize" downtown Boston and facilitated its current urban crisis. Among the studies on the "New Boston" are Stephan Thernstrom, *Poverty, Planning, and Politics in the New Boston: The Origins of ABCD* (New York, 1969); Walter McQuade, "Urban Renewal in Boston" (*Urban Renewal: The Record and the Controversy*, ed. James Q. Wilson [Cambridge, 1966], pp. 259–77); Martin Meyerson and Edward Banfield, *Boston: The Job Ahead* (Cambridge, 1966); Nancy Arnone, "Redevelopment in Boston" (Ph.D. diss., MIT, 1965); Langley Carlton Keyes, Jr., *The Rehabilitation Planning Game: A Study in the Diversity of Neighborhood* (Cambridge, 1969); Keyes, *The Boston Rehabilitation Program: An Independent Analysis* (Cambridge, 1970); Edward Banfield,

Big City Politics (New York, 1965); Banfield and Martha Derthick, eds., *A Report on the Politics of Boston* (Cambridge, 1960); John F. Collins, *Boston's Second Revolution* (New York, 1962); Edward J. Logue, "Boston, 1960-1967—Seven Years of Plenty" (*Proceedings of the Massachusetts Historical Society*, 84 [1972] : 82-96); and William Loring, Jr., et al., *Organization for Citizen Participation in Urban Renewal* (Boston, 1957). For community struggles to preserve neighborhoods, see Gordon Fellman, *The Deceived Majority: Politics and Protest in Middle America* (New Brunswick, N.J., 1973); Alan Lupo et al., *Rites of Way: The Politics of Transportation in Boston and the U.S. City* (Boston, 1971); and Dorothy Nelkin, *Jetport: The Boston Airport Controversy* (New Brunswick, N.J., 1974).

The politics of urban renewal more often than not destroyed low- and middle-income housing for the purposes of commercial revitalization. Herbert Gans' *The Urban Villagers: Group and Class in the Life of Italian-Americans* (New York, 1962 and 1982), a sensitive probe into community and kinship ties among Italian Americans in the West End, laid bare the unnecessary destruction of a viable low-income neighborhood simply because it was too close to downtown. Other works that are useful in this area are Marc Fried's *The World of the Urban Working Class: Boston's West End* (Cambridge, 1973); Samuel H. Beer and Richard E. Barringer, *The State and the Poor* (Cambridge, 1970); Manuel Carballo and Mary Jo Bane, *The State and the Poor in the 1980s* (Boston, 1984); Joe R. Feagin et al., *Subsidizing the Poor: A Boston Housing Experiment* (Lexington, Mass., 1972); and Ann Withorn, *The Circle Game: Services for the Poor in Massachusetts, 1966-1978* (Amherst, 1982). A system of federally supported urban economics that served the privileged and rewarded the commuter ended up punishing the multitude of disadvantaged city dwellers.

Boston's spatial tensions—neighborhoods versus downtown and suburbs—were too much even for her most successful politician, Kevin H. White. A voluble politico, White was "a mayor who survives," wrote Martha W. Weinberg in "Boston's Kevin White" (*Political Science Quarterly*, 96 [Spring 1981] : 87-106). Quite recently, in a superficial and hastily patched-together work, *Style versus Substance: Boston, Kevin White, and the Politics of Illusion* (New York, 1984), novelist/journalist George V. Higgins unfairly characterized White as "all style and no substance," a creation of the media. Other works on politics from the 1960s to the 1980s include Philip B. Heymann and Martha W. Weinberg, "The Paradox of Power: Mayoral Leadership on Charter Reform in Boston" (*American Politics and Public Policy*, ed. Walter D. Burnham et al. [Cambridge, 1978]); Boston Urban Study Group, *Who Rules Boston? A Citizen's Guide to Reclaiming the City* (Boston, 1984); Eric Nordlinger, *Decentralizing the City: A Study of Boston's Little City Halls* (Cambridge, 1972); George Washnis, *Municipal Decentralization and Neighborhood Resources: Case Studies of Twelve Cities* (New York, 1972); Arnold M. Howitt, "Strategies of Governing: Electoral Constraints on Mayoral Behavior in Philadelphia and Boston" (Ph.D. diss., Harvard University, 1976); and Daniel S. Pool, "Politics in the New Boston, 1960-1970" (Ph.D.

diss., Brandeis University, 1974). For a discussion of young Irish politicians as "the last of the breed" in the 1960s, see Edward M. Levine, *The Irish and Irish Politicians: A Study of Cultural and Social Alienation* (West Bend, Ind., 1966). One issue that demonstrated the mayor's constitutional ineffectiveness and that focused attention upon the interdependent network of the metropolitan system concerned the racial tensions elicited by the school busing order of federal judge W. Arthur Garrity.

Blacks made the long and arduous journey to greater Boston in the same search for jobs and equality of opportunity as did the other migrants to the city. Elizabeth Pleck's meticulously documented study of post-Civil War migration from the upper South, *Black Migration and Poverty: Boston, 1865-1900* (New York, 1979), described job discrimination and constant struggle against social prejudice. Her succinct conclusion was that "black economic progress did not fit the model of even the most limited example of nineteenth-century immigrant advance, that of Irish Bostonians."[18] For more on the black community in Massachusetts, one should consult Elizabeth H. Pleck, "The Two Parent Household: Black Family Structure in Late Nineteenth-Century Boston" (*Journal of Social History*, 6 [Fall 1972]: 1-31); Gerald N. Davis, "Massachusetts Blacks and the Quest for Education, 1638-1860" (Ph.D. diss., University of Massachusetts, 1977); George A. Levesque, "Black Boston: Negro Life in Garrison's Boston, 1800-1860" (Ph.D. diss., State University of New York, Binghamton, 1976); and Joseph P. Lynch, "Blacks in Springfield, 1868-1880: A Mobility Study" (*Historical Journal of Western Massachusetts*, 7 [June 1979]: 25-34).

Turn-of-the-century studies by South End settlement-house workers, such as John Daniels' *In Freedom's Birthplace: A Study of Boston's Negroes* (Boston, 1914), confirm Pleck's conclusion. While there were cases of black success stories—editor William Monroe Trotter of the *Guardian*, minister Peter Randolph, businessmen Julius Chappelle and William Wells Brown—and the appearance of a small black upper class, for the most part a life of menial labor and residential transience was the lot of black Bostonians. Stephan Thernstrom, in his *The Other Bostonians*, aptly summed up this dismal tale of denial of economic advancement: "There was virtually no improvement in the occupational position of black men in Boston between the late nineteenth century and the beginning of World War II."[19] Among the most useful works are John Daniels, "Industrial Conditions among Negro Men in Boston" (*Charities and the Commons*, 16 [October 7, 1905]: 35-39); Stephen R. Fox, *The Guardian of Boston: William Monroe Trotter* (New York, 1970); Peter Randolph, *From Slave Cabin to Pulpit* (Boston, 1883); Henry M. Field, *Bright Skies and Dark Shadows* (New York, 1890); Edward Farrison, *William Wells Brown* (Chicago, 1969); Adelaide C. Hill, "The Negro Upper Class in Boston—Its Development and Present Social Structure" (Ph.D. diss., Radcliffe College, 1952); Susie K. Taylor, *Reminiscences of My Life in Camp* (Boston, 1902, and New York, 1968); W. E. B. Du Bois, *The Black North in 1901: A Social Study* (New York, 1901); and Seaton W. Manning, "Negro Trade Unionists in Boston" (*Social Forces*, 17 [December 1938]: 256-

66). For a study of antebellum blacks, one should read James O. Horton and Lois E. Horton, *Black Bostonians: Family Life and Community Struggle in the Antebellum North* (New York, 1979).

The picture did not change after the onset of World War II. Malcolm X recorded the limitations of black opportunity in Boston and the delusions of the tiny black upper class: "What I thought I was seeing there in Roxbury were high-class, educated, important Negroes, living well, working in big jobs and positions. . . . I know now, of course, that what I was really seeing was only a big-city version of those 'successful' Negro bootblacks and janitors back in Lansing. The only difference was that the ones in Boston had been brainwashed even more thoroughly. . . . Under the pitiful misapprehension that it would make them 'better,' these Hill Negroes were breaking their backs trying to imitate white people."[20] The migration of large numbers of blacks began in earnest only after 1950, so that by 1980 they represented 22 percent of the population of Boston. Throughout this period, persistent discrimination led to menial labor positions, residential segregation, and unequal schooling.

Unlike Detroit or Atlanta, cities that experienced long-term and continuous heavy black migrations, Boston's blacks were never able to marshal significant political power because of their fewer numbers. From 1870 to 1940, blacks averaged only 1.4 to 3.1 percent of Boston's population. In 1950, blacks were 5 percent of the population, 9.1 percent in 1960, 16.3 percent in 1970, and 22 percent in 1980, or about 126,000 in a city of 562,000. Lacking a substantial middle class, competing for jobs with other ethnic groups in a city with a weak and narrow economic base for unskilled labor opportunities, facing a white power structure that resorted to racism to win elections, Boston's blacks were ghettoized in a fashion almost comparable to Jim Crow days in the South. By 1976 Michael Conzen and George K. Lewis, in their brief but lucid analysis of the city, *Boston: A Geographical Portrait* (Cambridge, 1976), stated with conviction that "blacks are more segregated in Boston than in most other large metropolitan areas."[21] Several other works that focus on the making of a black ghetto in Boston are Robert Coles, *The South Goes North* (Boston, 1967); U.S. Commission on Civil Rights, *Hearings Held in Boston, October 4-5, 1966* (Washington, D.C., 1967); Leon Mayhew, *Law and Equal Opportunity: A Study of the Massachusetts Commission Against Discrimination* (Cambridge, 1968); and Robert Rosenthal et al., *Different Strokes: Pathways to Maturity in the Boston Ghetto* (Boulder, Colo., 1976).

Peter Shrag's graphic study, *Village School Downtown: Boston Schools, Boston Politics* (Boston, 1967), illustrates the "balkanizing" of the city into contending "tribal domains" with a "garrison mentality." Jonathan Kozol's *Death at an Early Age: The Destruction of the Hearts and Minds of Negro Children in the Boston Public Schools* (Boston, 1970, 1985) told of his painful yet uplifting experiences teaching in racially segregated inferior schools and how he was fired for introducing a poem into the curriculum by black writer Langston Hughes. The black community, led by the NAACP and by leaders such as Mel King and

Royal Bolling, fought the racial injustice perpetrated by the city's public officials and by the obdurate state government. Judge W. Arthur Garrity's momentous *Boston School Decision* (Boston, 1974) ruled that the evidence was overwhelming that the Boston School Committee had "knowingly carried out a systematic program of segregation." A dissertation by J. Brian Sheehan, "The Boston School Integration Dispute: Social Change and Legal Maneuvers" (Ph.D. diss., Columbia University, 1981), provides a useful analysis, as do Emmett H. Buell, *School Desegregation and Defended Neighborhoods: The Boston Controversy* (Lexington, Mass., 1982); Robert A. Dentler and Marvin B. Scott, *Schools on Trial: An Inside Account of the Boston Desegregation Case* (Cambridge, 1981); and George Metcalf, *From Little Rock to Boston: The History of School Desegregation* (Westport, Conn., 1983).

Judge Garrity's busing order was not the product of paternalistic Yankee elites, but of suburban assimilated Irish. In "All in the Family: The Dilemmas of Busing and the Conflict of Values" (Formisano and Burns, *Boston, 1700-1980*, p. 245), J. Anthony Lukas theorized that the middle-class Irish repudiated the tarnished spoils-system politics of city hall for a new sense of regional politics based upon social responsibility. "Garrity is, of course, quite as Irish as most fourth-generation Irish Americans," declares Lukas. "His style is not so much Yankee as middle-class, the assimilationist mode of countless immigrant families who have made it into mainstream America." For the impact of the busing crisis on Boston family life, and on the role of the *Boston Globe*, see Lukas, *Common Ground: A Turbulent Decade in the Lives of Three American Families* (New York, 1985) and "The Siege of Morrissey Boulevard" (*New England Monthly*, 2 [August 1985]: 27-37, 76-81).

The working-class inner-city Irish, led by Louise Day Hicks and an organization known as ROAR, reacted to Garrity's decision with demonstrations and then with violence. The members of the group, Restore Our Alienated Rights, vowed: "I will not pledge allegiance to the Court Order of the United States, or to the dictatorship for which it stands, one law, under Garrity . . . with liberty and justice for none." Alan Lupo's detailed *Liberty's Chosen Home: The Politics of Violence in Boston* (Boston, 1977) chronicles the agonizing and vacillating actions taken by the Kevin White administration to protect public safety in the city. Daniel J. Friedman's *White Militancy in Boston: A Reconsideration of Marx and Weber* (Lexington, Mass., 1973) provides another perspective on the episode. But the issues were beyond the control of the mayor and the Boston police. Finally, federal marshalls were called into Boston to carry out a U.S. Federal District Court desegregation order promulgated because of a 1954 Supreme Court decision.

One way or another, the entire metropolitan community and the nation were somehow involved in the Boston school busing controversy. The grim findings of the U.S. Commission on Civil Rights report, *Desegregating the Boston Public Schools* (Washington, D.C., 1975), further demonstrated the intransigence of the Boston School Committee. Besides the School Committee, the report accused the Boston School Department, Mayor White, the Boston Police Department, the Boston Patrolmen's Benevolent Association, Boston's social service agencies, and the municipal court system of contributing to community defiance of Judge Garrity's decision. However, the blame extended beyond the city's limits: the area's religious leaders of all denominations, the metropolitan business community, the region's institutions of higher learning, the media (local and national), and the federal executive branch, including President Gerald Ford, all were cited for failing to act effectively to carry out the law of the land. A case in point, the school desegregation issue of Boston could not be confined to the artificial and fixed political boundaries of one city, because it was the product of an urbanized, interrelated society.

It should therefore be apparent that we must broaden our perspective of Massachusetts history to include the pervasive theme of urbanization. Yet much of the historical literature devoted to the state falls far short of this goal. Amid the profusion of specialized studies of the Bay State's history, one cannot find a single volume that tackles the general topic of modern urban Massachusetts. Similarly, one searches in vain for up-to-date monographs on municipal politics or even straightforward narrative accounts of major Massachusetts cities in the twentieth century. Another major omission is the absence of a religious history of the century. Aside from officially authorized works and biographies, we know next to nothing about the pivotal role played by the Catholic church in the state's recent past. In this area, Donna Merwick's *Boston's Priests, 1848-1910: A Study of Social and Intellectual Change* (Cambridge, 1973) is the only valuable and insightful work. The standard volume, commissioned by the church, is Robert Lord et al., *History of the Archdiocese of Boston*, 3 vols. (Boston, 1945). For portraits of Catholic prelates, the reader should see J. H. Cutler, *Cardinal Cushing of Boston* (New York, 1970); Joseph Dever, *Cushing of Boston: A Candid Portrait* (Boston, 1965); and John H. Fenton, *Salt of the Earth: An Informal Profile of Richard Cardinal Cushing* (New York, 1965). On Cardinal William Henry O'Connell, the works include O'Connell's autobiography, *Recollections of Seventy Years* (Boston, 1934); Dorothy G. Wayman, *Cardinal O'Connell of Boston* (New York, 1955); and Robert O'Leary, "Brahmins and Bullyboys: William Cardinal O'Connell and Massachusetts Politics" (*Historical Journal of Massachusetts*, 10 [January 1982]: 3-17). On Bishop John Bernard Fitzpatrick, the best study is Thomas O'Connor's *Fitzpatrick's Boston, 1846-1866* (Boston, 1984). Also useful is Kenneth Underwood, *Protestant and Catholic: Religion and Social Interaction in an Industrial Community* (Boston, 1957).

The list of significant but ignored subjects in the context of modern Massachusetts' urbanization should be of great concern: women's history, family history, class and social history, institutional and cultural history, ethnic and racial history, and environmental history; all beckon the attention of the professional scholar trained in urban studies. To discover the vital essence of modern metropolitan society necessitates full acknowledgement of the totality of Massachusetts' transformation into an urban commonwealth.

NOTES

1. Henry Adams, *The Education of Henry Adams: An Autobiography* (Boston, 1918), p. 240.

2. *The WPA Guide to Massachusetts* (Boston, 1937; reprint, New York, 1983), p. 50.

3. Hans Blumenfeld, "The Modern Metropolis," *Cities: A Scientific American Book* (New York, 1966), p. 41; Kingsley Davis, "The Urbanization of the Human Population," ibid., p. 5.

4. Francis X. Blouin, *The Boston Region, 1810–1850: A Study of Urbanization* (Ann Arbor, 1980), p. xii.

5. Robert W. Eisenmenger, *The Dynamics of Growth in New England's Economy, 1870–1964* (Middletown, Conn., 1967), pp. 60, 63, 75.

6. Alex Keyssar, "Social Change in Massachusetts in the Gilded Age," *Massachusetts in the Gilded Age; Selected Essays*, ed. Jack Tager and John W. Ifkovic (Amherst, 1985), p. 135.

7. Oscar Handlin, *Boston's Immigrants: A Study in Acculturation*, rev. and enl. ed. (New York, 1972), p. 82.

8. Sam Bass Warner, Jr., *Streetcar Suburbs: The Process of Growth in Boston, 1870–1900* (Cambridge, 1962), pp. 164–65.

9. Stephan Thernstrom, *The Other Bostonians: Poverty and Progress in the American Metropolis, 1880–1970* (Cambridge, 1973), p. 73.

10. Keyssar, "Social Change," p. 145.

11. Leslie G. Ainley, *Boston Mahatma* (Boston, 1949), p. 13; James Michael Curley, *I'd Do It Again* (Englewood Cliffs, N.J., 1957), p. 7.

12. John Stack, *International Conflict in an American City: Boston's Irish, Italians, and Jews, 1935–1944* (Westport, Conn., 1979), p. 24.

13. Jon C. Teaford, *The Unheralded Triumph: City Government in America, 1870–1900* (Baltimore, 1984), pp. 311–12.

14. R. C. Estall, *New England: A Study in Industrial Adjustment* (New York, 1966), p. 9.

15. A. A. Bright, ed., *The Economic State of New England: Report of the Committee of New England of the National Planning Association*, 2 vols. (New Haven, 1954), I, p. 10.

16. *Boston Globe*, May 1, 1984.

17. Warner, *Streetcar Suburbs*, p. 165.

18. Elizabeth H. Pleck, *Black Migration and Poverty: Boston, 1865–1900* (New York, 1979), pp. 7–8.

19. Thernstrom, *The Other Bostonians*, p. 194.

20. Malcolm X, *Autobiography of Malcolm X* (New York, 1964), p. 40.

21. Michael Conzen and George K. Lewis, *Boston: A Geographical Portrait* (Cambridge, 1976), p. 38.

8

WOMEN IN MASSACHUSETTS HISTORY BEFORE 1920

MARY J. OATES

ANY STUDY OF women in Massachusetts must of necessity be selective, not only in terms of time, but also with regard to issues, groups, and individuals considered. Certainly, in many respects their experiences reflect those of women in other parts of the country. But in a number of ways Massachusetts women faced unusual challenges resulting from evolving political, religious, economic, and educational institutions in the state as well as from its dominant civic and cultural traditions and values. These factors, in turn, strongly affected their responses and helped form unique elements in their contributions to its collective life and welfare. Traditional histories of Massachusetts have largely neglected half its population, but recent research by demographers as well as by social and economic historians, when considered with the writings of the women themselves, represents the beginning of a more comprehensive and balanced literature on the place and impact of women in its history. As yet, much of this work is found in dissertations and journal articles.

The standard reference works on outstanding individual women in the state continue to be Edward T. James and Janet Wilson James, eds., *Notable American Women, 1607-1950*, 3 vols. (Cambridge, 1971), and its companion volume, Barbara Sicherman and Carol Hurd Green, eds., *Notable American Women: The Modern Period* (Cambridge, 1980). Of over 1,800 entries in these volumes, 14 percent were women who were born and lived in Massachusetts or women who, although not born in the state, spent a substantial part of their lives there. Each article in these volumes indicates the major writings and achievements of each woman, and brief bibliographies, including manuscript sources, are provided.

There is no general bibliography limited to Massachusetts women, but Jill K. Conway's *The Female Experience in Eighteenth- and Nineteenth-Century Amer-*

ica: A Guide to the History of American Women (New York, 1982) is extremely valuable, since many of the works cited deal with Massachusetts women, and the author's essays are both authoritative and sensitive. Another useful bibliography is Janet Wilson James' *Changing Ideas about Women in the United States* (New York, 1981; reprint of Ph.D. diss., Radcliffe College, 1954).

Published and unpublished materials on Massachusetts women figure prominently in the holdings of several libraries in the state. Of special interest are the Schlesinger Library at Radcliffe College and the Sophia Smith Collection at Smith College, whose holdings are cataloged in *The History of Women in America: Catalogs of the Books, Manuscripts, and Pictures of the Arthur and Elizabeth Schlesinger Library*, 10 vols. (Boston, 1983), and *The Author, Subject, and Manuscript Catalogs of the Sophia Smith Collection*, 7 vols. (Boston, 1983). Significant materials may be found also at the Boston Public Library and at the American Antiquarian Society in Worcester.

Most colonial writers, when they discussed women at all, focused on female challenges to their subordinate position within the Puritan church. John Winthrop (*Journal: History of New England, 1630-1649*, vol. 1 [New York: 1908]) surveys the rise of the Antinomians and attempts to vindicate the church trial and excommunication of Anne Hutchinson. Her civil trial is recounted by Thomas Hutchinson (*The History of the Colony of Massachusetts Bay*, 2nd ed., vol. 2, appendix [London, 1760]). Lyle Koehler ("The Case of the American Jezebels: Anne Hutchinson and Female Agitation during the Years of Antinomian Turmoil, 1636-1640," *William and Mary Quarterly*, 31 [1974]: 55-78) challenges the long-standing contention of writers like Peter Oliver (*The Puritan Commonwealth, An Historical Review of the Puritan Government in Massachusetts in its Civil and Ecclesiastical Relations . . .* [Boston, 1856]) and Emery Battis (*Saints and Sectaries: Anne Hutchinson and the Antinomian Controversy in the Massachusetts Bay Colony* [Chapel Hill, 1962]) that Hutchinson's unorthodox behavior resulted from a lack of male spiritual direction and from her psychological instability. Koehler's cohesive study argues that her defenders and critics alike have emphasized the theology of the Antinomian controversy to the neglect of its critical significance as a social movement. Koehler concludes that the subordinate domain assigned Puritan women in home and society aroused a profound dissatisfaction in many, and therefore Hutchinson's aggressive struggle for equality within antinomianism presented an attractive model for her numerous supporters.

Ben Barker-Benfield ("Anne Hutchinson and the Puritan Attitude toward Women," *Feminist Studies*, 1 [1972]) argues perceptively that John Winthrop viewed Hutchinson as a sexual threat and that male subordination of Puritan women was generated by the psychological insecurity accompanying rapid societal change. J. F. Maclear ("Anne Hutchinson and the Mortalist Heresy," *New England Quarterly*, 54 [1981]) discounts such conclusions as modern versions of older "naively feminist" Hutchinson biographies, maintaining that Hutchinson's theological arguments at her church trial, particularly her denial of immortality of the soul, should be given more attention. Since the survival of society would be threatened if the most powerful inducement to moral living disappeared, ministers and magistrates quite logically moved swiftly and forcefully to suppress Hutchinson. But other outspoken women soon appeared in the state. In 1655 Quakers Mary Fisher, Anne Austin, and Mary Dyer commenced preaching the feared doctrine of sexual equality in Boston and, like Hutchinson, were viewed as social threats. The best source on Quaker women in the state, George Bishop's *New England Judged* (London, England, 1661), is supplemented by Mabel R. Brailsford's *Quaker Women, 1650–1690* (London, 1915) and G. Andrews Moriarty's "The True Story of Mary Dyer" (*New England Historical and Genealogical Register*, 104 [1950]). The significance of social factors in explaining the challenge of these women to civil order and hierarchy in colonial Massachusetts is clearly revealed by Koehler's data. While in the early years of the Massachusetts settlement under 2 percent of those brought before the General Court were women, by the late 1630s, immediately after the Hutchinson case, the figure stood at 6.7 percent and climbed to 9.4 percent in the 1640s. Like Hutchinson, many of these women were Antinomians.

The origins and effects of the witch trials that began in Massachusetts in the mid-seventeenth century have long been the subject of scholarly investigation. Marion L. Starkey (*The Devil in Massachusetts: A Modern Inquiry into the Salem Witch Trials* [New York, 1949]) chooses to emphasize collective hysteria among the young girls involved, while Paul Boyer and Stephen Nissenbaum (*Salem Possessed: The Social Origins of Witchcraft* [Cambridge, 1974]) give considerable attention to the significance of social and political events in their discussion. John Demos' impressive *Entertaining Satan: Witchcraft and the Culture of Early New England* (New York, 1982) uses psychology as well as social history to interpret the phenomenon. He rejects open sexual conflict as an explanation on the grounds that both men and women clearly understood their respective spheres. Nonetheless, women charged with witchcraft tended to be more assertive and unconventional than average, and in that sense they may have posed a challenge to conventional sexual roles. For example, the two exceptions Demos concedes, Anne Hutchinson and Anne Hibbins, openly moved away from women's designated sphere and questioned male authority. Mary Beth Norton ("The Evolution of White Women's Experience in Early America," *American Historical Review*, 89 [1984]) offers a perceptive assessment of how danger to social order and the welfare of future generations, perceived in Hutchinson's atypical behavior, evoked extreme response. Norton's contribution is supported by Carol F. Karlsen ("The Devil in the Shape of a Woman: The Witch in Seventeenth Century New England" [Ph.D. diss., Yale University, 1980]), who argues that the witchcraft phenomenon declined after it had served its purpose, that is, when women had once again become less aggressive and outspoken.

The state's white women differed from their counterparts in other early colonies not only in the extensive influence of the Puritan church in their lives, but also in the highly patriarchal structure of the Massachusetts family. (Very little is known about Indian women in Massachusetts. Mary Rowlandson, *The Narrative of the Captivity and Restoration of Mrs. Mary Rowlandson*, ed. Frederick L. Weis [Boston, 1930], offers some limited perspectives on their lives, based upon observations made in 1675 or 1676.) We are given valuable insights into the daily activities and religious experiences of white female colonists in a collection of letters from women to members of the Winthrop family (*Winthrop Papers*, 1, 5th series, Massachusetts Historical Society). Melville R. Cobbledick ("The Status of Women in Puritan New England, 1630-1660: A Demographic Study" [Ph.D. diss., Yale University, 1936]) provides a pioneer effort at systematic social analysis of women's place in colonial society, but the classic study of the close interaction of religion and domestic life within the colonial family remains Edmund S. Morgan's excellent study *The Puritan Family: Religion and Domestic Relations in Seventeenth-Century New England* (New York, 1944).

Despite the dearth of leadership opportunities for them within the Massachusetts church, women continued to join at high rates. Gerald F. Moran and Maris A. Vinovskis ("The Puritan Family and Religion: A Critical Reappraisal," *William and Mary Quarterly*, 39 [1982]: 29-63) reveal that although women accounted for 45 to 56 percent of church membership in urban centers like Boston, Charlestown, and Salem in the 1630s, by the 1690s the proportion stood at 70 to 76 percent, an increase they attribute to ministerial efforts to consolidate their authority by rendering all laity, not simply women, silent. Men were provoked to retreat from organized religion in favor of secular pursuits in which they could exert more authority. Mary Maples Dunn ("Saints and Sinners: Congregational and Quaker Women in the Early Colonial Period," *American Quarterly*, 30 [1978]) also advances our understanding of why this gender differential persisted over time. Women accounted for 71 percent of admissions to the Congregational church in the 1750s, and very high rates were sustained during the Second Great Awakening of 1780-1830.

Laurel Ulrich ("'Vertuous Women Found': New England Ministerial Literature, 1668-1735," *American Quarterly*, 28 [1976]) endeavors to analyze the position of women in the church in an innovative investigation of ministerial addresses and sermons. She concludes that the absence of sex-specific virtues in this literature indicates that women enjoyed equality in the spiritual realm, if nowhere else, restricted only by their role as childbearers. Margaret Masson ("The Typology of the Female Model for the Regenerate: Puritan Preaching, 1690-1730," *Signs*, 2 [1976]) also finds in Puritan doctrine limited support for sexual equality, although she acknowledges that reliance upon prescriptive literature does not permit firm resolution of the question of women's spiritual status. Lonna M. Malmsheimer ("New England Funeral Sermons and Changing Attitudes Toward Women, 1672-1792," Ph.D. diss., University of Minnesota, 1973) proposes that women's growing representation among church members resulted in some expansion of traditional understandings of their spiritual status and power, since the decline in the political power of the church by the late eighteenth century forced ministers eager to preserve influence to rely more heavily upon their female congregations for support. Barbara Easton's "Women, Religion, and the Family: Revivalism as an Indicator of Social Change in Early New England" (Ph.D. diss., University of California, Berkeley, 1975) employs early conversion testimonies to suggest that although women did not react openly against their subordinate position in the church until the mid-nineteenth century, growing numbers were expressing frustration about it. While in 1750 female and male testimonies resembled each other and were largely confined to expressions of remorse for sin, in succeeding decades, unlike men, women confessed more often to rebellion against God, the Scripture, and the ministers. Lyle Koehler's absorbing monograph, *A Search for Power: The "Weaker Sex" in Seventeenth-Century New England* (Urbana, Ill., 1980), argues for considerable caution in drawing conclusions about women's situation within the church until more research is undertaken on the behavioral responses of churchgoers, male as well as female, to clerical addresses and sermons.

John Demos' fine study *A Little Commonwealth: Family Life in Plymouth Colony* (New York, 1970) and Philip J. Greven, Jr.'s *Four Generations: Population, Land, and Family in Colonial Andover, Massachusetts* (Ithaca, N.Y., 1970), although not focused on women per se, provide useful depictions of colonial domestic life. Older, heavily descriptive studies by Alice Morse Earle (*Home Life in Colonial Days* [New York, 1898]); Margaret Winthrop (*Women of Colonial and Revolutionary Times* [New York, 1895]); Alice Clark (*Working Life of Women in the Seventeenth Century* [New York, 1919]); and Carl Holliday (*Woman's Life in Colonial Days* [Williamstown, 1968, reprint of 1922 edition]) deal more directly with women's experience.

In recent years, scholars have employed more innovative approaches in analyzing women's position within the household. Norton's "Evolution of White Women's Experience in America," for example, explores in depth why the expected subordination of Massachusetts wives to their husbands engendered tensions between the sexes. A major contribution to our understanding of women's experience is the excellent demographic and social study by Daniel Scott Smith ("Parental Power and Marriage Patterns: An Analysis of Historical Trends in Hingham, Massachusetts," *Journal of Marriage and the Family*, 35 [1973]), who traces a gradual erosion of parental control over daughters' lives. While in the early colonial period women could expect marriages to be arranged by fathers, after 1750 more daughters remained permanently single, and those who married were less apt to marry in birth order. These developments, according to Smith, indicate growing female autonomy in marriage decisions. Smith's dissertation ("Population, Family, and Society in Hingham, Massachusetts, 1635-1880," Ph.D. diss., University of California, Berkeley, 1973) incorporates valuable long-term data on Massachusetts family life.

The popular perception that widowhood brought few hardships to widows in colonial Massachusetts because they tended to be wealthier than single women and thus able to remarry quickly and return to a traditional family structure has been strongly criticized by Alexander Keyssar ("Widowhood in Eighteenth-Century Massachusetts: A Problem in the History of the Family," *Perspectives in American History*, 8 [1974]), who makes effective use of tax and court records to study sixty Woburn couples married between 1701 and 1710. He found that, on the average, women married at a later age than has generally been believed and outlived their husbands. Few remarried, and those without family became the responsibility of the community. Other dimensions of this question are addressed by Gary B. Nash ("The Failure of Female Factory Labor in Colonial Boston," *Labor History*, 20 [1979]) in an intriguing description of a futile effort by Boston elders to remove destitute widows from the poverty rolls by hiring them for a linen factory. Douglas Lamar Jones ("The Strolling Poor: Transiency in Eighteenth-Century Massachusetts," *Journal of Social History*, 7 [1975]) examines Essex County records to conclude that single women appear to have been just as likely to be impoverished as single men.

George Elliott Howard's early *History of Matrimonial Institutions* (Chicago, 1904), which reviewed in depth the changing marriage and divorce laws in colonial New England, has been supplemented by several excellent recent studies that merit attention. Seventeenth-century marriage and divorce laws have been the subject of careful analysis in D. Kelly Weisberg's "'Under Greet Temptations Heer': Women and Divorce in Puritan Massachusetts" (*Feminist Studies*, 2 [1975]). And eighteenth-century data have been skillfully mined by Nancy Cott in two essays, "Eighteenth-Century Family and Social Life Revealed in Massachusetts Divorce Records" (*Journal of Social History*, 10 [1976]) and "Divorce and the Changing Status of Women in Eighteenth-Century Massachusetts" (*William and Mary Quarterly*, 33 [1976]: 586-614), which provide superb examples of interdisciplinary research in family and women's history. Although women sued more often than men, Cott reports that before 1773 men frequently charged adultery while women rarely did. After the Revolution, judges honored Puritan doctrine on adultery more strictly, and women were more likely to be granted divorces on the same grounds as men. But since in desertion and cruelty suits women had greater success in winning separations than divorces, many remained legally and economically bound to their husbands. The place of the Massachusetts married woman remained legally ancillary to that of her husband, and in this regard the state's women had fewer rights than women in other colonies. C. Dallett Hemphill's ambitious review of court records ("Women in Court: Sex-Role Differentiation in Salem, Massachusetts, 1636 to 1683," *William and Mary Quarterly*, 39 [1982]: 164-175) strengthens James K. Somerville's conclusion that "before 1720 Salem wives and mothers generally exercised more control over landed property than was the case between 1721 and 1750" ("The Salem (Mass.) Woman in the Home, 1660-1770," *Eighteenth-Century Life*, 1 [1974]). N. E. H. Hull ("Female Felons: Women and Serious Crime in the Superior Courts of Massachusetts, 1673-1774" [Ph.D. diss., Columbia University, 1980]) sees some modification in societal views of women after 1650 in the fact that relatively fewer were charged with violent crimes and relatively more with thefts and burglaries. As prosecutions for witchcraft and adultery declined, women were less often singled out as public sinners and scapegoats.

While openly feminist statements were rare in mid-eighteenth-century Massachusetts, one cannot conclude that women were unconcerned about women's progress. Not unusual were businesswomen like Bostonian Elizabeth Murray Smith, whose views on the education of her nieces are sensitively explored by Mary Beth Norton ("A Cherished Spirit of Independence: The Life of an Eighteenth-Century Boston Businesswoman," (*Women of America*, ed. Carol R. Berkin and Mary Beth Norton [Boston, 1979]). That Smith was not unique is confirmed in the experiences of Massachusetts women recounted in Elizabeth W. Anthony Dexter's survey volume *Colonial Women of Affairs: A Study of Women in Business and the Professions in America before 1776* (Boston, 1924).

As early nineteenth-century industrialization took men from farming to wage work, the home was increasingly exalted as a safe refuge from a troubled and secular society, and the model woman became the lady at home. By the 1830s a number of Massachusetts women had taken the lead among editors and writers of prescriptive literature, women's magazines, and sentimental novels that aimed to convince readers that maternal and wifely duties were central to rather than part of their lives. Lydia Maria Child (*The Mother's Book* [Boston, 1831] and *The Frugal Housewife* [Boston, 1829]) was probably the best known of the group, which included also Sarah Josepha Hale and Catharine Sedgwick. Kirk Jeffrey ("Marriage, Career, and Feminine Ideology in Nineteenth Century America: Reconstructing the Marital Experience of Lydia Maria Child," *Feminist Studies*, 2 [1975]) expands our understanding of this unusual woman who exercised national influence in establishing women as models of morality and virtue and guardians of the family. According to Mary Kelley ("A Woman Alone: Catharine Maria Sedgwick's Spinsterhood in Nineteenth Century America," *New England Quarterly*, 51 [1978]), the collective message was intended for all women, as Sedgwick advocated that single women also assume the role of virtuous wives and model mothers in a somewhat wider community sphere.

Such intense concentration on the home produced some beneficial effects. In a rich and absorbing study, Nancy Cott (*The Bonds of Womanhood: "Woman's Sphere" in New England, 1780-1835* [New Haven, 1977]) argues that it fostered friendship ties among middle-class women, permitting them an informal but socially accepted forum on matters within the purview of female influence. Daniel Scott Smith ("Family Limitation, Sexual Control, and Domestic Feminism in Victorian America," (*A Heritage of Her Own*, ed. Nancy Cott and Elizabeth Pleck [New York, 1979]) analyzes Hingham marriages between 1820 and 1860 to document skillfully that women in this period were acquiring and using significant domestic authority in such critical areas as family size.

The uncritical but factually accurate essay by Ednah D. Cheney ("The Women of Boston," *Memorial History of Boston*, vol. 4, ed. Justin Winsor [Boston, 1881]), when read with her *Reminiscences* (Boston, 1902), provides a comprehensive review of local middle-class female organizations and the philanthropic causes they chose to support. As early as 1790 women had begun to organize into benevolent societies, thereby extending their maternal concerns beyond the home. Peter Holloran ("Boston's Wayward Children: Social Services for Homeless Children, 1800-1930" [Ph.D. diss., Boston University, 1982]) advances considerably our appreciation of the key role of the state's women in the area of child care. And Keith Melder's interpretation ("Ladies Bountiful: Organized Women's Benevolence in Early Nineteenth-Century America," *New York History*, 48 [1967]) puts in broader perspective the impact of one such pioneer organization, the Boston Female Society for Missionary Purposes, which was widely imitated by other women's groups nationally. The Boston Female Asylum, founded in 1800 by Hannah Morgan Stillman and her friends, was another such model institution. Its early development is well described in Abby L. Wade's informative *Reminiscences of the Boston Female Asylum* (Boston, 1844). Susan Lynne Porter ("The Benevolent Asylum—Image and Reality: The Care and Training of Female Orphans in Boston, 1800-1840" [Ph.D. diss., Boston University, 1984]) affirms that this asylum was an enlightened institution for its day, exhibiting an advanced and distinctively feminine approach to child care. A fascinating and insightful essay on the rise and decline of one of a number of women's associations in the state modeled on the Boston Female Asylum is given by Carol S. Lasser ("A 'Pleasingly Oppressive' Burden: The Transformation of Domestic Service and Female Charity in Salem, 1800-1840," *Essex Institute Historical Collections*, 116 [1980]). The establishment of domestic service as an appropriate and respectable employment for orphan girls is investigated in Lasser's "Mistress, Maid, and Market: The Transformation of Domestic Service in New England, 1790-1870" (Ph.D. diss., Harvard University, 1982).

Although women's charities were progressive in many respects, their policies tended to be constrained by class, religious, and ethnic attitudes of members. For example, Barbara M. Hobson ("Sex in the Marketplace: Prostitution in an American City, Boston, 1820-1880" [Ph.D. diss., Boston University, 1982]) presents evidence of strong hostility toward Irish Catholics in the New England Female Moral Reform Society. Still denied admission to the Boston Female Asylum in 1844 were black, Catholic, and illegitimate girls as well as those with criminal relatives. Porter plausibly defends asylum policy on Catholic girls, maintaining that it was in place only after 1825 in response to Bishop Benedict Fenwick's objections to the Protestant weekly worship and anti-Catholic textbooks. Nonetheless, his stand, when considered with the clearly discriminatory admission policies of many Massachusetts charitable agencies, resulted in early development of separate institutions for Catholic children where, as in Protestant establishments, women played critical roles. Holloran ("Boston's Wayward Children") is one of the few scholars to give serious attention to the philanthropic work of Catholic women in the state. He considers, for example, reasons for the early development of St. Vincent's Female Orphan Asylum in Boston, an institution founded in 1832 and heavily subsidized thereafter by the Sisters of Charity. Catholic sisters became more visible and numerically important in Massachusetts as its immigrant population increased after 1850. Mary J. Oates ("Organized Voluntarism: The Catholic Sisters in Massachusetts, 1870-1940," *Women in American Religion*, ed. Janet Wilson James [Philadelphia, 1980]) explores the charitable and educational works of these women as well as evolving attitudes of church and society toward them.

A compelling study by Anne M. Boylan ("Women in Groups: An Analysis of Women's Benevolent Organizations in New York and Boston, 1797-1840," *Journal of American History*, 71 [1984]) evaluates membership in eleven Protestant women's societies established in Boston and proposes that administrative experience acquired in benevolent groups organized before 1830 did not impel women to the reform and political action that marked later societies. This conclusion challenges the traditional view that the female benevolent societies served as direct antecedents to the reform societies of the 1840s. Boylan explains differences between benevolent and reform groups in the degree of heterogeneity within their respective memberships, with reform societies like the Boston Female Anti-Slavery Society far more diversified in religious affiliation and social class than the typical benevolent society. Reform society members tended to be more liberal and aggressive in approach, speaking before public audiences in support of secular causes that often reached far beyond church and home.[1] Such features of reform women are revealed sharply in the memoirs of Maria Weston Chapman (*Ten Years of Experience: Ninth Annual Report of Boston Anti-Slavery Society* [Boston, 1842]) and in Weston correspondence probed by Margaret Munsterberg ("The Weston Sisters and 'The Boston Controversy'," *Boston Public Library Quarterly*, 10 [1958]). Alma Lutz' monograph, *Crusade for Freedom: Women of the Antislavery Movement* (Boston, 1968), expands our awareness of the relative importance of Massachusetts women among abolitionist leaders, as does Blanche Glassman Hersh (*The Slavery of Sex: Feminist Abolitionists in America* [Urbana, Ill., 1978]). In Hersh's detailed study of fifty-one key abolitionists, one of every five has Massachusetts roots.

At the same time that a cult of domesticity was developing among middle-class women, textile manufacturers were beginning to seek female workers for new factories. By the 1820s, Massachusetts mill girls represented the first large group of industrial wage-earning women in America. Their recruitment and labor force experience are examined in informative studies by Pamela Jean Nickless ("Changing Productivity and the Utilizing of Native Women Workers in the American Cotton Textile Industry, 1825-1860" [Ph.D. diss., Purdue University, 1976)] and Mary Alice Feldblum ("The Formation of the First Factory Labor Force in the New England Cotton Textile Industry, 1800-1848" [Ph.D. diss., New School for Social Research, 1977]). Elfrieda McCauley ("Some Early Women Librarians in New England," *Wilson Library Bulletin*, 51 [1977], and "The New England Mill Girls: Feminine Influence in the Development of Public Libraries in New England, 1820-1860" [D.L.S. diss., Columbia University, 1971]) focuses on some of the non-pecuniary benefits of local mill towns to young women from isolated farms, including opportunities to attend Sabbath

Schools and evening lectures and courses and to use Sabbath School libraries. Social activities enjoyed by operatives in the boardinghouses are considered by McCauley to have fostered a community spirit that was analogous to that which developed later in residence halls at the women's colleges.

Several books and anthologies incorporate primary materials to give us the words of mill workers themselves. Among the best are Claudia L. Bushman's *"A Good Poor Man's Wife": Being a Chronicle of Harriet Hanson Robinson and Her Family in Nineteenth-Century New England* (Hanover, N.H., 1981); Lucy Larcom's *A New England Girlhood* (Boston, 1889); and *The Lowell Offering: Writings by New England Mill Women, 1840-1845*, ed. Benita Eisler (New York, 1977). While we acquire a rich appreciation of mill labor and life from the worker's perspective as well as an understanding of the factors that drew women to mills in the first place, these writings by early operatives tend to present an exaggeratedly positive image of many features of the mill experience. More balanced are later efforts well represented in Philip S. Foner, ed., *The Factory Girls: A Collection of Writings on Life and Struggles in the New England Factories of the 1840s* (Urbana, Ill., 1977). Thomas Dublin's substantial contribution as editor, *Farm to Factory: Women's Letters, 1830-1860* (New York, 1981), gives a perspective account of mill life in the antebellum years.[2]

Publications by Massachusetts mill girls reflected a growing willingness to organize to protest wage reductions or unfair treatment. The Factory Girls' Association commenced in the 1830s, and in the next decade the *Voice of Industry* served as an effective forum for the more aggressive Female Reform Association led by Sarah Bagley. The achievements and weaknesses of this important labor organization are addressed by Christina Lynne Zwarg ("Woman as Wife or Worker: The Success and Failure of Feminism in the Lowell Female Labor Reform Association, 1845-1848," [M.A. thesis, Brown University, 1974]). Because their grievances centered on wages and working conditions, issues they shared with male workers, Barbara J. Harris (*Beyond Her Sphere: Women and the Professions in American History* [Westport, Conn., 1978]) portrays mill women of the 1830s and 1840s as only marginally influential in the development of a feminist awareness in the state. But since collective action by working-class women was taking place coincidentally with early feminist efforts, it seems more plausible to assume that the two movements affected each other. Of special interest are studies by Thomas Dublin ("Women Workers and the Study of Social Mobility," *Journal of Interdisciplinary History*, 9 [1979]); Carl Gersuny ("'A Devil in Petticoats' and Just Cause: Patterns of Punishment in Two New England Textile Factories," *Business History Review*, 50 [1976]); and Hannah Josephson (*The Golden Threads: New England's Mill Girls and Magnates* [New York, 1949]), which together provide convincing evidence that mill workers became increasingly sophisticated in organizing as women and workers. Laurie Nisonoff ("Bread and Roses: The Proletarianisation of Women Workers in New England Textile Mills, 1827-1848," *Historical Journal of Massachusetts*, 9 [1981]) and Thomas Dublin ("Women, Work, and Protest in Early Lowell Mills: 'The

Oppressing Hand of Avarice Would Enslave Us,'" *Labor History*, 16 [1975])
succeed in showing that the organization of mill work and housing joined with
homogeneity in sex, birthplace, and age of early operatives to permit the growth
among them of a collective spirit and lasting sensitivity to their rights as women.
Massachusetts women who left the mills for marriage or teaching carried lessons
from the experience to their local communities or to the West.

As more-vulnerable Irish women began to replace native women in the 1840s,
worker turnover in Massachusetts mills increased and organized action diminished.
Barbara Easton ("Industrialization and Femininity: A Case Study of Nineteenth-
Century New England," *Social Problems*, 23 [1976]) identifies as a consequence
of this change a widening disparity between the lifestyles of the urban Protestant
wife and the working-class wife. Thomas Dublin's perceptive analysis (*Women at
Work: The Transformation of Work and Community in Lowell, Massachusetts,
1826-1860* [New York, 1979]) concludes that the differential in wages paid
native-born and Irish women was due not to work experience or educational differences but to discrimination. Dublin's study and an earlier one by Ray Ginger
("Labor in a Massachusetts Cotton Mill, 1853-60," *Business Historical Society
Bulletin*, 28 [1954]) demonstrate that living expenses in Massachusetts mill
towns remained relatively low before 1860, a feature that benefited Irish workers,
many of whom lived with their parents, permitting them to save, on the average,
between 25 and 50 percent of their wages.

As manufacturing in the state expanded to other industries, women had
greater choice of occupation. Judith A. McGaw's welcome contribution ("'A
Good Place to Work.' Industrial Workers and Occupational Choice: The Case of
Berkshire Women," *Journal of Interdisciplinary History*, 10 [1979]) seeks
to explain the contrasting choices of native-born and Irish-born workers. In
Berkshire County in 1880, textile mills attracted relatively more Irish and
younger women than did paper mills. Although wages paid in paper mills were
20 percent less than in cotton mills, native women preferred them for their
shorter days, more flexible schedules, and fewer shutdowns. Of wives whose
husbands worked in textile mills, McGaw found over four-fifths not in the labor
force, a sharp contrast to the 50 percent figure for wives whose husbands were in
paper mills. Hasia Diner underscores and clarifies this cultural difference in her
thorough study of a relatively unexplored group heavily represented in the state's
labor force. Her *Erin's Daughters in America* (Baltimore, 1983) provides strong
evidence that although many worked outside the home, in general Irish wives
preferred not to do so. Important research by Tamara Hareven and Maris A.
Vinovskis ("Marital Fertility, Ethnicity, and Occupation in Urban Families: An
Analysis of South Boston and the South End in 1880," *Journal of Social History*,
8 [1975]) complements Diner's work, providing explanatory data on the significantly larger numbers of children born to Irish than to native-born wives.

Occupational mobility among Massachusetts factory women varied not only
according to their ethnic origins and marital status but also by the environment
and location of the workplace. Libby Zimmerman ("Women in the Economy: A

Case Study of Lynn, Massachusetts, 1760–1974" [Ph.D. diss., Brandeis University, 1977]) elaborates on these differences in an informative study of Lynn women, whom she reveals as confronting a deeply entrenched sexual division of labor that severely hampered their integration into the labor force and their upward mobility. Her arguments gain support from Mary H. Blewett ("The Union of Sex and Craft in the Haverhill Shoe Strike of 1895," *Labor History*, 20 [1979]), whose perceptive study adds to a growing literature on the experience of working-class women. Skilled female workers in Haverhill were far more class-conscious than Irish women workers of Lynn, a variation that Blewett explains, in part, by their being largely single and native-born. Keith Melder ("Women in the Shoe Industry: The Evidence from Lynn," *Essex Institute Historical Collections*, 115 [1979]) concurs with such findings, but at the same time calls for more basic research in this emerging area of investigation.

Not all women workers in the state were employed in manufacturing. Carroll D. Wright's *The Working Girls of Boston* (Boston, 1889) is a fine pioneer survey that displays the variety of occupations engaging nineteenth-century women. It is nicely complemented by the work of Mary E. Trueblood ("Social Statistics of Workingwomen," *Massachusetts Labor Bulletin*, 18 [1901]). Useful also in advancing awareness of the work experience of the many women in domestic service are Mary W. Dewson's "Hours of Labor in Domestic Service" and "Social Conditions in Domestic Service" (*Massachusetts Labor Bulletin*, 8 [1898]; 13 [1900]). A report of the Massachusetts Bureau of Statistics of Labor ("Trained and Supplemental Employees for Domestic Service," *Annual Report, 1906* [Boston, 1907]) presents data on these workers, most of whom were single and either immigrants or daughters of immigrants. A demographic study by Peter R. Uhlenberg ("A Study of Cohort Life Cycles: Cohorts of Native Born Massachusetts Women, 1830–1920," *Population Studies*, 23 [1969]) finds that, across time and location, a consistently higher proportion of foreign-born women in Massachusetts were single than their American-born counterparts. Diner (*Erin's Daughters in America*) maintains that Irish women, despite their high representation in the manufacturing labor force, preferred domestic service to factory work. Albert Gibbs Mitchell's "Irish Family Patterns in Nineteenth Century Ireland and Lowell, Massachusetts" (Ph.D. diss., Boston University, 1976) sheds some light on this distinctive feature of Irish workers. But domestic service was confining and low paying, and women of Irish origin moved away from it as soon as they could. David M. Katzman's comprehensive study *Seven Days a Week: Women and Domestic Service in Industrializing America* (New York, 1978) indicates that while in 1900 over half of the Irish-born women workers in Massachusetts were servants (excluding laundresses), only 11.2 percent of second-generation women were similarly employed.

Unlike white women, black women in Massachusetts, whether married or single, had few job options beyond domestic work before 1920. McGaw's survey, for example, discovered not one of sixty-eight Berkshire County mills willing to employ a black woman in 1880. Yet a disproportionate number of these women were obliged to work outside the home. A valuable paper by Elizabeth H. Pleck ("A Mother's Wages: Income Earning among Married Italian and Black Women, 1896-1911," in Cott and Pleck, *A Heritage of Her Own*) reveals that among Cambridge and Boston families, 44 percent of black wives were employed, in contrast to only 27 percent of Irish wives and 16 percent of Italian wives.

Studies by James Oliver Horton and Lois E. Horton (*Black Bostonians: Family Life and Community Struggle in the Antebellum North* [New York, 1979]) and Donald M. Jacobs ("A History of the Boston Negro from the Revolution to the Civil War" [Ph.D. diss., Boston University, 1968]) permit us to gain some limited perspective on the lives of black women in the state before 1860, and Elizabeth Pleck ("The Two-Parent Household: Black Family Structure in Late Nineteenth-Century Boston," *Journal of Social History*, 6 [1972]) addresses their post-war experiences with considerable insight. Life within the small upper-class black community in Boston is illuminated in a study by Adelaide C. Hill, "The Negro Upper Class in Boston—Its Development and Present Social Structure" (Ph.D. diss., Radcliffe College, 1952).

The traditional view of the black urban family as less stable than the white family is sharply challenged in Elizabeth Pleck's sophisticated work *Black Migration and Poverty: Boston, 1865-1900* (New York, 1979). Her conclusions are underscored by Holloran ("Boston's Wayward Children"), who argues that female-headed households were no more common within the black community in 1870 than among Irish immigrant Bostonians. Negative assessments of black family stability based, in part at least, on the disproportionate number of black children appearing on the rolls of state reform schools are rendered dubious by Holloran's discussion of the outright refusal of most private reform institutions to admit black children.

Black women endeavoring to enter professions met nearly insurmountable barriers for much of the period. Scholarly publications on them and, more generally, on influential black women in the state are, unfortunately, extremely sparse. One exception is a well-documented and intriguing study by Ruth Bogin of "Sarah Parker Remond: Black Abolitionist from Salem" (*Essex Institute Historical Collections*, 110 [1974]). Remond had been strongly influenced by the acclaimed Massachusetts black feminist and abolitionist, Maria W. Stewart, author of *Productions of Mrs. Maria W. Stewart* (Boston, 1835) and *Meditations from the Pen of Mrs. Maria W. Stewart* (Washington, D.C., 1879). The best bibliographical source on these and such other prominent black women of the state as Mary Eliza Mahoney, Maria Baldwin, and Josephine Ruffin at this time remains *Notable American Women, 1607-1950.*

Even though early opportunities in church and government were minimal and their status in the home subordinate, Massachusetts women had always disseminated ideas in written form. The serious female writer frequently encountered isolation, lack of encouragement, and obstacles from publisher or preacher. The early historian Hannah Adams (*A Memoir of Miss Adams Written by Herself, with Additional Notes by a Friend* [Boston, 1832]) describes such experiences vividly. Although Adams was the best known of early Massachusetts authors, there were many others, including Phillis Wheatley, Mercy Warren, Hannah Webster Foster, Elizabeth White, Judith Murray, and Sarah Morton, whose challenges as serious writers were shared by their nineteenth-century successors. Recent research by Karen A. Dandurand ("Why Dickinson Did Not Publish" [Ph.D. diss., University of Massachusetts, 1984]) and Marilyn E. Matis ("'We Demand the Flame': The Assembly of Emily Dickinson's Female Audience" [Ph.D. diss., State University of New York, Buffalo, 1983]) expands our appreciation of the state's finest poet. Matis concludes that the Amherst writer became so discouraged by editors and publishers that she abandoned them midway in her career, "publishing" her poems after 1865 only through letters to a group of female friends.[3]

The most numerous group of writers were those catering to popular tastes. Jacqueline Hornstein ("Literary History of New England Women Writers: 1630–1800" [Ph.D. diss., New York University, 1978]) describes their efforts as tending heavily before 1770 toward pious autobiography and thereafter to sentimental romance. It was often the atypical and successful woman of the world like Susanna Rowson, whose novels included the immensely popular *Charlotte Temple* (1791), or Sarah Josepha Hale, founder of *Ladies' Magazine* in 1828 and editor of *Godey's Lady's Book* from 1837 to 1877, who, in best-selling publications, urged on other women lives of purity and domesticity. Isabelle Webb Entrekin (*Sarah Josepha Hale and Godey's Lady's Book* [Philadelphia, 1946]) and Dorothy Weil (*In Defense of Woman: Susanna Rowson (1762-1824)* [University Park, Pa., 1976]) ably assess these influential women.

Nancy F. Cott's acclaimed study, *The Bonds of Womanhood*, maintains that the reassuring tone of these publications apparently comforted women readers as they strove to embody in their own persons the virtues of the ideal wife and mother. While most of this literature was poorly written, the best of the genre has been judged positively in that it depicted strong-willed female characters. Recent studies reveal that after the Civil War popular female novels began to exhibit, at least indirectly, a more feminist character. Christine Stansell's interpretive discussion ("Elizabeth Stuart Phelps: A Study in Female Rebellion," *Massachusetts Review*, 13 [1972]) extends a conventional biographical treatment of Phelps provided by Mary Angela Bennett (*Elizabeth Stuart Phelps* [Philadelphia, 1939]) by arguing, for example, that Phelps' best seller, *The Gates Ajar* (1868), displays frank disaffection for patriarchal religion. And while Louisa May Alcott has been depicted as strongly promoting woman's domestic sphere, Eugenia Kaledin ("Louisa May Alcott: Success and the Sorrow of Self-Denial," *Women's Studies*, 5 [1978]) argues convincingly that the financially straitened author was not writing her convictions, but only what people wanted to read, or as Alcott put it, "rubbishy tales, for they pay best." Sarah Elbert (*A Hunger for Home: Louisa May Alcott and "Little Women"* [Philadelphia, 1984]) presents her as a true feminist who tried to reconcile societal norms on women's place in the home with their efforts to achieve independent identities. Noteworthy biographies of

Alcott include those by Madeleine B. Stern (*Louisa May Alcott* [Norman, Okla., 1950]) and Martha Saxton (*Louisa May: A Modern Biography of Louisa May Alcott* [New York, 1977]). Of primary importance also is *Louisa May Alcott: Her Life, Letters and Journals*, ed. Ednah D. Cheney (Boston, 1889).

Two of the state's best writers in this period, Sarah Orne Jewett and Mary Wilkins Freeman, have frequently been dismissed by such critics as Ronald L. Lycette ("Diminishing Circumferences: Feminine Responses in Fiction to New England Decline" [Ph.D. diss., Purdue University, 1970]) as local-color regionalists imprisoned by their upper-class backgrounds. Unable to deal with immigration, poverty, and industrial unrest, they concentrated on light, feminine subjects and their own "genteel tradition." Recent scholarship by Josephine Donovan ("A Woman's Vision of Transcendence: A New Interpretation of the Works of Sarah Orne Jewett," *Massachusetts Review*, 21 [1980]) and Laraine Flemming ("Women of More Than Local Color" [Ph.D. diss., State University of New York, Buffalo, 1983]) strongly disputes such conclusions, postulating rather that Jewett and Freeman had progressed well beyond most of their contemporaries by treating revolutionary issues in simple, familiar settings, a technique which ensured that their ideas would reach many women. A well-focused collection of essays on Jewett's work is Gwen L. Nagel, ed., *Critical Essays on Sarah Orne Jewett* (Boston, 1984). The annotated biography of Freeman by Edward Foster (*Mary E. Wilkins Freeman* [New York, 1956]) has been supplemented by Abigail Ann Hamblen's *The New England Art of Mary E. Wilkins Freeman* (Amherst, 1966) and by Perry D. Westbrook's *Mary Wilkins Freeman* (New York, 1967).

A few early women authors spoke directly to the issue of women's position in society. Constantia [Judith Sargent Murray] ("On the Equality of the Sexes," *Massachusetts Magazine*, 2 [1790]), for example, argued astutely that the best route to equality for women was improved intellectual training. Barbara Welter ("Mystical Feminist: Margaret Fuller, A Woman of the Nineteenth Century," *Dimity Convictions: The American Woman in the Nineteenth Century* [Athens, Ohio, 1976]) depicts Margaret Fuller as the single most influential American woman writing during the antebellum period. And Paula Blanchard (*Margaret Fuller: From Transcendentalism to Revolution* [Cambridge, 1978]) concludes that, despite its exhortatory style, Fuller's *Women in the Nineteenth Century* (Boston, 1845) contributed enormously to the development of a feminist perspective in America, serving as the manual for the 1848 Women's Rights Convention. Like Murray, Fuller advocated better education as the single most promising avenue to female independence. Studies by Marie Maguire McAllister ("The Educational Experience of Margaret Fuller" [Ph.D. diss., Boston College, 1984]) and Roberta J. Russell ("Margaret Fuller: The Growth of a Woman Writer" [Ph.D. diss., University of Connecticut, 1983]) add to a growing literature on this remarkable woman and consider the means she employed to stir Massachusetts women to action and independent thought.

While the importance of improved education to women's progress into the mainstream of society had long been addressed by female intellectual leaders, advance was slow. According to Cott (*The Bonds of Womanhood*), by the end of the colonial period 80 percent of Massachusetts males were literate, while the female literacy rate remained as it had for decades at 40 percent. And Jo Ann Preston ("Feminization of an Occupation: Teaching Becomes Women's Work in Nineteenth-Century New England" [Ph.D. diss., Brandeis University, 1982]) indicates that eighteenth-century town schools hired male teachers for boys in the winter months, with girls instructed by women only during the summer. But Linda Kerber in two major contributions ("The Republican Mother: Women and the Enlightenment—An American Perspective," *American Quarterly*, 28 [1976], and "Daughters of Columbia: Educating Women for the Republic, 1787-1805," *Our American Sisters*, ed. Jean E. Friedman and William G. Shade [Boston, 1976]) presents evidence that by 1800 there was increasing consensus not only that girls should be educated, but that their education should differ in some fundamental ways from that provided boys so that they might be prepared for their adult roles as domestic character models and caretakers of future citizens.

The first public high school for girls in Massachusetts opened in Worcester in 1824, and women were hired for its faculty. A Boston school established in 1825 saw nearly 300 girls applying for a seat in its single room, but, according to Ednah Cheney, ethnic bias contributed to its precipitous closing less than two years later: "Many young Irish girls had entered the school and had proved fine scholars; and an outcry was raised against education for the poorer classes, as unfitting them for domestic service."[4] Lowell opened a high school in 1832 that incorporated a Female Department with a four-term year, an arrangement that Elfrieda McCauley ("The New England Mill Girls") explains was introduced to allow local mill girls to attend for an occasional term without losing their jobs. Although more public high schools appeared thereafter in other Massachusetts towns with girls enrolling in large numbers, it was not until 1852 that Boston opened its Girls' High School. Lucy Woods (*A History of the Girls' High School of Boston, 1852-1902* [Cambridge, 1904]) gives an informative account of the early history of this institution.

Expansion of public education in the state brought with it rising demand for teachers, and therefore women entered classrooms at increasing rates. An innovative essay by Richard M. Bernard and Maris A. Vinovskis ("The Female School Teacher in Ante-Bellum Massachusetts," *Journal of Social History*, 10 [1977]) reports that by 1860 they accounted for 78 percent of the state's teachers. Since before 1850 they had little formal education beyond the elementary level, few opportunities for advancement arose. Although women were paid about 60 percent less than the average male teacher, the new profession had great appeal for young women, and, according to Carl F. Kaestle and Maris A. Vinovskis (*Education and Social Change in Nineteenth-Century Massachusetts* [New York, 1980]), about 20 percent of the state's white women in the nineteenth century taught school at some time during their lives.[5]

The need for better-trained women teachers was quickly recognized, and by 1843 Massachusetts had four normal schools, with the Framingham school, which opened in 1839 in Lexington, the first state normal school in the nation. The young women followed a tightly supervised regimen that has been described in a lively style and fascinating detail by seventeen-year-old Mary Swift (*The First State Normal School in America: The Journals of Cyrus Peirce and Mary Swift*, ed. Arthur O. Norton [Cambridge, 1926]). According to a careful investigation by David Asher Gould ("Policy and Pedagogues: School Reform and Teacher Professionalization in Massachusetts, 1840-1920" [Ph.D. diss., Brandeis University, 1977]), by the 1890s graduates of the normal schools were filling three-quarters of the vacancies in a typical town.

The late nineteenth century brought growing numbers of poor immigrant children to crowded urban schools of Massachusetts, a situation that aroused concern among Boston's upper-class philanthropic women. Barbara A. Beatty ("A Vocation from on High: Pre-School Advocacy and Teaching as an Occupation for Women in Nineteenth Century Boston" [Ph.D. diss., Harvard University, 1981]) sensitively documents the efforts of these women to introduce programs to benefit the very young child. Elizabeth Palmer Peabody and Lucy Wheelock, leaders of the kindergarten movement, encouraged Pauline Agassiz Shaw to fund twenty charity kindergartens that by 1886 were enrolling 1,300 Boston children. These women saw in the kindergarten movement a cause especially appropriate to women's motherly talents. Their ideas and methods are presented in Ruth M. Baylor's *Elizabeth Palmer Peabody: Kindergarten Pioneer* (Philadelphia, 1965); *Pauline Agassiz Shaw, Tributes Paid Her Memory* (Boston, 1917); and Lucy Wheelock's "The Kindergarten in New England" (Wheelock College, 1935).[6]

Testimonies on public education from the perspective of immigrant schoolgirl Mary Antin (*From Plotzk to Boston* [Boston, 1899] and *The Promised Land* [Boston, 1912]) and Boston public school teacher Marian A. Dogherty (*'Scusa Me Teacher* [Francestown, N.H., 1943]) reflect not only difficult cultural and language barriers but also a growing mutual affection and respect between teachers and their students. In fact, upper-class women tended to exhibit more class consciousness in their attitudes toward immigrants than did public school teachers. Despite generous donations of time and money in the cause of improved education, these women found it difficult to view these newcomers as fellow Bostonians. Some examples of their attitudes may be seen in the writings by Annie A. Fields (*How To Help the Poor* [Boston, 1883] and *Lend a Hand*, 1 [1886]) and Mary Mann (Cambridge *Chronicle*, May 11, 1878), who characterized poor children as "little savages from three to five, the pests of the street, their mouths full of profane and obscene language."

Parochial as well as public schools were attracting women to their faculties in these years, and their role in the education of working-class children in Massachusetts has been examined by Mary J. Oates in "Organized Voluntarism" and in "Professional Preparation of Parochial School Teachers, 1870-1940" (*Historical Journal of Massachusetts*, 12 [1984]). Like female public school teachers, sisters received about half the stipend paid religious brothers for instructing boys in the schools. Given heavy demand for teachers after 1880, sisters received less formal education than their public school counterparts.[7]

As long as liberal arts colleges in the state refused them admission, talented and ambitious women necessarily remained subordinate in professional fields or confined to volunteer activity. The lengthy struggle for higher education by Massachusetts women has been the subject of more intensive research than any other aspect of their experience in the state.[8] Mt. Holyoke College originated in 1837, with founder Mary Lyon insisting that the Mt. Holyoke Female Seminary resemble male colleges in every way, except that while the latter prepared clergy for the church, it would prepare women to teach. Its early history is lucidly detailed by Kathryn Kish Sklar ("The Founding of Mount Holyoke College," Berkin and Norton, *Women of America*), who indicates that by 1849 Mt. Holyoke Female Seminary was graduating more teachers than the normal schools of the state, as well as a large number of missionaries. Additional informative sources on this pioneer female institution include Edward Hitchcock's *The Power of Christian Benevolence Illustrated in the Life and Labors of Mary Lyon* (New York, 1858); Sarah D. Stow's *History of Mount Holyoke Seminary, South Hadley, Massachusetts, during the First Half Century, 1837-1887* (Springfield, Mass., 1887); Arthur Cole's *A Hundred Years of Mount Holyoke College: The Evaluation of an Educational Ideal* (New Haven, 1940); and Elizabeth Alden Green's *Mary Lyon and Mount Holyoke College: Opening the Gates* (Hanover, N.H., 1979). Louise Porter Thomas (*Seminary Militant: An Account of the Missionary Movement at Mount Holyoke Seminary and College* [South Hadley, Mass., 1937]) gives particular attention to the role of religion in this women's school, and Tiziana Rota ("Between 'True Women' and 'New Women': Mount Holyoke Students, 1837-1908" [Ph.D. diss., University of Massachusetts, 1983]) skillfully demonstrates that its religious traditions persisted well into the 1860s. The college's later years are examined by Rota and also by Charlotte K. Shea in a good interpretive study ("Mount Holyoke College, 1875-1910: The Passing of the Old Order" [Ph.D. diss., Cornell University, 1983]). David F. Allmendinger, Jr., ("Mount Holyoke Students Encounter the Need for Life Planning, 1837-1850," *History of Education Quarterly*, 19 [1979]) provides insight into Lyon's success at fund raising among middle-class women, a skill that permitted tuition at her school to be significantly lower than that at other local academies for girls.

An authoritative investigation by Sally Schwager ("'Harvard Women': A History of the Founding of Radcliffe College," [Ed.D. diss., Harvard University, 1982]) explores in depth the origins of another type of college for women originating in the state. Massachusetts women linked by family ties to Harvard's faculty or its graduates and led by Elizabeth Cary Agassiz, Anna Eliot Ticknor, and Katherine P. Loring petitioned in the 1870s for the admission of women to Harvard College. Although as upper-class Bostonians these women subscribed to traditional ideas on women's place, they saw no conflict between that outlook and their belief that women should be as well educated as men. Since their co-education proposal was quickly vetoed, they opened the Harvard Annex, a program of study for women that was to evolve in 1894 into Radcliffe College. Mary Hume Maguire ("The Curtain-Raiser to the Founding of Radcliffe College: The Search for a 'Safe, Promising, and Instructive Experiment,'" *Proceedings of the Cambridge Historical Society*, 36 [1955-1956]) maintains that early administrators of the college envisioned higher education for women to be largely a preparation for life in the home or in the classroom. But the graduates of the new colleges soon abandoned teaching as a leading professional choice. Elizabeth P. May's survey of Wellesley alumnae ("Occupations of Wellesley Graduates," *School and Society*, 29 [1929]) indicates that as work options widened somewhat, especially in social service, the high proportion of new college graduates who chose to teach fell sharply. While almost 80 percent of employed Wellesley graduates of 1880 taught school, among 1889-1893 graduates that proportion was only 33 percent.

Representative individual studies of Massachusetts women's colleges include L. Clark Seelye's *The Early History of Smith College, 1871-1910* (Boston, 1923); Sarah H. Gordon's "Smith College Students: The First Ten Classes, 1879-1888" (*History of Education Quarterly*, 15 [1975]); Dorothy Elia Howells' *A Century to Celebrate: Radcliffe College, 1879-1979* (Cambridge, 1978); Florence Converse's *Wellesley College: A Chronicle of the Years 1875-1938* (Wellesley, 1939); and Jean Glasscock, ed., *Wellesley College. 1875-1975: A Century of Women* (Wellesley, 1975). Smith, Wellesley, and the Harvard Annex are considered in several early essays by John Tetlow ("The Eastern Colleges for Women: Their Aims, Means, and Methods, Parts I and II," *Education*, 1 [1881]). Barbara Miller Solomon's *In the Company of Educated Women: A History of Women and Higher Education in America* (New Haven, 1985) incorporates a valuable and cohesive interpretation of the development of the Massachusetts colleges. Also worth noting in this regard is Helen Lefkowitz Horowitz' *Alma Mater: Design and Experience in the Women's Colleges from Their Nineteenth-Century Beginnings to the 1930s* (New York, 1984).

Intense bonds among female friends had long marked women's lives. Cott (*The Bonds of Womanhood*) demonstrates that late eighteenth-century women, reacting to their narrow domestic sphere and restricted social position, sought solace and support in female friendships. In her "Passionlessness: An Interpretation of Victorian Sexual Ideology, 1790-1850" (*Signs*, 4 [1978]), Cott explains how women's peculiar capacity for pure spiritual love was seen reflected in these relationships, and therefore they continued to receive social approval throughout the nineteenth century. William R. Taylor and Christopher Lasch ("Two 'Kindred Spirits': Sorority and Family in New England, 1836-1846," *New England Quarterly*, 36 [1963]); Carroll Smith Rosenberg ("The Female World of Love and Ritual: Relations between Women in Nineteenth Century America," *Signs*, 1 [1975]); and Judith Ranlett ("Sorority and Community: Women's Answer to a Changing Massachusetts, 1865-1895" [Ph.D. diss., Brandeis University, 1974]) together provide rich and enlightening perspectives on nineteenth-century female support relationships.

Two excellent studies by Patricia Palmieri ("Patterns of Achievement of Single Academic Women at Wellesley College, 1880-1920," *Frontiers*, 5 [1980], and "In Adamless Eden: A Social Portrait of the Academic Community at Wellesley College, 1875-1920" [Ed.D. diss., Harvard University, 1981]) give clear evidence that single faculty women were able to enjoy close friendships and lead satisfying, active lives outside marriage and domesticity. Raised for the most part in liberal families active in social and political causes, they could more easily avoid domestic life in favor of a profession without incurring opposition than could women from more traditional backgrounds. The tightly knit college environment provided them with a supportive structure and an invigorating sense of working together in an exalted mission. These close ties enriched their emotional lives and encouraged professional achievement.[9] Margaret Rossiter's fine study, *Women Scientists in America: Struggles and Strategies to 1940* (Baltimore, 1982), emphasizes the critical importance of the women's colleges in providing opportunities for early women Ph.D.'s to undertake professional careers in higher education. In general, before 1920 single women were better able to assume long-term leadership roles in education and in the professions than were married women. Alice Freeman's promising career as president of Wellesley College, for example, ended after only six years upon her marriage in 1887, and her biographer-husband George Herbert Palmer (*The Life of Alice Freeman Palmer* [Boston, 1908]) documents the widespread public praise she received on her retirement.

By the 1880s graduate education for women in all fields had become essential for the development of qualified faculty for the women's colleges. Many at this time were required to enroll at European universities since few American graduate programs were yet open to them. In 1881 seventeen pioneer college women, most from Massachusetts, established the Association of Collegiate Alumnae (which in 1921 became the American Association of University Women) to raise funds to endow graduate fellowships and to provide a public forum for the growing ranks of female college graduates. Marion Talbot and Lois Kimball Mathews Rosenberry (*The History of the American Association of University Women, 1881-1931* [Boston, 1931]) illuminate the early years of this important female organization. A major question entertained at its first meetings was whether the women's colleges were educating women to be assertive and independent thinkers interested in pursuing careers that ranged beyond the domestic. Roberta Wein ("Women's Colleges and Domesticity, 1875-1918," *History of Education Quarterly*, 14 [1974]) ably demonstrates that although instruction in the colleges improved over time, they were not in 1918 successfully challenging the traditional prescription of home and family as women's pre-emptive sphere. Joyce Antler's "'After College, What?': New Graduates and the Family Claim" (*American Quarterly*, 32 [1980]) documents the ambitions and conflicts represented in the choices of Wellesley College graduates of 1897 and identifies explanatory features of the tensions that could be observed between home and professional obligations.

The career of Ellen Richards provides a useful case in point. A study by Caroline L. Hunt, *The Life of Ellen H. Richards* (Boston, 1912), confirms that even the best-educated women, whether graduates of women's colleges or of co-educational institutions, were ambivalent about the proper role of their sex in society. As MIT's first female student, Richards had earned a B.S. in chemistry in 1873, followed by an M.A. from Vassar as well as doctoral study at MIT, where, as a female, she was denied the Ph.D. degree. After 1890 her research interests at MIT turned from chemistry to the new field of home economics, which she thereafter energetically promoted for public high school and college women. This shift to a "female field" by so prominent an advocate of women's higher education as Richards has been judged to have hindered female progress in a convincing essay by Jill K. Conway ("Perspectives on the History of Women's Education in the United States," *History of Education Quarterly*, 14 [1974]). Richards' professional choices seemed to reflect broader female efforts to deal in conventional and socially acceptable ways with a growing and pervasive uneasiness about their assigned roles. That household responsibilities weighed on middle-class women in Massachusetts before 1920 is revealed in provocative early essays by the founder of the Cambridge Cooperative Housekeeping Society, Melusina Fay Peirce ("Cooperative Housing, I-IV," *Atlantic Monthly*, 22 [1868]; 23 [1869], and *Cooperative Housekeeping: How Not to Do It and How to Do It: A Study in Sociology* [Boston, 1884]). She proposed creative ways for housewives to acquire greater independence. Dolores Hayden's substantive contributions ("Charlotte Perkins Gilman and the Kitchenless House," *Radical History Review*, 21 [1979], and "Two Utopian Feminists and Their Campaigns for Kitchenless Houses," *Signs*, 4 [1978]) explore and evaluate proposals like Peirce's.

Massachusetts women venturing outside the academic world to other professions had long met great hurdles. Acceptance in traditionally male fields especially remained a formidable enterprise, as Sally Gregory Kohlstedt ("In from the Periphery: American Women in Science, 1830-1880," *Signs*, 4 [1978]); Joan Burstyn ("Early Women in Higher Education: The Role of the Anderson School of Natural History," *Boston University Journal of Education*, 159 [1977]); and Margaret Rossiter (*Women Scientists in America*) ably show. In major scientific associations, for example, women could hold only nominal affiliation before the 1880s.

Efforts of Massachusetts women to enter the medical profession were early and persistent. Harriot K. Hunt, a privately educated Boston physician, graphically describes her experiences in *Glances and Glimpses; or Fifty Years Social, Including Twenty Years Professional Life* (Boston, 1856; reprinted New York, 1970). Public rebuffs by Harvard Medical School of Hunt's petition to attend lectures in 1847 and 1850 helped to mobilize the nascent movement for a local women's medical school. Her concern for women's health led her to establish the Ladies' Physiological Institute of Boston in 1843, a society thoroughly considered by Martha H. Verbrugge ("The Social Meaning of Personal Health: The Ladies'

Physiological Institute of Boston and Vicinity in the 1850s," *Health Care in America*, ed. Susan Reverby and David Rosner [Philadelphia, 1979]). Regina Markell Morantz ("Making Women Modern: Middle-Class Women and Health Reform in Nineteenth-Century America," *Journal of Social History*, 10 [1977]) suggests that the "cult of scientific domesticity" among early health reformers represented a first step by women into the medical profession. Some local women became wealthy by capitalizing on the women's health movement. A valuable study of one such entrepreneur is Sarah J. Stage's *Female Complaints: Lydia Pinkham and the Business of Women's Medicine* (New York, 1981).

In 1862 Dr. Maria Zakrzewska founded in Boston the New England Hospital for Women and Children, an institution owned, managed, and generously supported by women. Mary Roth Walsh (*"Doctors Wanted: No Woman Need Apply": Sexual Barriers in the Medical Profession, 1835-1975* [New Haven, 1977]) gives an authoritative and compelling account of Boston medical women and an absorbing analysis of the development of this institution. Physicians like Zakrzewska and Lucy Sewall, the hospital's first resident physician, were unacceptable to many in the medical establishment who publicly debated whether their physiology permitted strenuous, concentrated work. Such charges were effectively rebutted by hospital physicians Emily F. Pope, Emma L. Call, and C. Augusta Pope (*The Practice of Medicine by Women in the United States* [Boston, 1881]) in an exhaustive survey of the health of 430 women doctors. Denied admission to the Massachusetts Medical Society, local women physicians in 1878 formed their own New England Hospital Medical Society.

Tensions arose in the 1880s at the New England Hospital between long-time staff physicians and young interns less convinced of the merits of an all-female hospital. Significant research has appeared on the implications of the dispute in Virginia Drachman's "Female Solidarity and Professional Success: The Dilemma of Women Doctors in Nineteenth-Century America" (*Journal of Social History*, 15 [1982]) and *Hospital with a Heart: Women Doctors and the Paradox of Separatism at the New England Hospital, 1862-1969* (Ithaca, N.Y., 1984) and in Helena M. Wall's "Feminism and the New England Hospital, 1949-1961" (*American Quarterly*, 32 [1980]). Zakrzewska's convictions concerning the importance of the all-female institution may have been prophetic, since Walsh testifies to the adoption after 1900 of admission quotas by local medical schools. While 30 percent of the Boston University medical graduates between 1898 and 1918 were women, by 1939 there was no female contingent in the graduating class. Similarly, the 1900 medical graduates at Tufts University included 42 percent women, but a decade later the figure was only 7.6 percent. Eugene Declercq and Richard Lacroix ("The Immigrant Midwives of Lawrence: The Conflict between Law and Culture in Early Twentieth-Century Massachusetts," *Bulletin of the History of Medicine*, 59 [1985]) add new dimensions to discussions concerning women's place in the medical profession.

Little research has yet been undertaken on efforts by Massachusetts women to enter the ministry and the legal profession. Ednah Cheney ("The Women of

Boston") reports that although women composed nearly a quarter of the enrollment at Boston University in 1879, only one was enrolled in law and two in theology. And an early survey by Elva Hubbard Young, "The Law as a Profession for Women" (*Association of Collegiate Alumnae Journal*, 3 [1902]), identified only nine women practicing law in the state. Such records make the late nineteenth-century achievements of Mary Baker Eddy, founder of Christian Science, especially remarkable. A charismatic and effective leader, she established a church, centered in Boston, that emphasized women's special position before a healing, maternal God. Maintaining in *Science and Health* (Boston, 1910) that "we have not so much authority for considering God masculine as we have for considering Him feminine," Eddy provided women equal opportunity with men to become readers and practitioners, with the result that by 1895 four-fifths of her followers were women. Although Christian Science has been termed "the Sentimental Heresy institutionalized" (by Gail Parker, "Mary Baker Eddy and Sentimental Womanhood," *New England Quarterly*, 43 [1970]), it seems clear that Eddy went far beyond sentimentalism in her bold challenge to mainstream views of women's place in organized religion. Eddy spoke often on women's rights, but her relative inaction in the suffrage movement has prompted Phillida Bunkle ("Sentimental Motherhood and Domestic Education, 1830-1870," *History of Education Quarterly*, 14 [1974]) to term her anti-feminist. Nonetheless, her autobiography, *Reminiscences, Prose Works* (Boston, 1925), and the evidence provided by her biographers Robert Peel (*Mary Baker Eddy: The Years of Trial* [New York, 1971]) and Julius Silberger (*Mary Baker Eddy: An Interpretive Biography of the Founder of Christian Science* [Boston, 1980]) suggest that so narrow a definition of feminism would exclude from its ranks one of the most unorthodox and influential women of Massachusetts.[10]

Massachusetts women made significant progress in the field of prison reform, moving from activities in female societies to full participation on state prison boards. Mary J. Bularzik's informative study, "The Dedham Temporary Asylum for Discharged Female Prisoners, 1864-1909" (*Historical Journal of Massachusetts*, 12 [1984]), focuses on the work of Hannah Chickering, who in 1864 prevailed upon a number of female friends to join her in establishing an institution where former inmates could be trained for sewing or domestic service and then aided in finding employment. A similar reformatory for girls and women was opened by the Sisters of the Good Shepherd in Roxbury in 1867, and a good account of this institution is provided in Holloran, "Boston's Wayward Children."

It was the asylum experience that convinced Chickering and Ellen Cheney Johnson of the need for separate reform facilities for women prisoners, who in the 1870s still shared jails and workhouses with male prisoners. Estelle B. Freedman's splendid study, *Their Sisters' Keepers: Women's Prison Reform in America, 1830-1930* (Ann Arbor, 1981), devotes substantial attention to the Massachusetts reformers and their institutions. One such institution, the Lancaster School for Girls, has been examined in an excellent study by Barbara Brenzel (*Daughters of the State: A Social Portrait of the First Reform School for Girls in North*

America, 1856-1905 [Cambridge, 1983]). As a consequence of a highly organized petition drive by Massachusetts women's groups, a prison for adult women was authorized by the Massachusetts legislature in 1874. The Sherborn Reformatory soon became the best-known women's reform institution in the nation, with all its administrators women by 1900. Isabel C. Barrows ("The Massachusetts Reformatory Prison for Women," *The Reformatory System of the United States*, ed. Samuel J. Barrows [Washington, D.C., 1900]) and Mary J. Bularzik ("Sex, Crime, and Justice: Women in the Criminal Justice System of Massachusetts, 1900-1950" [Ph.D. diss., Brandeis University, 1982]) present rich evidence of the numerous challenges the institution confronted throughout its history. Under the strong and progressive leadership of Superintendent Ellen Cheney Johnson between 1884 and 1899 the treatment and education of female prisoners were significantly advanced. Isabel C. Barrows ("Ellen Johnson and the Sherborn Prison," *New England Magazine* 21 [1899-1900]) elaborates on Johnson's role as a national leader for women's prison reform. Johnson herself explains her reform philosophy in a valuable monograph (*Modern Prison Management, The Underlying Principles of Prison Reform, as Applied in the Reformatory Prison for Women at Sherborn, Massachusetts* [Boston, 1899]).

Massachusetts women had an enduring impact on prison reform, moving into powerful advocacy positions within state institutions and on political commissions and boards. Some, like Mary Dewson, progressed from prison work to political careers. James T. Patterson ("Mary Dewson and the American Minimum Wage Movement," *Labor History*, 5 [1964]) ably shows how Dewson, as administrator of the women's parole department of the state industrial school system between 1900 and 1912, became convinced of the strong connections between poverty and delinquency. Her belief that the best way to solve the delinquency problem was to press for a minimum wage prompted her to undertake political campaigns for such legislation at state and national levels.

For the most part, careers in public service were rare among Massachusetts women before 1920. Their political focus remained centered on mobilizing citizens for women's suffrage. Dimensions of nineteenth-century suffrage efforts as seen by a participant are revealed in Harriet Jane Hanson Robinson's *Massachusetts in the Woman Suffrage Movement, 1774-1881* (Boston, 1883). Dale Baum's insightful essay, "Woman Suffrage and the 'Chinese Question': The Limits of Radical Republicanism in Massachusetts, 1865-1876" (*New England Quarterly*, 56 [1983]) also advances our understanding of the early years of the struggle. By 1879 Massachusetts women had gained the limited right to vote for town school committees as well as to be elected to them.

Since the state had an unusually large representation of anti-suffragists, the campaign for an amendment to its constitution was bitter and ultimately unsuccessful. In the immediate postbellum era, the Boston-based American Woman Suffrage Association, led by Lucy Stone and Julia Ward Howe, tended to be far more conservative than the National Woman Suffrage Association, based in New York. Julia Ward Howe (*Reminiscences, 1819-1899* [Boston, 1900]); Deborah Pickman Clifford (*Mine Eyes Have Seen the Glory: A Biography of Julia Ward Howe* [Boston, 1979]); and Mary Hetherington Grant ("Private Woman, Public

Person: An Account of the Life of Julia Ward Howe from 1819 to 1868" [Ph.D. dis., George Washington University, 1982]) together provide valuable perspectives on Howe's thinking. Mary Livermore, another early suffragist, established in 1874 the Massachusetts Woman's Christian Temperance Union. Although both suffrage and temperance were appropriately female and middle-class causes, the sturdy link that developed in the public mind between them affected working-class support for the suffrage cause. Janet Zollinger Giele ("Social Change in the Feminine Role: A Comparison of Woman's Suffrage and Woman's Temperance, 1870-1920" [Ph.D. diss., Radcliffe College, 1961]) enriches our understanding of a number of critical issues related to suffrage strategy. Women's participation in political reform, although often confined to "women's concerns," was persevering, as fine studies by Polly Welts Kaufman ("Boston Women and City Politics: Nurturers and Protectors in Public Education, 1872-1905" [Ph.D. diss., Boston University, 1978]) and Lois Bannister Merk ("Massachusetts and the Woman-Suffrage Movement" [Ph.D. diss., Radcliffe College, 1956, revised 1961] and "Boston's Historic Public School Crisis," *New England Quarterly*, 31 [1958]) ably document.

A stimulating investigation by Sharon Hartman Strom ("Leadership and Tactics in the American Woman Suffrage Movement: A New Perspective from Massachusetts," *Journal of American History*, 62 [1975]) argues that the failure of an 1895 municipal suffrage referendum pushed Boston women to organize new suffrage societies. The smallest but most progressive and influential of these was the Boston Equal Suffrage Association for Good Government, founded in 1901 by Pauline Agassiz Shaw, Mary Hutcheson Page, and Maud Wood Park. Park and Inez Haynes enlisted local college students and alumnae for the College Equal Suffrage League, which by 1908 boasted a national membership. In time, cooperation between suffrage women and the Massachusetts Women's Trade Union League led middle-class and working-class women to greater awareness of their mutual dependence. The league's report (*The History of Trade Unionism among the Women in Boston* [Boston, n.d., c. 1907]) is noteworthy here.

Scholars have endeavored to determine why increasing numbers of Massachusetts citizens were attracted to anti-suffrage forces after 1890. James J. Kenneally ("The Opposition to Woman Suffrage in Massachusetts" [Ph.D. diss., Boston College, 1963]) and Jane Jerome Camhi ("Women against Women: American Antisuffragism, 1880-1920" [Ph.D. diss., Tufts University, 1973]) shed considerable light on this phenomenon. Although anti-suffragist women defended their position as a way to protect women in the home, the integrity of the family, and the stability of society, a fear of change and an unwillingness to share political power with groups they considered inferior lay behind the stand of a sizeable group of upper-class women. Their attitude is exemplified in comments by Bostonian Margaret Deland ("The Change in the Feminine Ideal," *Atlantic Monthly*, 105 [1910]). James Kenneally's "Catholicism and Woman Suffrage in Massachusetts" (*Catholic Historical Review*, 53 [1967]) supports the view that the negative attitude of the Catholic church on the suffrage question crucially affected the low participation rate of working-class women in the movement.

The Civil War had motivated many Massachusetts women to public action not only in the cause of suffrage but also for social reform. An intriguing personal testimony of the effect of the war on one reformer is Mary Livermore's *My Story of the War: A Woman's Narrative of Four Years Personal Experience* (Hartford, 1889). Dorothea Dix, prison reformer and long-time advocate for the insane poor, had served as superintendent of army nurses, and Clara Barton also had worked independently in war hospital wards. The postwar activities of these Massachusetts women significantly helped to advance nursing as a profession for women. The New England Woman's Club, founded in 1868, and listing Julia Ward Howe as an early and long-term president, represented an important new postwar female organization in the state. The club enlisted women not only to support public as well as private institutions aiding girls and women, but also to identify and meet needs neglected by existing agencies. In 1877 the club established the nationally acclaimed Women's Educational and Industrial Union, which undertook more ambitious projects and offered a wide array of services to middle-class as well as working-class women.

Yet according to John P. Rousmaniere ("Cultural Hybrid in the Slums: the College Woman and the Settlement House, 1889–1894," *American Quarterly*, 22 [1970]), by the 1890s growing numbers of unmarried college graduates were seeking more direct and tangible opportunities to use their educations to reform society than were provided through the women's clubs. Faculty of the Massachusetts women's colleges took the lead in encouraging young women to enter the public domain through personal involvement with the urban poor. Katharine Coman, Vida Scudder, and Katharine Lee Bates of Wellesley organized the College Settlement Association, which opened its Boston settlement, Denison House, in 1892. Their activities and personal observations are well presented by Dorothy Burgess (*Dream and Deed: The Story of Katharine Lee Bates* [Norman, Okla., 1952]); Katharine Coman ("The Wellesley Alumnae as Social Servants," *Wellesley Magazine*, 13 [1904]); Vida Dutton Scudder (*On Journey* [New York, 1937]); and Caroline Williamson ("Six Months at Denison House," *Wellesley Magazine*, 3 [1895]). Zilpha Drew Smith played a pivotal role in the development of more sophisticated approaches to urban poverty and social reform, and the professionalization of social work owes much to her leadership as general secretary of the Boston Associated Charities from 1879 to 1903. Her perspectives on those whom settlement social workers served are reflected in her study, *Deserted Wives and Deserting Husbands: A Study of 234 Families Based on the Experience of the District Committees and Agents* (Boston, 1901). Linda Gordon ("Single Mothers and Child Neglect, 1880–1920," *American Quarterly*, 37 [1985]), using records of the Massachusetts Society for Prevention of Cruelty to Children, provides a fascinating and pathbreaking analysis of the experience of many Massachusetts women with organized charity.

Like some prison reform leaders, Denison House members occasionally moved to the political arena, applying skills acquired in settlement work more broadly to the cause of the less fortunate. Peter J. Frederick ("Vida Dutton Scudder: The Professor as Social Activist," *New England Quarterly*, 43 [1970]) and Theresa Corcoran ("Vida Scudder and the Lawrence Textile Strike," *Essex Institute Historical Collections*, 115 [1979]) focus on Scudder's progression from involvement in settlement reform to the Christian Socialist Movement, which she perceived to be a more radical way to preach the Social Gospel. Mercedes M. Randall (*Improper Bostonian: Emily Greene Balch* [New York, 1964]) chronicles the life of another early Wellesley faculty member and settlement worker who turned to radical pacifism, receiving for her achievements the 1946 Nobel Peace Prize.

Traditionally, women's role in the history of Massachusetts was judged a marginal one in that few histories of the state mentioned them, and those that did referred only to a few well-known figures or to wives of prominent men. There was little suggestion that these atypical individuals had much in common with the rest of the women in the state. They were simply exceptions to the rule that women belonged, for the most part, in the private, domestic sphere and had no place or direct influence on the civic, religious, educational, and social life of Massachusetts. But, in fact, recent scholarship effectively disproves such judgments. The representative literature discussed in this essay attests to the need to reformulate traditional interpretations and to continue recent efforts to recognize and assess objectively the significant and often crucial contributions of female citizens to Massachusetts history. While their opportunities were long constrained by societal perceptions of what they could legitimately accomplish, they moved nonetheless to utilize their skills and numerical strength to form women's organizations where they could assume leadership positions and choose the social causes that would benefit from their financial support and volunteer labor. Their many associations directly addressed the most neglected groups in society, with girls and women of particular concern.

Women's role in the public and parochial schools of the state was dominant and pervasive, despite the fact that they did not achieve much upward mobility in the teaching profession before 1920. Their struggle on behalf of quality higher education for half the citizens of Massachusetts led to the establishment of several of the nation's earliest and finest women's colleges, all of which depended for moral as well as financial support on the state's women and their organizations. Women's entrance into male-dominated professions, accomplished with extreme difficulty in most instances, served to broaden the professional visions of men as well as women by encouraging new perspectives and approaches and by identifying overlooked social needs.

Working-class women played key roles in the development of Massachusetts industry and labor organizations from the mills of Lowell and Lawrence to the Women's Trade Union League. Although these women had little success in moving out of sex-segregated occupations, especially if they were members of immigrant or minority groups, over time they encouraged their daughters, whose educational opportunities surpassed their own, to avoid domestic work and factories in favor of teaching and clerical work.[11] In a relatively short time, daughters of Massachusetts working-class families were well represented on college faculties and in the professions.

By 1920 Massachusetts women had begun to examine the position of women as a whole when determining organized action. Although upper-class and working-class women had found it difficult, at times, to work together in the past, especially on labor and suffrage issues, they recognized by 1920 that in many ways all women were still "outsiders." Many areas of women's experience in the state remain to be investigated. But research currently available clearly documents that in developing a collective power and in bringing critical issues to the fore through social programs, education, political action, and writing, Massachusetts women, although bound by tradition, circumvented it to make a lasting impact on the state and on the nation.

NOTES

1. See also Boylan's "Timid Girls, Venerable Widows and Dignified Matrons: Life Cycle Patterns among Organized Women in New York and Boston, 1797–1840," *American Quarterly*, 38 (1986): 779–97.

2. Of interest also are Christopher D. Dale's "From Household Laborers to Millhands: A Study of Women in the Transition to Industrial Capitalism in Antebellum New England" (Ph.D. diss., University of Kentucky, 1984), and Patricia A. Gagnon's "The Educational Experiences of Antebellum Lowell Mill Women" (Ph.D. diss., Boston College, 1986). Personal reactions of immigrant workers sixty years later are presented in Lucille O'Connell's "The Lawrence Textile Strike of 1912: The Testimony of Two Polish Women," *Polish American Studies* 36 (1979): 44–62.

3. The poet's career is examined in a wider context in Joanne A. Dobson's "Emily Dickinson and Mid-Nineteenth-Century American Women Writers: A Community of Expression" (Ph.D. diss., University of Massachusetts, 1985).

4. The education of a typical middle-class woman is described in Joan M. Maloney, "Mary Toppan Pickman: The Education of a Salem Gentlewoman, 1820–1850," *Essex Institute Historical Collections*, 123 [1987]: 1–28.

5. See also Madelyn Holmes, "The 'Unsung Heroines': Women Teachers in Salem before the Civil War," *Essex Institute Historical Collections*, 122 (1986): 299–310.

6. See also recent studies by Judith Roman, "'The Spirit of Charles Street': A Life of Annie Adams Fields, 1834–1915" (Ph.D. diss., Indiana University, 1984), and Louise Swiniarski, "Elizabeth Peabody: A Pioneer in the Kindergarten Movement in America," *Essex Institute Historical Collections*, 123 (1987): 206–29.

7. The social and educational work of Catholic sisters is addressed by Mary J. Oates in "'The Good Sisters': The Work and Position of Catholic Churchwomen in Boston, 1870–1940," *Catholic Boston: Studies in Religion and Community, 1870–1970*, ed. Robert E. Sullivan and James M. O'Toole (Boston, 1985): 171–200.

8. An excellent overview is provided in Patricia M. King's "The Campaign for Higher Education for Women in Nineteenth-Century Boston," *Massachusetts Historical Society Proceedings*, 93 (1981): 59–79.

9. Also valuable are Palmieri's "Here Was Fellowship: A Social Portrait of Academic Women at Wellesley College, 1895–1920," *History of Education Quarterly*, 23 (1983): 195–214.

10. See also Margery Fox, "Protest in Piety: Christian Science Revisited," *International Journal of Women's Studies*, 1 (1978): 401–16.

11. Clerical work as a career for women is considered by Carole Srole in "'A Position that God Has Not Particularly Assigned to Men': The Feminization of Clerical Work, Boston, 1860–1915" (Ph.D. diss., UCLA, 1984).

9

VOICES FROM THE PAST: ORAL HISTORY IN MASSACHUSETTS

JOHN J. FOX

IN 1978 THE Oral History Research Office at Columbia University celebrated its thirtieth birthday. In many ways this marked the coming of age of oral
history as a research methodology. Many present at the luncheon were active in
the Oral History Association and could look back to 1966 when James Mink,
university archivist at UCLA, hosted the meeting that led to the formation of
the association. In their luncheon chatter they recalled how, in the early years,
their colleagues in the historical profession looked down upon the movement
that they were part of. To many of the critics, Barbara W. Tuchman, who had
been featured at one of the association's early meetings, said it all.

With the appearance of the tape recorder . . . we now have through its creature
Oral History, an artificial survival of trivia of appalling proportions. To sit down
and write a book, even of memoirs, requires at least some effort, discipline and
perseverance which until now imposed a certain natural selection on what survived in print. But with all sorts of people being invited merely to open their
mouths, and ramble effortlessly and endlessly into a tape recorder . . . a few
veins of gold and a vast mass of trash are preserved which would otherwise have
gone to dust.[1]

Invariably, the conversations turned to Allan Nevins (1890-1971), who is
considered the "father" of oral history, although at the 1966 meeting at Lake
Arrowhead, California, he disclaimed the credit.[2] Nevins began the movement in
1938 when in his introduction to *Gateway to History* he "suggested establishing
'some organization which made a systematic attempt to obtain, from the lips
and papers of living Americans who have led significant lives, a fuller record of
their participation in the political, economic, and cultural life of the last sixty

years.'"[3] Heeding his own call, Nevins established the country's first oral history project at Columbia ten years later. He was motivated by his fear that modern means of communication would eventually deny to the scholar much of the traditional primary source materials. It was clear to him that fewer and fewer people were depending upon written communication as a means of transmitting their thoughts and views. He was also concerned that people tended not to keep diaries, letters, papers, or other written documents. In the past, these materials had served as the primary sources for the historical researcher. To ensure that his research would not suffer from a lack of source material, Nevins turned to interviewing. One has to assume that Professor Nevins in 1948 could not have predicted that his solution to a problem of scholarship would become as important as it has.

It may well have been that the failure of oral history to quickly gain professional respectability was caused by the inability of its practitioners to clearly define what it was. Possibly William W. Moss comes the closest to defining oral history in the *Oral History Program Manual*:

Oral History is difficult to define exclusively. It is far easier to talk about it than to pin down the boundaries between what is and what is not oral history. . . . Oral history interviewing is a systematic collection, arrangement, preservation and publication (in the sense of making generally available) of recorded verbatim accounts and opinions of people who were witnesses to or participants in events likely to interest future scholars. It is basically an information-collecting technique.

It is safe to say that oral history is a data-gathering process that must maintain the same high standards of scholarship followed by historians using the more traditional methods of research.[4]

Although Nevins had turned to oral history as a means of doing research on individuals who had become the movers and shakers of the nation, it was not too long before it attracted less-traditional historians who saw it as providing an opportunity to do history from the "bottom up." Influenced by the turmoil and changes of the late sixties and early seventies, they came to share the views of Jesse Lemisch. In an essay that appeared in *Towards a New Past: Dissenting Essays in American History*, Lemisch challenged the writing of history only from the perspective of the winners or rulers. If we are not to be taken in by the "dominant mythology," we must be sympathetic to the "victims of historical processes," he insisted:

This sympathy for the powerless brings us closer to objectivity; in practice, it leads the historian to describe past societies as they appeared from the bottom rather than the top, more from the point of view of the inarticulate than of the articulate. Such an approach will have two components. It will continue to examine the elite, but instead of using them as surrogates for the society beneath them, it will ask how their beliefs and conduct impinged on that society. Having determined the place of those who rule, it will study the conduct and ideology of the people on the bottom: this is nothing less than an attempt to make the inarticulate speak. This second task is perhaps more difficult than the first. But both can be and indeed must be done if our generalizations about past societies are to have more than limited validity.[5]

The debate within the ranks of oral history first developed at the Arrowhead meeting. Ten years later the association was still discussing the merits of "elite" versus "non-elite" history. Professor Alice Hoffman, past president of the Oral History Association, in an article published in the 1976 volume of the *Oral History Review*, clearly summarized the position of those who looked upon oral history as a vehicle by which history could be made democratic:

Oral history provides us with an opportunity to write a type of history that heretofore has received very little attention. . . . Now for the first time we have a technique which enables us to evaluate the experiences of many people, and, in so doing to arrive at a much truer picture.

. . . If we are truly to understand our times, we need to understand those events of the past as experienced by a much wider segment of the population than has previously been thought worthwhile to record and preserve. Oral History does allow us to open avenues for shared experience to those who have no other means to express their sense of history.[6]

Since then, the debate has been rather subdued, although it still continues. The issue can still give rise to lively discussions at the association's annual meeting. To a degree, part of this can be attributed to the nation's bicentennial. Many communities looking for ways to commemorate the 200th anniversary of the Declaration of Independence initiated an oral history project. In most cases the intention was to preserve the history of the community by interviewing long-time residents. The tapes, it was promised, would be collected and placed in a repository, such as the local library, so that they would be available to those who wanted to hear voices from the past. All of the projects were undertaken with good intentions, but often they were undertaken by individuals who knew little about oral history.

In all too many cases, the tapes that were collected ended up in shoe boxes gathering dust, unknown and unavailable to those who might use them. Librarians and archivists, used to handling and storing printed documents, knew little about what was necessary to access or preserve the tapes. When placed in a repository, they were often left uncataloged and never became part of the collection. Even when cataloged, they frequently were left untranscribed or unindexed, thus forcing the user to go through the tedious task of searching for the portion that he wanted. Can there be little wonder that most of these tapes have lain unused? When oral history is misused like this, it gives the methodology a bad name. There is no need for this. With proper training, responsible individuals can generate materials that would help to preserve the twentieth-century history of their community and that would be of archival value.

There is another recent movement that has influenced oral history. In the last ten years there has been a reawakened interest in local or community history. Since the professionalization of history in the early twentieth century, those who have been interested in local history have been saddled with the derogatory title of "antiquarianist." Respectable scholars, it was held, did not "waste" their time on events at the local level. In order to understand the nation's history, they maintained, it was necessary to get the "big picture." Despite their opposition, the movement went forward.

Some of the same factors that accounted for the rise of the "new history" helped to turn some historians' attention to community history. These historians understand that each community has stories to tell, which, if uncovered, would help us to better understand the community, its residents, and their relation to the nation's history. Some, trained in the methods of history and in the techniques of oral history, began to make important contributions to scholarship. Their work was encouraged by the American Association for State and Local History. It also encouraged historical societies and museums to undertake new programs that highlighted the daily world of the ordinary person. Through its publication of *History News*, the technical leaflet series, and books, it has done yeoman service in providing professional guidance.[7] The Essex Institute in Salem was one of the museums that recognized this movement and saw it as an opportunity to broaden community interest in the institute. The institute, which for over 150 years had been the attic of the Brahmins, put together an award-winning exhibit on "Life and Times in Shoe City: The Shoe Workers of Lynn." In this exhibit, Ann Farnam, museum curator, aided by Keith Melder, skillfully weaved together an exhibit that used both traditional and newer methodologies such as oral history. Professor John Fox, Salem State College, and Professor R. Wayne Anderson, Northeastern University, assumed the responsibility for the oral history segment. Fox and Anderson were both conducting oral history classes at their institutions and employed their students to conduct the majority of the interviews with shoe-factory owners, workers, family members, and community leaders. The exhibit attracted people to the museum who in the past either had been unaware of its existence or unmoved to enter its galleries.

In its fight for acceptance, oral history has had to overcome several hurdles. Among these have been the charge that it is not a valid research tool because the memory of the interviewees cannot be trusted to be reliable, especially if the events that they are recalling took place many years ago. Critics maintain that in the intervening years the interviewees may have been influenced by many factors that cloud their recollections of a particular event. The age of one at the time of the event can also influence how it is remembered.[8]

Those who are seriously involved in oral history have never made the claim that memory is infallible or that they are the finders of truth. John Neuenschwander, a respected oral historian and past president of the Oral History Association, alerts oral historians to the fact that there is still no clear-cut answer to the questions of reliability of memory. Yet this does not mean that oral historians must enter the interview process with the fear that they cannot gain information and recollections that will be of value in putting an event into perspective. It seems reasonable to believe that if trained oral historians prepare themselves fully in written sources and if they follow the historical method, the interview that they and the interviewee jointly produce should be of value. At the community level, this is another problem. Volunteers who are at first excited by a project may soon lose their enthusiasm and make little or no effort to prepare themselves.[9]

A recent survey that attempted to document the use of oral history in Massachusetts suggests that the fascination with oral history has begun to decline. Several reasons may account for this trend. Before addressing that subject, it is important to discuss the survey. As of 1984 there had been no systematic survey to determine the state of oral history in Massachusetts. In an attempt to meet this need, a questionnaire was developed and mailed to historical societies, historical commissions, museums, college history departments, college libraries, and public libraries. For various reasons, some institutions were not included in the survey.[10] In July 1984, 497 questionnaires were mailed. Each contained a stamped and addressed return envelope. The returns trickled in throughout the summer and into the fall. In the end 243 were returned. Since the mailing it has become apparent that the questionnaire had some weaknesses. Thus the results of the survey are only suggestive of the current status of oral history in Massachusetts.

Of those returned, 41 indicated an ongoing program or a program that had been completed. 202 institutions responded that they are not and have not ever been actively involved in oral history. For purposes of tabulating the survey, the 41 positive responses were put into the following categories: public libraries, colleges and universities, historical societies, historical museums, historical commissions, and others. The statistics, which will be presented below, do not agree with the number of positive returns because some of those responding did not provide all the information requested.

One hundred thirty-six public libraries returned the form. This was the greatest number of responses within the six categories. Of this number sixteen indicated that they had an oral history collection. Most collections contain less than twenty-five interviews. The Newton Free Library has over fifty, and Ipswich Public Library and Stoneham Public Library have over seventy-five. Most interviews are an hour or less in length. The libraries in Stockbridge, Lincoln, Reading, and Westborough indicated that their collection had been used for publications.

Like most public institutions, libraries have suffered under Proposition 2½. As a result they need to depend upon grants, gifts, and volunteers if they are going to carry out an active oral history program. Funding is the most serious drawback. Some of the libraries have received funds under various LSCA programs. The Marstons Mills Public Library has just received an LSCA Title II grant that it is going to use to undertake a "Living History of Marstons Mills." This program will include some oral history interviews. Several libraries have received grants from the Massachusetts Foundation for Humanities and Public Policy and the Massachusetts Council on the Arts and the Humanities. Some have received donations from civic-minded individuals and businesses. When the grant ends or the funds dry up, frequently the oral history program comes to an end.

Eleven of the sixteen libraries indicated that they use volunteers. In nearly all cases, volunteers are used for interviewing and transcribing. From the survey data, it appears that only the Brimfield Public Library has formed a steering committee composed of community residents. Of those libraries responding, only Newton Free Library has developed a working relationship with an institution of higher education in its region. In collaboration with the Institute for Boston Studies at Boston College, Newton has undertaken an active program to do oral histories of the villages that make up the city of Newton. Under the title of "Work in Newton, 1920–1950" they have completed four villages.[11]

Out of forty-eight colleges and universities that responded, nine indicated that they were conducting oral history projects or served as a repository for tapes that were being collected by faculty members or alumni. As is the case with the public libraries, most collections are rather small, averaging 25 or fewer interviews. Greenfield Community College Library has over 100 interviews in its collection, mainly coming from the Pioneer Valley Studies program at the college. University of Lowell Library has "about 150" interviews. The majority of the interviews in all collections are an hour or less. Only Lowell and Regis College indicated that the average length of their interviews was longer than one hour.[12]

The University of Lowell has one of the most active programs in the state. Presently it is conducting four projects: (1) the Alumni Oral History Project; (2) the Family Oral History Project; (3) the Immigrant Oral History Project; and (4) the Mill Workers of Lowell Project, which is being conducted in conjunction with Lowell National Historical Park. It has completed work on St. Jeanne D'Arc Oral History Project and the Rogers Hall School for Girls History Project. Libraries at Western New England, Mount Holyoke, Smith, and Regis are conducting projects that focus on alumnae, faculty, administration, and staff. Shea's Library at American International College is the repository for tapes collected by the Oral History Center at the college. The center, one of the first in the state, under the direction of Dr. Theodore Belsky has conducted projects on the Summit House of Mt. Holyoke, Development of Quabbin Reservation, Holyoke Community College, History of Recent Educational Reform in Massachusetts, and several social and economic histories of communities in the Springfield area. Material from the collections at Massachusetts College of Art, University of Lowell, and American International College has been used in publications or other forms of production. Salem State College and Endicott College have conducted some oral history projects on a less formal level. The Bates Center at Salem State has acquired some interviews relating to the political careers of Congressmen George and William Bates. The College Alumni Association sponsors, in conjunction with a graduate oral history class, "A Noble Past: An Oral and Documentary History of Salem State." For the past several years Endicott College has sponsored a project that focuses on the history of Beverly.

Funding seems to be less of a problem for these institutions than for the public libraries, mainly because the programs are being sponsored and supported by alumni or are part of course requirements. In either case, little or none of the institution's budget has to go to supporting the oral history program. In most cases the only direct cost is library staff time for accession and cataloging.

Only twelve historical societies replied to the survey. Of these, six are conducting oral history programs. As is the case with the libraries, most societies have twenty-five or fewer interviews. Only the Sharon Historical Society and the Duke's County Historical Society indicated that they had collected more than twenty-five interviews. Sharon also indicated that the average length of its interviews is over two hours. Nahant's interviews are between one and two hours. The interviews of the other four societies are one hour or less. None of the six indicated that their material has been used in publications.

The most interesting project being conducted seems to be that of the Old Dartmouth Historical Society in New Bedford. It has an archive of approximately thirty tapes. Most of these are interviews with former whalemen. The projects of the other societies are mainly reminiscences with selected citizens in the community. None indicates that it plans to undertake an in-depth study of the social, economic, and political institutions of the community. Funding does not appear to be a major consideration for the societies. Most of the projects are conducted by volunteers working on their own and supplying their own tape and equipment. From the questionnaire, it appears that only the Sharon Historical Society has made a firm commitment to oral history, having established an oral history committee.

One of the weaknesses of the questionnaire was that it did not ask the respondents to be specific about programs and projects that are no longer active. It is safe to assume that some of the historical societies conducted programs as part of their bicentennial celebration. There is a need to know where these tapes are deposited if they are to be available for research purposes. Interviews, unknown and hidden away on a dusty shelf, being destroyed by improper environmental conditions, are of no more value than an artifcat that remains unfound or that has been destroyed.

Three of the four historical commissions that responded to the survey indicated that they were currently conducting oral history projects. The Conway Historical Commission indicated that an oral history project had been conducted for the bicentennial and that a planning committee was "gearing up to continue such a project." The most ambitious program is "In the Days of Strawberries and Streetcars," which is being conducted by the Concord Historical Commission. Leyden, a small town of about 600, is conducting an oral history program "which is designed to outline the changes which have occurred in town over the last 100 years." The commission plans to use the material to produce a radio program and a traveling slide/tape show. The Concord program has recorded over seventy-five interviews, while the other two have recorded less than twenty-five.

The Concord program, now in its ninth year, is one of the oldest and most successful programs in the state. Much of the credit for this must go to Renee Garrelick, who has served as director since the program's inception. Garrelick who is a writer, has successfully used interviews as the basis for articles in the *Concord Journal.* She has also produced a soft-cover booklet, and presently she is preparing a book for the town's 350th anniversary.

Historical commissions, which are created under state legislation, are responsible to the local governing body and thus may have an easier time than other organizations in getting community funds to carry out particular projects. In the case of Concord and Leyden the program is funded. In Concord the oral history program director receives a stipend for each project. In Leyden the program director is paid. Historical commissions are also free to seek funding from granting agencies and to solicit donations.

After the survey was completed, Wakefield established an historical commission. Currently, this commission is in the process of structuring a program entitled "Wakefield, 1900-1980: A Changing Community." The first project in the program will be "Strangers No More." This project will produce a documentary history of the experiences of selected immigrant families who settled in town after the turn of the century. The documentary, which will be based on interviews, will be shown on local cable television.

Five historical museums replied to the survey. Of these, one has an ongoing oral history program. The other two have in the past conducted limited programs or serve as repositories for interviews collected by others. Neither the number of interviews in their collections nor the length of the interviews varies significantly from other institutions that responded. Only the Hancock Shaker Village took the time to complete the questionnaire fully. Its project is currently limited to conducting interviews with women who lived at the village as children. From the point of scholarship, this project has the potential to be important.

Undergraduate interns have conducted two projects for the Connecticut Valley Historical Museum. One dealt with the celebration of Christmas during the depression, while the second concentrated on family lifestyle during the depression. Pilgrim Hall Museum has in its archive "a small scattered collection of oral histories" that are chiefly the reminiscences of local residents. The Essex Institute has some uncataloged and unindexed interviews with individuals who were connected to the Lynn shoe industry.

Nineteen institutions that did not fit in one of the above categories also replied. Of these, two are involved with oral history. The Institute for Boston Studies at Boston College sponsors an oral history project that is part of the public history course. The students conduct interviews for the "Work in Newton, 1920-1950" program of the Newton Free Library. The other institution that is actively collecting interviews is the Archive of American Art/New England Art Center. The archive, a division of the Smithsonian Institution, has a worldwide rather than local or state focus. Within its American Visual Arts program it conducts interviews with contemporary artists and art world figures. Currently it has over seventy-five interviews in its collection. Babson College has an ongoing project relating to Roger Babson. The Episcopal Diocese of Massachusetts' Library and Archives is just beginning to conduct some interviews. As of the time it responded to the questionnaire, it had not yet established an oral history program.

For those who support oral history as a legitimate research methodology, the survey causes some concern. Out of the forty-one institutions, only sixteen indicated that they use a legal release form. Unlike other research documents that one can find in a repository, interviews can only be used legally if the party to the interview has signed a release. Although most of the interviews that have been collected could be used without any legal complications, the chance that this would not always be the case, no matter how remote, still exists. Colleges and public libraries tend most frequently to use the release form. This is not surprising. As professionals in the information field, they should be well aware of the 1978 Copyright Law. Still, three college libraries and five public libraries do not use the forms. Five historical societies, three museums, and two commissions indicate that they also do not require a form to be signed. It would be easy to suggest that those not using the form are just being negligent, but there may be a better explanation. Only two of the forty-one belong to the New England Association of Oral History, and none belongs to the Oral History Association. This clearly suggests that there are many individuals conducting interviews—"doing oral history"—who are unaware of the guidelines that they should be following. If oral history at the local level is ever to be more than an interesting diversion, it is necessary that those involved know what professional standards are expected.

Only eighteen institutions have begun a program of transcribing their tapes. Of these, eight are colleges and three are public libraries. While none of the eighteen has transcribed all of its tapes, all are working toward that goal. It is easy to understand the reluctance on the part of an institution to undertake a transcription program—it is expensive. Each hour of tape can generate twenty to forty pages of transcription. Yet, there is a very good reason why the tapes should be transcribed: transcriptions are much easier to use. Of those institutions transcribing, only two follow professional guidelines. The others do verbatim transcripts.

In the case of the latter institutions this suggests that the tapes are not returned to the interviewee for review. This step is important because frequently, on reviewing the final edited transcript, the interviewee may find something in the tape to be incorrect and wish to correct it, or he may indicate that he has additional information to add. With his review and approval of the transcript, the tape can be put into the collection with the knowledge that it represents the interviewee's best recollection. Nothing could be more destructive to a program than to have one or more interviewees claim that their material is inaccurate.[13]

It may well be that an institution has neither the staff, resources, nor time to undertake a full-fledged transcription program. At the very least it can provide an index of the tape interview. Of the forty-one, nineteen do; eight are college libraries and nine are public libraries. A tape index is an easy thing to produce and would be extremely helpful to users. All that is necessary is to list by either the digital counter numbers on the recorder or by five-minute segments the major topics that are included on the tape. A tape index allows the user to quickly find the material that he is interested in. No one wants to waste time listening to material that is not relevant to his interest. Researchers who have worked with printed documents have developed the art of skimming to a science. The index provides them with the means to skim the tape. Tapes that are not transcribed or indexed will not be used for serious research.

In terms of accessibility, most of the interviews are available for use without restrictions. Interviews on which restrictions have been placed appear more frequently in college collections than in other institutions (although other collections may have some interviews that are restricted). The explanation may well be that these collections hold interviews on subjects that are controversial and the interviewee agrees to be interviewed only if promised that the interview, or portions of it, will be sealed for an agreed-upon period of time. The restrictions placed on interviews once again point to the need for legal release forms. In these forms the restrictions can be spelled out. Restrictions on portions of interviews also underline the importance of a transcript. A transcript can make available to users that portion of the interview that the interviewee is not concerned will be construed as being defamatory, libelous, or causing what Willa Baum refers to as "social injury." In programs where transcripts are not made, a user copy, with the approval of the interviewee, could be made in which the restricted material has been edited out. Under no circumstances should the master copy (the original interview tape) be tinkered with; the master tape should be considered a primary document, and as such it must not be mutilated by erasing or editing.

A final statistic: only three of the forty-one institutions indicated that they have a published listing or catalog of their oral history collection. Not surprisingly, two of them are college libraries and the other is a public library. One public library indicated that its tapes are listed in the card catalog. This could well be the case for other libraries. It would seem that the failure to have some consistent system of listing interviews—one that both staff and users are familiar with—is a major shortcoming for a program. The question arises concerning who will be able to find the interview and related material when those who have put the program together are no longer involved. One public library indicated that this is a problem for them.

For several reasons it is difficult to identify works that are based on oral history. Works produced for a local community seldom ever go beyond that community's boundary and thus never become known to a wider audience. This is especially true of written works. Works, whether books, exhibits, multimedia productions, radio productions, or video documentaries, that are funded by a granting agency have a better chance of being more widely known. But even in these cases the agency's mailing list determines who will know. The failure of these works to be sent to professional journals for peer review is another factor. In some cases the community may see its project as local and feel no need or obligation to share it with a broader audience. This is a poor attitude. Only by sharing can we learn from others.

There are some published works that can be identified as being based on oral history. They include *Surviving Hard Times: The Working People of Lowell* by Dr. Mary H. Blewett; *From Hearing My Mother Talk: Stories of Cambridge Women*, compiled by Cindy Cohen; *Justice in Everyday Life: The Way It Really Works*, edited by Howard Zinn; *Not So Long Ago: Oral Histories of Older Bostonians* by Lawrence Elle; *A Dialogue with the Past: Oral History Accounts of Boston's Ethnic Neighborhood and People*, edited by Robert C. Hayden; and "Salt, Haying, Farming, and Fishing in Salisbury, Massachusetts: The Life of Sherb Eaton (1900-1982)" and "The Salisbury Beach Dodgem: A Smashing Ride (1920-1980)" by Betsy H. Woodman.[14]

Oral history lends itself well to video or multimedia productions. Because of production costs, it is frequently necessary for producers, especially those who are working independently, to seek outside funding. For the last several years the Massachusetts Foundation for Humanities and Public Policy has been supportive of such undertakings. Those that they have funded include "And That's How We Did in the Mill: Women in the Lowell Textile Mills," a video documentary by Martha K. Norkunas; "Fall River Women: Workers, Wives, and Mothers," a slide/tape production by Joyce Munroe; "The Old Quabbin Valley," an award-winning 16-mm color and sound film documentary by Lawrence Hott; "Women on the New Right," a radio series on the "grass-roots women of the New Right" by Carol Pierson; and "Points de Vue Franco-Americains" a series of thirteen bilingual one-hour radio interviews by Dr. Eloise Briere.

It should be noted that an oral history program does not have to generate publications or media material. A particular program can be committed to collecting interviews and related materials for archival accession. The institution's main purpose in undertaking this type of program would be to acquire interviews that reflect the community's best recollections and perceptions of its recent past. This could be a commitment that the local historical society assumes.

Institutions and programs that were not included in the survey also need to be identified if this report is to fully reflect the status of oral history in Massachusetts. Without doubt, the largest oral history collection in the state is that which has been collected by the John F. Kennedy Library. Its collection of over 1,300 interviews contains a great deal of material that would be of importance to researchers who are interested in the presidency and the executive branch, John F. Kennedy, Robert F. Kennedy, and Massachusetts politics from the end of World War II to the assassination in 1963. *Historical Materials in the John*

Fitzgerald Kennedy Library indicates that over three dozen interviews have been made with local friends, colleagues, associates, and state politicians.[15]

Since its beginnings in 1976, the "Black Women's Oral History Project," which is affiliated with the Schlesinger Library at Radcliffe College, has interviewed over seventy women who, whether or not they had a national reputation, were important in the black movement. Many of these individuals have played a significant role in American life. Among those who have been interviewed are Rosa Parks, the woman whom some have called the "Mother of the Civil Rights Movement;" Ellen Jackson, the founder in Boston of Operation Exodus, which eventually developed into the highly successful METCO program; Melinea Cass, the late activist who was revered as the "first lady of Roxbury;" Muriel Snowden, cofounder of Freedom House in Boston, and Addie William, who after being born to slaves spent fifty years teaching school in Virginia. This project is the basis for "Women of Courage," a traveling photographic exhibition of the interviewees. The official opening was held at the Schomburg Center for Research on Black Culture in New York City on December 13, 1984. The Schlesinger Library is also conducting the "Women in the Federal Government" oral history project. Both projects are under the direction of Ruth Hill, the library's audiovisual librarian.

For the last several years Eartha Dengler has run the highly successful and well-respected Immigrant City Archive in Lawrence. Committed to documenting the history of immigrants to this industrial region, she has conducted extensive interviews on a wide range of subjects including ethnic culture, ethnic organizations, working, immigration, and neighborhood. Presently the archive, in conjunction with Merrimack College's Political Science Department, is videotaping interviews with community politicians. As a result of the various projects the archive has a collection of 125 tapes, all of which are open and indexed. The archive is also a depository for ten interviews that were done for the Museum of American Textile History (formerly the Merrimack Valley Textile Museum). These, plus five other interviews, have been fully transcribed. The archive's oral history collection, along with related materials, is extremely valuable for scholars who are studying the interrelationship between immigrants and the community. The collection has served as source material for several students' papers and for a dissertation that will be published.

The Oral History Office of the Department of History at Northeastern University, which is under the direction of Dr. R. Wayne Anderson, has developed a collection of 192 interviews dealing with shoe workers, fishermen, immigrants, World War I, and Boston area communities, along with several minor topics such as merchant seamen and transportation. The fishermen and shoe workers collections are of research quality and have been used as source material for professional papers, articles, and a chapter in a forthcoming book on Georges Bank. The interviews, related slides, and other collateral material are available to scholars and others who are interested in these areas.

The Oral History Office of MIT between 1975 and 1978 collected 103 interviews for the Recombinant DNA History Collection. The project, which was under the direction of Professor Charles Weiner, interviewed scientists, legislators, lobbyists, environmentalists, journalists, university administrators, and citizen review board members concerned with the use of recombinant DNA technology. This collection is housed in the Institute Archives and Special Collection of the Libraries along with other oral history collections. These other collections are "Women Scientists and Engineers," "The Physical Science Study Committee," "Ocean Engineering," and "Computers at MIT." Under the policy of the archives, the taped interviews in all cases are closed. Typed transcripts approved by the interviewees are open to researchers. The archivist has indicated that for those transcripts for which there are yet no gift agreements, the libraries would contact interviewees and ask them for permission to open the transcripts. This is an important collection that should prove valuable to researchers.

On the community level, an interesting project is the Cambridge Women's Oral History Project. The purpose of this project is to record the recollections of women who live in the neighborhoods or are from the various ethnic groups that make up the community. This project, which has been ongoing for over five years and is under the direction of Cindy Cohen, is unique in that it involves women of all ages. The interviews are conducted by high school students. This project is intended to do more than just produce archival material. As end products, it has produced a booklet (*From Hearing My Mother Talk*) and a slide/tape presentation ("Let Life Be Yours: Voices of Cambridge Working Women") and has given rise to the Cambridge Women's Quilt Project.

It was earlier mentioned that the fascination with oral history has begun to decline. Let us now turn to that topic as we begin an assessment of oral history in Massachusetts. It appears to those who watch the oral history movement closely that Alex Haley's popular book *Roots* and the television miniseries of the same name, along with the bicentennial, were the impetus that caused the movement to "take off." It is inevitable that any movement that has a meteoric rise will also have a sharp decline. Therefore, it is not surprising that such a decline is taking place in the field of oral history. There are some factors that help to put the decline into perspective. (1) Those who originally became involved with oral history within institutions outside of the academic community have done what they wanted to do. In a sense, they played with it long enough and have now turned their attention to other things. This does not suggest that they no longer have an interest in oral history, but it does indicate that they no longer have the drive or feel the urgency to continue in this area. (2) Oral history no longer is a "new" way of doing history and as such does not receive the publicity that it once did. Ten years ago it was being written about in newspapers, news magazines, and more general magazines. Everyone was encouraged to become "his own historian" and save his family from historical extinction. (3) The promise of oral history was never fulfilled. Somehow it came to be believed that this "new method" would provide us with an inexhaustible supply of historical material. Indiscriminate taping by untrained volunteers provided in too many cases recollections or perceptions that were of interest to few and of value to none. (4) For those institutions that were interested in developing a professional program, it quickly became apparent that oral history was an expensive undertaking in both time and money. With limited resources, the institutions came to believe that they could better devote their time and efforts to undertakings that would bring a better return. (5) In terms of history, we who live in the birthplace of American civilization still have a hard time focusing on the twentieth century as an historical period. A walk through most of our museums and historical societies establishes rather clearly that most are tied to our "golden age" and have not yet developed a consistent collection policy for the century that is rapidly fading into the historical past.

This chapter was undertaken with the intention of discussing oral history as a methodology and relating its potential as a research tool for Massachusetts history. As the chapter is brought to a close, it is sad to note that the majority of the oral history collections identified in Massachusetts do not appear to be of value to serious researchers who are interested in producing works that will help us to better understand the community or that will help us to integrate the community and its institutions into the national picture. It should be noted that there are some scholars working out of institutions of higher education and being supported by the institution or by outside funding agencies, who have undertaken oral history programs that meet the standards of the professional associations.[16]

An evaluation of oral history in Massachusetts strongly indicates that the lack of professionalism is the most serious problem. It would be easy to let those involved off the hook by writing that they are amateur rather than trained historians, or to say that theirs is a labor of love and thus we cannot expect the same high quality that we would from those who follow history as a vocation. These and other excuses are feeble. Whether we are talking about libraries, colleges, historical societies/museums, or commissions, we are talking about institutions that claim that they are committed to preserving the community's history. If this is the case, then it is important that those who are responsible for historical preservation within the institution follow professional standards. This is not an impossible task.

First, the institution should invite a professional historian, one who has an interest in community/local history, to serve as a consultant. In this role he can help design a program that will be of historical worth while helping the community to put its past into perspective. Second, the institution should belong to the appropriate professional associations. Through their publications, the institution can quickly become familiar with the territory. Its staff can learn what manuals are available to help them; they can become familiar with the professionals in the field; they can attend workshops and meetings sponsored by the associations where they will learn the process and where they can ask questions and get answers. In a sense, membership in these organizations will ensure that they do not waste their time recreating the wheel. Third, there should be created, possibly in the state archives, a Community History Resource Center that could serve as a clearinghouse for the types of projects being pursued and as a repository for selected materials, including those that relate to oral history, that would be of value to other institutions and interested individuals. Fourth, the state historical commission, which is headed by the secretary of the commonwealth, should be adequately funded and should undertake a wide range of programs geared to the preservation of the state's history. Pennsylvania is a fine example of how such a commission can effectively operate. Fifth, the historical societies, commissions, museums, and other interested parties should join together in creating a strong state historical society to serve as an umbrella organization and to provide guidance and training. The failure of Massachusetts to have such an organization, which is common in most other states, has been a hindrance to the professionalization of local and community history. Finally, those using oral history methodology to collect interviews, to write books and articles, or to create video and radio documentaries and multimedia productions should inform the professional associations of what they have in their collection or what they have produced. There are two reasons why this should be done: the associations through their publications will make other scholars and interested individuals aware of the material and thus help it to have a broader dissemination; and it will provide an opportunity for peer review and evaluation. This process is important if we are to ensure that individual oral history collections are of value to scholars.

What Concord, Leyden, and the University of Lowell are doing and what Wakefield plans to do is what can be done with "good" oral history. If used properly, it can help people to look back in time and assess the changes that have taken place during the last eighty-five years. It provides the community with one more resource by which to judge how these changes, in whole or in part, have influenced the development of the community, and whether they have been beneficial in terms of the quality of life. For the younger members, oral history can help them come to understand the community in which their parents' generation grew up. Further, it should help them realize that all those born before World War I were, in a practical sense, if not by the calendar, born into the nineteenth century, and those still alive will die in the twenty-first century.

It is not the intention of this chapter to discuss in detail the use of oral history within the educational curriculum, but this use should be briefly mentioned. Since the success of Eliot Wigginton's *Foxfire* in the mountains of Georgia, some teachers in Massachusetts have turned to oral history as a means of enlivening the students' experience. Although they claim that they are doing "oral history," in reality they are not. Their purpose is to teach skills upon which the students can build their education. The preservation of a community's past is secondary to this primary goal. After this has been said, it would be unfair not to acknowledge that some inspiring teachers have joined with their students in producing material that is of archival worth. In some communities, students involved in cultural journalism have produced magazines in which community history and folkways have been highlighted. For this we should be grateful. But we should recognize that these undertakings are not permanent; they exist only as long as the interest of the teacher and the students remains. This is not the answer to preserving the community's past.

There are several colleges in Massachusetts where oral history courses are taught. In these institutions, the course is under the direction of a professor who is a trained historian and who has a commitment to oral history. Usually the students work on a project designed by the professor or on one for a local agency. Unlike the courses in secondary school, these courses can produce material that meets professional standards and thus will prove of value to other scholars. But there is a weakness here also. Too frequently, these courses fail to get minimum enrollment and thus run sporadically. A community cannot depend upon these courses to capture the voices from the past.

Oral history, coupled with modern technology, has provided our generation with an opportunity to preserve for the first time in a systematic way the recollections and perceptions of both the kings and the commoners. But these recollections perceptions will be of value to those who will take on the responsibility of writing our generation's history only if they can withstand the historian's scrutiny. Of this, those who gather must always be aware. To accept a lesser standard is unacceptable. For to do so would make real the fear expressed by Barbara Tuchman.

NOTES

1. Barbara W. Tuchman, "Distinguishing the Significant from the Insignificant," *Radcliffe Quarterly*, 56 (October 1972): 9-10.

2. Nevins told those gathered at the first meeting that he wanted to dispose "of the myth that I had anything to do with the founding of oral history. It founded itself. It has become a patent necessity, and would have sprung into life in a dozen places, under any circumstances." Allan Nevins, "The Uses of Oral History," *Oral History at Arrowhead: Proceedings of the First National Colloquium on Oral History*, ed. Elizabeth I. Dixon and James V. Mink (Los Angeles, 1967), pp. 25-37.

3. David K. Dunaway and Willa K. Baum, *Oral History: An Interdisciplinary Anthology* (Nashville, 1984), p. 27.

4. Elizabeth I. Dixon, "Definition of Oral History," Dixon and Mink, *Oral History at Arrowhead*, p. 14; William W. Moss, *Oral History Program Manual* (New York, 1974), p. 7. Moss, the archivist at the Smithsonian, was formerly the senior archivist at the John F. Kennedy Presidential Library.

5. Jesse Lemisch, "The American Revolution Seen from the Bottom Up," *Towards a New Past: Dissenting Essays in American History*, ed. Barton J. Bernstein (New York, 1969), pp. 5-6.

6. Dixon, "Definition of Oral History," p. 4; "Who Are the Elite, and What is a Non-Elitist?," *The Oral History Review, 1976*, pp. 1–5. For a discussion of the democratic nature of oral history see Paul Thompson, *The Voice of the Past: Oral History* (New York, 1978).

7. *History News* is published monthly. Books published by the association that would be useful to those interested in the use of oral history in community studies include David K. Dunaway and Willa K. Baum, *Oral History: An Interdisciplinary Anthology* (Nashville, 1984); David E. Kyvig and Myron A. Marty, *Nearby History: Exploring the Past around You* (Nashville, 1982); Barbara Allen and Lynwood Montell, *From Memory to History: Using Oral Sources for Historical Research* (Nashville, 1981); Brad Jolly, *Videotaping Local History* (Nashville, 1982); Willa K. Baum, *Oral History for the Local Historical Society* (Nashville, 1974); and Willa K. Baum, *Transcribing and Editing Oral History* (Nashville, 1977).

8. For a different type of incident that seems to show how the nature of an event can affect memory, see Tamara K. Hareven and Randolph Langenbach, *Amoskeag: Life and Work in an American Factory City* (New York, 1978), p. 32.

9. John A. Neuenschwander, "Remembrance of Things Past: Oral Historians and Long-Term Memory," *The Oral History Review, 1978*, pp. 44–53; Thompson, *Voice of the Past*.

10. The list was developed from listings in American Association for State and Local History, *Directory of Historical Societies and Agencies*, 12th ed. (Nashville, 1978); Bay State Historical League, *Directory of Historical Agencies in Massachusetts* (Boston, 1983); *Community Resources Directory* (Salem, Mass., 1981); American Historical Association, *Guide to Departments of History* (Washington, D.C., 1984); and the Massachusetts Library Association's listing of public libraries.

11. The four villages are Nonantum, West Newton, Auburndale, and Newton Highlands.

12. It is not clear if these two institutions were indicating that the interview sessions were longer than one hour, or that more than one one-hour interview session was held with a majority of the interviewees.

13. The following works provide basic information on transcribing: Willa K. Baum, *Transcribing and Editing Oral History* (Nashville, 1977); Cullom Davis et al., *Oral History: From Tape to Type* (Chicago, 1977); Mary Jo Deering and Barbara Pomeroy, *Transcribing without Tears: A Guide to Transcribing and Editing Oral History* (Washington, D.C., 1976); and Shirley Stephenson, *Editing and Indexing: Guidelines for Oral History*, 2nd printing with revisions (Fullerton, Calif., 1983). For a different perspective on transcribing see Edward D. Ives, *The Tape-Recorded Interview: A Manual for Field Workers in Folklore and Oral History* (Knoxville, 1980).

14. Mary H. Blewett, *Surviving Hard Times: The Working People of Lowell* (Lowell, 1982) (material in this book is based on tapes in the University of Lowell collection); Cindy Cohen, compiler, *From Hearing My Mother Talk: Stories of Cambridge Women* (Cambridge, 1979); Howard Zinn, *Justice in Everyday Life: The Way It Really Works* (New York, 1975); Lawrence Elle, *Not So Long Ago: Oral Histories of Older Bostonians* (Boston, 1980); Robert C. Hayden,

ed., *A Dialogue with the Past: Oral History Accounts of Boston's Ethnic Neighborhood and People* (Newton, 1979); Betsy H. Woodman, "Salt, Haying, Farming, and Fishing in Salisbury, Massachusetts: The Life of Sherb Eaton (1900–1982)," *Essex Institute Historical Collections*, 119 (July 1983): 165–81; Betsy H. Woodman, "The Salisbury Beach Dodgem: A Smashing Ride (1920–1980)," *Essex Institute Historical Collections*, 120 (October 1984): 277–313.

15. *Historical Materials in the John Fitzgerald Kennedy Library* (Boston, 1981).

16. Although it is difficult to identify all those who have used oral history for serious research, there are individual scholars at most of the state's institutions of higher education who have. In many cases they or their students have conducted the interviews. It is believed that many of these tapes have not been placed in a repository that would be open to other scholars. Too frequently, the interviews remain in the possession of the scholar or author. There are also those outside of the academic field who conduct interviews as a means of gathering material for their research.

PART TWO

ARCHIVES AND SOURCES

INTRODUCTION: SOURCES AND REPOSITORIES

PERSONS WHO INTEND to make use of Part 2 of this *Guide to the History of Massachusetts* should realize that in a one-volume work such as this one it is impossible to do more than touch upon the more important archives and repositories. This work has its predecessors, and researchers should be aware of the uses one may make of them. C. A. Flagg's *Guide to Massachusetts Local History* (Salem, 1907) is obviously hopelessly outdated, but the more recent work of the Committee for a New England Bibliography can be of major use to any researcher interested in any topic related to the history of Massachusetts or any of its cities or towns. Special mention should be made of John D. Haskell, Jr., *Massachusetts: A Bibliography of Its History* (Boston, 1976). Although this work is merely a listing of books and articles without any attempt to distinguish their accuracy, significance, and usefulness, it does provide the closest thing to a comprehensive listing of works on the history of the state and its cities and towns. The Committee for a New England Bibliography is continuing with its work, and it promises to update the 1976 edition and to expand it by including doctoral dissertations as well as the more important master's theses. During the Great Depression, the Historical Records Survey completed a study of available resources in the state, which was published as *A Guide to Depositories . . . in Massachusetts* (Boston, 1939). That *Guide* can be useful, especially for the smaller repositories.

In terms of published state records, a useful listing is found in the *Harvard Guide to American History* (Cambridge, 1954), pp. 130-32. Newspapers can provide a gold mine of information on the various cities and towns and on specific events and developments in history. The American Antiquarian Society and the Boston Public Library possess the most extensive newspaper collections in the state, with excellent coverage of newspapers from the colonial period to the present from various cities and towns in Massachusetts. For published and unpublished diaries, one should consult William Mathews, *American Diaries: An Annotated Bibliography of American Diaries prior to . . . 1861* (Berkeley, 1945), and H. M. Forbes, *New England Diaries, 1602-1800: A Descriptive Catalogue of Diaries, Orderly Books, and Sea Journals* (Topsfield, Mass., 1923).

In addition to the sources described herein, the historian would be well advised to consult the *National Union Catalog of Manuscript Collections*, which provides "collection-level" descriptions of more than 54,000 collections from 1,300 repositories, and adds about 2,000 each year. For materials related to Massachusetts that have been deposited in the National Archives, one should consult *Guide to the National Archives of the United States* (Washington, D.C., 1974), and the researcher should certainly be aware of the existence of the Regional Archives Branch of the Federal Archives and Records Center at 380 Trapelo Road, Waltham, Massachusetts 02154 (617 647-8100). The Regional Archives Branch maintains and makes available for research about fourteen thousand cubic feet of records of Federal agencies in New England, dating from 1789 to the present. These include records of the U.S. District and Circuit Courts, records relating to Customs and Coast Guard activities at New England ports, records of the U.S. Army Corps of Engineers for the Boston and Providence district offices, records of the Office of Scientific Research and Development (World War II laboratories at Harvard and MIT), the Northeast Region of the Bureau of Public Roads, the First Naval District and Shore Establishments in New England, and smaller groups of records of other federal agencies. In addition, the regional archives branch has over 35,000 rolls of microfilm containing copies of documents located in the National Archives. These include microfilm copies of the existing federal population census schedules, taken every ten years, for all states from 1790 to 1910, with the exception of the 1890 census schedules, which were destroyed by fire in 1921. In addition, there are microfilm copies of non-population census schedules for Massachusetts from 1850 to 1880, and of some schedules of a special census of Union veterans and widows of veterans in 1890. There also are microfilm copies of applications for pension and bounty land warrants issued to veterans of the Revolutionary War and microfilm copies of military service records of those who served in the Revolution. There also is a microfilm index to compiled service records of volunteer soldiers who served during the War of 1812. The Federal Archives Record Center also has records of immigrants who applied for American citizenship, from U.S. district and circuit courts in Massachusetts (1790-1950), as well as copies of naturalization records from Federal, state, county, and municipal courts in Massachusetts from 1790 to 1906. Finally, there are copies of most passenger arrival lists for the ports of Boston (March 1891 to July 1920) and New Bedford (1902 to 1919). An annotated listing is available on request.

Persons with an interest in aspects of Massachusetts history that relate directly to Great Britain and Ireland (such as colonial relations with the mother country or Irish immigration to the state) ought to consult Charles M. Andrews, *Guide to the Materials for American History, to 1783, in the Public Record Office of Great Britain*, 2 vols. (Washington, D.C., 1912); Charles M. Andrews and F. G. Davenport, *Guide to the Manuscript Materials for the History of the United States to 1783 in the British Museum, in Minor London Archives, and in the Libraries of Oxford and Cambridge* (Washington, D.C., 1908); and B. R. Crick et al., *A Guide to Manuscripts Relating to America in Great Britain and Ireland* (London, 1961). The Library of Congress has obtained typewritten, microfilm, or photostatic copies of most important manuscripts in European archives, and a list is provided in G. G. Griffin, *A Guide to Manuscripts Relating to American History in British Depositories Reproduced for the Division of Manuscripts* (Washington, D.C., 1946).

Record keeping is governed by state law, and the various cities, towns, and counties therefore are supposed to follow published and accepted standards for maintenance and use of governmental sources. Birth, death, and marriage records are maintained by the city or town clerk. When searching for material, however, the historian ought to be aware that borders and names of many towns have changed over the years. A good source for finding out about changes in town jurisdictions and names is *Historical Data Relating to Counties. Cities, and Towns in Massachusetts*, prepared by the secretary of state's office. Massachusetts land deeds and probate and divorce records are kept by the county seats. A good example of the situation regarding town records was provided by Ellen M. Coty in "Research Aids: Genealogy in Western Massachusetts," *Historical Journal of Western Massachusetts*, 6 (Spring 1978): 45-47.

Finally, in some cases a repository has a published guide, and these should be secured and utilized as a much more extensive reference tool than this book can possibly be. Where appropriate, the archival descriptions below include specific reference to those guides. No effort has been made to include the hours repositories are open because they are subject to frequent change.

AMERICAN ANTIQUARIAN SOCIETY
185 Salisbury Street
Worcester, Mass. 01609-1634
(617) 755-5221

The American Antiquarian Society (AAS) is a learned society that maintains a research library of American history and culture. Founded in 1812 in Worcester, the society's mission is to collect, preserve, and make available for research use the printed record of the United States. Specializing in the American period to 1877, the society's holdings number close to 3 million books, pamphlets, broadsides, manuscripts, prints, maps, and newspapers.

Many of the society's manuscript collections are rich sources for early Massachusetts history. They cover a broad variety of topics and include early American book trades and book collecting; early New England diaries; papers of eighteenth- and nineteenth-century New Englanders, particularly those in the religious, political, and military worlds; and papers and records of central Massachusetts families and volunteer associations from 1750 to 1870. The collections are particularly strong for the central Massachusetts area. The society's manuscript collections were cataloged during the 1970s with the assistance of the National Endowment for the Humanities. They are described in *Catalogue of the Manuscript Collections of the American Antiquarian Society*, 4 vols. (Boston, 1979). Collection descriptions for all collections are available at the library and may be photocopied.

The society, a member of the Research Libraries Group, Inc., has begun cataloging manuscript acquisitions and holdings using the new MARC format for archival and manuscripts control (AMC), and these records are available in the RLIN data base. The society's own archival records, 1812 to the present, are currently being arranged and described. To facilitate research use, a finding aid and AMC records will be generated for this material.

The society's research facilities are open to experienced adult researchers, following presentation of two forms of identification (one with a picture) and an interview with a senior staff member. Graduate students must also present a letter of introduction from the faculty member supervising their research project. Limited photoduplication services are available. For information about AAS collections and their use, please write to the curator of manuscripts.

Barbara Trippel Simmons

ANDOVER NEWTON THEOLOGICAL SCHOOL
FRANKLIN TRASK LIBRARY
169 Herrick Road
Newton Centre, Mass. 02159
(617) 964-1100 ext. 252

Andover Newton Theological School is related to American Baptist Churches in the U.S.A. and the United Church of Christ. The collections document Baptist and Congregational history. Although some personal papers relate to national denominational work and foreign missionary activity, the majority of collections relate to New England history. In addition to the archives of Andover Newton and the two predecessor schools, Andover Theological Seminary (founded 1807) and Newton Theological Institution (founded 1825), collections include personal papers of sixty-five individuals and families, records of twenty-six state and regional Baptist and Congregational organizations, and records of forty-eight Baptist and Congregational churches. The collections date from 1665 to the present, although only three collections predate 1700.

The Merrill Department of Rare Books and Special Collections also includes rare books, library collections, and records of New England Baptist Library and Backus Historical Society, as well as a collection of Bibles given by the American Board of Commissioners for Foreign Missions. A description of representative collections related to Massachusetts history follows:

The papers of Isaac Backus (7 feet) include personal papers from 1746 to 1806 and correspondence and narratives chronicling the Separate Baptist struggle for religious freedom from 1660 to 1806, as well as the records of the Warren Baptist Association. This is an important collection, as Backus was not only minister in Middleborough from 1756 to 1806 and author of a three-volume history of the denomination, but traveled extensively in New England, helping organize churches and settle disputes among Baptist groups.

The papers of Jonathan Edwards (4 feet) include correspondence of the minister who became known as the father of the Great Awakening (1703-1758), as well as sermon notes, and memoranda on cases of church discipline and theological and philosophical subjects. In addition, this collection includes Edwards' family papers and the sermons of James Pierpont (1660-1714), Jonathan's father-in-law.

The papers of Irah Chase (2 feet) include correspondence, sermons, addresses, lectures, literary manuscripts, student lecture notes at Andover Theological Seminary, and notes on readings. Chase graduated from Middlebury College in 1814 and Andover Theological Seminary in 1817. After serving as a missionary in Virginia, he became an educator, coming to Massachusetts in 1825 to inaugurate the Baptist seminary, Newton Theological Institution. He taught biblical theology from 1825 to 1838 and church history from 1838 to 1845.

The papers of Edwards Amasa Park (9 feet) include correspondence, sermons, lectures, notes on theological subjects and on his readings, and newspaper clippings. Park taught at Andover Theological Seminary from 1836 to 1881 and was considered one of the greatest preachers of his time. He was on the editorial staff of *Bibliotheca Sacra* for 56 years as coeditor (1844-1852), editor (1852-1884), and associate editor (1884-1900).

The papers of Alvah Hovey (12 feet) include autobiographical essays, his diary, correspondence, sermons, addresses, lectures, literary manuscripts, student lecture notes from Dartmouth College and Newton Theological Institution, notes on biblical texts and theological subjects, and newspaper clippings. Hovey taught at Newton Theological Institution beginning in the late 1840s and served as president from 1868 to 1898.

The Records of the Brethren (one foot, 1808-1870) document the evolution of foreign missionary work from its beginnings at Williams College in 1808, to Andover Theological Seminary. Andover students who petitioned for financial support from the General Association of Massachusetts (Congregational) stimulated the establishment of the American Board of Commissioners for Foreign Missions, the first foreign missionary organization in this country. The collection includes a minute book and correspondence, as well as record books of Brethren at Lane Theological Seminary, Auburn Theological Seminary, and Princeton Theological Seminary.

The Records of the Society of Inquiry Respecting Missions (4 feet, 1811-1920) include minute books of the general society and committees, correspondence, papers read at monthly meetings and annual public meetings, catalogs of the library, and documentation of a survey on religious condition of colleges that was conducted from 1856 to 1878. Although this was an organization of students at Andover Theological Seminary, members often corresponded after becoming missionaries, so there is valuable information on various fields of mission work in letters written to the group.

The library is the depository for the archives of The American Baptist Churches of Massachusetts (TABCOM, 1969 to the present) and its predecessor organizations, the Massachusetts Baptist Missionary Society (1802-1835), the Massachusetts Baptist Convention (1824-1969), and the Boston Baptist Bethel City Mission Society (1921-1969). The library also has the records of TABCOM-affiliated organizations, including the American Baptist Women of Massachusetts (1924 to the present), the Massachusetts Baptist Foundation for Campus Ministry (1966 to the present) and its predecessor organization, the Baptist Student Foundation (1950 to 1966), and the Northern Baptist Education Society (1830 to the present) and its predecessor organization, the Massachusetts Baptist Education Society (1814-1830). The library also has the records of fourteen associations affiliated with TABCOM, as well as the records of forty-five American Baptist churches.

Diana Yount

ARCHIVES OF THE
ARCHDIOCESE OF BOSTON
**2121 Commonwealth Avenue
Brighton, Mass. 02135
(617) 254-0100**

The Archives of the Archdiocese of Boston preserves and makes available the records of the Roman Catholic church in eastern Massachusetts, covering the entire period from 1788 to the present. Included are records and papers of the bishops and archbishops of Boston, as well as those of the Catholic clergy, women religious, and laypersons. In addition, there are large collections pertaining to local parish life and the activities of church-related charitable, educational, and social service organizations and institutions. The holdings include paper records in the form of letters, diaries, and other documents; they also include photographs, motion pictures and videotapes, sound recordings, oral history interviews, and some artifacts. The collections are described fully in James M. O'Toole, *Guide to the Archives of the Archdiocese of Boston* (New York, 1982).

The archives makes its holdings available to interested researchers of all kinds. Topics covered may include local history, parish history, genealogy, and the social and religious history of New England. Of particular interest to genealogists is the collection of baptismal and marriage records of all Catholic parishes dated before 1910. The archives also conducts a variety of educational programs, including adult education programs centering on parish history and anniversary celebrations and making primary sources available to classes of local high school students. In addition, the archives engages in other outreach activities, including exhibits, presentations to local civic and church groups, and a regular column on history and archives in the archdiocesan newspaper, *The Pilot.*

ARCHIVES OF THE
CONTEMPORARY BOSTON AREA
WOMEN'S MOVEMENT
46 Pleasant Street
Cambridge, Mass. 02139
(617) 354–8807

The Archives of the Contemporary Boston Area Women's Movement is an independent and privately supported archives that collects the records and other source material relating to the history of Boston-area feminist organizations from 1968 to the present. The archives has a total of 90 cubic feet of organizational records, over 3,000 books and pamphlets, a periodical collection of 120 serials, and 25 cubic feet of flyers, brochures, and newspaper clippings relating to the contemporary women's movement.

The archives' holdings include the records of early Boston-area groups such as Bread and Roses (1969–1971), one of the first socialist-feminist organizations in the country; Female Liberation (1970–1974), active in the reproductive rights movement; and Cell 16, publishers of an early radical feminist theoretical journal, *No More Fun and Games* (1968–1975). These three groups were highly influential in both the local and national women's movement, and their records add considerably to our knowledge and understanding of the movement's formative days. Materials within these collections include position papers, minutes of meetings, correspondence, financial records, publications, and press releases.

Another major collection is that of the Women's Center (Women's Educational Center, Inc.), 1971 to the present. The center, one of the oldest community-based women's centers in the country, is a resource and referral center for the women of Boston and its surrounding communities as well as an umbrella organization providing meeting space and financial support for a number of Boston-area women's groups and projects. The center collection includes financial and administrative records, correspondence, minutes of meetings, photographs, publications, staff logs, and clippings. Records of affiliated groups include those of the Boston Area Rape Crisis Center (1972 to the present); Lesbian Liberation (1971 to the present); the publications *Second Wave* (1970–1984), *Sister Courage* (1974–1978), and *On Our Way* (1971 to the present); Boston Women's Pentagon Action (1983–1986); Women against Violence against Women (1979–1984); and the Abortion Action Coalition (1976–1980).

All collections are open for research use, but there are some restrictions on the use of sensitive material where individuals are mentioned. Photocopying is permissible only by staff members.

Elizabeth Bouvier

ARTHUR AND ELIZABETH SCHLESINGER LIBRARY
RADCLIFFE COLLEGE
10 Garden Street
Cambridge, Mass. 02138
(617) 495-8647

This library, founded as the Women's Archives in 1943, focuses on the history of women in America. It includes a book collection of almost 30,000 volumes, more than 400 periodicals, and vertical files of clippings and pamphlets on individual women, organizations, and subjects of interest to researchers on the history of women in America.

The manuscript holdings provide source materials on such topics as women's rights and suffrage, social welfare and reform, pioneers in the professions, family history, health, and child rearing, as well as women in politics, labor, and government service. In terms of material related to Massachusetts, this collection is especially rich, including the papers of penologists Jessie Donaldson Hodder and Miriam Van Waters, pioneering female physician Dr. Elizabeth Blackwell, suffragist Lucy Stone, author Caroline Wells Healey Dall, leaders of the League of Women Voters (Dorothy Kirchwey Brown, Sara Rosenfeld Ehrmann, Eunice Mannheim, and Maud Wood Park), Congresswoman Edith Nourse Rogers, and Boston Municipal Court Judge Jennie Loitman Barron.

A number of collections relate to the conditions of women's employment and their participation in the labor movement. The correspondence, diaries, and scrapbooks of Harriet Jane Hanson Robinson and her daughter Harriette Lucy Robinson Shattuck include letters from Lucy Larcom and other Lowell mill girls and provide information on nineteenth-century working conditions. Material on twentieth-century factory work and union organizing is found in the autobiography and other papers of Mary Kenney O'Sullivan. Efforts to mobilize public opinion in support of improved working conditions are found in the records of the Consumers' League of Massachusetts (established in 1898) and in the papers of John Graham Brooks, a founder of the National Consumers' League.

The library's collection is rich in materials related to the education of women in the state. The extensive papers of Abigail Adams Eliot, cofounder of the Eliot-Pearson School of Child Study at Tufts University, and Katharine Taylor, the progressive educator who directed the Shady Hill School in Cambridge from 1921 to 1949, are especially important. The library also has the correspondence of numerous university professors, including historian Helen Maud Cam, the first woman on the faculty of arts and sciences at Harvard, and Dr. Alice Hamilton, industrial toxicologist and first woman to teach at Harvard (Harvard Medical School, 1919-1935). Female college presidents are well represented in the collection, including Elizabeth Cary Agassiz and Ada Louise Comstock of Radcliffe and Sarah Gibson Blanding of Vassar. Ella Lyman Cabot's papers document her interest in ethics and religious education. There are many diaries and letters written by schoolgirls and schoolteachers, including papers of Abigail Williams May, who served on the Boston School Committee from 1873 to 1875. Fannie Fern Andrews began the Boston Home and School Association in 1907 to bring parents into active participation in the public schools, and her files on that organization, and on others concerned with peace education, are maintained in the library. Organizations concerned with education of women include the American Association of University Women (AAUW, Massachusetts state division and Boston chapter), and the Berkeley Street School Association.

In the areas of medicine and public health, the library includes the papers of the pioneer female physician Elizabeth Blackwell and of Eliza Taylor Ransom, a Boston physician who founded the first Twilight Sleep Hospital in America. Other health professions are well represented, including the papers of Ethel Cohen, a pioneer in medical social work, Mary Sewall Gardner, a national leader in public health nursing, Edith T. Garfield, a psychologist who sought to implement new concepts of care for children in the Boston Floating Hospital, Elizabeth Prince Rice, associate professor of public health social work at the Harvard School of Public Health, and Maida Herman Solomon, psychiatric social worker and educator. Researchers with an interest in aspects of sex, reproduction, and marriage will find useful data in the files of the Birth Control League of Massachusetts and the Massachusetts Society for Social Health, in the papers of birth control activists Lucile Lord-Heinstein, Florence Clothier, and Sarah Bradley Gamble, and in the files of Mass Choice.

Social welfare and reform are well represented in the library. The abolition movement is chronicled in the papers of various well-known reforming families, including the Beechers, the Stowes, the Lorings, and the Blackwells. Elizabeth Hewes Tilton worked for the temperance cause, prison reform was the concern of Jessie Hodder and Miriam Van Waters, and Elizabeth Glendower Gardiner Evans advocated the full range of reform causes of her era. One large and several small Emma Goldman collections document her friendships and her work for free speech and anarchism. Various settlement houses are documented in the collection, including the records of Denison House, in Boston's South End, and the North Bennet Street Industrial School, a trade school and settlement house founded in 1879 as the North End Industrial Home. The early history of social work can be found in the papers of Eva Whiting White, who was head worker at Elizabeth Peabody House from 1909 to 1944, professor at Simmons College from 1922 to 1950, and president of the Women's Educational and Industrial Union from 1929 to 1952. The library also has records of various institutions that have served women, including the Home for Aged Women (founded in Boston in 1849), Rutland Corner House (established in 1877), and the Women's Educational and Industrial Union (1877), all still active.

Numerous organizations have placed their archives in the library, including the Ladies' Physiological Institute of Boston and Vicinity (founded in 1848), the New England Women's Club (founded in 1869), the Saturday Morning Club of

Boston (founded in 1871 by Julia Ward Howe), the League of Women for Community Service (a social service and civic organization of black women that began about 1916), and the Fragment Society (founded in 1812 as a sewing circle to provide clothing to indigent families).

Business is represented, mainly by the massive records of the Lydia E. Pinkham Medicine Company of Lynn.

In recent years the library has developed several important projects that certainly will add to the material available on black women, and working conditions in nineteenth- and twentieth-century Massachusetts. These include ongoing oral histories, cooperative microfilming, and collecting projects.

The holdings are described in the Arthur and Elizabeth Schlesinger Library on the History of Women in America, *Catalogs of Manuscripts, Books, and Periodicals*, 10 vols. (Boston, 1984). For more specific information on the holdings, researchers should consult this work prior to their arrival at the library. Anyone with a research interest in the history of women in Massachusetts would be wise to schedule a lengthy visit to the Schlesinger Library.

Eva Moseley

BERKSHIRE ATHENAEUM
LOCAL HISTORY AND LITERATURE SERVICES
One Wendell Avenue
Pittsfield, Mass. 01201
(413) 499-9486

The Berkshire Athenaeum, Pittsfield's public library, was incorporated in 1872. Its local history collection, inaugurated by Harlan H. Ballard, librarian from 1888 to 1934, now includes the genealogical collections, the Shaker Collection, the Herman Melville Memorial Collection, and the Berkshire Authors Collection.

The local history collections include the William Williams Collection, consisting of two boxes of over one thousand items dating fron 1734 to 1838. These include the personal papers, reports, and commissions of Col. William Williams written during the French and Indian War, early proprietors' records of Pontoosuck (Pittsfield), and other documents and correspondence of this period. There is a four-volume typewritten and indexed transcription. The local history collection includes a considerable amount of cataloged manuscript material, including eighteenth- and nineteenth-century business ledgers, documents and records of various towns in Berkshire County, sermons of the Rev. Thomas Allen, Regimental Order books and other records of the 49th Massachusetts Volunteer Militia, and a portfolio of letters and other documents related to Shays' Rebellion, as well as a transcription of General Lincoln's Order Book (1787), made from the original that was formerly in the collection of the Berkshire Athenaeum, and an account book of Colonel Ashley's First Massachusetts Regiment dated 1780. The library has seven boxes of executions (1762-1768) from the Berkshire County Court of Common Pleas.

The Berkshire Agricultural Society Papers (1811-1901) include account books from 1824 to 1859, addresses from 1811 to 1854, reports from 1816 to 1823 and 1859 to 1893, exhibitors' entries, lists, premiums, and miscellaneous correspondence and pamphlets.

The Berkshire Medical Institution Collection (6 feet) includes manuscript theses of graduates from 1823 to 1867, annual catalogs from 1832 to 1867, catalogs of graduates from 1823 to 1867, and matriculation and lecture tickets from 1827 to 1866, as well as miscellaneous records and papers from 1822 to 1871.

The library has 250 items of personal correspondence by and to Governor George N. Briggs, dating from 1832 to 1861. The Taft Papers consist of two boxes of early legal documents relating to western Massachusetts, of which one box contains account books and documents of the Tenth Massachusetts Turnpike Corporation. The Maplewood Institute Collection contains records, photographs, annual reports, lectures, and catalogs from 1842 to 1883 of this private educational institution for young women. The Cyrus and Daniel Williams Papers (1797-1850) contain personal papers, estate papers, financial records, business agreements, and civic and religious papers of two Stockbridge merchants. The Hinsdale Family Papers include letters, deeds, and journals of the Rev. Theodore Hinsdale (journals dated 1787, 1795, and 1804, and justice of the peace records from 1799 to 1815 and 1849 to 1855).

The photograph collection includes the Erwin H. Kennedy Collection of early photographs of Pittsfield dating from 1850 to 1911 (5 portfolios). Additional photographs in the collection include the Gravelle Collection of photographs of people and sites in Pittsfield during the early 1940s.

The Shaker Collection (17 feet) includes manuscript letters, records, and treatises by Shakers, especially those from Mt. Lebanon, as well as books, drawings, music, and rare pamphlets. A more complete listing of this collection is in Mary L. Richmond's *Shaker Literature*, 3 vols. (Hanover, N.H., 1977).

The Genealogical Collections include the Rollin H. Cooke Collection (6 feet) of town, church, and cemetery records of Berkshire County towns, the Elmer I. Shepard Collection (40 file drawers) containing research notes, vital records, and probate records of families from Berkshire County, western Massachusetts, other New England states, and New York, and the William Bradford Browne Collection (9 boxes) of research notes and collected historical information of the late genealogist and town clerk of North Adams, primarily relating to northern Berkshire families. The latter collection includes copies of Stafford Hill-New Providence (Cheshire) First Baptist Church records.

BOSTON ATHENAEUM
101½ Beacon Street
Boston, Mass. 02108-3777
(617) 227-0270

The Boston Athenaeum is an independent research library founded in 1807 by a group of literary-minded Bostonians who had in 1905 joined to edit the *Monthly Anthology and Boston Review*. Qualified guest researchers wishing to use the collection should apply in advance. Special collections include nineteenth-century tracts, eighteenth- and nineteenth-century Boston newspapers, books and tracts from the libraries of John Adams, John Quincy Adams, and Charles Francis Adams (some including manuscript notes), and nineteenth-century prints and photographs.

Among the newspaper holdings are the *Boston Evening Post* from 1740 to 1775, the *Boston Newsletter* from 1710 to 1775, and the *Boston Gazette* from 1723 to 1798. The library also has a good representation of early New England and colonial newspapers, some on microfiche or microfilm. These include the *Boston Post Boy* from 1734 to 1775, the *American Weekly Mercury* from 1719 to 1746, the *New England Weekly Journal* from 1727 to 1741, and the *New England Courant* from 1721 to 1726.

The Athenaeum's collection of historical prints and photographs is one of its major strengths. The collection includes advertising prints, drawings, music sheets, portraits, street scenes, and views by most of the important Boston printmakers and artists of the nineteenth century. The photograph collection contains approximately 20,000 daguerreotypes, ambrotypes, and photographs, and includes portraits and views that document the history of New England itself. The Athenaeum also has a large collection of architectural drawings, including works by Nathaniel J. Bradlee and George Minot Dexter.

Other collections include the library of General Henry Knox (Washington's secretary of war), material relating to the Sacco and Vanzetti case, selected papers of Obadiah Rich, a founder of the Athenaeum, and the Athenaeum archives. The latter provides an exceptional source of information about Boston people and events, as well as the book trade and nineteenth-century library development.

BOSTON PUBLIC LIBRARY
Rare Books and Manuscripts
Copley Square
Boston, Mass. 02117
(617) 536-5400

The Boston Public Library has collections that are undoubtedly indispensable sources for the history of the state of Massachusetts. Among them are the following:

1. The Papers of Judge Elijah Adlow include about 10,000 legal documents relating to Suffolk County, Massachusetts.

2. The Papers of Ellis Ames, Boston lawyer, include about 2,000 letters and documents relating to nineteenth-century legal cases, land deeds, and so on.

3. The Anti-Slavery Collection consists of books, manuscripts, broadsides, and photographs. The collection of manuscripts is popularly referred to as the Garrison Papers. This rare collection (16,000 items) consists of the letters and papers of William Lloyd Garrison and his associates on *The Liberator* editorial staff in the American Anti-Slavery Society from the 1830s through the 1870s.

The Anti-Slavery Collection also includes books, broadsides, and photographs of nearly 4,000 items, including the travels and histories of fugitive slaves. The collection is closely connected with the Civil War Collection, which includes soldiers' diaries as well as letters and books from both sides of the fighting forces.

4. The Boston Latin School Collection (c. 5,000 items) contains correspondence, records, documents, reports, and photographs from the nineteenth and early twentieth centuries of or relating to the Boston Latin School, the oldest educational institution in continuous existence in the country. The printed material consists of works published by and for the Boston Latin School: yearbooks, invitations, programmes, school journals, and so on. The collection also contains volumes by classical authors, Latin and Greek grammars, and materials donated by the Boston Latin School Alumni.

5. The Boston School Committee Collection consists of the original documents and related papers of the Boston School Committee from 1792 through 1870. They presently comprise approximately 45 bound volumes of minutes and some 90 linear feet of supporting papers. These documents are basic materials for research on American education and are used extensively for such programs as ones on the early public education of blacks and females.

6. City of Boston Records include Tax Assessors records commencing with 1789 and including tax bills for Paul Revere; City Clerk files beginning in 1629 and including a document dated 1670 that records a meeting between Sagamore Suamauge of the Abenaki (and his council and sachems) and Lt. John Capen on the matter of land purchase; and Building Department records including building plans for more than one hundred years. These collections of an evolving city

provide rare source material for urbanologists, architects, historians, and other scholars.

7. The Mellen Chamberlain Autograph Collection includes about 20,000 letters and documents relating to American and European history and literature (1897).

8. The Felicani Archives consists of thousands of letters, manuscripts, documents, broadsides, pamphlets, and relics collected by Aldino Felicani, the treasurer of the Defense Committee for Nicola Sacco and Bartolomeo Vanzetti. These magnificent archives have been described by one antiquarian bookman as the "most detailed, thorough, and complete research resource dealing with the trial itself, the lives of the defendants, . . . No other collection can approach it in research importance."

9. The Franco-American Collection. Rarities abound in this collection of parish histories, early New England and U.S. directories compiled by Bourbonniere, historic pamphlet material on French settlements in Louisiana and the Canadian colony of Winooski, Vermont, Paquin's history of the French-Canadians of Chicago, and Jehin de Prume's study of French Americans in New York City.

10. The Walter Lewisson–Washington Collection contains about 6,000 volumes on the life and times of George Washington, many of which were printed before 1800. Many of these deal with Washington in Massachusetts, honors conferred on him, memorials, and so on.

11. The Library of Wendell Phillips contains about 3,000 books and pamphlets collected by the noted abolitionist covering all aspects of the anti-slavery movement.

12. Pre-Revolutionary Documents of Boston and Massachusetts consists of more than 12,000 documents, with letters and other papers bearing such signatures as Paul Revere and Sam Adams. Included are the town records of Boston, Dorchester, Roxbury, and Charlestown for the period 1634–1789. These early documents are an historian's mother lode, containing as they do commentaries and reports on the Battle of Bunker Hill, the Boston Massacre, the historic Tea Party, and other events.

13. The 20th Regiment Collection includes about 8,000 volumes on the Civil War and Massachusetts in the military.

These collections are the ones dealing directly with the history of the state of Massachusetts. There are many others on various subjects that, while not dealing directly with history, are part of the history of the state, for example, literary and theatrical collections. The library also possesses a marvelous collection of Massachusetts newspapers on microfilm.

Laura V. Monti

BOSTON UNIVERSITY
MUGAR MEMORIAL LIBRARY
Special Collections
771 Commonwealth Avenue
Boston, Mass. 02215
(617) 353-3696

The Twentieth Century Archives at Boston University has been written about extensively as the most comprehensive and significant part of Special Collections. It has become a major research collection of international status and is most fully described in the published guide *Special Collections at Boston University* (Boston, 1981), as are the other book and manuscript collections.

All serious researchers are welcome to consult the holdings of Special Collections. In the case of twentieth-century manuscript material, researchers should check that no restrictions have been made by donors. In any case, a preliminary phone call is advised as a consultation with library staff on research topics and materials.

The Rare Book Collection of Boston University contains several areas of historic Massachusetts interest. Early Americana is held in both printed and manuscript form in the Bortman Collection. Two thousand books and manuscripts document the first two centuries of colonial America, with emphasis on the early history of New England, church history, military affairs, and the history of Canada and the West Indies. Colonial documents include British account books that tabulate imports and exports from the colonies, 1698 to 1764; ships' logs and maritime papers; a manuscript from the 1680s of "Meditations, Prayers and Pious Devotions" by David Dunster; an early manuscript volume of sermons, including one sermon of possible attribution to Anne Hutchinson; a commonplace book of Richard Saltonstall; addresses and petitions of colonial governors to English monarchs; and letters of John Eliot, the Mathers, and John Cotton.

Manuscripts relating to the War of Independence have important content. Two British reports on the Stamp Act of 1765; a chaplain's diary with an eyewitness account of the siege and evacuation of Boston in 1776; a resolution of the Massachusetts General Court calling up troops in 1777; and General Henry Clinton's report to his superiors on "The State of His Majesty's Forces in North America" (1781) are present. Military manuscripts record the British government's expenditures on arms between 1688 and 1697 and the supplies issued by the Admiralty to troops in North America between 1715 and 1750. Municipal documents are held in depth, such as deeds, marriage certificates, and grant papers.

The collections of books, pamphlets, and broadsides dealing with the Revolutionary and federalist periods are quite extensive, and include orations and proclamations following most of the military encounters of the war, contemporary newspaper accounts of the war, and numerous charters, bills, and military papers, both British and American, relating to the conduct of the war. More than 100 Massachusetts election sermons from 1733 to 1883 and 150 Fourth of July orations from 1781 to 1871 record significant political and social opinions and events in New England affairs.

The Bortman Collection holds several generations of family papers of the Mayhew and the Foxcroft families of New England. The Mayhew Papers (1648-1774) include personal papers, literary manuscripts, commonplace books, and the correspondence of Jonathan Mayhew (1720-1766). The Foxcroft Papers (1690-1770) contain the correspondence, religious writings, autobiography, and miscellaneous papers of the Reverend Thomas Foxcroft (1697-1769), minister of the First Church of Boston, and his immediate family, with many sermons, papers on the history of local churches, and correspondence with religious leaders, among them Cotton Mather, Samuel Sewall, and Isaac Watts.

Another family archive is that of the lineal and collateral families descendent of George Morton (1585-1624), one of the early settlers of Plymouth. The collection numbers over 10,000 items, mostly dating from the nineteenth and twentieth centuries. This collection of his family papers was given by H. C. Robbins Landon, contemporary American musicologist, and is part of the Twentieth Century Archives.

Two separate libraries on deposit at Boston University form the holdings on military history. The working library and archives of the Massachusetts First Corps of Cadets and the library of the Military Historical Society of Massachusetts create a specialized subject collection of more than 7,500 printed volumes and approximately 200 linear feet of manuscripts. The First Corps of Cadets, chartered in 1741 as the bodyguard of the governor of the Province of Massachusetts Bay, is the oldest military unit in continuous existence in the United States. The corps took an active part in the War of Independence, the Civil War, and both world wars. Its library of more than 3,500 volumes was formed between 1860 and 1910, though works printed much earlier are present. The Archives of the First Corps of Cadets depicts the part played by the corps during the Revolutionary War. Among other events it protected life and property during the Stamp Act upheavals and the Hutchinson Riots. Manuscripts from this era include a letter from George Washington to John Hancock and prewar correspondence of Boston's Revolutionary leaders, including Samuel Adams and William Palfrey. The corps was called into action during the Lawrence mill strike of 1912 and the Boston police strike of 1919, and these records of daily activities and reports of duty constitute a primary source of labor history.

The library of the Military Historical Society of Massachusetts features regimental histories and publications of veterans' organizations of Massachusetts. It contains pamphlets on military groups and heroes of Massachusetts.

The Historical Manuscript Collection contains a notable group of letters and documents of American statesmen from the Revolutionary period to the twentieth century. Edward C. Stone donated a collection of letters and documents of the signers of the Declaration of Independence that includes a rare Button Gwinnett petition, in his hand, to Governor James Wright of Georgia, dated 1769; a collection of letters and documents of the signers of the Constitution; and two sets of letters and documents of the presidents of the United States. Purchases and other holdings have expanded these collections from the original nucleus of the gift by Edward Stone.

Two highlights of American manuscripts are an eleven-page letter of April 15, 1814, from John Jay (1745–1829), first chief justice of the United States, to his friend John Murray, Jr.; and a bound manuscript of Charles Sumner's speech "Issues of the Presidential Election," delivered October 30, 1869, at the Cambridge City Hall.

Central to the Irving P. and Helen Joy Fox Collection is a group of letters to Silas Deane (1737–1789), a member of the Continental Congress and a diplomat. Letters dating from 1775 to 1782 were sent to Deane on his diplomatic mission to France by Benedict Arnold, George Washington, the Count d'Estaing, General Philip Schuyler, John Jay, and Benjamin Franklin.

The Boston Mercantile Library Association Records depict another side of Massachusetts life during the nineteenth century. Organized for the purpose of improving the "intellectual and moral condition of young men engaged as merchants' clerks," the association sponsored a reading room and lending library, debates, and lectures on "improving" topics. Contained in thirty-six volumes and four manuscript boxes are records of meetings, correspondence and catalogs, addresses, account books, lists of members, visitors' books, scrapbooks, and publications dating from 1820 to 1903.

The nucleus of the strong Black Americana Collection came to Boston University as the personal library of Edward Starr. The Rare Book Collection holds many nineteenth-century slave narratives; documents on the abolition of the slave trade in the eighteenth and nineteenth centuries; and contemporary printings of early writers such as Phillis Wheatley and Frederick Douglass.

The Richards Collection, a gift of Paul C. Richards, Boston University, Class of 1960, consists of more than 4,000 manuscripts, 1,500 etchings and engravings, hundreds of signed photographs and documents of state from American and European sources, and historical recordings. Among these riches are letters of Cotton Mather, Emerson and Thoreau, Louis Agassiz, and many U.S. presidents from George Washington to Gerald Ford. Fifty letters and manuscripts of the Unitarian clergyman, teacher, and statesman Edward Everett (1794–1865) represent his social and cultural interchanges with contemporaries. A letter dated March 21, 1862, from Louis Agassiz to President Lincoln proposes government patronage of a botanical expedition to the Rocky Mountains.

Boston publishing firms of the nineteenth century are represented by the strong collection of 1,000 volumes published by Ticknor and Fields, present in varying printings and bindings. Gift of the *Boston Globe*, this book collection represents many first editions of the Massachusetts Transcendentalists, British writers, and of American authors writing on health, travel, scientific works, and biography. Years of publication range from 1836 to the 1860s. At the close of the century, the firm of Copeland and Day is represented with several hundred imprints between 1893 and 1899.

The Boston University Archive holds both individual and institutional collections of Massachusetts interest. Although the university originated in 1839 and was chartered in 1869, the earliest records in the archive are those of the New England Female Medical College (1848-1873). United with Boston University in 1873, the New England Female Medical College formed the School of Medicine.

The university's own records begin with course catalogs for 1873-1874 and the first annual report of the president for that year. The Massachusetts Society for the University Education of Women was founded as the Boston University Women's Education Society in 1875, and the archive holds minutes, yearbooks, and other records of this society.

As do most university archives, the Boston University Archive holds yearbooks, catalogs, student and faculty publications, financial records, files of various organizations, scrapbooks, photographs, and newspapers and journals, documenting in many different forms the history of the university. The monthly journal published by the students of the College of Liberal Arts, *The Beacon*, is present in its complete run of 1876 to 1951.

Administrative and faculty collections of manuscripts include the papers of the first president, William Fairfield Warren, president from 1873 to 1903; Daniel L. Marsh, president from 1926 to 1951; and Harold C. Case, president from 1951 to 1968. Other significant collections include the extensive office files of William Marshall Warren, dean of the College of Liberal Arts from 1904 to 1937, and the correspondence of his successor, Ralph W. Taylor, from 1937 to 1956.

Noteworthy faculty collections include those of Melville M. Bigelow (1846-1921), one of the first School of Law faculty members and later dean of the School of Law; Dallas Lore Sharp (1870-1929), the well-known lecturer and naturalist; and the papers of Edgar S. Brightman (1884-1953), known as the American advocate of the philosophy of personalism. Edward C. Stone (1878-1964), donor of one part of the university's Abraham Lincoln Collection, a graduate of the School of Law and a member of the Massachusetts State Senate, has a personal collection of voluminous business and personal files displaying his many interests and roles. Other collections of notable Massachusetts interest are those of Dr. Dudley Sargent (1881-1924), an early proponent of preventive medicine through physical education, and the book collection on folk arts formed by Elizabeth Burchenal (1877-1959), president of the American Folk Dance Society.

The History of Nursing Archive, established in 1966, holds a book collection of over 1,650 titles, including Florence Nightingale's writings, and over one hundred manuscript collections comprising the personal and professional papers of nursing leaders, records of schools of nursing and public health organizations, and other professional nursing organizations. Collections with Massachusetts interest include records of the Boston City Hospital School of Nursing, organized by Linda Richards in 1878, the Children's Hospital School of Nursing in Boston (1889–1978), and the papers of the Beth Israel Hospital Nurses' Alumni Association (1916 to the present). The Children's Hospital School of Nursing Collection contains minutes and committee reports, student records, administrative correspondence, course materials, photographs, and related material.

The History of Nursing Archive also includes the papers of the Nursing Council of the United Community Services of Boston, the Massachusetts Nurses Association, and the Massachusetts League for Nursing. The papers of the Boston Visiting Nurse Association include reports, correspondence, records of cases and visits by nurses, and photographs. Reports on this group's work during the Chelsea Fire of 1908 are of special interest.

Turning from medical to musical collections, the Boston Symphony Orchestra's cultural influence on Boston is portrayed in its archive. The archive consists of scores and of tape recordings and videotapes of performances, to which additions are regularly made. The library of the Boston Symphony Orchestra holds over two hundred bound volumes of nineteenth-century manuscript copies of mainly Italian opera scores with full orchestration, and some printed editions of scores. Among scores commissioned by the trustees on the fiftieth anniversary of the orchestra in 1930 are Arthur Honegger's *Symphonie*, Ottorino Respighi's *Metamorphosean Mode XII*, Igor Stravinsky's *Symphonie de Psaumes*, Serge Prokofiev's *Symphony No. 4*, and Paul Hindemith's *Konzertmusik für Streichorchester und Blechbläser.* Other twentieth-century scores include Randall Thompson's *The Last Words of David*, commissioned in honor of Serge Koussevitsky's twenty-five years as director of the orchestra in 1949, and Walter Piston's *Symphony No. 8*, dedicated to Erich Leinsdorf.

Tape recordings of the Boston Symphony Orchestra concerts are deposited in the Music Library of the University Libraries. Starting in 1958, over a thousand tapes have been deposited of many hundreds of Boston concert performances under the successive direction of Charles Munch, Erich Leinsdorf, William Steinberg, Seiji Ozawa, and guest conductors, as well as the Boston Pops performances under the direction of Arthur Fiedler and of guest conductors.

The Robert Frost Collection deserves mention in this survey of Massachusetts sources. Since Frost grew up in Massachusetts, took courses at Harvard University, and taught there and at Amherst College, he can be claimed as a poet of at least partial Massachusetts provenance. Donated to the University by Paul C. Richards in honor of his parents, the Frost Collection, one of the nation's largest and most comprehensive, contains literary manuscripts, notebooks, letters, books, proof copies, journals, Christmas cards, and many types of memorabilia. Manuscript versions of more than sixty poems highlight the collection, which also includes two holograph notebooks from different periods in Frost's career. The book collection preserves nearly all of Frost's published books in all variant formats. Books, manuscripts, photographs, and artworks from the collection are on exhibit in the Robert Frost Room in the Mugar Library.

The Twentieth Century Archives contains the papers of many influential Massachusetts citizens, deceased and living. The list of individuals in the guide *Special Collections at Boston University* may be consulted for specific names. Two notable twentieth-century people whose collections have recently been added are Arthur Fiedler and Dr. Howard Thurman.

The Arthur Fiedler Collection, given to Boston University by Mrs. Ellen Fiedler in 1982, contains some 5,000 individual items, including scores, books, recordings, photographs, manuscripts, and memorabilia ranging from ceremonial swords to batons. Founder of the Esplanade concerts in 1929, director of the Boston Pops Orchestra for more than forty years, Arthur Fiedler (1894–1979) was known and addressed by his first name by admiring Bostonians of all classes. His influence continues to be felt in the musical life of the city and the state.

The collection of scores of all types made by Mr. Fiedler is notable in quantity and type. The collection holds more than 300 orchestra full scores, many signed by Mr. Fiedler, written by such important musicians as Ernest Bloch, Walter Piston, Knudage Riisager, and Ned Rorem. Mr. Fiedler collected over 2,000 miniature scores for his working collection. Other types of scores held in quantity are string orchestra, band music, opera, piano, and choral scores, and orchestra parts. A rare and important first edition of the full score of Mozart's *Don Giovanni* is a highlight, as is the second edition of the complete parts of Beethoven's *Symphony No. 7 in A*.

Fiedler's personal library, part of the collection, contains over 300 books on music, many presentation copies from the authors to Arthur Fiedler. Items drawn from the collection are on display in the Arthur Fiedler Reading Room in the Mugar Library.

The Howard Thurman Archive, a collection of the personal papers of one of the most distinguished religious leaders of the twentieth century, was given to Boston University in 1984 by Mrs. Sue Bailey Thurman. Dr. Howard Thurman (1900–1981) has been a profound influence on the twentieth century through his teaching, ministry, and writings. As professor of religion and theology at Morehouse College, at Howard University, and at Spelman College, as professor of spiritual resources and disciplines at Boston University (1953–1964), as dean of Marsh Chapel (1953–1964), as minister-at-large and dean emeritus (1965–1981) at Boston University, and as a lecturer at more than 500 colleges and author of twenty-three books, Dr. Thurman propounded and developed his spiritual and intellectual beliefs for several generations of Americans. From his collection at Boston University, hundreds of tape recordings and transcripts of his sermons, lectures, meditations, and prayers are available for research.

In summation, the Special Collections Department holds rich resources of Massachusetts history in its diverse book and manuscript collections.

Katherine Cain

DANVERS ARCHIVAL CENTER
PEABODY INSTITUTE LIBRARY
15 Sylvan Street
Danvers, Mass. 01923
(617) 774-0554

The Danvers Archival Center is a department of the Peabody Institute Library of Danvers, Massachusetts. Conceived in 1970 as a part of the Danvers Historical Commission Master Plan, the idea was to collect and place in one central location, protected from fire and atmospheric and insect damage, all the written and printed materials relating to the history of Danvers, Massachusetts.

Through the cooperation of the Danvers Historical Society, Town Clerk, Public Library, and many other groups, the Archival Center was initially outfitted in the basement of the Historical Society headquarters at 13 Page Street. In 1972 a town archivist was appointed to collect, preserve, conserve, and care for the historic materials as well as act as a resource person for town history matters. In 1981 the Archival Center moved to new, expanded quarters at the Peabody Institute Library at 15 Sylvan Street in Danvers. Approximately 2,500 square feet is divided between a reading room and a storage area. The area is waterproof, fire resistant, secure, and has its own climate control system. The archivist is a department head of the library and an assistant town clerk.

The significance of the Archival Center rests with the fact that it is the first of its kind to bring together such a large collection of public and private records of a single community for purposes of preservation and accessibility to researchers. The archives houses probably the most extensive and varied collection of materials relating to an individual municipality in New England. The collections on permanent deposit include the local history holdings of the Historical Society, the library, numerous churches and town organizations, and the official records of the Town of Danvers.

The Archival Center collects through gift, purchase, and, in cases where the material belongs to still-functioning corporate organizations, permanent deposit materials on paper relating to the history and development of Salem Village and Danvers, Massachusetts. Items collected include books, pamphlets, monographs, manuscripts, periodicals, maps, photographs, newspapers, audio and video tapes, films, broadsides, microforms, and architectural drawings. Collections include the following:

1. Printed materials on local history. Included in this segment of the collections is the printed material relating to the Town of Danvers, from general histories of Essex County and Danvers to volumes devoted to specialized topics such as the *Danvers Historical Society Collections* from 1913. There are complete runs of the *Statement of the Accounts of Danvers* from 1845, *Valuations of Danvers* from 1856, *Danvers School Reports* from 1839, *Street Poll Lists* from

1890, and numerous biographies of Danvers notables, including Israel Putnam, John Greenleaf Whittier, Samuel Parris, John Endicott, Samuel Holten, George Peabody, and Grenville Dodge. Augumenting the printed collection are general reference sets important to local study, including *Acts and Resolves of the Province of Mass. Bay*; *Journals of the House of Representatives of Massachusetts*; *Essex County Quarterly Court Records and Files*, 1636–1686; and the *Essex Institute Historical Collections* from 1859.

2. Genealogy. While the Archival Center does not attempt to gather an all-encompassing collection of family histories, it does endeavor to acquire genealogies of important Danvers families, including the Putnam and Porter families. Reference volumes for genealogy include vital records to 1850 of most Massachusetts towns and of Massachusetts soldiers and sailors in the Revolution, War of 1812, and Civil War, the *Essex Antiquarian*, and the *New England Historical and Genealogical Register*. Also of aid to the genealogical researcher are the town manuscript vital records dating to 1917 and federal census records for Danvers from 1790 to 1910.

3. Witchcraft. The Ellerton J. Brehaut witchcraft collection is perhaps the most complete collection of printed materials relating to the 1692 witchcraft hysteria in Salem Village (present day Danvers). Included in this collection are well over 1,000 items. The collection includes originals or copies of all the early imprints relating to the Salem Village witchcraft hysteria, as well as a number of seventeenth-century English volumes on the subject. First editions include Mather's 1693 *Wonders of the Invisible World*, Calef's 1700 *More Wonders*, Hale's 1702 *Modest Enquiry*, Upham's 1834 *Lectures* and 1867 *Salem Witchcraft*, Woodward's 1864 *Records*, and many of the books that were used by witchcraft scholars. Documents include the only signature by mark of Giles Corey and documents of many more of the notables. Chief among the primary sources within the collection is the three-volume typescript copy set *Salem Witchcraft*, containing the verbatim transcription of the witchcraft papers constituting the most complete source in existence of the hysteria. Also augmenting the collection are the manuscript records of the First Church of Danvers.

4. Manuscript Collection. Among the over 500 volumes and 75,000 manuscript Town Records are the *Salem Village Records of Transactions*, 1672–1715, town meeting, tax, and valuation records from 1752, and the vital, fire, school, selectmen, military, town clerk, town treasurer, overseers of the poor, police, electric light, library, assessors, and street records. Non-municipal records include account books, daybooks, journals and diaries, deeds, wills, and inventories from as early as the seventeenth century, records of numerous organizations, including the First Church, Maple Street Church, Baptist Church, Methodist Church, Episcopal Church, and Historical Society, collections of correspondence, and a great variety of other manuscript materials.

There are a number of other specialized collections, including a group of over 100 Revolutionary War period broadsides and a 250-piece collection relating to the abolition movement, much of it belonging to reformer Parker Pillsbury.

Richard B. Trask

ESSEX INSTITUTE
JAMES DUNCAN PHILLIPS LIBRARY
132 Essex Street
Salem, Mass. 01970
(617) 744-3390

The Essex Institute is a private non-profit historical society and museum whose mission is to collect, preserve, study, and interpret the material culture of Essex County, Massachusetts, from the seventeenth century to the present. Through six museum galleries, seven historic houses, and a research library, the Essex Institute serves as a "keeper of the past" for a region that boasts a history and culture of national significance.

The James Duncan Phillips Library contains over 300,000 printed items, 4,000 linear feet of manuscripts, and approximately 100,000 photographs. The library is a center for the study of New England and American history and culture, with particular emphasis on biographical data and historical information on local towns in Massachusetts. The library contains several distinctive collections of published works. These include works by and about Nathaniel Hawthorne (a collection considered to be the most complete in existence), the Frederick Townsend Ward China Library (an outstanding assemblage of Western-language material on imperial China), books and photographs of Samuel Chamberlain, early American almanacs, nineteenth-century American hymnbooks, broadsides, cookbooks, trade catalogs, and seventeenth- and eighteenth-century English imprints.

The manuscript holdings at the Essex Institute contain over 1,000 separate collections, dating from the early seventeenth to the twentieth century. Created by individuals (both prominent and obscure) and institutions in Essex County, the collections encompass a broad range of record types. Included are letters, diaries, account books, family papers, business records, military and legal papers, sermons, genealogies, local and organizational records, and the institute's archives.

Over half of the Essex Institute's manuscript collections relate to the long and complex history of maritime trade activities emanating from Salem and other Essex County ports. During Salem's heyday of commercial activity (c. 1790-c. 1840) her ships traded with Asian, African, European, South American, and East and West Indian ports. At its peak, Salem was the sixth busiest port in the United States. Documentation of this voluminous importation and exportation of goods is preserved in the business and personal records of merchant families, international businesses, and associated industries such as insurance companies and shipwrights. Additional insight into the shipping industry is available through the financial records, personal diaries, and correspondence generated by ships' captains and officers, agents overseeing trade in the foreign ports, and sailors. The Essex Institute also houses Custom House papers for Salem, Newburyport, Marblehead, and Gloucester, and over 1,500 ships' logbooks. These materials constitute an outstanding resource for the study of early shipping in the United States.

An additional strength of the manuscript collection is the wealth of personal and business records documenting the history of Essex County and its people, institutions, and culture. Account books and correspondence provide evidence of the wide variety of commercial enterprises in Essex County. Business records of local industries, from shoemaking to the railroad, highlight the evolution of Essex County commerce from the seventeenth to the twentieth century. The day-to-day affairs of housewives and businessmen are related through diaries, correspondence, and financial papers. Cultural activites in Essex County are well represented through the records of local artists, authors, and societies. Military, church, and civic records also help document Essex County history. Collections of special note are the Salem witchcraft trial documents and the papers of philanthropist George Peabody and inventor Nathan Read.

The following list highlights a few of the collections at the Essex Institute. Interested researchers should contact the curator of manuscripts for unpublished finding aids and additional topics.

Merchant Families

Crowninshield (George and sons)
Curwen (George and Samuel)
Derby (Richard and Elias H.)
Hathorne (John and Benjamin H.)
Pickman (Benjamin)

Associated Maritime Industries

Brackley R. Peabody (shipmaster)
Essex Fire & Marine Insurance Company
French Spoilation Claims
Joseph Perkins (pilot)
Nathaniel Kinsman (China agent)
Salem Marine Insurance Company

Literary and Societal

Ipswich Anti-Slavery Society
Lucy Larcom
Mary Abigail Dodge
Mozart Association
Nathaniel Hawthorne
Salem Female Employment Society

Merchant Businesses

B. W. Stone & Bros.
John Bertram
N. L. Rogers & Bros.

Ropes Emmerton & Co.
Stone Silsbee & Pickman

Local Businesses

Phillips Family (lumber trade/railroad forwarding)
Salem & Boston Stage Company
Salem Iron Factory
Samuel Fowler (tannery)
Thomas Perley (tailor)

Miscellaneous

Andrew Dunlap (attorney)
Asa Lamson (climatology)
Edward S. Rogers (viticulture)
John J. Currier (mayor)
Nathan Read (inventor)
Northey family (Quakers)
Witchcraft Trial Papers

FORBES LIBRARY
20 West Street
Northampton, Mass. 01060
(413) 584-8399

The Forbes Library has a large collection of sources of interest to the historian of the state and the region. The larger holdings include the Kingsley Collection (720 feet) on Northampton and Hampshire County history, the Massachusetts History Collection (120 feet) containing town and county histories and vital statistics, and the Genealogy Collection (120 feet) on Northampton, Hampshire County, and New England. Another important collection is that compiled by Sylvester Judd, including 62 volumes of records, vital statistics, and histories of western Massachusetts and northern Connecticut. There also is a Manuscript Collection (60 feet) containing letters, papers, genealogies, account books, and diaries recording the history of persons and events in Hampshire County. The Stephen Strong Collection contains the letters and private papers of Governor Caleb Strong. The Walter Corbin Collection contains photographs of Florence and vicinity, and the Northampton and Hampshire County Picture Collection includes three drawers of photographs of Northampton and Hampshire County.

The library contains the *Daily Hampshire Gazette* from 1786 to the present; there is a two-volume index covering the period from 1786 to 1937, and sixteen drawers of typed index cards covering the period from 1951 to the present.

There are four drawers of microfilm vital statistics, records of court cases, and probate records, all related to Hampshire County. This collection includes microfilm census records for Hampshire County, 1810, 1850, 1860, 1870, 1880, and 1910.

The World War I Collection contains four drawers of scrapbooks and cardex of soldiers from Hampshire County who served in that war. The World War II Collection contains four drawers of information on soldiers, sailors, and marines of Hampshire County who served in that war.

The Calvin Coolidge Room contains letters, papers, scrapbooks, and memorabilia relating to Calvin and Grace Coolidge, as well as various secondary sources (210 feet).

Other sources in the Forbes Library include the Gerald Stanley Lee Collection (fifteen pamphlet boxes of letters, papers, and journals of Stanley Lee, the clergyman, writer, and professor), the Benjamin Smith Lyman Collection (two drawers of letters, papers, and books of the renowned geologist), and the Clarence Hawkes Collection (four drawers of books and papers of the Hadley writer and naturalist).

Elise Bernier-Feeley and Daniel Lombardo

HARVARD DIVINITY SCHOOL
THE ANDOVER-HARVARD THEOLOGICAL LIBRARY
45 Francis Avenue
Cambridge, Mass. 02138
(617) 495-5788

The Andover-Harvard Theological Library of the Harvard Divinity School is one of the almost one hundred libraries that form the Harvard University Library system. The University Library has more than 11 million volumes, and the Andover-Harvard Library has almost 400,000 volumes, which is about half the holdings in the field of religion available at Harvard. For 150 years the Divinity School has had a close relationship with the liberal religious movement, although it has always been a non-denominational school. But its association over decades with the Unitarians, and later the Universalists, has made it the leading center for the study of those denominations. Both the American Unitarian Association and the Universalist Church of America had their roots and their headquarters in Boston. In 1961 they merged as the Unitarian Universalist Association, which also has its main offices in Boston.

The Harvard Divinity School library holds the archives for these three groups and the archives of the Unitarian Service Committee, which was established in Boston in 1940 (now the Unitarian Universalist Service Committee). The library has, in addition, hundreds of collections representing the papers of Unitarian and Universalist ministers, local churches, conferences, state conventions, and related organizations. Many of these are Massachusetts-based. It also has the papers of former faculty members of the Divinity School, many of which have pertinent value for the cultural and religious life of the state. Examples are the archive of Paul Tillich, one of the most significant theologians of this century; the papers of Samuel Howard Miller, minister at Old Cambridge Baptist Church (1935-1959) and a dean of the Divinity School (1959-1968); and the papers of Edward Caldwell Moore, Plummer Professor and chairman of the Board of Preachers at Harvard University (1915-1929), and of his family, which document with letters and scrapbooks life in Cambridge for a generation. These collections include sermons, addresses, lectures, correspondence, church and family records, official documents, diaries, scrapbooks, photographs, tapes, and some microfilms. Supporting them is a large collection of books, serials, and pamphlets relating to liberal Christianity that is particularly strong in its holdings from the eighteenth to the twentieth century. The archival and manuscript collections at Andover-Harvard are available for research use, and registers are provided for those that have been processed and cataloged. Unitarian Universalist books not in the rare book collection or otherwise restricted, and microfilms may be borrowed through interlibrary loan. Photocopying services are available at the library.

THE UNIVERSALIST CHURCH OF AMERICA (UCA)

Universalism as an organized movement emerged in America in the eighteenth century, but the idea of the salvation of all individuals is traced to the early church. While a number of preachers were proclaiming the doctrine before 1770 (Elhanan Winchester in the Philadelphia area and Jonathan Mayhew and Charles Chauncy in Massachusetts), John Murray, an itinerant minister from England, is considered to be the founder of the denomination. Murray served churches in Gloucester and Boston (1774-1815) and was a prime mover in bringing the scattered Universalist churches together in their first convention at Oxford, Massachusetts (1785). Murray's manuscripts were destroyed by mildew, but most of the few items that have survived, chiefly letters, are at Andover-Harvard. The second major Universalist figure was Hosea Ballou (1771-1852), whose most lasting ministry was at the Second Universalist Society in Boston. Ballou was the most original thinker the denomination produced (see his *A Treatise on Atonement*, which is still in print), and his views prevailed among Universalists for a century. Theodore Parker felt that Ballou "wrought a revolution in the thoughts and minds of men" that accomplished more than all of the politicians of his day. Ballou's papers at Andover-Harvard include his correspondence and his valuable sermon workbook. The definitive history of this denomination is Russell E. Miller's recent study, *The Larger Hope*, 2 vols. (Boston, 1979 and 1985).

In the Andover-Harvard collection are the papers of the more significant Universalist ministers of Massachusetts, including Thomas Whittemore (1800-1861), editor and publisher for thirty years of the leading Universalist newspaper, the *Trumpet and Universalist Magazine*, and a representative in the Massachusetts legislature from Cambridge; Edward Turner (1776-1853), a leader in the Restorationist movement in the church; Hosea Ballou II (1796-1861), scholar and first president of Tufts University; William Wallace Rose (1889-1969), prominent minister of the large church in Lynn; Roger F. Etz (1886-1950), a general superintendent of the UCA and minister for many years at Charlestown and Medford; and Clarence Russell Skinner (1881-1949), teacher of the social gospel and dean of the Universalist seminary at Tufts University and the church's most widely respected twentieth-century theologian.

Their papers are supplemented by the official record books (minutes, vital statistics, financial accounts, Sunday School, youth and women's groups) of the following organizations: the Massachusetts Universalist Convention, the Massachusetts Association of Universalist Women, the Massachusetts Universalist Home Missionary Society, the Massachusetts Universalist Sabbath School Association, Bethany Union for Young Women in Boston, the Clara Barton Birthplace Camp, the Massachusetts Universalist Sunday School Association, and churches located in Amesbury, Boston, Brighton, Cambridge, Charlestown, Chatham, Dana, Dorchester, Duxbury, Holliston, Hyde Park, Jamaica Plain, Leominster, Lexington, Marblehead, Marion, Marlborough, Medford, New Bedford, Newton, Oxford, Plymouth, Quincy, Rockland, Roxbury, Salem, Salisbury, South Adams, Sutton, Warren, Watertown, and West Amesbury. In addition, all of the extant archival records of the Universalist Church of America, chiefly of the twentieth century and especially helpful for information on Massachusetts ministers and churches, are at Andover-Harvard. For another description of these resources, see Alan Seaburg, "The Universalist Collection at Andover-Harvard," *Harvard Library Bulletin*, 27 (1980): 443-55.

TIIE AMERICAN UNITARIAN ASSOCIATION (AUA)

While the American Unitarian Association was founded in 1825, American Unitarian beginnings in fact came out of the controversy about the nature of God within New England congregationalism during the previous generation. The concept that God is a unity and not a trinity, however, had been a lively debate within European Christianity since the Reformation. When the liberal minister Henry Ware was appointed by the Harvard Corporation to be Hollis Professor of Divinity in 1805, and when the Boston minister William Ellery Channing preached an ordination sermon in Baltimore in 1819 that stated bluntly and clearly the liberal position, Unitarian Christianity became its own separate community in the new Republic.

Andover-Harvard has a large and extensive Unitarian collection that includes the archives of the AUA for the nineteenth and the twentieth centuries, and that of its successor organization, the Unitarian Universalist Association. Prominent in these archives are thousands of letters received from ministers and laypersons by the various secretaries of the AUA from 1825 through 1902. These are arranged chronologically, and access to them is available through several recently prepared indexes. In addition, the library has more than 200 linear shelf feet of official records of the AUA from 1900 onward that contain invaluable material on Massachusetts ministers and churches and on the work of the national headquarters at 25 Beacon Street, Boston. Besides the archives of the parent organization, the library holds archives from a number of other Massachusetts groups, such as the Boston Association of Ministers (1755-1947), the Tuckerman School on Beacon Hill (1918-1933) for the training of women as parish assistants and religious educators, the Society for Propagating the Gospel among the Indians and Others in North America (1806-1858), the Unitarian Club of Boston (1881-1945), the Cape Cod Conference (1870-1922), and the Cambridge Association of Ministers (1809-1943).

Massachusetts, as the most important early region of Unitarianism, produced consequently its share of leading ministers. William Ellery Channing (1780-1842) was the first major American Unitarian theologian. While he served only one church, the Arlington Street Church in Boston, his influence was national in scope. Most of his manuscripts have not survived, but Harvard has much of what is extant at Andover-Harvard and Houghton Library. This includes drafts of the famous Baltimore sermon, "Unitarian Christianity," which is still the most widely read of all Unitarian sermons. The papers of Emerson are at Houghton. Those of the third leading Unitarian with a national reputation, Theodore Parker (1810-1860), are mainly at Andover-Harvard, the Massachusetts Historical Society, and the Boston Public Library. Best known for his sermon, "The Transient and Permanent in Christianity," he preached to large crowds at the Melodeon Theater and later at the Music Hall in Boston and was a gadfly to both contemporary Unitarians and the orthodox in all denominations. Andover-Harvard has several of his journals, many manuscript sermons, and some correspondence. Another important minister was Edward Everett Hale (1822–1909). He served the South Congregational Church (Unitarian) in Boston for fifty years, wrote many books, and authored the famous story, "The Man without a Country." Almost all his sermons have been preserved, as well as countless letters. For this century, the collection includes papers of Samuel Atkins Eliot, Frederick May Eliot, Louis Craig Cornish, and Dana McLean Greeley, all Harvard graduates, all presidents of the AUA, all active in the religious and social life of this state. These major collections are supported by manuscripts of other figures vital to the history of this region, such as William Rice at Wellesley, Samuel McChord Crothers at Cambridge, and the Henry Wilder Foote family of Salem, Boston, and Cambridge.

As with the Universalists, the library holds records of many Unitarian churches both defunct and active. These include, for example, the Arlington Street Church and several Boston churches now closed, the First Parish in Cambridge, and records for such places as Somerville, Malden, and Holyoke. The records of Sherborn and Marblehead are on microfilm. These records are enriched by a unique ongoing program that microfilms the newsletters of most Unitarian Universalist churches in Massachusetts, thereby adding another dimension to the study of religious history. For more data, see Alan Seaburg, "Some Unitarian Manuscripts at Andover-Harvard," *Harvard Library Bulletin*, 26 (1978): 112-20.

Alan Seaburg

HARVARD UNIVERSITY LIBRARIES

University Archives
Pusey Library
Cambridge, Mass. 02138
(617) 495-2461

Houghton Library-Manuscript Division
Harvard University
Cambridge, Mass. 02138
(617) 495-2449

Harvard Theatre Collection
Harvard College Library
Cambridge, Mass. 02138
(617) 495-2445

Littauer Library
Littauer Center
Harvard University
Cambridge, Mass. 02138
(617) 495-2106

Francis Countway Library of Medicine
10 Shattuck Street
Boston, Mass. 02115
(617) 732-2170

Harvard Law School Library
Manuscript Division
512 Langdell Hall
1545 Massachusetts Avenue
Cambridge, Mass. 02138
(617) 495-4550

Baker Library
Manuscripts and Archive Department
Harvard Business School
Boston, Mass. 02163
(617) 495-6411

Carpenter Center for the Visual Arts
The Harvard Film Archives
24 Quincy Street
Cambridge, Mass. 02138
(617) 495-4700

Peabody Museum Archives
11 Divinity Avenue
Cambridge, Mass. 02138
(617) 495-2248

The addresses are in the order of mention in the description given below. It should be noted that many of the libraries in Cambridge are in Harvard Yard and have no street addresses.

The Harvard University libraries contain numerous manuscript and archival collections related to the history of Massachusetts. The Harvard University Archives, located in the Pusey Library, houses the records of the Harvard Corporation since 1643, the Board of Overseers since 1650, the faculty since 1725, and the treasurer since 1725. The archives also contains minutes of meetings, correspondence, reports, financial and student files, and other records related to administrative subdivisions of the university, including the Faculty of Arts and Sciences and academic departments, libraries, museums, and other research institutions (such as the Harvard Economic Research Project and the Peabody Museum), and the graduate faculties of design, divinity, education, government, and law. The archives house records of a large number of student organizations, some dating from the eighteenth century. The collection also includes the personal papers of a large number of the men and women who have contributed to the administration and faculty of the university. There also are a large number of undergraduate diaries, as well as lecture notes taken by various students over the years. For a more complete description, see Clark A. Elliott, *A Descriptive Guide to the Harvard University Archives* (Cambridge, 1974).

The Houghton Library, part of the Harvard College Library, contains a massive collection of manuscripts, including 36 boxes containing the papers of William James, 9 volumes of personal papers of Abbott Lawrence, 100 volumes of personal papers of Josiah Royce, 40 boxes of personal correspondence of Jared Sparks, and 200 boxes of the papers of Charles Sumner. The collection also houses 25 boxes of the papers of Emily Dickinson and her family; 250 literary manuscripts, 2,800 letters sent and 15,000 letters received by Henry Wadsworth Longfellow; 24 volumes and 39 boxes of the papers of Amy Lowell; 14 boxes of the papers of James Russell Lowell; and 3 volumes of the papers of Archibald MacLeish. There are 8 boxes of the papers of Louisa May Alcott and her father Amos Bronson Alcott; 17 notebooks, 100 literary manuscripts, and 54 letters of Edward Bellamy; and 26 boxes and 700 pieces related to Henry James. Other authors represented by large collections include Gamaliel Bradford, Ralph Waldo Emerson, James Thomas Fields, Charles Eliot Norton, Horace Elisha Scudder, and Henry David Thoreau. Abolitionists and reformers represented in the collection include Dorothea Lynde Dix, Margaret Fuller, William Lloyd Garrison, Thomas Wentworth Higginson, Julia Ward Howe, and Samuel Gridley Howe. The papers of Henry Lee Higginson include a large amount of material on the Boston Symphony Orchestra. The papers of the sea captain and merchant James Hunnewell consist of 15 volumes and 16 boxes of material. There also are 75 volumes of logs of whaling and merchant ships covering the years from 1753 to 1879. The archives of the American Board of Commissioners for Foreign Missions, 1812-1945 (45 stack sections) are on deposit in the library. For a more complete description of the collections at the Houghton Library, one should consult *The Houghton Library, 1942-1982* (Cambridge, 1982).

The Harvard College Library also houses the massive Harvard Theatre Collection, consisting of an estimated 5 million pieces. The focus is on the history of performance throughout the world, especially the English and American stage and the history of the dance. Areas such as cinema and popular entertainment (for example, fairground, circus, minstrel, and vaudeville) are all well represented. The collection contains over 3 million playbills and programs, approximately 500,000 photographs, 250,000 engraved portraits and scenes, 15,000 scenery and costume designs, and nearly 5,000 promptbooks, in addition to manuscripts, journals, newspaper clippings, and scrapbooks.

The Industrial Relations Collection in the Littauer Library contains a large collection relating to labor unions and labor-management relations, including records of the National Maritime Union, Boston Local, papers of the Glaziers Union, Boston Local 1044, and labor-management arbitration decisions by umpires and arbitrators (12,000 pieces). The collection is especially strong in labor-management agreements between 1935 and 1947 and continuing to the present day. The Littauer Library also houses transcripts of the National War Labor

Board from 1942 to 1946 and documents relating to cases considered by the board. The collection also contains the records of the Boston regional office of the Office of Defense Transportation from 1942 to 1944 and the working papers of the Boston regional office of the Office of Price Administration from 1941 to 1946.

The Francis Countway Medical Library in Boston possesses a large and growing manuscript collection, including the records of the Harvard Medical School faculty, papers of a large number of important physicians and surgeons from the early colonial period to the present, and the records of various medical organizations and societies. Individual collections include those of Benjamin Waterhouse, Oliver Wendell Holmes, Walter Bradford Cannon, and Paul Dudley White. In addition, the library houses the records of the Massachusetts Medical Society, as well as the institutional records of various hospitals, including the Massachusetts General Hospital.

The Law School Library houses a manuscript collection with an emphasis on persons and projects related to Harvard Law School. The geographic emphasis is on New England, and chronologically the papers are strongest for the period from 1895 to 1965. Individual collections include those of Louis D. Brandeis, Zechariah Chafee, Jr., Felix Frankfurter, Learned Hand, Oliver Wendell Holmes, Jr., and Roscoe Pound. For a more complete description, see Erika S. Chadbourn, "Documenting the American Legal Scene: The Manuscript Division of the Harvard Law School Library," *Harvard Library Bulletin*, 30 (January 1982): 55-73.

The Baker Library of Harvard's Graduate School of Business Administration (in Boston) houses a large number of collections relating to the economic history of Massachusetts. These include records of generic industries, such as papers on farming, lumbering, fishing, whaling, mining, quarrying, sugar refining, textile manufacture, woolen goods manufacture, tailoring and hat making, manufacture of wood products, manufacture of textile machinery, shipbuilding and repair, wire manufacture, manufacture of jewelry and watches, pottery manufacture, chemical manufacture, and leather manufacture (primarily boots and shoes). Although the collection is national in scope, much of it relates to business in New England, especially in Massachusetts. Among the largest collections, for instance, are the records of the Dwight Manufacturing Company from 1832 to 1933 (936 volumes, 141 boxes, and 10 crates), the Pepperell Manufacturing Company from 1839 to 1928 (1,000 volumes and 95 boxes), and the Slater Companies of Massachusetts and Rhode Island from 1793 to 1926 (1,250 volumes, 430 boxes, and many crates). Among the records of the publishing and printing industries are the records of the *Boston Gazette* from 1867 to 1941 (300 volumes, 52 boxes, and 9 crates), and account books and letter books of Ticknor and Fields from 1847 to 1900 (117 volumes). There also are 50 volumes of records of Boston's theaters and museums.

The collection includes a great deal on retail selling, including the records of general stores from 1685 to 1927, food stores from 1747 to 1878, shoe stores from 1830 to 1932, jewelry stores from 1830 to 1925, hardware stores from 1800 to 1869, department stores from 1826 to 1942, peddlers from 1849 to 1877, advertising firms from 1830 to 1919, and real estate firms from 1643 to 1921. Records of financial services cover banking, insurance, and stock exchange operations. Legal services are covered by 78 volumes and 12 boxes.

The Baker Library manuscript collection also includes numerous records of governmental services, including tax and customs records from 1658 to 1888 and letters from railroad men to William Zabena Ripley, the economist who served as special examiner on railway consolidations for the Interstate Commerce Commission (1921-1923). For a useful description of the collection in the Baker Library, see Robert W. Lovett, *List of Business Manuscripts in Baker Library*, 2nd ed. (Boston, 1951), and Robert W. Lovett and Eleanor C. Bishop, *Manuscripts in Baker Library: A Guide to Sources for Business, Economic, and Social History*, 4th ed. (Boston, 1978).

Transportation is well covered in the collection, including the records of the Boston and Albany Railroad (337 volumes, 10 boxes, and 9 crates), as well as papers related to the history of electric railroads in Massachusetts and elsewhere. In the area of water transportation, there are 105 volumes and 20 boxes related to coastal shipping, as well as 337 volumes and 139 boxes on ocean shipping. The Hunnewell Family Papers consist of 83 bundles and 17 boxes, chiefly relating to James Hunnewell, the sea captain and merchant. Another massive collection is the Heard Family Papers from 1754 to 1898, which include the papers of Augustine Heard, the sea captain and China merchant. The Hancock Family Papers from 1712 to 1854 contain 14 boxes of the papers of John Hancock (chiefly business records). There are numerous ships' logs and records of wharves and docks.

The Carpenter Center for the Visual Arts (in Cambridge) contains a photographic archive with some 45,000 items dating from 1840 to the present. Among the leading collections housed in the center are the Social Ethics Collection on social reform in America, 1895-1910, and the Social History of America Collection (1929-1955). The Massachusetts Transportation Authority Collection contains glass plates on the building of the Boston subway.

The Peabody Museum archives includes the daybooks of the first and second curators, Jeffries Wyman and Frederic Ward Putnam, and the correspondence of Charles Pickering Bowditch, as well as other collections related to archaeology and anthropology.

HISTORIC DEERFIELD MEMORIAL LIBRARIES
Deerfield, Mass. 01342
(413) 774-5581

The Memorial Libraries of Historic Deerfield, Inc., contain the book and manuscript collection of the Pocumtuck Valley Memorial Association (PVMA; established in 1870 by George Sheldon and others), as well as the Henry N. Flynt Library of Historic Deerfield, Inc. The collection represents the life and thought of one small Connecticut Valley town from the seventeenth century to the present, and the holdings are indispensable for researching the history of Franklin and Hampshire counties. The older printed books in the collection include genealogies, local authors and imprints, sermons, hymnals, town histories, publications of the Massachusetts State Commissioner of Education and the Massachusetts Board of Agriculture, and numerous travel accounts.

An extensive collection of manuscript town records is available at the library. These include the Book of the Proprietors of the Common Field of Deerfield for the years from 1734 to 1860, numerous warrants for town meetings, and a substantial number of minutes of eighteenth- and nineteenth-century town meetings. There also are large collections of the papers of various Deerfield town officers, including persons who served as treasurer, tax collector, assessor, town clerk, overseers of the poor, and town and district school committee members.

The library also has a large collection of microfilms of local records that were in private or institutional hands. These include 12 reels of official records of the Town of Deerfield, 2 reels of records of various Deerfield churches, 1 reel of account books and miscellaneous town business records, and 1 reel of early Deerfield Academy records. The library also has microfilm copies of the records of the Hampshire County Probate Court (1660-1820), the Franklin County Probate Court (1812-1866), and the Hampshire County Court of Common Pleas and General Sessions (1677-1788), as well as town, state, and federal tax inventories and schedules from 1768 to 1900. In addition, there is microfilm of the U.S. census schedules for Franklin County from 1800 to 1910 and a WPA transcript of the diary of Rev. Stephen Williams of Longmeadow, which covers the years from 1715 to 1782.

The library possesses a nearly complete file of the *Greenfield Gazette* and its successors from 1792 to 1932. There is also a complete file of the *Springfield Republican* from 1857 to 1954, and microfilms of the *Hampshire Gazette* from 1786 to 1852, the *Turners Falls Reporter* from 1872 to 1922, and early Springfield newspapers. There are also miscellaneous bound volumes of Franklin and Hampshire County newspapers, most of which were short-lived.

The library houses transcriptions of probate inventories for Deerfield residents from 1674 to 1834; a computerized six-volume file of craftsmen working in the Massachusetts portion of the Connecticut Valley before 1850, representing 180 crafts; a research file on textiles and notions available in Deerfield, from 1780–1820; and various reference indices, bibliographies, and finding aids to resources in the Deerfield collections and beyond.

Records of several churches have been preserved in the PVMA collection. These include records of the First Church and other churches of Deerfield, the Baptist church of Shelburne, and the First Church of Hawley (from 1788 to 1809), as well as the diary of Rev. Roger Newton (1737–1816) of Greenfield. There are manuscript sermons from the early eighteenth to the nineteenth century, including more than 200 sermons of Rev. Jonathan Ashley (1712–1780) and 227 sermons of Rev. Samuel Williams (1743–1817), who was minister of Bradford, Massachusetts, and Hollis Professor of Mathematics and Natural Philosophy at Harvard College. There also are 93 sermons by Rev. Jonathan Grout (1763–1835) of Hawley and a bound volume of 30 sermons preached at Conway and neighboring towns in the 1820s by Rev. Edward Hitchcock (1793–1864), who later was president of Amherst College.

Social historians will be interested in the records of voluntary societies that have been preserved in this library. Dating from the nineteenth and early twentieth centuries, these include the Deerfield Temperance Society, the Deerfield Social Society, the Young Ladies Literary Society, the Adelphi (literary society) of Deerfield, the Female Benevolent Society of the Town of Deerfield, the Greenfield Dorcas Society, the Franklin Harvest Club, the Myron E. Stowell Post Number 84 of the Grand Army of the Republic, and the records of the Pocumtuck Valley Memorial Association.

The manuscript collection includes representation from more than one hundred families, with the collections ranging from two or three items of a genealogical nature to more than two hundred boxes of correspondence. Among the more notable collections are those of the Barnard family of merchants, tavernkeepers, farmers, and minor writers, the Dickinson family of farmers and merchants, the Higginson family of Boston, which came to Deerfield in the mid-nineteenth century to escape industrial progress and urban growth, and the Hoyt family, which includes the papers of Elihu Hoyt, who represented the town in the General Court during a time of agricultural and economic change and crisis. The manuscript collection includes more than 375 account books and daybooks of local origin, kept by craftsmen, farmers, merchants, professional men, storekeepers, and tavernkeepers. Among these are the account books and daybooks of the merchant Joseph Barnard (1717–1785), the merchant Elijah Williams (1712–1771), the physician Dr. William Stoddard Williams (1762–1829), and a group of 20 daybooks and 1 account book kept by the Ware family in the early nineteenth century.

The collection includes numerous diaries, along with a card catalog approach as well as notes and study aids. These include the diaries of Elihu Ashley (1750–1817), kept when he was an apprentice physician in Deerfield and Worthington from 1773 to 1775. Other important diaries are the journals and travel accounts of Elihu Hoyt (1771–1833) when he was Deerfield's legislative representative from 1803 to 1833, and the journals of Samuel Willard (1775-1859), a Unitarian minister who assumed the pulpit of the First Church of Deerfield (the diary covers the years from 1806 to 1808). Among the later diaries are those of Agnes Gordon Fuller (1838-1924), who began her journal in 1855 at the age of sixteen and continued to her death at the age of 85.

From the 1880s to the 1920s, Frances Stebbins Allen and Mary Electa Allen photographed the people, buildings, and surroundings of Deerfield, and a large number of their original prints are preserved in the PVMA collection.

JOHN F. KENNEDY LIBRARY
Columbia Point
Boston, Mass. 02125
(617) 929-4534

The John F. Kennedy Library is one of seven presidential libraries administered by the National Archives and Records Administration. Dedicated on October 20, 1979, the library collects, preserves, and makes available the papers and memorabilia of John F. Kennedy. Through its archives, museum, and educational activities, the library provides scholars and the general public with opportunities to gain insights into the people, issues, and events of mid-twentieth-century America.

The papers of John F. Kennedy are the heart of the Kennedy Library as well as the foundation of other library programs. They comprise approximately one-third of the more than 30 million pages of documents housed in the library. Aside from being the single most comprehensive collection of Kennedy-related material anywhere, the papers represent a collection of major significance in the study of mid-twentieth-century American history, politics, and government. The papers of John F. Kennedy cover the period from 1917 to 1963 and total 4,164 linear feet of material. They are further divided into personal papers, pre-presidential papers, and presidential papers.

The Personal Papers of John F. Kennedy (1917-1963, 20 feet, 5 rolls of microfilm) consist of personal materials previously scattered through other collections or located in other institutions. They have been assembled into a collection for greater convenience of research use. Included in the collection are academic records donated by Harvard University and records of the "Athenia" affair donated by the Department of State. Here researchers can also find biographical material, correspondence, book manuscripts for *Why England Slept* and *Profiles in Courage*, senator's notes, and presidential doodles.

The Pre-Presidential Papers (1947-1960, 430 feet) are the official papers covering John F. Kennedy's fourteen-year career as congressman and senator. They reflect his major official interests and activities of the period. Included are correspondence files, speech files, subject files, legislative files, campaign files, and materials from the 1960 presidential transition period.

The Presidential Papers cover the period from 1961 to 1963 and total 3,476 feet of material. They are further divided into three major subcollections (President's Office Files, National Security Files, and White House Central Files), several collections of miscellaneous presidential files, and the files of individual members of the president's White House staff.

The President's Office Files (73 feet) are the working files of President Kennedy as kept by his personal secretary in the White House Oval Office. Included are correspondence files, speech files, press conference files, legislative files, staff memoranda, subject files, a countries file, and presidential recordings.

The National Security Files (175 feet) are the working files of McGeorge Bundy, special assistant to the president for national security affairs. Portions are closed due to national security classification or because they have not yet been processed by library staff. Significant amounts of material are available, however, making this collection a critical resource for understanding U.S. foreign relations during the 1960s. Materials include embassy cablegrams, intelligence memoranda and analyses, records of National Security Council meetings, National Security Action Memoranda, and other types of material filed among several series, in particular an extensive countries file.

The White House Central Files (1,725 feet) were designed as a reference service for the president and his staff and to document White House activities. The Central Files consist of four major subdivisions. The Subject File (440 feet) is the main file kept by the Central File room in the White House. It consists largely of inactive correspondence, reports, memoranda, etc., organized by subject according to an alphanumeric system. The Name File (1,247 feet) serves essentially as an index to the Subject File. It contains a copy of the first page of incoming or outgoing White House correspondence marked to indicate where the complete file is located. The Chronological File (8 feet, closed), contains President Kennedy's outgoing correspondence. The Security Classified File (30 feet, closed) contains national security classified material withdrawn from the Subject File by the staff of the Central File room.

Other presidential materials (1,503 feet) include Bureau of the Budget Bill Reports, the White House Social Files (closed), and files of individual members of the president's staff. Among the latter are the papers of Lawrence O'Brien (special assistant to the president for congressional relations, 72 feet), Pierre Salinger (press secretary to the president, 111 feet), Myer Feldman (deputy special counsel to the president, 14 feet), Sanford Fox (staff assistant for social affairs, 16 feet), August Heckscher (special consultant on the arts, 20 feet), Lee White (assistant special counsel to the president, 10 feet), and Harris Wofford (special assistant to the president, 6 feet).

Other collections of personal papers of note are the papers of David Bell (director of the Bureau of the Budget, 25 feet), John Kenneth Galbraith (economist and ambassador to India, 75 feet), Walter Heller (chairman of the Council of Economic Advisors, 50 feet, 116 rolls of microfilm), Robert F. Kennedy (brother of the president, attorney general, and senator from New York, 1,300 feet), Burke Marshall (assistant attorney general for civil rights, 21 feet), Arthur M. Schlesinger, Jr. (author, historian, and special assistant to the president, 132 feet), and Theodore Sorensen (special counsel to the president, 45 feet).

To supplement documentary resources, the Kennedy Library maintains a collection of more than 1,100 oral history interviews, of which approximately 650 are open for research use. Included are interviews with leaders in politics, government, business, labor, journalism, etc. In addition, the library has a special library that consists of more than 35,000 cataloged volumes, and an audiovisual department that holds nearly 150,000 still photographs, more than 6.5 million feet of motion picture film, and over 7,000 sound recordings.

Historical Materials in the John Fitzgerald Kennedy Library (Boston, 1981), which lists and briefly describes all library holdings, is available free of charge to those intending to conduct research at the library.

Ronald E. Whealan, Head Librarian

MASSACHUSETTS HISTORICAL SOCIETY
1154 Boylston Street
Boston, Mass. 02215
(617) 536-1608

The Massachusetts Historical Society was organized in 1791 for the purpose of collecting, preserving, and making available the sources for the study of American history. It was the first organization of its kind in North America and the first institution in the world to devote its attention exclusively to collecting Americana. Today, the library owns a distinguished collection of rare books, more than 300,000 books and pamphlets, more than 5,000 maps, and some 23,000 broadsides, as well as extensive holdings of almanacs, directories, atlases, and other reference works.

From the outset, the society has been active in publishing. A series entitled *Collections*, still current, publishes valuable manuscripts owned by the library. The Massachusetts Historical Society *Proceedings* publishes papers read at monthly meetings and records the annual history of the society. There is an annual facsimile publication of volumes of *Journals of the House of Representatives of Massachusetts*, of which no full set of originals exists. Sibley's *Harvard Graduates*, now in seventeen volumes, contains biographical sketches of all Harvard graduates from the earliest times. In addition, there are continuing programs that publish the early papers of the Winthrop and Adams families. The library's microfilm publications, now well in excess of one million frames, are distributed by University Microfilms International of Ann Arbor, Michigan, from whom a catalog may be obtained.

The manuscript collection consists of an estimated 14 million pieces and is considered the most distinguished in North America outside the Library of Congress. A catalog of the manuscript holdings has been issued in nine folio volumes and has been distributed internationally.

In the area of Massachusetts history, the society houses the largest manuscript collection related to the history of the state, from the early colonial period into the twentieth century. Indeed, for researchers interested in major topics in early American history, the Massachusetts Historical Society is likely to be indispensable.

The collection is so extensive that any brief description can only note in passing the most important persons represented. Futhermore, due to the size of the collection, it must be divided into chronological segments in order to provide a sense of the scope involved. The society's holdings include a large collection of papers of families that were important in American as well as Massachusetts history. The Adams family collection, for instance, includes the papers of John Adams, John Quincy Adams, Charles Francis Adams, and Henry Adams, as well as significant material relating to Abigail Adams (Mrs. John

Adams), Louisa Catherine Adams (Mrs. John Quincy Adams), and Marian Adams (Mrs. Henry Adams). Other important persons represented in family papers are the merchant and United States representative Nathan Appleton, the clergyman and advocate of teacher-training schools Charles Brooks, the architect Charles Bulfinch, the colonial jurist Richard Dana, the state chief justice Francis Dana, the attorney and writer Richard Henry Dana, the physician and scientist John Jeffries, the lawyer and patriot Josiah Quincy, the legislator and city reformer Josiah Quincy, Governor James Sullivan, and the surgeon and Harvard Medical School professor John Collins Warren.

Members of the "state's" representatives to the Continental Congress represented in the collection include John Adams, Thomas Cushing, Francis Dana, Nathan Dane, Elbridge Gerry, John Hancock, Robert Treat Paine, Theodore Sedgwick, James Sullivan, and George Thacher. Colonial governors represented in the collection include Jonathan Belcher and John Winthrop, and state governors from the late colonial and early national period include Elbridge Gerry, John Hancock, James Sullivan, and Increase Sumner. Jurists represented in the collection include William Cushing, John Davis, Robert Treat Paine, Samuel Sewall, Joseph Story, Increase Sumner, and George Thacher. Clergymen represented in the collection include Jeremy Belknap, John Lathrop, Cotton Mather, Increase Mather, Samuel Mather, Ebenezer Parkman, William Pratt, and Joseph Sewall. A large number of shipowners, manufacturers, and merchants are represented in the collection, including Nathaniel Cutting, Caleb Davis, Joseph Palmer, Sir William Pepperell, Paul Revere, William Rotch, Samuel Phillips Savage, and Samuel Waldo.

When we turn to the nineteenth century, the society's collection continues to include persons who were important in the history and culture of Massachusetts. These include governors John A. Andrew, George Boutwell, Edward Everett, John Davis Long, Marcus Morton, and William Eustis Russell. Other persons important in the state's political life include Samuel T. Armstrong, Dwight Foster, Henry Cabot Lodge, Jonathan Mason, Harrison Gray Otis, John Phillips, Josiah Quincy, Lemuel Shaw, Charles Sumner, and Daniel Webster. Among the papers of nineteenth-century merchants are those of Nathan Appleton, Samuel Cabot, Franklin Gordon Dexter, James Hunnewell, Thomas Lamb, Amos Lawrence, Amos Adams Lawrence, and Edward Silas Tobey. Religious leaders represented include Noah Worcester, whose papers relate to the Massachusetts Peace Society, and Theodore Parker. Educators and writers represented in the collection include Alexander Hill Everett, James Thomas Fields, William Bentley Fowle, Mark Hopkins, Samuel Gridley Howe, Horace Mann, Francis Parkman, James Ford Rhodes, George Ripley, Mercy Otis Warren, and Justin Winsor. In the areas of science and medicine, the collection includes the papers of Jacob Bigelow, William Eustis, William T. G. Morton, Frederick Cheever Shattuck, Lemuel Shattuck, John Warren, and John Collins Warren.

The society's holdings also include transcripts of instructions to governors of Massachusetts from 1631 to 1775, miscellaneous papers from 1200 to 1952, papers relating to Shays' Rebellion, and records of the Assistant Fire Society from 1783 to 1819, the Bunker Hill Monument Association from 1825 to 1919, the Humane Society from 1787 to 1903, the Independent Christian Society from 1791 to 1840, the Massachusetts Anti-Suffrage Association from 1895 to 1921, the Massachusetts Colonization Society from 1842 to 1911, the New England Freedmen's Aid Society from 1862 to 1873, and the Society of the Cincinnati from 1765 to 1911.

For a more detailed listing of holdings, see the *Handbook of the Massachusetts Historical Society, 1791-1948* (Boston, 1949). There are extensive reports of acquisitions in the *Proceedings* of the society.

**MASSACHUSETTS INSTITUTE OF TECHNOLOGY
ARCHIVES AND SPECIAL COLLECTIONS**
Room 14N-118
Library
Cambridge, Mass. 02139
(617) 253-5688

The Institute Archives and Special Collections at MIT gathers unpublished material including official records of the institute, personal and prefessional papers of the faculty, staff and students, published material about the institute, and MIT theses and technical reports. The collection chronicle the founding and growth of each of MIT's schools and courses. The archives house significant material about MIT's programs in architecture, management, and the humanities, The development of science and engineering education and research is particularly well documented. It also houses several collections of rare books on the early history of science and technology.

MIT's influence extends far beyond Cambridge, of course, and as a result the archives includes materials revealing the institute's effect on the Boston area and its wide role in contemporary society. Many collections document the evolution of modern science and engineering and its impact on society, as well as the role of scientists and engineers in the formation of science policy.

The official records of the institute reflect MIT's role in statewide educational and economic development. The William Barton Rogers Papers cover his decision to move to Boston and pioneer in the field of technical professional education. Later presidential records document the beginnings of cooperative education in electrical engineering around the turn of the century, and other archival records reveal the roots of Route 128 and the electronics/computer industry in eastern Massachusetts. The biotechnology industry in Massachusetts is documented in the administrative records of the institute, in the personal papers of biologist David Baltimore, and in the Recombinant DNA Oral History Collection which covers the debates in the late 1970s, including the Cambridge City Council hearings on research hazards.

Another important collection in the archives is the papers of John Ripley Freeman (1855-1932). These papers document Freeman's activities as a consulting engineer on hydraulics projects throughout the world. Massachusetts historians might be interested in the material in the collection related to Freeman's work with the Boston Metropolitan Water Board on the Charles River Dam. The papers of sanitary engineer Allen Hazen complement this collection. Hazen's hydraulics projects included extensive public water analysis in towns across Massachusetts.

And the "new Boston" can be examined as it developed in the later 1960s and early 1970s by studying architect Devin Lynch's plans for Copley Square.

The research materials in the Institute Archives are complemented by the photographs, instruments, biographical files, and other holdings in the MIT Museum (265 Massachusetts Avenue, Cambridge).

MASSACHUSETTS STATE ARCHIVES
220 Morrissey Boulevard
Boston, Mass. 02125
(617) 727-2816 or 727-2817

The Massachusetts State Archives is the repository for the permanently valuable non-current records of the Commonwealth of Massachusetts and the state agencies of which it is comprised. Collecting is confined to the public records generated by state agencies and their predecessors. The Massachusetts Archives does not collect private manuscripts.

Chronologically, the holdings of the archives extend from the early settlement era of the Massachusetts Bay Colony (1620s) down to the near-recent past. Included is a particularly strong assemblage of seventeenth- and eighteenth-century records (Massachusetts Archives Series). In addition, there are ten volumes of colonial records and maps that were copied from French archives in the nineteenth century. Another important collection is the Eastern Lands Papers, consisting of records of the General Court, special commissions and land agents relative to the settlement of the eastern lands in Maine, boundary disputes, and the separation of the State of Maine in 1820. Included in the collection are maps, committee reports, surveyors' records, fiscal material, and correspondence. Currently, the collecting policy of the archives is directed toward the accessioning of records that more fully illustrate the development of public institutions and policies within the Commonwealth of Massachusetts.

The holdings of the Massachusetts Archives can be divided into several component parts. Of these, the most prominent are legislative materials, gubernatorial records, records of the State Treasurer and Secretary of State, files of administrative agencies, military records, and genealogical records. Highlights drawn from these categories follow:

The Legislative Collection contains journals of the General Court from 1628 to the present, as well as engrossed Acts and Resolves from 1686 to the present. There are letter books from 1763 to 1776, including letters to the agent in Great Britain. The collection includes original papers generated in the legislative process, from 1775 to date, including bills, petitions, remonstrances, committee reports, and other papers referred to the legislature by government officials. These include messages from the governor, reports of special commissions and state agencies, claims, and correspondence. Bill packets are held for both enacted and unenacted legislation. Committee files, dating from the 1970s, are available for the committee on taxation, committee on public service, committee on commerce and labor, and the senate ways and means committee.

Executive letter books, held by the archives, contain incoming correspondence of the governor for the years 1853 to 1893, and outgoing correspondence for the years from 1861 through 1925. The term of Governor John Andrew (1861-

1866) is especially well-documented. Broader holdings of more recent governors date from the mid-1960s to the 1980s. There are also journals of the Governor's Council from 1628 to the present at the archives, and council files from 1780 to the present include records of special commissions appointed by the governor and council, appropriations, and petitions for pardons, paroles, respites, and commutations.

Other constitutional offices for which the archives holds records are the State Treasurer and the Secretary of State. A large and varied quantity of records document Treasury affairs from 1692 down to the twentieth century. These include account books, ledgers, journals, cashbooks, and wastebooks, which are comprehensive for the colonial and early statehood periods. Among the materials in the Treasury files are sheriffs' returns, records of taxes and loans, special accounts relating to the disposition of Loyalist estates, and the operations of the Troy and Greenfield Railroad Company. Material in the records of the Secretary of State include commissions and qualifications of officeholders, acceptances of local option statutes, election returns from 1780 to the present, political and candidate and state convention returns from 1938 to 1968, initiative petitions, docket books and statements of lobbyists from 1891 to the present, renditions and extraditions, medical examiners' returns for deaths from 1885 to the present, state census schedules for 1855 and 1865, and other special censuses, maps and plans from 1636, and records of the state geographical and topographical surveys, tax valuations from 1738 to 1786, and correspondence and other administrative material.

Administrative records are held for all other executive offices, as well. Office files and correspondence are available for the Executive Offices of Administration and Finance, Educational Affairs, Environmental Affairs, and Human Services. Within these umbrella agencies, records of subordinate departments and divisions include public health, public welfare, mental health, corrections, youth services, labor and industries, education, harbor and land commissioners/waterways, arbitration and conciliation, rate-setting commission, consumers' council, Metropolitan District Commission, and the Massachusetts Bicentennial Commission. Frequently, these records extend back to predecessor agencies such as the State Board of Charities and the Harbor and Land Commissioners. The records of the State Board of Charities include lists of alien passengers entering the port of Boston from 1848 to 1891. Metropolitan District Commission records include approximately 15,000 negatives detailing the construction of the Quabbin Reservoir. An expanding collection of institutional records involves material from the Monson and Tewksbury almshouses, state hospitals at Tewksbury, Pondville, Rutland Heights, North Reading, and Westfield, the Danvers and Belchertown mental institutions, and the prisons at Charlestown, Framingham, Concord, Norfolk, and Walpole.

The holdings of military records are particularly strong for the colonial and Revolutionary War periods. A variety of muster rolls (from 1710 through Shays' Rebellion) and other military accounts document well the events of the Revolutionary and colonial wars. Records of the Massachusetts Board of War, Commissary General, and Quartermaster provide great detail for an understanding of the prosecution of the Revolutionary War and the War of 1812 in Massachusetts. Similarly, a considerable portion of material reveals the position and activities of the commonwealth during the brief period of Shays' Rebellion. Records of the Adjutant General primarily for the Civil War include muster rolls, issue books, and correspondence with most pertaining to the agent for state troops (1861–1867). Records also include state Revolutionary War pension records and Maine land grant bounties, and claims for state pay from veterans of the Spanish-American War.

Genealogists find the archives' holdings of vital records particularly useful. Comprised of Registers of Births, Marriages, and Deaths throughout the commonwealth, these materials cover the years from 1841 through 1890. State and federal census records, also available in the archives, are used to good effect in combination with the vital records, as is the card file that indexes the names of aliens entering the port of Boston during the period from 1849 to 1890. The archives also include microfilm copies of local records in Massachusetts that were filmed by the Church of Jesus Christ of Latter Day Saints. The WPA Historical Records Survey (1936–1942) documents the inventories of manuscript collections and county, municipal, and church records.

While certain materials are subject to restriction by law (e.g., records containing personal data), most of the holdings are available upon request. Several staff members are available to assist patrons with their inquiries. Persons may use the automated shelf list as a guide to the holdings, and most parts of the collection are also detailed in inventory sheets that can be used by patrons at the main desk in the research area.

MUSEUM OF AMERICAN TEXTILE HISTORY
800 Massachusetts Avenue
North Andover, Mass. 01845
(617) 686-0191

The Museum of American Textile History (MATH), formerly known as the Merrimack Valley Textile Museum, is devoted to preserving and chronicling the history of the American textile industry. The museum has several departments. There is a collection of preindustrial textile tools and equipment, and industrial technology is preserved in over 250 pieces of textile machinery. Textiles themselves, both hand and machine made, are also collected. The museum also has a library of technical and historical reference materials. In addition to the 35,000 books, the library's resources include trade catalogs, broadsides, and a major collection of prints, photographs, and other images related to textiles. The library is also the repository for the business papers of many textile manufacturers and for the many other kinds of manuscript materials related to the history of the American textile industry and the people who were part of that history.

Much of the history of Massachusetts is the history of the textile industry. At MATH, the manuscript materials relative to this history range from single items to collections of many linear feet. There are individual letters of mill girls, draft books of hand weavers, and student notebooks. A business collection may be as small as ten boxes from the Ware Company, or as large as the several hundreds of boxes and volumes from the Essex Company and the Stevens companies.

The Ware Company collection is a small jewel among the treasures. Only four linear feet, these materials chronicle an ambitious but short-lived (1823-1829) enterprise in the central Massachusetts town of Ware. Its correspondence files are rich in information about the management of the factories from Boston, the supply and transportation of raw materials, and the labor force in Ware.

Among the most heavily used collections at MATH is that of the Essex Company (1845-1946). A land and water power company, it developed the city of Lawrence. One hundred linear feet of records document the many aspects of the company's work in engineering, city planning, and corporate management. The papers include executive and engineering correspondence, payrolls, engineers' field notebooks, and many plans and drawings.

At present the largest collection (640 linear feet) is that of the Stevens Companies (1811-1972). The Stevens Woolen Mill, opened in 1813, was the beginning of a family business that grew to include ten New England mills and parented the present J. P. Stevens Company. The business records are extensive for the period from 1830 to 1920. Among the richest records in this collection are time books, payrolls, and the many letters from employees to the three generations of Stevens men who owned and ran the mills. The collection also includes many personal family papers that can provide much social and even political history, for Moses T. Stevens served in the Massachusetts legislature and spent two terms in the U.S. Congress.

These three collections are only a sampling of the manuscript materials available at MATH. The collection also includes the substantial records of machinery manufacturers like Davis & Furber, Crompton & Knowles, the Mason Machine Works, and the Whiten Manufacturing Company, all Massachusetts firms of major importance. There are also records of many other textile mills, such as the Appleton Company (1815-1926) or the Uxbridge Cotton Mills (1840-1924). All the business collections have a variety of records for investigation.

The business records have all been organized and described in a uniform manner based on the model developed at the Baker Library of the Harvard Business School. Each company's records are arranged in the following order: Organization and Administration, Executive, Financial, Purchasing, Sales, Labor, and Production. Finding specific record types in any collection is relatively easy, and as each collection is in the same order, it is also easy for a researcher to compare the available materials in several different collections.

The scope of MATH's collections can only be suggested in this brief summary. However, there is a published guide to the museum's manuscript holdings, *The Merrimack Valley Textile Museum: A Guide to the Manuscript Collections* (New York, 1983). There is also an in-house inventory of manuscripts acquired since the guide was published.

Dorothy Truman

MUSEUM OF OUR NATIONAL HERITAGE
33 Marrett Road (Route 2A)
Lexington, Mass. 02173
(617) 861-6559

The Museum of Our National Heritage is a bicentennial project sponsored by the Scottish Rite Masons of the Northern Jurisdiction of the United States. It is a general American history museum and library presenting traveling and cooperative exhibitions on a wide variety of subjects. The permanent collections are twofold. General American history collections include maps, prints and paintings, photographs, decorative arts objects, costumes, and textiles that are used in the changing exhibition program.

The research collections of the museum and library are on the history of fraternal organizations in America. This collection includes the archives of the Supreme Council of the Scottish Rite of Freemasonry of the Northern Jurisdiction, whose headquarters share the museum grounds in Lexington. Other collections include certificates, regalia, publications, photographs, and manuscripts of Masonic and other fraternal organizations, as well as decorative arts objects with the symbolism of the various groups. Organizations represented in the collection include Freemasons, Odd Fellows, Red Men, Patrons of Husbandry, temperance organizations, labor organizations, and ethnic and mutual benefit societies. The museum has also begun to collect photographs and inventories of collections in individual lodges and other museums in order to assemble an archive of available fraternal materials for scholarly research.

Barbara Franco

NEW BEDFORD FREE PUBLIC LIBRARY
613 Pleasant Street
New Bedford, Mass. 02740
(617) 999-6291 ext. 15

The Free Public Library was incorporated in 1852, making it the second tax-supported public library in the country. In 1864 Librarian Robert C. Ingraham began to collect systematically material related to the history and genealogy of southeastern Massachusetts, the Society of Friends, and American whaling. These areas remain the strengths of the collection.

The collections related to American whaling are most extensive. The New Bedford Customs House Records include crew lists and shipping articles (1807-1922), seamen's protection papers (1834-1869), merchant manifests (1808-1890), whaling manifests (1815-1890), cod fishing bonds (1829-1867), mackerel fishing bonds (1843-1867), coasting trade licenses (1808-1812), bonds for licenses of vessels (1825-1898), and register bonds (1800-1809 and 1840-1869).

The library possesses logbooks from upwards of 450 voyages. The bulk are whaling logbooks from the 1830s until World War I. The whaling logbooks are listed in *Whaling Logbooks and Journals: an Inventory of Manuscript Records in Public Collections* (New York, 1986).

The library has the records of several leading whaling agents. These include those of Charles Waln Morgan, with letter books (1819-1846), business accounts (1818-1858) including the accounts of the Wareham Paper Company (1836-1838), and logbooks of the whaleships *Abigail, Clarice, Condor, Hector, Maria,* and *Pioneer.* The records of J. and W. R. Wing and Company include letter books (1899-1900 and 1905-1908), business accounts (1849-1924), and logbooks for 32 whaleships. The papers of Charles R. Tucker include letter books (1836-1838), business accounts (1836-1875), and logbooks for 23 whaleships. The papers of William Rotch of Nantucket, France, Great Britain, and New Bedford include letter books (1782-1792) and business accounts from 1772 to 1806. The papers of Swift and Allen include logbooks of 17 whaleships. The papers of Dennis Wood include abstracts of voyages of American whaleships (5 volumes, 1831-1873). Wood was director of the Mutual Marine Insurance Company, as well as being a merchant and whaling agent.

Other business records related to whaling include the Maritime Insurance Records of the Bedford Insurance Company, the Mutual Marine Insurance Company, and the Fairhaven Mutual Marine Insurance Company. In addition, the library possesses the business records (1867-1901) of the George S. Homer Whale Oil Refinery, of a sailmaker, Alfred M. Chapman, of a whale-oil merchant, Isaiah Franklin Terry, and of William James Rotch, president of the New Bedford Cordage Company and Rotch Wharf Company.

Non-whaling business records include the letter books (1846-1862) of Andrew Robeson, president of Robeson's Print Works in Fall River, the minutes of the Board of Directors of Old Colony Railroad (1839-1873), the minutes of the Board of Directors of the New Bedford Bridge Corporation (1796-1872), and records of the New Bedford architectural firm of Caleb Hammond and Son (c. 1894-1904).

Military records in the collection include the orders (1808-1816 and 1821-1839), roster (1814-1819 and 1828-1840), applications for discharges (1835-1840), and letter book (1833-1839) of the Massachusetts Militia, Fifth Division, Second Brigade, led by Lt. Col. Benjamin Lincoln and Maj. Gen. James D. Thompson. In addition, the library has the orders (1821-1833) of the First Brigade and the orders (1855-1861) of the First Division, Second Brigade. The records of Camp Meigs, Readville (Hyde Park), Massachusetts, include orders, guard reports, and correspondence (1862-1865), and discharges (1863-1864). The bylaws, roster, and orders (1840-1849) of the New Bedford Guards are also in the collection, along with the journals of the Home and Coast Guard, Company C, kept while it was stationed at Fort Taber, New Bedford, and Fort Phoenix, Fairhaven (May-October 1861). Finally, the library has the records of William Logan Rodman Post No. 1 of the Grand Army of the Republic (1866-1928), including minutes of meetings, a letter book (1868-1879), and "Personal War Sketches" of the members.

The library has several important collections related to libraries and education. These include the records of the Encyclopedia Society (1799-1826), of the New Bedford Social Library (1806-1852), the New Bedford Free Public Library (1852 to the present), and the New Bedford Academy (later Fairhaven Academy) (1798-1841).

Religious records include the minutes of meetings (1837-1851 and 1867-1922) of the First Christian Church of Acushnet, manuscripts of 685 sermons (1857-1893) delivered by Rev. William James Potter of the First Congregational Society (Unitarian) of New Bedford, and four volumes of diaries (1813-1881) of Rev. Moses How of the Christian churches in Methuen, Salem, New Bedford, and Portsmouth, New Hampshire.

Municipal records in the collection include town meetings (1674-1787) of the Town of Dartmouth, town meetings (1787-1847) and tax records (1787-1848) of the Town of New Bedford, and the records (1845-1882) of the Overseers of the Poor of the City of New Bedford.

Personal papers in the collection include letter books (1858-1926) of William Wallace Crapo, member of the state House of Representatives (1857), member of the U.S. House of Representatives (1875-1883), and attorney in the "Alabama Claims" hearings. The library also contains the correspondence (1807-1817), family papers, and business accounts of Paul Cuffe (1759-1817), black merchant and master mariner who was involved in the resettlement of black Americans in Sierra Leone. The papers of James Bunker Congdon (1802-1880) include documents and notes collected for a projected history of New Bedford. Finally, the

Pardon Gray Seabury Collection includes documents and notes collected by Rev. Pardon Seabury (1796–1875) concerning the history of Freetown and Fall River, Massachusetts, as well as Tiverton and Little Compton, Rhode Island. Included are the minutes of the meetings of the proprietors of the Pocasset Purchase (1694–1821) and a book of the descendants and grantees of the original proprietors of the Freeman's Purchase.

The Genealogy Room focuses on the families of southeastern Massachusetts, including families of British, French-Canadian, Acadian, Portuguese, Cape Verdean, and Afro-American descent. The collection includes U.S. censuses from 1790 to 1910, New Bedford immigration lists from 1823 to 1942, Canadian "repertoires de mariage," New Bedford newspapers back to 1792, and genealogical compilations by Emma Pierce, Elisha Leonard, Warren Ladd, and George Randall. The Melville Whaling Room contains a card index of a quarter of a million names from whaling crew lists and seamen's protection papers.

Finally, the library possesses several hundred volumes relating to the Quakers from Britain, America, and Europe. The earliest is an anti-Quaker book of 1655 by Richard Baxter. The library also has runs of Quaker periodicals, such as the *American Friend* and the *Friend's Quarterly Examiner*.

Paul Cyr

OLD DARTMOUTH HISTORICAL SOCIETY
NEW BEDFORD WHALING MUSEUM
18 Johnny Cake Hill
New Bedford, Mass. 02740
(617) 997-0046

The Old Dartmouth Historical Society was founded in 1903 to encourage and promote an interest in the history of the area that now comprises New Bedford, Dartmouth, Fairhaven, Acushnet and Westport, by collecting, preserving, and interpreting to the public the documentary and material evidence of its past. With the establishment of the Whaling Museum a few years later, the society determined to make its collection of materials on the history of American whaling "the most comprehensive of any nationally and internationally." The Whaling Museum Library, housed in a facility completed in 1981 and designed specifically to meet the needs of rare and fragile material, contnues to collect with these goals in mind.

There are over 15,000 books, pamphlets, maps, charts, broadsides, and periodicals in the library as well as 1,800 reels of microfilm and access to 15,000 photographic negatives. The microfilm collection includes copies of logbooks belonging to the society. Copies of an additional 1,500 logbooks in institutions and private libraries are part of the International Marine Archives. This microfilm collection also contains records of whaling, merchant, and exploration voyages copied from the national archives of the United States, Great Britain and France. United States consular despatches from a dozen ports in the Pacific area from 1812 to 1906 are also included.

The book collection emphasizes local and maritime history. The Charles F. Batchelder collection, acquired by the library in 1975, is the largest body of printed material on the history of American whaling ever assembled. The Charles A. Goodwin collection contains works of more general maritime interest including biographies, narratives of voyages and discoveries, seamen's navigation manuals, and histories of ships and shipbuilding.

The manuscripts occupy approximately 750 linear feet and include more than 1,000 logbooks, primarily of whaling voyages during the age of sail, 1745-1927. Other records of the American whaling industry are to be found in the papers of agents and owners, such as William Rotch, Jr., 1789-1863; John Russell Thornton, 1841-1894; Thomas Knowles & Company, 1844-1889; and Swift & Allen, 1831-1893. The correspondence, owner and crew accounts, bills and receipts, consular and customs papers, shipbuilding and outfitting records, tell the story of one of our country's earliest and most profitable industries. Old Dartmouth's venture capitalists sent ships to all parts of the globe in search of whales, and in doing so opened new areas to trade and commerce in the Pacific basin and even more remote areas. Whalemen were among the first to explore the Arctic and Antarctic regions and to record in their journals the appearance and behavior of indigenous peoples.

Also in the manuscript collection are the papers of local organizations, businesses and families that illustrate the nature of social and commercial development in a maritime community. The records of the Dartmouth Monthly Meeting, 1699-1965, and the First Unitarian (formerly Congregational) Church in New Bedford, 1730-1977, Friends Academy, 1810-1980, and New South School House, 1808-1827, are records that show how the two dominant religious groups in the area acted and interacted.

Other documentation for social history can be found in records of charitable organizations such as New Bedford Child and Family Service, 1842-1960, and in rich collections of family papers such as that of the Corys of Westport, Massachusetts. Occupying forty feet, these latter papers concern four generations of a family involved in shipping, shipbuilding, whaling, weaving, a general store, and town offices. The Paul Cuffe collection, 1811-1828, records the career of an Afro-American merchant and philanthropist who owned several vessels and was involved in business ventures with the Corys.

The role of women is highlighted by diaries and letters written at home and at sea, as well as in other records of domestic life. The business papers of the Hathaway family, 1811-1888, record New Bedford's involvement in the China trade. The records of the New Bedford Cordage Company, 1839-1968, Pierce Manufacturing Corp., 1868-1948, and the New Bedford Rayon, Inc., 1926-1974, illustrate the city's later industrial development.

The last half of the nineteenth century saw a rapid growth of the arts in the New Bedford area. The papers of artists R. Swain Gifford, 1722-1968, and Clement Nye Swift, 1872-1947, as well as authors Daniel Ricketson, 1840-1918, and Charles Agard, 1882-1962, are also part of the collection.

Judith Downey

OLD STURBRIDGE VILLAGE
1 Sturbridge Village Road
Sturbridge, Mass. 01566
(617) 347-3362

The Old Sturbridge Village collections are comprised of several distinct parts: curatorial collections, library collections, photographic (visual resource) collections, archives, and archaeological collections. The curatorial collections consist of material culture artifacts illustrative of the daily lives of inland rural New Englanders from 1790 to 1840. These collections include household furnishings and implements, fine and decorative arts objects, tools and products of trades, crafts, and industries, agricultural equipment, and textiles and clothing. In the course of sixty years of development, the collections have evolved particular strengths in specific areas. Old Sturbridge Village's collections of clocks, clothing, decorated vernacular furniture, and lighting devices are of national significance. The collections of glass, other textiles, firearms and militia accoutrements, and hand tools, are of regional note, while decorated tinware, labeled vernacular furniture, pewter and britannia, and folk art are of growing importance.

The Old Sturbridge Village Research Library collection focuses on the history and material culture of inland rural New England from 1790 to 1840. Within the structure of this well-defined historical period, the library's collection contains primary sources and supportive secondary materials dealing with all aspects of community life. There are substantial collections of New England local histories, eighteenth- and nineteenth-century maps and atlases, books printed before 1850 (particularly textbooks, juveniles, and advice books), and manuscripts including account books, diaries, letters, and miscellaneous papers of ordinary rural people. Thematically the library is particularly strong in the areas of nineteenth-century town and county histories, law, health and medicine, agriculture, the decorative arts, architecture, and traditional rural crafts. The collection also includes a significant array of primary resources on microfilm and microfiche, manuscript census schedules, property deeds, probate records, and town directories, as well as modern scholarly books and journals. Although the collection concentrates on New England, it also includes materials that contribute to the understanding and interpretation of the region and its particular lifestyle within the broad context of American history.

Microfilm copies of New England newspapers to 1860 and significant original issues of central Massachusetts publishers are available. Gravestone rubbings are a small collection.

The Old Sturbridge Village Archives consists of those records that constitute the biographical history of the institution and, as such, have continuing and permanent administrative, legal, fiscal, informational, and historical value.

The Old Sturbridge Village Visual Resource Library acquires and maintains a collection of photographic images that document the history of the village, its buildings, collections, and programs, as well as photographic images that depict life in the towns of inland rural New England. Photographic materials include original negatives and antique and contemporary photographic prints, including daguerreotypes, ambrotypes, tintypes, and special format prints such as card photographs (cartes de visite, cabinet cards, etc.), stereographs, and postcards, as well as large-format transparencies, 35mm slides, and lantern slides.

The Archeology Department seeks to preserve those material culture objects and fragments thereof that have been recovered during the course of archaeological excavations organized by Old Sturbridge Village. Excavations take place at a variety of rural inland New England historical sites identified through documentary research as a part of the museum's general research program.

The Curatorial and Archeological collections are available only by appointment.

PILGRIM HALL MUSEUM
75 Court Street
Plymouth, Mass. 02360-3891
(617) 746-1620

The library and archives of the Pilgrim Society are housed in Pilgrim Hall Museum. Since its founding in 1820, the society has collected books, manuscripts, and other materials related to the Plymouth colonists and the history of the colony and town. The collections of books, maps, photographs, and archival holdings are an unrivaled source of information about the Pilgrims. The collections cover from the early seventeenth century to the present. The library and archives are open to the public by appointment.

The reference collection includes more than 12,000 books, pamphlets, and periodicals. The nucleus of the collection focuses on the Pilgrims, their English background, their religion, and their historical significance. The local history collection includes street directories, census materials, church histories, books on town events and celebrations, and extensive vertical subject files. Important sources include Plymouth Colony Records from 1620 to 1692, Plymouth County Court Records from 1685 to 1859, Records of the Town of Plymouth from 1636 to 1783, Plymouth Church Records from 1620 to 1859, and vital records and town histories of Plymouth County towns.

The manuscript collection includes the papers of Plymouth families and records of local businesses, civic organizations, and churches. Major topics covered are family history, local industry, shipping, and social movements. A guide to the manuscripts collection is available.

The collection of maps, plans, and architectural drawings and atlases (manuscript and printed) is a major source for studying the Plymouth area. Among the highlights of the collection are Samuel Champlain's map of Plymouth Harbor (1605/1613) and William Hack's manuscript "Description of New England in America" (c. 1656-1707). There is also a photograph collection of over 5,000 images of Plymouth street scenes, houses, events, and people (1865 to date). It includes the A. S. Burbank collection of 1,200 glass-plate negatives (1859-1921).

The library has several runs of Plymouth newspapers (1786, 1822-1917), along with an index (1822-1921) to the *Old Colony Memorial*, Plymouth's longest-running newspaper.

SOCIETY FOR THE PRESERVATION
OF NEW ENGLAND ANTIQUITIES
HARRISON GRAY OTIS HOUSE
141 Cambridge Street
Boston, Mass. 02114
(617) 227-3956

Since its founding in 1910, the special purpose of SPNEA's library has been to collect and preserve a record of New England's architectural heritage in association with its surrounding landscape and material culture. The present collections consist of nearly one million items, nearly half of which are visual in format. Collectively, these document the building traditions of New England as a whole—its cities, suburbs and rural areas—representing structures of all types, styles, and time periods viewed from the perspective of regional artists and photographers, both professional and amateur. Supplementary information about the history, design, and construction of individual buildings will be found in related collections of manuscripts, architectural drawings, maps, and printed matter.

PHOTOGRAPHIC COLLECTIONS

Photographs are the major specialization of this library. The collections consist of images in all media, from daguerreotypes and ambrotypes, historically the first commercially viable photographic processes, to modern prints and postcards. They include an impressive number of over 70,000 negatives, the majority of them original glass plates or film negatives exposed by photographers throughout New England from the 1880s to the mid-1940s. Photographs are arranged by type.

Daguerreotypes and Ambrotypes

This collection consists of approximately 800 uncataloged items, ranging from 1/16″ to full plates and dating from the early 1840s to the early 1860s. The majority are cased portraits, many of them identified. The work of several of New England's leading daguerreotypists is represented, including Southworth and Hawes, Whipple, Heywood, Chase, Plumbe, and many others. There is a small but significant quantity of architectural views, including fourteen daguerreotypes by Calvin Philco Wheeler, taken in Plymouth in the early 1850s.

Cartes de Visite

Chronologically, the "carte de visite" era overlaps with the waning popularity of daguerreotypes and ambrotypes as the predominant medium of photographic portraiture. The earliest cartes de visite in this collection date from c. 1858, though the majority cluster between 1862 and 1866. Not surprisingly, nearly 95 percent of the material is portraiture, including military, political, literary, and theatrical personalities, as well as "ordinary people" from infancy to old age, either New Englanders or photographed by New England photographers. However, nearly 250 architectural or scenic views have been identified and are separately filed by localities. Most of these are Boston views. The total size of the carte de visite collection amounts to approximately 4,000 images, many still in their original and highly decorative albums.

Stereo Views

The majority of stereo views are arranged by localities. Boston is particularly well covered by nearly 1,500 views of churches, streets, public buildings, the harbor, and parks, in some cases intertwined with noteworthy events such as the Peace Jubilees of the 1860s and early 1870s, the Centennial Parades of 1876, and the tragic aftermath of the Great Fire of 1872. Outside of Boston, the best-represented communities include Portland, Maine; Newport, Rhode Island; Newburyport, Massachusetts; Lawrence and Lowell, Massachusetts (emphasizing industrial and manufacturing subjects); and Oak Bluffs, Massachusetts. The latter is of special interest because of the coverage of camp meetings and the cottage architecture that replaced the earlier fanciful tents with equally fanciful building forms. John Soule, N. W. Pease, and the Bierstadt Brothers are but a few of the other major photographers represented in this important collection. In the "small photo files" approximately 1,500 stereos are arranged by subjects, including housing, farming, and occupations and trades; religion; and shipping and railroads. A small number are filed by photographer's name alone, though it should be stressed that many more examples of the work of individual photographers will be found under specific localities.

Postcards and Snapshots

Although postcards are currently enjoying a vogue as "collectibles," they are used in this library as an important source of documentary information about a variety of commercial, residential, civic, and industrial buildings that were often ignored by photographers in search of the "picturesque." To say "We were here" fortunately has left a record of many hamlets and small towns that otherwise would have gone unrecorded in the photographic record, not to mention the major resorts and main streets that have now lost their earlier glory. Nearly the entire collection of approximately 5,000 postcards, dating from the 1890s to the 1930s, is filed by localities. Of related interest are the 8" x 10" photographic proofs from which two Boston postcard manufacturers—Thomson & Thomson and the New England News Company—prepared their postcard views. The geographic scope of the postcard collection is similar to that of the stereos; Boston is most richly documented, followed by resorts and important manufacturing centers throughout New England. Snapshots and prints smaller than 4" x 5" comprise an important part of the postcard and small photo file. These are also arranged by localities and subjects. The small photo file includes a wide range of subjects, especially those relating to transportation. Included are several hundred views of sailing vessels, arranged by vessel name; trains and railroad stations; and miscellaneous vehicles of all types.

Standard-Size Photographic Prints

This is the most sizeable and most complex of the library's photographic holdings, containing an estimated 100,000 items, dating from the 1860s to the present. This collection is a rich archive of the work of individual New England photographers and photographic firms.

Standard prints are filed by localities if the content is primarily architectural in nature. Others are filed by subjects or under personal names. The collection includes media of all types, from albumen prints to modern silver prints. Fragile or unusual albumen prints, dating from the late 1850s to the early 1890s, have been removed to a separate file, and the original image replaced by a xerox. The arrangement of files is simple: subdivisions are by the name of each New England state, further subdivided by the name of city or town, followed by street or structure names. Do not be alarmed by the folders marked "Ancient" and "Modern." These are catchall categories that refer to the age of the structure represented, not to the antiquity of the photograph. "Ancient" comprises structures from the seventeenth century to the mid-nineteenth century. Filing errors occur, however, so consult both. Such folders are used when there is not enough material relating to an individual structure or street to justify an individual folder. For access to photographs filed by subject, consult the list of subject headings.

Major collections include photography by Arthur Haskell, Baldwin Coolidge, Wilfred French, Henry Hadcock, the Halliday Historic Photograph Company, the Soule Art Photo Company, Thomson & Thomson/New England News Company, Boston Building Department, Hiram Harlow Collection, Fred Quimby, Harriet Curtis, Emma Coleman, George Noyes, William Clark, Wallace Nutting, Mary Northend, Horace Chandler, the Marine Photographs of Nathaniel L. Stebbins and Henry G. Peabody, the Boston and Albany Railroad Archive, the Donald Howe Collection of Quabbin Valley Views, the Codman Collection of Family Photographs, and views of residential interiors, 1,500 prints, dating from the mid-1870s to c. 1920. The archives of the Boston Transit Commission and Boston Elevated Railroad Company document the planning, building, and completion of Boston's subway system.

The print collection consists of approximately 2,500 woodcuts, engravings, lithographs, and wood engravings, dating from the 1830s to the 1920s. Material relating to Boston and vicinity (including Cambridge) has been cataloged and is described in an inventory, cross-indexed by the names of artists, engravers, or lithographers, printers, subjects, streets, and structure names. Nearly 500 pencil, ink, watercolor, and pastel sketches and more finished works add a further dimension to the documentation of many New England buildings and regional landscapes, though their viewpoint is necessarily more subjective and often less detailed than photographic and printed information. Over 5,000 illustrated trade cards, billheads, and manufacturers' catalogs provide a rich source of visual documentation for the study of New England's material culture in the nineteenth and early twentieth centuries.

The library maintains a collection of over 500 maps of New England localities and 150 bound atlases. The majority relate to Boston and vicinity, with especially good coverage for the period between 1800 and 1900.

Next to photographs and prints, architectural drawings constitute the library's most sizeable holdings. Over 10,000 individual drawings have been cataloged and are accessible by means of a card index arranged by localities and architects' names.

This is also a major repository for material generated by the Historic American Buildings Survey in the 1930s. HABS's collections include over 125 complete sets of full-scale survey drawings of historic buildings throughout New England, supplemented by forty-three albums of photographs by staff photographers.

Prior to the formation of HABS in 1933, Norman Isham, J. F. Kelley, G. F. Dow, Alfred Shurrocks, Frank Chouteau Brown, Donald Millar, Thomas T. Waterman, and others systematically combed New England in search of surviving buildings from the first and second period of its architectural history. Much of their work was inspired by William Sumner Appleton, the founder of SPNEA, which led the movement to document and preserve early regional building traditions. The efforts of these individuals resulted in hundreds of drawings—some little more than rough sketches, others carefully drawn and measured plans, elevations, and details. Besides such "historic" material, the architectural drawing collections include substantial holdings of the commissioned work of firms or individual architects, among them Arthur Little and Herbert Browne; Ogden Codman, Jr.; Luther Briggs; Frank Chouteau Brown; Arland Dirlam; Jacob Luippold; George Clough, Halfdan Hanson, Julius Pomeroy, and William Place, among others. Asher Benjamin, Alexander Parris, Samuel McIntire, Richard Upjohn, Edward Casey, and others are represented by more scattered holdings.

MANUSCRIPT COLLECTIONS

As a consequence of its ownership of historic properties throughout New England, SPNEA has acquired several sizeable collections of family manuscripts. The most notable of these are the Papers of the Bowen Family; the Codman Family Papers (100 linear feet); the Casey Family Papers (70 linear feet); the Jewett Family Papers; the Business Papers of Harrison Gray Otis; the Rundlet-May Family Papers; the Sayward Family Papers; the Marrett Family Papers; the Parson Smith Papers; and the Coffin Family Papers.

Of special interest to the study of New England's economic history is a collection of over 150 account books (not including those in family manuscript collections). These reflect the activities, expenditures, and personnel of various specialized occupations, as well as the consumption patterns of households, from c. 1750 to the 1880s, with particular strengths in textile production (both domestic and commercial), carpentry, agriculture, and merchandising practices of general stores.

Correspondence generated by SPNEA from its founding in 1910 has been microfilmed through 1973. Not only is this a leading resource for the study of the historic preservation movement in New England, but it is also a rich source of information about the history and background of SPNEA properties.

SPECIAL COLLECTIONS

"Special collections" consist of small holdings of materials whose relevance to architectural subjects is peripheral but which nevertheless reflect the society's interest in New England's material culture as a whole. These include greeting cards, calling cards, tickets of admission, other printed ephemera (such as paper samples, menus, theater programs, and programs for special events), copybooks, school catalogs, monitorial maps and schoolgirl albums, farmer's almanacs, and religious tracts.

Ellie Reichlin, Director of Archives

SPRINGFIELD ARMORY NATIONAL HISTORIC SITE
One Armory Square
Springfield, Mass. 01105
(413) 734-8551 or 734-6477

The library associated with the Springfield Armory Museum at the Springfield Armory National Historic Site is an important centei for research into the Springfield Armory and related subjects. The original records generated at the armory while it was a functioning institution (1795-1968) have nearly all been transferred to the National Archives or to other military installations. The most significant of these records, however, have been microfilmed by the National Archives and are available for research use. These records are part of Record Group 156 (Office of the Chief of Ordnance), and are predominantly from the period up to and including World War I. Some 300 reels will be available when the program is completed. In addition, there are several reels of microfilm in other categories, notably copies of scrapbooks formerly maintained by the Springfield Armory.

The library has acquired the bulk of the working photo collection amassed by the former Springfield Armory. This embraces over 18,000 images on various media, such as prints, film negatives, glassplate negatives, lantern slides, and film slides. The photos are organized into sixteen subject categories, and a finding aid exists for the print portion of the collection. Copies of finding guides are available for a fee. Due to staff limitations, requests should be made well in advance.

The collection also includes approximately 180 movie films, most in 16-mm format. These are mostly technical films of development and testing of weapons or news films concerning events or operations at the armory. The period covered by these films extends from the early 1940s to the closing of the armory. There is a finding aid for this portion of the collection.

Another category of audiovisual holdings is the growing collection of oral history interviews, emphasizing former employees of Springfield Armory. Most of these cover the period after 1940, but a few go back earlier. An effort is being made to index these tapes for easier research access, but many have not been completed.

The library has also acquired a significant segment of the former Springfield Armory collection of maps and drawings, totaling approximately 8,000 items. This collection includes architectural drawings, maps of armory property, and mechanical drawings and instructional charts related to weapons development. Generated primarily by the engineering department, these documents date from the early nineteenth century to the present, but the majority are from the twentieth century. This portion of the collection is indexed in a card-catalog format and organized by area and building.

Some primary data has survived at this site. Twelve linear feet of loose papers, including technical reports, individual papers, and memorabilia, have been organized in a vertical file and are in the process of being indexed. The manuscript collection includes the papers of John C. Garand and John D. Pedersen. Garand, the inventor of the M-1 rifle, pursued his career as an employee of the armory, while Pedersen was under contract to the armory in the 1920s and developed competing designs.

There is also a collection of source material: Post Orders from 1861 to 1943, Memoranda from 1910 to 1972, Annual Reports from 1901 to 1956, World War I and World War II "house organs," and histories of the armory, including a detailed doctoral dissertation by Derwent S. Whittlesey (University of Chicago, 1920) and a manuscript by Constance M. Green compiled in the 1940s. There is also a sizeable collection of army training and field manuals. The library also contains more than 1,000 general reference titles, 47 percent of which are devoted to military science.

The library is open by appointment only.

Larry Lowenthal

SPRINGFIELD CITY LIBRARY
Genealogy and Local History Department
220 State Street
Springfield, Mass. 01103
(413) 739-3871, exts. 230 and 272

The Springfield City Library Genealogy and Local History Department was created in order to document the political, economic, social, and cultural history of Springfield and the Connecticut Valley. The sources include city directories from 1845 to date, family vital records from 1636 to 1850, the Pynchon colonial records from 1638 to 1690, death, ordination, and marriage newspaper notices from 1786 to 1850, municipal reports from 1852 to 1958, voting lists from 1884, maps, atlases, and scrapbooks, high school and college yearbooks, *Springfield Republican* annual building reports from 1859 to 1916, vertical files, church and business histories, trade journals, and Springfield newspapers on microfilm from 1786 to date. The department also maintains a collection of over 20,000 photographs that record the history of Springfield individuals, groups, events, institutions, and business and industry. The collection is particularly strong in its coverage of the late nineteenth and early twentieth centuries.

The archives contain approximately 2,000 linear feet of correspondence, account books, business records, and other manuscripts, ranging from seventeenth-century documents of the founding Pynchon family to twentieth-century buisness records and personal papers. An extensive collection of nineteenth-century Connecticut Valley business records and a large number of papers documenting colonial times in and around Springfield represent the archives' special strength.

The business collections, totaling over 800 linear feet of material, include mill records, insurance company records, an arms manufacturer's papers, and various account books of eighteenth-century and early nineteenth-century Connecticut Valley merchants. The Ames Sword Company, with the bulk of the material dating from 1831 to 1888, documents the development of the largest manufacturer of swords in nineteenth-century America. The documents also record the Ames Company's active role in the manufacture of cannons, pistols, ammunition, and machine guns, and its involvement in arms production during the Civil War. The Farr Alpaca Company, which was a large mill operation in Holyoke, Massachusetts, from 1874 to 1940, is documented by a largely complete collection of account books, stock ledgers, time books, correspondence, and other material.

Springfield is known for the importance of its insurance industry, which is documented in the archives by two large collections, the Mass Mutual Insurance Company Collection, the Springfield Fire and Marine Insurance Company Collection, and the Monarch Insurance Company Collection. The Mass Mutual Company, founded in Springfield in 1851 and now one of the largest organizations of its type in the country, is documented by a wide variety of material, including annual reports, company periodicals, executive correspondence, photographs, and a variety of other types of material. The Springfield Fire and Marine was founded in 1849 and was an important nationwide company until its absorption by Monarch Insurance Company of Springfield in 1960. The collection includes a wide variety of material documenting every aspect of the company's existence in Springfield.

The Springfield Library Archives also includes an extensive collection of records from the Package Machinery Company, originally from Springfield and now based in East Longmeadow. The company was formed in 1913 when several wrapping-machine companies merged to form the Springfield concern, and by 1937 it had become the largest machine-wrapping operation in the world. The records of Package Machinery (including correspondence of the president, financial records, Board of Directors minutes, memoranda, and other material retained by the President's Office) originated from the papers of Roger L. Putnam (1894-1972), whose father helped found the company and who himself served on the Board of Directors or as president of the company for over five decades.

The library archives also retains a large collection of personal papers. Of particular interest is the extensive collection of Roger L. Putnam, who was a three-term Springfield mayor (1937-1943), an officer in the Truman administration, and a candidate for governor of Massachusetts (1942), in addition to his business activities. Putnam's papers, amounting to 96 linear feet of material, include his business and personal correspondence, files on political activities, the records of his work on the Massachusetts Board of Higher Education, and personal and family records. They date from 1920 to 1972.

The papers of Donald L. Macaulay (1896-1980), a Massachusetts State Supreme Court justice (1956-1971), an unsuccessful candidate for mayor of Springfield (1937 and 1939), and a pilot during World War I, consist of personal and business correspondence, records of his Springfield law practice, personal files concerned with his judicial work, and memorabilia from his days as a pilot. The collection dates from 1915 to 1980 and consists of 10 linear feet of material.

The William Lathrop Collection consists of his personal correspondence between 1820 and 1837. Of particular interest are the letters between William and his father, Samuel Lathrop, a U.S. congressman from western Massachusetts (1819-1827), an unsuccessful candidate for governor of Massachusetts (1824), and president of the Massachusetts State Senate (1829-1830).

The library archives also holds partial collections of several other figures important to Springfield history, including John Pynchon (1621-1703), the son of the founder of Springfield and a leader of the settlement during the second half of the seventeenth century; George Bliss (1764-1830), a member of the Massachusetts Senate (1805); John Worthington (1719-1800), a colonel in the Massachusetts Militia, a member of the Massachusetts House of Representatives (1765-1769), attorney-general for Massachusetts (1769), and a loyalist during the

Revolution; Abel Chapin (1756–1831), who served in the Revolution and commanded a company of government troops during Shays' Rebellion; and Chester William Chapin (1798–1883), president of the Connecticut River Railroad (1850–1853), founder and president of the Agawam National Bank, and a U.S. congressman (1875–1877).

Other collections of interest include the Records of the Springfield Day Nursery, a day-care service and kindergarten serving the city since 1882; the Springfield Cemetery Collection, which includes account records and other material associated with the cemetery since 1842; and the Springfield Library and Museums Association President's Office Records (1857 to the present). The Springfield Library Director's Office Records (1871 to the present) include all annual reports of the library, files of the Library Training Class (1898–1946), and correspondence of several of the directors. Of particular note is the correspondence of John Cotton Dana, Director of the Springfield City Library (1898–1902).

Guy A. McLain, Jr.

UNIVERSITY OF LOWELL
Center for Lowell History
Lydon Library
Lowell, Mass. 01845
(617) 452-5000

The Center for Lowell History at the University of Lowell was established to assure the safekeeping, preservation, and availability for study and research of materials in unique subject areas, particularly those related to the Merrimack Valley and the University of Lowell.

Since its opening in 1976, the Lowell Museum Corporation had acquired several private collections as well as books, photographs, and manuscripts. In cooperation with the University of Lowell, the museum decided to house all of its collections and materials in Special Collections. This includes a number of important manuscript collections. The Flather Collection contains the textile library of John Rogers Flather and the Boott Mill Company Records from 1903 to 1954. This collection is said to be the best example of a twentieth-century textile company archive available in New England.

For many years the books and manuscripts collected by the Lowell Historical Society were kept in a locked area of the Lowell City Library. This collection is the largest and most heavily used within Special Collections, containing a wide variety of resources from diaries and company records to photographs and videotapes, and provides materials that are indispensable for understanding the history of Lowell. In addition to the material collected by the Lowell Historical Society, other collections were donated to the university that provide information on the early history of the town. Among the most important is the Proprietors of Locks and Canals Collection, which consists of materials from those who provided engineering skills, capital, and managerial know-how to build the canal system that supported an enormous complex of textile mills in the city. This collection includes architectural and engineering drawings and photographs. In 1963 Professor Lewis Atwell Olney donated his library of books and periodicals on textile chemistry. Since that time additional materials on textiles and other closely related topics have been acquired, forming a large collection on the development of textile technology.

The Genealogy Collections include the U.S. census for Middlesex and Essex counties, the Massachusetts census, accelerated index for Massachusetts, and vital records for Massachusetts, as well as a wide selection of maps, atlases, city directories, and town histories. The Lowell Newspaper Collection includes several runs of very early newspapers that came from the Lowell Historical Society, including the *Middlesex Standard*, the *Chelmsford Courier*, and the *Vox Populi*. In addition, the university has purchased on microfilm complete runs of most of the local newspapers available.

Special Collections houses the records of a number of historically important corporations. In 1978 arrangements were made to house the historic railroad materials collected by the Boston and Maine Railroad Historical Society. This collection consists of some of the Boston and Maine Railroad Company records, as well as periodicals, books, maps, timetables, and photographs related to New England's railroads. The Middlesex Canal Association Collection contains the archives of the association, which was formed to promote and preserve the history of the Middlesex Canal. This collection includes books, manuscripts, maps, photographs, and paintings. The manuscripts include the records of the Middlesex Canal Company, which provided transportation between Lowell and Charlestown from 1803 to 1853.

The Manning Collection consists of correspondence, professional writings, project reports, and photographs by Warren H. Manning (1860-1938), a landscape architect and a founder of the American Institute of Landscape Architects. Working out of Billerica, his firm completed over 1,600 projects throughout the United States. The Davis Collection contains the professional papers and the music library of books and scores by Katherine Kennicott Davis (1892-1980), a prolific composer best known for "The Little Drummer Boy."

A number of oral history projects have been completed, with hundreds of taped interviews gathered, indexed, transcribed, and published. The library also has a significant photograph collection. This includes the Coggeshall Collection, consisting of a large number of original photographs and negatives taken by John Ingersoll Coggeshall (1857-1912), an engraver, photographer, and painter. In addition, the Photograph Collection contains over 20,000 historic photographs in the various collections at the University; they were separated from their original collections with cross-references maintained for the record. This allowed extensive subject, name, and geographic indexes to be developed.

The Tsongas Collection consists of the congressional papers of Paul E. Tsongas, who served in the U.S. House of Representatives from 1974 to 1978 and in the U.S. Senate from 1978 to 1984.

Finally, the University of Lowell Archives contains the records of the State Normal School and Lowell Textile School, both of which were established in Lowell in the mid-1890s. The archives includes photographs, newspapers, yearbooks, and administrative records of the former institutions as well as the University of Lowell.

Martha Mayo

UNIVERSITY OF MASSACHUSETTS, AMHERST
Archives and Manuscripts Department
Library
Amherst, Mass. 01003
(413) 545-2780

The Archives and Manuscripts Department at the University of Massachusetts at Amherst houses the official records of the university and the historical collections of the campus community. Many of these records have larger implications for the history of the commonwealth. The records and publications of the Extension Service and the Agricultural Experiment Stations, for just two examples, document such subjects as commercial farming, rural life, recreation, and science and technology in Massachusetts over the past century. Similarly, many past presidents, faculty, university officials, and students captured in the more than 3,500 linear feet of records have served the state in political, administrative, and private capacities either before or after their stay at the university.

Archives and Manuscripts, as part of its responsibility in connection with the major public research institution in the state, also collects extra-university archival and manuscript collections that document aspects of the history of the commonwealth, focusing particularly on the social and industrial history of the state. The most significant of these collections, described here, reveal the range of holdings. They include records from labor unions, businesses, social service agencies, and private voluntary organizations, as well as the papers of individuals—including the original correspondence and writings of Great Barrington native W. E. B. Du Bois—who reflect something of the ethnic, racial, social, and political diversity of the peoples of Massachusetts. The extra-university collections, which comprise over 1,000 linear feet, span the years from 1700 to 1985, but the bulk date from the past 120 years.

The collections include the records of a number of corporations. Among them are the American Writing Paper Company Records (1899-1966, 9 feet), consisting of the records of fourteen western New England papermaking companies, centered primarily in Holyoke, which merged in 1899 to form the American Writing Paper Company. This collection includes board of directors minutes, blueprints, land transactions, merger agreements, and printed material, but the bulk of the collection is comprised of the labor files, which include contracts, correspondence, grievances, and negotiations.

The George H. Gilbert Company Records (1841-1930, 29 feet) document how two Ware entrepreneurs, Charles Stevens and George H. Gilbert, formed a partnership to manufacture broadcloth and cloakings. Ten years later the partnership dissolved, and each partner carried a part of the business into separate establishments. The George H. Gilbert Company began the manufacture of high-grade woolen flannels, which it continued until it ceased operations in 1930. The records, comprising cash books, production records, time books, weavers' accounts, and correspondence (1846-1886), document the operation of Gilbert and Stevens and later the Gilbert Company for almost a century. Through the labor accounts (1851-1930) one can trace the phases of the varying ethnic composition of the work force, Irish, French-Canadian, and eventually Polish, as well as the family orientation of the mills.

The Northampton Cutlery Company Records (1868-1984, 40 feet) yield details about the employment of some immigrant and working-class families in the region, as well as about the technology used in the cutlery-manufacturing process. Included are ledgers, cash books, inventory records, trial balance sheets, payroll ledgers, personnel files, some correspondence, and other business records.

Among the labor records in the archives are those of the Boston Joint Board of the Amalgamated Clothing Workers of America from 1916 to 1979, the Northampton Labor Council, AFL-CIO, Minutes from 1933 to 1985, and the United Brotherhood of Carpenters and Joiners of America (Springfield and Holyoke District Council Records from 1885 to 1975, 27 feet). Included in the latter collection are minutes of some locals as well as the district councils, local membership records, local and district financial records, contracts, subject files, and the correspondence of the Springfield District Council from 1920 to 1968. The locals represented in the collection include Local 96 (Springfield French-speaking), Local 177 (Springfield English-speaking), Local 222 (Westfield), Local 685 (Chicopee French-speaking), Local 1881 (Holyoke English-speaking), Local 390 (Holyoke French-speaking), and Local 1503 (Amherst).

Among the social service agencies represented in the archives are the records of the Belchertown State School Friends Association (1954-1986, 10 feet), which was established to promote improved conditions at the school and promote better treatment of retarded citizens in the state. Another important collection is that of the Children's Aid and Family Service, Inc., covering the period from 1910 to 1981 (3.5 feet). These records trace its growth from volunteer beginnings to the complex professionalism of the agency as it is now. They also reflect the social attitudes of the community through the years. The Hampshire Community Action Commission Records (1965-1984, 12.5 feet) document the federally funded programs for the poor, including Head Start, Alcoholism Prevention, Hispanic Center, day care, Energy/Winterization, and Youth Work Experience.

The Traprock Peace Center Records (1979-1986, 2.5 feet) document the activities of that Deerfield center, which organized the first successful attempt in the United States to get a nuclear weapons moratorium referendum on the ballot and passed in the 1980 general state election. The Valley Peace Center Records (1967-1973, 14 feet) document the history of this Amherst organization, which was established to oppose the Vietnam War, to counsel young men regarding the selective service draft, and to support programs directed at related social and political problems.

The Great Barrington History Collection (1734-1900, 2.5 feet) was originally gathered by Charles Taylor for his 1883 history of Great Barrington. The collection includes Court of Common Pleas decisions (1784-1803), deeds and sales (1765-1865), indentures and leases (1806-1815), sheriffs' writs (1800-1827), genealogical research (1800-1900), land surveys, estate inventories, and subject notes.

The Swift River Valley Collection (1730-1940, 12.5 feet) contains a wide variety of documents collected by Donald Howe for his history of the towns now buried under the Quabbin Reservoir, which was built in 1938-1939 to supply water for the Boston area. Some of the records are from organizations such as the Women's Missionary Society of Enfield (1885-1928), the Storrsville Lyceum Debating Society (1842-1846), the Enfield Fire Department (1911-1938), and the Enfield Congregational Church (1831-1939). Also included in the collection are many account books from local businesses and manufacturers, some making palm-leaf hats, as well as the earliest account books of the Enfield selectmen and schools and the Fifth Massachusetts Turnpike Company. There also are family papers, particularly those of the Howe family of Enfield, and the journals (1858-1865) of Marcus Emmons (farm laborer and enlistee in Company K, 21st Regiment, Massachusetts Volunteers during the Civil War). Among the personal papers in the archives are the ornithological papers of Arthur Cleveland Bent (1866-1954), author of *Life Histories of North American Birds*, published between 1919 and 1942. This includes Bent's journals (1887-1942) detailing his daily ornithological activities in Taunton and elsewhere, and the field notebooks (1880-1909) of Owen Durfee of Fall River.

The Maurice A. Donahue Papers (1960-1971, 34.5 feet) document the work of Donahue, who was elected to the state House of Representatives in 1948 and to the Senate in 1950, becoming majority leader in 1958 and Senate president from 1964 to 1971. While in the Senate, he sponsored the Willis-Harrington Commission on Education, the Boston campus and Medical School of the University of Massachusetts, state scholarships for needy students, and commissions to improve vocational education, to study problems of urban school systems, and to extend educational facilities in the state.

The W. E. B. Du Bois Papers (1803-1985, 166 feet) reflect the activities of the educator, sociologist, editor, author, and crusader for the rights of blacks. The collection covers his education at Great Barrington, at Harvard University, and in Germany, his participation in the founding of the Niagara Movement (with William Monroe Trotter and George Washington Forbes), the NAACP, *Crisis* magazine, and the Pan-African movement, his teaching at Wilberforce and Atlanta universities, his extensive speaking, writing, and international travel, and his years in Ghana at the end of his life. The collection consists of correspondence (1877-1965), editorial files for *Crisis* magazine (1910-1934), manuscripts of speeches, articles, newspaper columns, and non-fiction books, as well as a variety of other sources.

The John W. Haigis Papers (1903-1974, 8 feet) document the interests of the founder, editor, and publisher of the *Greenfield Recorder* and founder of radio station WHAI in Greenfield. He served as a bank officer in Franklin County and in several town offices in Montague. He was a state representative from 1909 to 1913, a state senator from 1913 to 1915 and 1923 to 1927, and state treasurer from 1929 to 1930. He was Republican candidate for lieutenant governor in 1934 and governor in 1936. The collection consists of scrapbooks (1903–1936), speeches in transcript and on records, campaign materials, photos, and a tape of an interview (1974) with Leverett Saltonstall about Haigis.

The Hudson Family Papers (1807–1963, 3 feet) document the activities of abolitionist Erasmus Darwin Hudson, Sr., (1806–1880) on behalf of the Connecticut and American Anti-Slavery societies between 1838 and 1849. Included in journals and correspondence are his descriptions of these efforts in Massachusetts as well as other states. Hudson, a pioneer orthopedic surgeon and inventor of prosthetic devices, lived at times in Massachusetts, particularly in the utopian community, the Northampton Association of Education and Industry (1842–1843) and in Springfield. The collection includes his journals (1832–1845), correspondence with family and fellow anti-slavery organizers, and writings. The collection also includes the papers of his son, Erasmus Darwin Hudson, Jr., a physician, his daughter Clara Hudson of Plainfield, and of the extended family's Fowler, Shaw, Clarke, and Cooke branches.

The Howes Brothers Photographic Collection (1882–1907, 0.5 feet) consists of 200 study prints selected from the 20,000 negatives on microfilm in the Library. Alvah, Walter, and George Howes traveled the Pioneer Valley of Massachusetts taking photographs of the residents, thereby documenting pictorially the customs, fashions, architecture, industry, technology, and economic conditions of rural New England at the turn of this century. The original glass plates are housed in the Ashfield Historical Society.

Among the extensive papers related to the history of the university, as well as the history of agriculture in the state, are the Kenyon Leech Butterfield papers (1889–1945, 12 feet) and the William Smith Clark papers (7 feet). Butterfield was an agricultural economist, rural sociologist, and college president (Rhode Island College of Agriculture and Mechanic Arts, then the Massachusetts Agricultural College [now the University of Massachusetts]) from 1906 to 1924, Clark was a faculty member at Amherst College and then president of the Massachusetts Agricultural College from 1867 to 1879. Clark's papers include correspondence covering his student days at Amherst College (1844–1848), his service in the Civil War with the 21st Regiment of Massachusetts Volunteers, his mission to Hokkaido, Japan, and his presidency of Massachusetts Agricultural College.

Linda Seidman and Kenneth Fones-Wolf

YALE UNIVERSITY LIBRARY
Manuscripts and Archives
Box 1603A, Yale Station
New Haven, Conn. 06520
(203) 436-0907

The Manuscripts and Archives Department of the Yale University Library is the principal repository for historical manuscripts and official records of the university, including its publications. These documents are collected, arranged, and described in order to provide convenient access for all interested researchers; they are consulted by Yale students and faculty and attract scholars from the United States and throughout the world.

Holdings relating to the history of Massachusetts include collections of original manuscripts, microform copies of manuscript material in other repositories, and records in the Yale University Archives about Massachusetts alumni.

There are about fifty collections of original manuscripts pertaining to Massachusetts, including personal papers, family papers, and business records especially relating to shipping and railroads. Personal and family collections include those of Samuel Benjamin (1753-1824), officer in the Massachusetts Continental Line, who participated in the battles of Lexington and Bunker Hill; the Bidwell family, principally Barnabas Bidwell (1763-1833), lawyer and politician; the Bromfield family of Boston, with material relating to Richard Clarke (1711-1795), Boston merchant who was involved in prerevolutionary activities about the tax on tea; Walter Chapman, an officer in the 36th Massachusetts Infantry during the Civil War who commanded a brigade of Afro-American troops; Justus Forward (1730-1814), pastor of the Congregational Church in Belchertown; the Frost family (1710-1923) of Andover; Edward Thornton Hartman (b. 1869), urban planner and state consultant for the Massachusetts Department of Public Welfare (1923-1929); Herman Haupt (1817-1905), railroad builder of the Hoosac Tunnel in 1857; Selden Huntington (1786-1846), a merchant in Springfield; Jonathan Lee (1786-1866), pastor of the Congregational Church in Otis; Edward J. Logue (b. 1921), lawyer, politician, and urban planner and administrator who worked in Boston in the 1960s; Edwards Amasa Park (1808-1900), theologian and professor at Andover Theological Seminary and collector of papers of Eliphalet Pearson, president of the Board of Trustees of Andover and of records of the Massachusetts Society for Promoting Christian Knowledge (1804-1821); Edward Tallmadge Root (1865-1948), secretary of the Massachusetts Federation of Churches (1904-1930) and candidate in Massachusetts for governor (1940) and senator (1944) for the Prohibition party; the Strong family (1667-1925), including Noah Lyman Strong, an official of the Boston Custom House during the Civil War, and his daughter Josephine Elizabeth Strong, a teacher of freedmen during and after the Civil War; Mabel Loomis Todd (1856-1932), editor of the writings of Emily Dickinson and founder of the Amherst Historical Society; David Peck Todd (1855-1939), professor of astronomy at Amherst College; the Loomis-Wilder family of West Springfield, Cambridge, and Ashfield, including Eben J. Loomis and his wife Mary Alden Wilder Loomis, friends of Henry and Maria Thoreau; and the Whitney family of Northampton (1778-1951), including Josiah Dwight Whitney (1819-1896), geologist and Harvard professor, and Maria Whitney (1830-1910), teacher at Smith College.

Special subject collections include the Nantucket Collection (1663-1822), containing papers of the Gardner, Pinkham, Swain, and Coffin families; the Massachusetts Railroads Collection (1822-1909); the American Revolutionary War Collection (1775-1786), including documents from Massachusetts; the Old Colony & Fall River Railroad Company Records (1863-1893); the Shipping Collection (1794-1915), including some material from Massachusetts; the Turnpikes Collection (1790-1898), which includes records of the Tenth Massachusetts Turnpike Company and the Hartford and Worcester Railroad Turnpike Company; and the Whaling Logs Collection (1830-1970), which includes two logs of whalers sailing from New Bedford and Provincetown.

Holdings of microforms of manuscript collections and archival records held by other repositories are substantial. Collections of personal and family papers include the Adams family (1639-1889), consisting primarily of the papers of John Adams, Abigail Adams, John Quincy Adams, Charles Francis Adams, Sr. and Jr., Henry Adams, and Brooks Adams; Timothy Pickering (1745-1829), cabinet officer, Indian commissioner, and Massachusetts congressman; transcripts of political papers of Elbridge Gerry (1744-1814); Nathan Perkins (1777?-1845), a clergyman in Amherst; and John William Appleton, a Civil War officer of the Massachusetts 54th Regiment (Colored). Business records include letter books (1846-1850) of Perkins & Brown, wool dealers of Springfield, and Boston ship registers (1789-1829). There are extensive city and town records, including 90 microfilm reels of the Massachusetts Archives publication of seventeenth- and nineteenth-century records; town records of Gloucester (1642-1830); town records of Acton, Bedford, Carlisle, Concord, Lexington, and Lincoln (1635-1886); census records (1861, 1865) and probate court records (1650-1850) of Suffolk County; and nearly 4,000 microfiches of Massachusetts vital records (1629-1984) for about seventy cities and towns.

Judith Ann Schiff

OTHER MANUSCRIPT REPOSITORIES

There are literally hundreds of other manuscript repositories in Massachusetts, and each of them possesses materials of importance to the researcher. That is especially the case with the local city or town historical society or museum, which often collects materials related to the history of the specific city or town. Although it is impossible to cover all the smaller historical societies or museums, in order to provide the reader with an awareness of the rich collections often available there, we would like to provide brief descriptions of several of them that in many ways are typical.

Among the leading local history collections are those of the Immigrant City Archives, which restricts itself to the historical development of Lawrence, which was founded in 1845 as a model factory town, and it does so with an exceptional level of completeness. In 1976 Immigrant City Archives was founded to save some of the rich heritage of Lawrence, and it began to collect and preserve printed material, oral histories, organizational records, letters, diaries, photographs, and memorabilia related to the experience of living and working in Lawrence. The collection now includes over 1,000 slides on the history of the city, over 150 oral histories (all of which are line indexed and some transcribed), over 1,000 photographs, and memorabilia of businesses, organizations, clubs, schools, and so on. The manuscript collection includes organizational records, diaries, ledgers, and city documents. Among the special collections are that of the YMCA from 1892 to the present, the International Institute from 1913 to 1934, and the City Mission from 1859 into the 1950s. Among the ethnic materials are papers of the Workmen's Circle (Jewish), the Lithuanian National Catholic Church, the German School (1872-1960), the Free Bed Society and other German clubs, and records of the French Catholic churches and schools. The ethnic collection is growing and already contains material on Hispanic, Indo-Chinese, Irish, Italian, Lebanese, Polish, Portuguese, and other immigrant groups.

Although the Immigrant City Archives is a unique repository, the commonwealth contains a number of other very fine historical societies that preserve materials related to the history of the specific cities or towns. In this book it is impossible to mention more than a handful of these important organizations, and persons who are interested in local history certainly should take advantage of the resources collected and made available through them. The Bay State Historical League (The State House, Box 247, Boston, Mass. 02133) published in 1986 the most comprehensive listing of historical societies, historical commissions, museums, archives, and research facilities in the state, which should be consulted by the prospective researcher (*1986 Directory of Historical Agencies in Massachusetts*).

Typical of the very fine local historical societies are the Dedham Historical Society, the Lexington Historical Society, and the Northampton Historical

Society. The Dedham Historical Society possesses thousands of papers dating back to 1638, relating to the history of Dedham and Norfolk County. Included in the holdings are records of local churches (from 1638) and diaries and sermons of early ministers. The collection includes records of an agricultural society (1849-1882), a cotton manufacturing company from 1807 to 1826), two teachers' associations (1830-1832 and 1848-1907), a turnpike corporation (1802-1856), two fire companies (1800-1886), a fruit growers' protective association (1865-1870), and two library associations (1854-1889) Among materials of statewide significance, the society has the papers of U.S. representative Fisher Ames and of educator and representative Horace Mann, including his lecture notes taken as a law student in Litchfield, Connecticut.

The Lexington Historical Society celebrated its one hundredth anniversary in 1986, and in the past century the society has acquired a significant amount of important material relative to the history of the Town of Lexington and its inhabitants. Among the collections are the papers of the following Lexington families, which include deeds, account books, business records, and correspondence: Robbins-Stone, Greene, Parker, Cutler, Muzzey, Redman, Fiske, Brown-Bacon, Winship, Ballard, and Blake. Also part of the manuscript holdings are the account book and interleaved almanac diary of Lexington's activist minister, the Reverend Jonas Clarke (1730-1805). In addition, the society is repository for the organizational and business records of the Lexington Girl Scouts, the Old Belfry Club, the Lend-a-Hand Society, and the Lexington Tennis Association. Also among the holdings are five volumes of student journals pertaining to the studies in the first normal school in America. Still other school records include the town district school files of 1814, 1833, and 1839.

Further records include the minutes of town meetings and selectmen's meetings from 1692 to 1815, plus random Selectmen's correspondence and town warrants from the eighteenth, nineteenth, and twentieth centuries. Several local collectors have contributed to the archival holdings of the Lexington Historical Society over the years, including broadsides, governor's proclamations, U.S. postal records of the nineteenth century, and the correspondence of Christopher Kilby to Thomas Hancock.

The society's resources include copies of newspapers from the eighteenth century, newspaper accounts of the American Revolution Centennial celebration, and bound copies of the local newspaper, the *Lexington Minute-man* from 1880 to 1960. Other items in the collection encompass maps (in limited number) and 75 linear feet of books, which include town reports, town directories, local histories, religious tracts, and Acts and Resolves of Massachusetts. Among the graphic art resources are drawings, paintings, intaglio prints, and lithographs. Finally, the society possesses a strong collection of photographic prints and negatives pertaining to the town, some dating from the 1860s. Two noteworthy titles within this area are the Fred S. Piper Collection and the Burr Church Collection, both dealing with the town from 1900 to 1925. Finally, the society holds about fifty hours of oral history interviews.

The Northampton Historical Society, like its counterparts in Dedham and Lexington, collects and owns papers and items related to the local history of the town from the seventeenth century to the present day. Included in the collection are 34 feet of ephemera, arranged alphabetically by subject (i.e., business, education, religion, etc.), 8 large file drawers of newspaper clippings, 9 feet of account books, and 9 feet of photographs. There also are 14 feet of photo albums, about 350 daguerreotypes, 2½ boxes of stereopticon views, and 2 boxes of postcards. There are 20 feet of miscellaneous papers, including the Stoddard-Williston Collection, the Whitmarsh Papers (owners of a silk mill), the Shaw-Hudson letters (physicians), the Pratt letters (architects), and the Parsons letters (descendents of Cornet Joseph Parsons). The French-Bliss Collection contains 18 feet of material on the Mount Holyoke family. The society owns the Shepherd House and contains 17 feet of the Shepherd Collection.

In addition to city and town historical societies and public library local history rooms, there are some excellent libraries that possess important material for Massachusetts history. Special attention should be paid to the Sophia Smith Collection of Smith College, in Northampton. The Sophia Smith Collection is the second largest archive on the history of women in America (the largest being the Schlesinger Library at Radcliffe). Included in the collection is a wide range of material related to the history of women in Massachusetts. There is an exceptional collection of secondary works, including periodicals. In addition, the manuscript collection is extensive, including important materials especially for social history and women's history. These include the records of the New England Hospital for Women and Children and for the Planned Parenthood League of Massachusetts, and four massive collections of family papers, of the Everett Hale family, the Coffin, Garrison, Ames, and Bodman families. There also are smaller collections related to women's rights, suffrage, and education. Finally, there are papers related to Northampton activities of the New England Freedman's Aid Society, the Ladies' Army Aid Society, and the League of Women Voters.

The Sophia Smith Collection is housed at Smith College, and as the commonwealth has a large number of colleges and universities, there are even more repositories, especially for records of the various institutions of higher education. One of the most important college repositories is the Amherst College Archives, located in the Robert Frost Library, in Amherst. In addition to extensive college records, the Amherst College Archives has collections that should be of great interest to persons interested in Massachusetts history. The Amherst College Weather Station Records, for instance, is a significant collection of data collected from 1852 to the present. Like many other college archives, the one at Amherst College possesses the papers of faculty and alumni, and in the case of Amherst College, these include a number of important collections. The Benjamin K. Emerson Papers include geological notebooks based on Emerson's research in New England. The President Edward Hitchcock Papers include material on the two official geological surveys of Massachusetts (1832 and 1840), as well as correspondence with leading scientists of the nineteenth century. The Dr. Edward Hitchcock Papers include correspondence and diaries that document the earliest professorship of physical education and hygiene in the United States. The Frank L. Boyden Papers document aspects of the history of Deerfield Academy, as Boyden was headmaster from 1902 to 1969. The Henry W. Boynton Papers help document the history of Phillips Academy, Andover, where Boynton was head of the department of English literature. The Rev. James Taylor Papers provide insight into the life of a clergyman who was pastor of the Sunderland Church. Finally, the Hills Family Papers document family life in western Massachusetts from the middle of the nineteenth century to the turn of the twentieth century. The Special Collections at Amherst College include the Robert Frost Collection, the Emily Dickinson Collection, and the Richard Wilbur Collection. Since each of these three individuals played prominent roles in the history of American literature, with Wilbur being named by President Ronald Reagan as poet laureate of the United States, their papers document the literary world from the 1840s to the present. Other college archives, like the one at Amherst College, possess collections that are of great importance to the historian, and if a researcher finds a relationship between his or her topic and any college, he or she would be wise to contact the archivist about collections that might prove to be indispensable.

With all of these repositories in Massachusetts, it is clear that historians are blessed with a wealth of source material that can document virtually every aspect of the state's history, as well as the history of every city and town. Finally, it should be recommended that amateur researchers contact professional historians for assistance, and that town historical agencies seek professional assistance before devoting large sums of money to historical projects that can be completed with far less money, and with greater expertise, if done by competent professional personnel. The Institute for Massachusetts Studies, at Westfield State College, for instance, has provided assistance to the Springfield Library and Museums Association for several important projects, resulting in impressive publications that meet the high standards of modern historical research. Upon request, the staff of the institute is pleased to provide assistance, especially to the smaller towns that do not have direct access to trained personnel.

INDEX

ABOUT THE CONTRIBUTORS

ELISE BERNIER-FEELEY is Reference Librarian at the Forbes Library, where she is responsible for the reference, genealogy, and local history collections, and for all manuscripts except those in art, music, and the Calvin Coolidge Memorial Room Collection. She received her undergraduate degree from the University of Massachusetts at Amherst, and in 1982 graduated with highest honors from Southern Connecticut State University school of library science and instructional technology. A member of Beta Phi Mu, the international library science honor society, she is also the recipient of the Frederick H. Cramer Award for excellence in the study of history.

ELIZABETH BOUVIER is Survey Archivist for the Boston Municipal Archives and Records Project, where she is responsible for the appraisal of data from departmental survey returns and the evaluation of records management procedures. She is also a consultant to the Archives of the Contemporary Boston Area Women's Movement (Women's Educational Center). Ms. Bouvier holds bachelor's and master's degrees in history, and did graduate work in history and archival methods at the University of Massachusetts at Boston.

FRANCIS J. BREMER is Professor of History at Millersville University of Pennsylvania. He received his B.A. from Fordham College and his M.A. and Ph.D. from Columbia University. He is the author of *The Puritan Experiment: New England Society from Bradford to Edwards* and has edited *Puritan New England* (with Alden T. Vaughan) and *Anne Hutchinson: Troubler of the Puritan Zion.* He has published articles on seventeenth-century New England in the *William and Mary Quarterly,* the *Proceedings of the American Antiquarian Society,* the

New England Quarterly, and elsewhere. He is the editor of the Winthrop Papers for the Massachusetts Historical Society.

KATHERINE CAIN is the Rare Book Selector for the Boston University Library. As well as purchasing rare books and selecting book gifts for the collection, she manages acquisitions for the Contemporary Authors Collection and the Mystery Collection. She is enrolled in the Master of Liberal Arts degree program at Boston University. She received her M.L.S. degree from Southern Connecticut State University in 1981. Prior to her work in Boston, Ms. Cain served as acquisitions assistant at the Beinecke Library of Yale University.

JOSEPH CARVALHO III is Director of the Connecticut Valley Historical Museum, of the Springfield Library and Museums Association. He holds a B.A. in history from Westfield State College, an M.A. in history from the College of William and Mary, and a master of library science degree from the University of Rhode Island. He has published many articles on various aspects of library science and archive administration, as well as history, and he served as editorial associate of the *Dictionary of American Medical Biography* (Westport, Connecticut, 1984). He is author of *Black Families of Hampden County* (Boston, 1984). Before accepting the position at the museum, Mr. Carvalho served as supervisor of local history and genealogy of the Springfield City Library, and he has been involved in various projects related to aspects of the history of Springfield. Since 1978, he has been associate editor of the *Historical Journal of Massachusetts.*

PAUL CYR is the Curator of Special Collections at the New Bedford Free Public Library. He received a B.A. in English from Providence College, and an M.A. in English and a Master's of Library Science from the University of Rhode Island. Prior to his present position, he was a hand bookbinder. He is a contributing editor of *Spinner: People and Culture in Southeastern Massachusetts* and is also the librarian of the Achushnet (Massachusetts) Historical Society.

BRUCE C. DANIELS is Professor of History at the University of Winnipeg, where he serves as coeditor of the *Canadian Review of American Studies.* He received his education at Syracuse University and the University of Connecticut, where he earned his doctorate in early American history. He is a specialist in the colonial city, is author of *The Connecticut Town: Growth and Development, 1635-1790* (1979), *Dissent and Conformity on Narragansett Bay: The Colonial Rhode Island Town* (1983), and is editor of *Town and County: Essays on the Structure of Local Government in the American Colonies* (1978). He serves as a member of the board of reviewers of the *Historical Journal of Massachusetts* and has written articles for that journal as well as for *William and Mary Quarterly* and others focusing on early American history.

JUDITH M. DOWNEY has been Manuscript Librarian of the Old Dartmouth Historical Society since 1981. She received her M.S. in library and information science from Simmons and her B.A. from the University of Massachusetts/Amherst. Ms. Downey has served as the president of the Local History and Genealogy Section of the Massachusetts Library Association since 1982. As the compiler of *Whaling Logbooks and Journals 1613-1927: An Inventory of Manuscript Records in Public Collections* (New York, 1986), she was the recipient of the John Lyman Award for the Best Maritime Reference Book of 1987.

KENNETH FONES-WOLF is the University Archivist of the University of Massachusetts, Amherst, and Head of the Archives and Manuscripts department. He graduated from the University of Maryland, received an M.L.S. from the University of Wisconsin and a Ph.D. in history from Temple University. He is author of *Trade Union Gospel: Religion and the Labor Movement in Philadelphia, 1865-1915* (Philadelphia, 1988).

JOHN J. FOX is Professor of History at Salem State College. He received his undergraduate education at North Adams State College and received a master's degree from Lehigh University. After having taught in the Pittsfield public school system, in 1964 he became a member of the faculty at Salem State College. He has been active in local, state, and national organizations devoted to the use of oral history and is executive secretary of the New England Association of Oral History, having served as its president from 1974 to 1979. He is book review editor of the *Oral History Review*. He is author of *Oral History: Window to the Past* (1977), and "Window on the Past: A Guide to Oral History," *Choice* (June 1980).

BARBARA FRANCO is Assistant Director of the Museum of Our National Heritage, where she is responsible for museum programs in the areas of education, collections, and exhibitions. She received her B.A. in history from Bryn Mawr College and an M.A. in museum training from the Cooperstown Graduate Program. She has worked at the museum since 1974 as curator of collections and coordinator of exhibits. Before coming to the Museum of Our National Heritage, Ms. Franco was curator of decorative arts at Munson-Williams-Proctor Institute, in Utica, New York.

JOHN W. IFKOVIC is Associate Professor of History at Westfield State College, where he has served as associate director of the Institute for Massachusetts Studies and associate editor of the *Historical Journal of Massachusetts*. He holds a bachelor's degree from Fordham University, a master of arts in teaching degree from Yale University, and a Ph.D. in history from the University of Virginia. He is coeditor of *Massachusetts in the Gilded Age: Selected Essays* (Amherst, 1985) and author of articles on various aspects of Connecticut and New England history, including *Jonathan Trumbull, Jr., 1740-1809. A Biography* (New York, 1982).

MARTIN KAUFMAN is Professor of History at Westfield State College, where he also serves as director of the Institute for Massachusetts Studies and editorial director of the *Historical Journal of Massachusetts.* He has been interested in state and local history for many years, and in 1972 he initiated the *Historical Journal of Western Massachusetts*, serving as its editorial director until 1980, when it became the *Historical Journal of Massachusetts.* He is author of *Homeopathy in America: Rise and Fall of a Medical Heresy* (Baltimore, 1971), *American Medical Education: Formative Years, 1765-1910* (Westport, Connecticut, 1976), and *The University of Vermont College of Medicine* (Hanover, New Hampshire, 1979). He is editor-in-chief of the *Dictionary of American Medical Biography* (Westport, Connecticut, 1984) and of a similar work on nursing (Westport, Connecticut, 1988).

JACK LARKIN is Chief Historian at Old Sturbridge Village, having been there since 1971. His undergraduate studies were completed at Harvard University and his graduate work in American history at Brandeis University. He is author of articles on early nineteenth-century American history appearing in *American Quarterly* and the *Proceedings of the American Antiquarian Society.* He is also author of *Infinite Details: Everyday Life in America, 1790-1840* (New York, 1988).

DANIEL LOMBARDO is the Curator of Special Collections at the Jones Library in Amherst, Massachusetts, where he is responsible for historical and literary collections, including those of Emily Dickinson and Robert Frost. He graduated summa cum laude from the University of Connecticut in 1974 and was elected to Phi Beta Kappa. He received a Master's of Library Science degree from the University of Southern Connecticut and completed two internships at the Yale Center for British Art. Mr. Lombardo is the author of *Tales of Amherst: A Look Back* (Amherst, 1986), *A Directory of Craftsmen in the Connecticut Valley of Massachusetts Before 1850* (1987), and numerous articles for publications such as *Vermont Life, Library Journal, Microform Review*, and the *Historical Journal of Massachusetts.* He also has been a consultant for television productions of PBS, Thames Television (London), and independent filmmakers.

LARRY LOWENTHAL is the Historian at the Springfield Armory National Historic Site, a unit of the U.S. National Park Service. He has held that position since October of 1979 and has been a permanent employee of the National Park Service since 1970. He received a B.A. in history from Rutgers University, where he was elected to Phi Beta Kappa and awarded a Woodrow Wilson Fellowship. He also holds a M.A. in history from Yale University. In addition to writing articles pertaining to the Springfield Armory, Mr. Lowenthal is interested in railroad history and has written books and articles on that subject.

GERALD W. McFARLAND is Professor of History at the University of Massachusetts, Amherst. He holds a B.A. from the University of California, Berkeley, and an M.A. and Ph.D. from Columbia University. He has taught at the University of Massachusetts for the past twenty-three years. He is author of *Mugwumps, Morals, and Politics, 1884-1920* (Amherst, 1975) and *A Scattered People: An American Family Moves West* (New York, 1985), and has had articles published in the *Political Science Quarterly, The Journal of American History*, *The Historian*, and *American History Illustrated*, and a host of others, including the *Historical Journal of Massachusetts*.

GUY A. McLAIN, JR., is Archivist for the Springfield City Library and Museums Association. He received his undergraduate education in history at the University of Massachusetts, at Amherst, and received his M.L.S. from the University of Rhode Island. Before coming to Springfield, he was processing archivist at the University of Massachusetts Archives. He has been active in the New England Archivists, serving on the task force on the image of archives and on the program committee. He is author of the *Guide to the Massachusetts Mutual Insurance Company Archives* (Springfield, 1984) and an article on "Steam Power on the Connecticut," which was published in the *Historical Journal of Massachusetts* (June 1986), pp. 135-45.

MARTHA MAYO is Head of the Center for Lowell History (formerly Special Collections), at the University of Lowell. She is responsible for directing the Public Service and Technical Service functions of the center. She holds a B.A. in American history from the University of Maine, at Orono and an M.A. in Library Science from the University of Illinois, at Champaign-Urbana. Initially hired as special collections librarian at Lowell Technological Institute, she became head of special collections with the merger of Lowell State College and Lowell Technological Institute. Recently, she was asked to create and head the new Center for Lowell History, to be located at the Patrick J. Mogan Cultural Center.

LAURA V. MONTI is the Keeper of Rare Books and Manuscripts at the Boston Public Library, where she is in charge of various collections of rare books and manuscripts dating from the thirteenth to the twentieth centuries. She received her undergraduate education and her master's of library science degree at the National University of Buenos Aires, and her Ph.D. from the Catholic University of America. She received her diploma of archivist from one of the earliest courses of American University and the National Archives of the United States. Her training in rare books was at the Folger Shakespeare Library, in Washington, D.C. Before coming to Boston in 1979, Ms. Monti was for sixteen years head of special collections at the University of Florida in Gainesville, where she organized the University Archives.

EVA MOSELEY is Curator of Manuscripts at the Schlesinger Library, Cambridge, where she is responsible for America's largest collection related to the history of women. She holds B.A. and M.A. degrees from Radcliffe College and has been with the Schlesinger Library since 1971, when she started as the library's first part-time manuscripts assistant. She has been active in the Society of American Archivists, serving three years on the council, on the editorial board, on the program, local arrangements, and nominating committees, and having been the first chairperson of the manuscript repositories professional affinity group (which is now a section of the SAA). She also edited an issue of the *American Archivist*. In addition to the SAA, Ms. Moseley has been active in the New England Archivists, having attended its founding meeting. She edited the NEA newsletter for six years, chaired three of its program committees, and is currently editing a publication on documenting the region. She was cofounder of the Boston Archivists Group and the Harvard/Radcliffe Archives Group and has lectured in archives and public history classes, conducted oral histories, and helped with programs and acquisitions of the Medford Historical Society. Her publications include two articles on documenting women's history (both in *The American Archivist*), "The Lydia E. Pinkham Medicine Company," in *Shop Talk* (Boston Public Library, 1975), and "One Half Our History: An Exhibit at Widener Library," in *Harvard Library Bulletin* (1984).

MARY J. OATES is Professor of Economics at Regis College (Massachusetts), where she has served on the faculty since 1967. She holds her B.A. from the Catholic University of America and an M.A. and Ph.D. from Yale University. She is author of *The Role of the Cotton Textile Industry in the Economic Development of the American Southeast, 1900–1940* (1975) and is editor of *Higher Education for Catholic Women: An Historical Anthology* (1987). She has also written essays in various collections and articles in the *American Quarterly*, *Signs: Journal of Women in Culture and Society*, and the *Historical Journal of Massachusetts*.

ROBERT A. O'LEARY is a member of the faculty at the Massachusetts Maritime Academy, in Buzzards Bay, Massachusetts. His undergraduate work was completed at Georgetown University, and he holds a master of arts in teaching degree from the University of Massachusetts, Amherst. He received his Ph.D. in American history from Tufts University, where he researched aspects of twentieth-century Massachusetts history and American Catholic history. His writings have appeared in the *Historical Journal of Massachusetts*, and he has participated in numerous programs related to aspects of recent Massachusetts history.

WILLIAM PENCAK is Associate Professor of History at the Pennsylvania State University's Ogontz Campus. He received his B.A., M.A., and Ph.D. from Columbia University, and he has written extensively on the history of seventeenth-century New England. He is author of *War, Politics and Revolution in Provincial Massachusetts* (Boston, 1981) and *America's Burke: The Mind of Thomas Hutchinson* (Lanham, Maryland, 1982), as well as numerous articles. He has held Andrew

Mellon (Duke University, 1979-1980) and National Endowment for the Humanities Fellowships (Shelby Cullom Davis Center, Princeton University, 1982-1983).

ELLIE REICHLIN is Director of Archives and Curator of Photographic Collections at the Society for the Preservation of New England Antiquities, where she oversees the collection, administration, and interpretation of an extensive collection of documentary photographs, architectural drawings, manuscripts, and ephemera relating to New England's architecture and daily life. She received her undergraduate training at Sarah Lawrence College, her master's degree in anthropology from the University of Rochester, where she is a candidate for the Ph.D. She also holds an M.L.S. degree from Simmons College. Before becoming director of the archives at SPNEA, Ms. Reichlin was on the staff of the Peabody Museum of Harvard University.

JUDITH ANN SCHIFF is Chief Research Archivist of the Yale University Library's division of manuscripts and archives, where she specializes in American history, New Haven history, and the history of Yale University. In addition, she is a biographer of Charles and Anne Morrow Lindbergh. She holds master's degrees in American history and in library science from Southern Connecticut State University and is currently working on a doctorate in American history at Columbia University. A founder and past president of New England Archivists, Ms. Schiff serves as archives director of the Jewish Historical Society of New Haven.

ALAN SEABURG is Curator of Manuscripts for the Andover-Harvard Theological Library of the Harvard Divinity School. He is responsible for collecting, cataloging, and servicing the library's manuscript and archival collections, which consist chiefly of materials relating to the Divinity School and to the Unitarian and Universalist traditions in America and Europe. His undergraduate work was done at Tufts University, where he also received his ministerial degree. His library science degree was earned at Simmons College, and he has done postgraduate work at Boston University. Before coming to Harvard, Mr. Seaburg served as librarian for the Crane Theological School of Tufts University and as archivist for the Unitarian Universalist Association.

LINDA SEIDMAN is the Manuscripts Curator in the Archives and Manuscripts Department, University of Massachusetts Library, at Amherst. Her principal responsibilities are processing, describing, and providing access and reference service for extra-university manuscript collections. She graduated from Oberlin College and received the M.L.S. degree from the University of Rhode Island, where she also received archival training.

JACK TAGER is Professor of History at the University of Massachusetts, Amherst. His undergraduate work was completed at Brooklyn College, and he holds a masters degree from the University of California at Berkeley. His doctoral studies were done at the University of Rochester, which awarded him a Ph.D. in 1965. He taught at Ohio State University before coming to the University of Massachusetts in 1967. He is coeditor of *Massachusetts in the Gilded Age: Selected Essays* (Amherst, 1985) and is author of *The Intellectual as Reformer: Brand Whitlock and the Progressive Movement* (Cleveland, 1968). He is a specialist in urban history and was coeditor of *The Urban Vision: Selected Interpretation of the Modern American City* (Chicago, 1970).

RICHARD B. TRASK is Town Archivist for Danvers, Massachusetts, having served in that capacity within the Peabody Institute Library of Danvers since 1972. He received his undergraduate training at Salem State College and received his M.A. in history from Northeastern University in 1970. Mr. Trask was director of the Samuel Parris archaeological excavation, is curator of the Rebecca Nurse Homestead, is a long-time member of the Danvers Historical Commission and Historic District Commission, and has served as historical consultant for the PBS television production "Three Sovereigns for Sarah," concerning the 1692 Salem witchcraft hysteria.

BARBARA TRIPPEL SIMMONS is Curator of Manuscripts at the American Antiquarian Society, where she is responsible for the preservation, organization, and use of the society's manuscript collections and archival records. She received her undergraduate degree from Colby College and a master of arts in library science from the University of Michigan. She was previously project archivist at the Massachusetts Institute of Technology's institute archives and assistant curator of manuscripts at the Historical Society of Pennsylvania.

DOROTHY TRUMAN is Manuscript Specialist and Archivist at the Museum of American Textile History in North Andover, Massachusetts. In addition to managing the museum's collection of business records and other documents related to the history of the textile industry, she is responsible for the museum's own archives. She is a graduate of Wellesley College, holds an M.A. in history from Columbia University, and studied archival theory and practice at the University of Massachusetts. In addition to her work at the textile museum, Mrs. Truman has inventoried the records of the town of Boxford, Massachusetts, and catalogued the collections of the Boxford Historical Society.

RONALD E. WHEALAN is Head Librarian at the John F. Kennedy Library, where he supervises reference service and administers printed materials collections. He received a B.A. in history from Boston State College, a M.A. in history from Northeastern University, and a M.L.S. from Simmons College. He has been a librarian at the Kennedy library since 1978.

DIANA YOUNT is Associate Director and Special Collections Librarian at Franklin Trask Library of Andover Newton Theological School. She received undergraduate training at Point Loma College and received a M.A. degree in the history of religions and Islamic studies from the Hartford Seminary Foundation. In addition, she received her library science degree from Simmons College. She received a certificate in archives administration from the American University/ National Archives program.